THE NOBEL FACTOR

Milton Friedman receives the Nobel Prize from King Carl XVI Gustaf of Sweden, Stockholm, 10 December 1976. (Photo by Jan Collsioo/Scanpix Sweden/Sipa USA)

THE NOBEL FACTOR

THE PRIZE IN ECONOMICS, SOCIAL DEMOCRACY, AND THE MARKET TURN

AVNER OFFER
GABRIEL SÖDERBERG

PRINCETON UNIVERSITY PRESS
Princeton and Oxford

Library of Congress Cataloging-in-Publication Data

Names: Offer, Avner, author. | Söderberg, Gabriel, 1978- author.
Title: The Nobel factor : the prize in economics, social democracy, and the
    market turn / Avner Offer, Gabriel Söderberg.
Description: Princeton, NJ : Princeton University Press, 2016. | Includes
    bibliographical references and index.
Identifiers: LCCN 2016003438 | ISBN 9780691166032 (hardback : alk. paper)
Subjects: LCSH: Economic history. | Socialism—Scandinavia—History. |
    Economic policy. | Nobel Prizes—History. | BISAC: BUSINESS & ECONOMICS /
    Economic History. | POLITICAL SCIENCE / Public Policy / Economic Policy. |
    HISTORY / Europe / Scandinavia.
Classification: LCC HC54 .O345 2016 | DDC 330.079–dc23 LC record available at
    https://lccn.loc.gov/2016003438
British Library Cataloging-in-Publication Data is available
This book has been composed in DIN 1451 Std & Sabon Next LT Pro.
Printed on acid-free paper. ∞
Printed in the United States of America
10 9 8 7 6 5 4 3 2 1

I conceive that a thing may have been repeated a thousand times without being a bit more reasonable than it was the first time.

William Hazlitt,
Table Talk or Original Essays on Men and Manners (1822)

CONTENTS

FIGURES

TABLE

ABBREVIATIONS

AEA—American Economic Association
ATP—Swedish supplementary pension system (Allmän Tilläggspension)
BIS—Bank of International Settlements
DSGE—dynamic stochastic general equilibrium
ESO—Expert Group for Studies in Public Economics (Expertgruggpen för Studier i Offentlig Ekonomi)
FOREX—foreign exchange
GDP—gross domestic product (domestic measure of economic output, disregarding output of overseas assets)
IMF—International Monetary Fund
IUI—Industrial Institute for Economic and Social Research, Stockholm (Industrins Utredningsinstitut); currently Research Institute of Industrial Economics' (Institutet för Näringslivsforskning).
LDC—less developed countries
LIBOR—London Interbank Offered Rate (benchmark financial market interest rate in the UK)
LO—Swedish manual workers trade union federation (Landsorganisationen i Sverige)
MCE—market-clearing equilibrium (see figure 5.3)
NBER—National Bureau of Economic Research (United States)
NCM—New Classical Macroeconomics
NPW—Nobel Prize winner
OECD—Organization of Economic Co-operation and Development
PPP—purchase price parity (exchange rates determined by comparing commodity prices in the relevant economies)
SAF—Swedish employers federation (Svenska Arbetsgivareföreningen)
SAP—Swedish Social Democratic Party (Sveriges Socialdemokratiska Arbetarparti)
SNS—Centre for Business and Policy Studies, Stockholm (Studieförbundet Näringsliv och Samhälle)

TCO—Swedish non-manual workers trade union federation
(Tjänstemännens Centralorganisation)
VAR—vector auto-regression (a method of statistical estimation that
makes extensive use of persistence in the data, and does not explicitly test
theoretical models)
WashCon—Washington Consensus

NOBEL PRIZE WINNERS IN ECONOMICS, 1969–2015

1969—Ragnar Frisch, Jan Tinbergen
1970—Paul A. Samuelson
1971—Simon Kuznets
1972—John R. Hicks, Kenneth J. Arrow
1973—Wassily Leontief
1974—Gunnar Myrdal, Friedrich August von Hayek
1975—Leonid Vitaliyevich Kantorovich, Tjalling C. Koopmans
1976—Milton Friedman
1977— James E. Meade, Bertil Ohlin
1978—Herbert A. Simon
1979—Sir Arthur Lewis, Theodore W. Schultz
1980—Lawrence R. Klein
1981—James Tobin
1982—George J. Stigler
1983—Gerard Debreu
1984—Richard Stone
1985—Franco Modigliani
1986—James M. Buchanan Jr.
1987—Robert M. Solow
1988—Maurice Allais
1989—Trygve Haavelmo
1990—Harry M. Markowitz, Merton H. Miller, William F. Sharpe
1991—Ronald H. Coase
1992—Gary S. Becker
1993—Robert W. Fogel, Douglass C. North
1994—John C. Harsanyi, John F. Nash Jr., Reinhard Selten
1995—Robert E. Lucas Jr.
1996—James A. Mirrlees, William Vickrey

1997—Robert C. Merton, Myron S. Scholes

1998—Amartya Sen

1999—Robert A. Mundell

2000—James J. Heckman, Daniel L. McFadden

2001—George A. Akerlof, A. Michael Spence, Joseph E. Stiglitz

2002—Daniel Kahneman, Vernon L. Smith

2003—Robert F. Engle III, Clive W. J. Granger

2004—Finn E. Kydland, Edward C. Prescott

2005—Robert J. Aumann, Thomas C. Schelling

2006—Edmund S. Phelps

2007—Leonid Hurwicz, Eric S. Maskin, Roger B. Myerson

2008—Paul Krugman

2009—Elinor Ostrom, Oliver E. Williamson

2010—Peter A. Diamond, Dale T. Mortensen, Christopher A. Pissarides

2011—Thomas J. Sargent, Christopher A. Sims

2012—Alvin E. Roth, Lloyd S. Shapley

2013—Eugene F. Fama, Lars Peter Hansen, Robert J. Shiller

2014—Jean Tirole

2015—Angus Deaton

PREFACE AND ACKNOWLEDGMENTS

The temper of the times changed around 1970. In the rich societies of the West, two golden decades of full employment and affluence gave way to hard times and hard faces. The reasons given for this 'market turn' are not the same as those that justified and motivated it. Much of the reasoning was economic. How did economic doctrines work, and what work did they do? The Nobel Prize in economics (first awarded in 1969), conveniently defines the economics of its time. It provides a point of reference for the conflict of two protean doctrines, neoclassical economics and social democracy, each of them vying to shape the post-war decades. Sweden established the Nobel Prize and was also an archetype of social democracy. It went through the local episode of a larger story, and we range more widely still. Ostensibly, the two doctrines sang from different scriptures. In practice, they mutated to accommodate each other, which is not to say that their marriages are happy ones.

To go directly to the story of the Nobel Prize, begin with an introduction in the first section of chapter 2 and then continue to a sustained narrative in chapters 4 to 6. Chapter 3 probes deeper into inter-war historical roots.

Before we begin, thanks are due to those who helped. In the spirit of the topic, the benefactors formed an unacknowledged public-private partnership. Our home institutions, the universities of Uppsala and Oxford, and All Souls College at Oxford, have given ample release from teaching and administration. Uppsala and All Souls provided good places to work in, and exquisite companionship. Nuffield College made its rich library available. Colleagues obligingly added some of our usual tasks to their other obligations. Our universities responded generously to matching opportunities offered by the Leverhulme Trust (to AO), and the Institute for New Economic Thinking (INET), two foundations established (more than eight decades apart) by big-hearted capitalists. At Oxford, the History Faculty and All Souls College also provided small grants for particular needs. The book was completed before Gabriel took employment at the Bank of Sweden, and no information acquired in the course of his work there has been used in the book.

In Sweden, Professor Assar Lindbeck spent a day with AO in a wide-ranging interview that extended (the following evening) into a stimulating dinner session. Professor Jörgen Weibull facilitated this interview and enhanced the dinner with informed interventions. We also spoke in Sweden with Professors Lars Magnusson and Janken Myrdal, and with Peter Nobel. Many thanks to them all.

Samuel Bjork co-wrote chapter 6. He developed an algorithm for the Bass model, and used the data we collected to estimate the Bass curves shown in that chapter and its appendix. Philip Mirowski went some of the way with us, and left due to differences of opinion. His acute advice has left its mark, and we parted amicably. Colleagues and friends have helped, listened and responded. Christopher Lagerqvist set up the Oxford-Uppsala collaboration that initially brought us together. Seminar and conference papers were presented in twelve countries on four continents. Many thanks for the invitations, the pointed comments, and the experience of different towns, faces, and outlooks. Friends and colleagues (and three research assistants, also named here) have also read particular chapters or discussed our ideas, including Sundas Ali, Tony Atkinson, Samuel Bjork, Sarah Caro, Vincent Crawford, Paul David, James Fenske, Tamar Frankel, Tim Leunig, Johannes Lindvall (far beyond the call of duty), Meng Miao, Philip Mirowski, Tom Nicholas, Henry Ohlsson, Andrew Scott, Claudio Sopranzetti, David Stuckler, and Julia Twigg. The whole typescript has been read by Pamela Clemit, Shamim Gammage, Max Harris, and Romesh Vaitilingam, who have saved us from error and have shown us the light. Faults that remain are ours alone. Two readers for the publisher were painstaking and sympathetic. Their contribution has sharpened the precision and point of what we have to say. Shamim Gammage provided excellent technical assistance. Sarah Caro and Hannah Paul (for the publisher) gave encouragement, forbearance, and guidance.

Gabriel, looking forward, thanks his wife Mao, and sends a greeting to little Li who will get it when she grows up and learns to read. Avner, looking backwards, is grateful to Leah, his wife, for decades of companionship, support, intelligence, and insight.

Avner Offer and Gabriel Söderberg
December 2015

Notes: When two dates are given in a footnote reference, the first indicates the date of original publication, the second the date of the edition used. The location of archival items in the footnotes can be found in the list of archives that precedes published references in the bibliography.

Chapter 6 draws on Bjork, S., A. Offer and G. Söderberg (2014). 'Time Series Citation Data: The Nobel Prize in Economics', *Scientometrics*, 98,1, 185–196, with kind permission from Springer Science+Business Media. © Akadémiai Kiadó, Budapest, Hungary 2013.

THE NOBEL FACTOR

INTRODUCTION

In the academy, economists are among the few who aspire to tell society how it should manage. They rarely speak with a single voice, but that does not diminish their confidence. Society treats them with bafflement and respect. What do they really know and how do they know it? Where does their authority come from and how far is it justified? Economic theorizing may be speculative, but its impact is powerful and real. Since the 1970s, it has been associated with a large historical trend, the 'market turn' of our title: the rising ascendancy of market liberalism, a political and social movement that (like economics) holds up buying and selling as the norm for human relations and for social organization. How good a warrant did economics provide for the 'market turn'? And is it an improvement on what went on before?

JUST WORLD THEORY

On the evening of 10 December 1969, in the grand setting of Stockholm's Concert Hall, the Dutch economist Jan Tinbergen took his place behind the year's Nobel laureates in physics, chemistry, medicine, and literature to receive the very first 'Prize in Economic Science in Memory of Alfred Nobel'. The other Nobel Prizes had all been given every year since 1901. Alfred Nobel himself, a prolific inventor and businessman of genius, would not have created a prize for economics. He wrote in a letter that he 'hated business with all [his] heart', and he considered himself a social democrat.[1] In the ceremony, the economist Tinbergen was made to stand apart from the other recipients, and was the last to receive his award, after the laureate in literature Samuel Beckett, the Irish avant-garde dramatist, novelist, and poet.

---

1.   Ahlqvist et al., 'Falkst Pris i Nobels Namn' ['False Prize in Nobel's Name'] (2001); Nobel, 'Alfred Bernhard Nobel' (2001), 260.

Now economics is difficult to master, but Beckett is difficult too. Is economics more like physics or literature? Most Nobel economists would dismiss this question, but let it linger for now.

The validity of economics would matter less if it were not used constantly to implement courses of social action in the purported interests of 'efficiency', often without specifying clearly what the benefits might be and for whom. These policies affect the livelihood and well-being of individuals and nations, as well as large financial and business interests. The arguments of economists are supposed to have a special authority, quite different from the pleadings of other parties: they are the counsel of reason, disinterested and objective. They stand apart from the claims of sectional and private self-interest; and also from those that emanate from metaphysical sources like religious sanction or the people's will. There is an irony here, which economists rarely acknowledge: they consider private self-interest to be the prime motivator, but not of their own advice.

Economics is a cluster of doctrines, not always consistent with each other, which mean to provide a simplified but essentially correct model of social reality. Its claim to authority is twofold: that the theory is compelling in itself; and that it is confirmed by observation or consequences. Theory comes first: its simplified accounts of reality have an elegance, even beauty, that arises from their being at odds with everyday intuitions, while at the same time bringing order to the confusion of experience. Economics is not easy to master, but is easy to believe. Since the 1980s, economic methodologists (scholars who appraise the methods and purpose of economics) have largely been content to leave it at that and to focus on the internal validity of theory, the various ways in which it is meant to hang together and work.[2] The main reason for this focus is that a good deal of economic theory is not borne out by either experience or results.

'The great tragedy of science,' the Victorian biologist Thomas Huxley said in 1870, 'is the slaying of a beautiful hypothesis by an ugly fact.' At the risk of being unfashionable, we part ways with present-day methodologists and go back to simpler times, in which theory, to be considered valid, had to accord with experienced reality. Confronting theory with evidence is not simple or easy, and we do not mean to dismiss the many writers who point this out. One of us has tried it himself, confronting George Akerlof's economic the-

---

2. Kincaid, *Oxford Handbook of the Philosophy of Economics* (2009); Mäki, *Philosophy of Economics* (2012).

ory of 'the market for lemons' (recognized by a Nobel Prize in 2001) with the facts of the historical used-car market, the subject of Akerlof's article.[3] A key premise was found to be wrong, the theory as stated was not genuinely testable, and some of its predictions were not borne out. Our reason for insisting on reality is that theory is not only about how to understand the world (epistemology), or how the world is constituted (ontology)—it is also about how life should be conducted, that is, theory is 'normative'. So much hangs on the benefits and sufferings that economics has the power to inflict that we have to insist on asking, 'Is it true and does it work?'[4] Other sources of authority can do without that kind of justification: commitment and inner belief have no need for external confirmation. Authority is often resistant to argument and evidence. Officials, priests, prophets, and leaders do not always submit to the test of consequences. But the Enlightenment in Europe and America ordained a quest for truth by means of critical argument and evidence. The sciences abide by this method, and economics, when it aspires to the same esteem, is presumed to do so as well.

What are the 'norms' that economics lays down? They start from the laudable principle of maximizing well-being, or 'welfare'. Welfare, however, is defined merely as what individuals want, and only that. That is the principle of 'methodological individualism'. A social improvement takes place when somebody can get more of what they want, without depriving anybody else. This is a 'Pareto improvement' (after Vilfredo Pareto, the Italian economist). When there is no slack, nobody can gain without somebody else losing. We get there by means of exchange: people sell what they want less of (including their labour), and buy what they want more of. Everybody has something to sell. If everyone trades freely, the system achieves a benign equilibrium, which is 'Pareto efficient'. This was supposedly anticipated in the eighteenth century by Adam Smith as being like the work of an 'invisible hand'.[5]

In such a system, everyone gets the value of what they can sell, and what they get is what they are due. This imaginary marketplace belongs with a larger set of doctrines, 'Just World Theories'. The concept comes from social psychology, but is used differently here.[6] The idea is simple: a Just World Theory says that everyone gets what he deserves. If the Spanish Inquisition burned heretics, that was only what they deserved. If peasants were starved

---

3. Akerlof, 'The Market for Lemons' (1970); Offer, 'The Markup for Lemons' (2007).
4. As per Blaug, 'Why I Am Not a Constructivist' (1994), 118–119.
5. Offer, 'Self-Interest, Sympathy, and the Invisible Hand' (2012).
6. Rubin, 'Who Believes in a Just World?' (1975); Lerner, *Belief in a Just World* (1980).

and exiled in Soviet Russia, they got what they deserved. Likewise the Nazis and the Jews. Just World Theories are ubiquitous; they are political, religious, ethnic, gendered, and cultural. They justify the infliction of pain.

Market liberalism is also a 'Just World Theory' of this kind. Milton Friedman, Nobel Prize winner (henceforth, NPW) in 1976 wrote, 'The ethical principle that would directly justify the distribution of income in a free market society is, "To each according to what he and the instruments he owns produces."[7] In other words, everyone gets what they deserve. The initial endowment of property and ability, and the consequent market outcomes, are both (as Friedman says) ethically deserved. The free market economy is not only efficient, it is also just, a natural order which it is futile to resist. The norm of individual desert justifies the inequalities and hardships of market society. These are the laissez-faire doctrines of nineteenth-century classical liberalism. Not every economist would accept their ethical value, but the assumption that marginal revenue equals marginal product is pervasive in economic modelling.

Market liberalism is radical. If you genuinely believe that the pursuit of individual self-interest maximizes collective welfare, then collective action in any form is likely to be harmful and to reduce welfare. As we shall see, this doctrine is actually the point of departure for a good deal of policy-related economic analysis since the 1970s. It is deeply counter-intuitive, but can it be true? Here is a role for the Nobel Prize, to provide disinterested scientific validation. Self-interest/market-clearing 'invisible hand' doctrines are inconsistent with most efforts at organized social betterment, and especially with social democracy.

SOCIAL DEMOCRACY AGAINST ECONOMIC DOCTRINE

In the last third of the nineteenth century, trade unions and social democratic parties arose to resist this presumption.[8] Their movements first entered government in Australia before World War I, and in northwestern Europe after its conclusion. Social Democracy (as we shall call it) had different priorities from those of the economics of its day. In economic theory, action is driven by the preferences of the autonomous individual. In Social Democracy, the basic impulse was not gratification but obligation, the basic unit not the individual but the group, family, class, and nation. The prime objective

---

7. Friedman, *Capitalism and Freedom* (1962), 161–162.
8. Deane, 'Scope and Method of Economic Science' (1983).

was not acquisitive, but to achieve security, and more specifically, to cope with life-cycle contingencies. In contrast to the personal cravings that motivate action in economic theory, Social Democracy was driven by the social problem of how to cope with dependency.

In the course of the life cycle, every person goes through periods when they cannot provide for themselves. Early motherhood, infancy and childhood, education, illness, unemployment, disability, and old age are all costly and time-consuming.[9] In conditions of dependency, there is nothing to sell except a claim on humanity, no product to bargain with, no 'two feet' to stand on, and little foresight or capacity to calculate. The 'welfare' problem is how to transfer resources from producers to dependents over the life cycle. In the inter-war years, unemployment threatened almost every manual-working household with losing the very means of existence.

The difference between Social Democracy and economic market doctrines is easy to draw. It is about how to deal with uncertainty. For each individual, the timing and extent of dependency is uncertain. In the aggregate, however, for society as a whole, the magnitude of dependency is known, and its future extent can be predicted actuarially. In Social Democracy, mutual support takes place now, as lateral transfers from one generation to another, from producers to dependents, paid for by taxes. In such a system of social insurance, the risks of dependency are pooled. How much is transferred is decided in a political equilibrium between taxpayers and recipients, but, over time, everyone contributes and everyone benefits.[10] In contrast to Friedman, in Social Democracy (also a Just World Theory), everyone deserves what they get. It extends an entitlement to the sources of well-being to the whole of the nation-state. In Sweden, Social Democracy was designated 'The People's Home.' In the words of its leader,

> The basis of the home is commonality and mutuality. A good home is not aware of any privileged or slighted, no darlings and no stepchildren. You see no one despise the other, no one who tries to gain advantage of others.... In the good home you find equality, compassion, cooperation, helpfulness.[11]

Social Democracy was more evenly gendered, with a focus not on the marketplace, but on family and home. It was not until thirty years after

---

9. Offer, 'Economy of Obligation' (2012).
10. Hills, *Good Times, Bad Times* (2014).
11. Per Albin Hansson, Swedish Parliament, *Andra Kammarens Protokoll* Nr 14–19 [Second Chamber Debates], no. 3, 28 January 1928, 11.

its foundation that a woman, Elinor Ostrom, first won the Nobel Prize in economics—the only one so far.

In economics, in contrast, the risk is borne by every individual. Each person's problem is how to transfer financial claims safely over time, from now, when premiums are paid or savings banked, to the future, when dependency might occur. Security is a commodity like any other, purchased in financial markets as insurance and savings, each person according to a sense of how much he or she can afford. Risks are pooled by insurance companies and banks. Individuals rely for security on commercial contracts.

Apart from these different takes on the future, there is overlap between the two doctrines: for production, both rely on private ownership and management; on distribution through markets, more or less competitive; and on government for a set of public and collective goods like defence and roads.

Late-Victorian economic doctrine answered the need for an intellectual response to the workers' challenge, to trade unions, to socialism, to the land reform movement, and to Social Democracy.[12] Liberal economists upheld the existing property order and its inequalities. In Western Europe, North America and Australasia, Social Democracy eventually prevailed over fascism and communism, established welfare states, safeguarded the structures of capitalism, and dominated policy during the first three post-war decades. It sustained economic growth and distributed it more equally. To do this, it had to challenge the assumptions of neoclassical economics, and sometimes to reject them.

In contrast to the competitive free-for-all of orthodox economics, Social Democratic parties in post-war Europe (and in the English-speaking countries) defined a cluster of collective aspirations:

- Collective insurance against life-cycle periods of dependency, regulated and administered by government and paid for through progressive taxation.
- Good-quality affordable housing, by means of rent control, new construction, mortgage subsidies, and public or collective ownership.
- Secondary and higher education, land use planning, scientific research, culture, sports, roads and railways.

---

12.   Deane, 'Scope and Method of Economic Science' (1983); Mirowski, *Effortless Economy of Science* (2004), chs. 13–14; Gaffney and Harrison, *Corruption of Economics* (1994).

- A mixed economy with extensive public services, some national-ized firms, but leaving private ownership to manage production and distribution.
- A special concern for disadvantaged groups.[13]

The United States also went along with a good deal of this programme, and if it failed to provide universal healthcare entitlement, it did provide one for the old and the indigent.

All this seemed to be expensive: it was administered by governments and paid for out of taxes, so government expenditure in northwestern Europe rose to between 40 and 50 percent of GDP by the end of the 1970s. But voters approved: for taxpayers in the aggregate, this spending provided more benefits than costs.[14] It shifted buying power from times of plenty to times of need. Earners supported those temporarily dependent: mothers, children, students, the unemployed, disabled, sick, and aged. In their turn, producers could anticipate support when they entered dependency in the course of the life cycle. Taxation was progressive, so those with more also gave more, and took out proportionately less. Where benefits were high and universal (that is, provided equally for all), those with lower incomes benefited proportion-ately more.[15] Inequality in advanced countries fell to the lowest levels since the Middle Ages.

COMPETING VISIONS

It is not far-fetched to regard World War II as a consequence of the policy failures of inter-war economic orthodoxy.[16] In 1944, with war still raging, two publications set out different visions of the future by two economists who received the Nobel Prize on the same day thirty years later. One was *The Postwar Programme of Swedish Labour*, published by the ruling Social Democratic Party in Sweden, and co-written by the economist Gunnar Myrdal (his portrait is on our jacket, with his Nobel Peace Prize–winning wife, Alva).[17] The other was *The Road to Serfdom*, published in Britain by Friedrich von Hayek.[18]

---

13. For Norway and Sweden, Sejersted, *Age of Social Democracy* (2011).
14. Lindert, *Growing Public* (2004), II; Hills, *Good Times, Bad Times* (2015).
15. Rothstein and Steinmo, 'Social Democracy in Crisis?' (2013), 99.
16. Chapter 3, below.
17. Landsorganisationen, *Postwar Programme of Swedish Labour* (1946, originally published 1944).
18. Hayek, *Road to Serfdom* (1944).

Swedish Social Democracy had come to power in 1932 and kept Sweden out of the war.[19] Its 1944 programme is a high point of Social Democratic aspiration. It condemned inter-war economics for tolerating unemployment and poverty; the war had mobilized productive resources even in neutral Sweden, which might serve as a model for peace. A detailed list of twenty-seven challenges fell under three headings: 'Full Employment' (as the main guarantee of security), and 'Fair Distribution and Higher Living Standards' (implying redistribution from capital to labour). A third item, 'Greater Productive Efficiency and Increased Industrial Democracy', set out the target of economic growth. This was the most distinctive feature of Swedish Social Democracy: it was Gunnar Myrdal's innovation to argue that security and equity for all were also productive, that there was no contradiction between efficiency and equity.[20] The fervour for improvement had a dark side, a certain lack of sympathy for those who might be incapable of work due to mental or social incapacity.[21] Overall, however, it was an articulate, sober and democratic challenge to economic orthodoxy.[22]

For Hayek, an Austrian professor at the London School of Economics, Social Democracy was the first stop on *The Road to Serfdom*. It could open the way to tyranny. The book belies its austere reputation: Hayek conceded some need for social insurance and other government interventions. If he was uneasy about the 'social' aspect of Social Democracy, he was also wary of the 'democratic' side. Freedom as the opposite of tyranny did not entail democracy. It had to be protected from majorities.[23] 'I would prefer temporarily to sacrifice ... democracy,' he said in an interview in Chile in 1981, 'before having to do without freedom.'[24]

Serfdom was an immediate hit in Britain, and even more so in the United States, where it was published by the University of Chicago Press.[25] It gained enormous circulation, over a million copies in a *Reader's Digest* abridged edition, and a cartoon version in the popular weekly magazine *Look*, also distributed gratis by General Motors and General Electric. The cartoons left out the section on social insurance. The book was quickly translated into Swedish as

---

19. Berman, *The Social Democratic Moment* (1998).
20. Andersson, *Between Growth and Security* (2006), ch. 2.
21. Andersson, ibid., ch. 3; Myrdal, *Nation and Family* (1941), ch. 6 (revision of Alva and Gunnar Myrdal, *Kris i Befolkningsfrågan* [1934]).
22. Landsorganisationen, *Postwar Programme of Swedish Labour* (1946), 3–5.
23. Burgin, *Great Persuasion* (2012), 116–120, esp. 119.
24. Caldwell and Montes, 'Friedrich Hayek and His Visits to Chile' (2014), 47.
25. Söderberg et al., 'Hayek in Citations' (2013), 66–67.

well, where it became a focal point for resistance to Social Democracy, whose electoral hold on power was never secure.[26] Hayek's slippery slope view of Social Democracy has since been grotesquely falsified: no societies on earth are further from serfdom than the Nordic welfare states. Mixed economies with high levels of government intervention have reliably sustained political and economic freedoms for many decades, while laissez-faire and totalitarian regimes have not.[27] But then Hayek consistently dismissed any scientific standing for economics, up to and including his Nobel Prize Lecture.

Hayek, who had been marginalized as an economist by John Maynard Keynes in Britain, was now lionized in the United States. He transformed his literary and financial success into a political project. Business foundations paid for an international gathering of economists, journalists, and businessmen at the Mont Pèlerin Hotel in Switzerland in April 1947. After several days of deliberation, the participants launched the Mont Pèlerin Society. From that year onwards, the regular meetings of the society, funded by American foundations at comfortable venues, became the intellectual focus of resistance to Social Democracy.[28] For about two decades, the society was controlled by Hayek, who vetted all new members. The first meeting assembled some of the leading anti-labour intellectuals in Europe and America, including several future winners of the Nobel Prize: Hayek himself, Milton Friedman, George Stigler, Bertil Ohlin, and Maurice Allais (though the last two declined to join).[29] Another participant, the philosopher Karl Popper, author of *The Open Society and its Enemies* (1945), advocated opening society meetings to external critics, but Hayek would not agree.[30] 'Freedom' was not the same as an open mind.

Many years later, the course of the society was described by Milton Friedman (NPW, 1976) to Max Hartwell, its official historian,

> The threat to a free society that we envisaged at the founding meeting of the Mont Pèlerin Society is very different from the threat to a free society that has developed over the intervening period. Our initial fear was of central planning and extensive nationalization. The developing threat has

---

26. Lewin, *Planhushållningsdebatten* (1967), 267–273.
27. Alves and Meadowcroft, 'Hayek's Slippery Slope' (2014).
28. Mont Pèlerin Society Papers, Hoover Institution Archives, Stanford University, and Liberaalarchief, Ghent; Hartwell, *History of the Mont Pèlerin Society* (1995); Walpen, *Die offenen Feinde und ihre Gesellschaft* (2004); Mirowski and Plehwe, *The Road from Mont Pèlerin* (2009); Burgin, *The Great Persuasion* (2012), ch. 3.
29. Allais did so later.
30. Burgin, *The Great Persuasion* (2012), 95.

been via the welfare state and redistribution. Unfortunately, the threat did not disappear but simply changed its character. Nonetheless, I believe it is very important to point out this change in character in interpreting the so-called re-emergence of liberalism. In the words of a song from an ILGWU musical of many years ago, 'Pins and Needles', 'One step forward, two steps backward, that is the way we progress.'[31]

This last sentence is rich in deliberate irony (this is also the title of a pamphlet by Lenin).[32] The musical came out of the New York Jewish immigrant culture which Friedman also came from; it was written and produced by members of the International Ladies Garment Workers Union with a cast of cutters, basters, and sewing machine operators, and played on Broadway more than a thousand times from 1937 to 1940. It was also performed at Franklin D. Roosevelt's White House. When Friedman's letter was written in 1985, the quotation had been sadly borne out, but it is also a humorous reference to the Mont Pèlerin Society's own long game of gradualism, which eventually achieved remarkable success, not least in capturing the prestige of the Nobel Prizes awarded to eight of its members.

THEORY AND PERFORMANCE

The Nobel Prize testifies to the formidable stock of theory underpinning economics. To be sure, only a minority of economists joined the Mont Pèlerin Society or supported its goals, but some of the most prominent among them were Nobel Prize winners. The ascendancy of market liberalism began around the same time as the creation of the prize. We could tell it this way: In December 1967, Milton Friedman delivered the American Economic Association's presidential address.[33] The message was incendiary: the Keynesian economic policies associated with Social Democracy no longer kept either unemployment or inflation at bay. For the next seven years, Friedman became among the most cited economists of all, temporarily overtaking Adam Smith, the permanent citation leader.[34] That speech signalled a move in the historical chess-game between the two doctrines: On the one hand, Social Democracy, a political movement which set out to reduce insecurities

---

31. Friedman to Max Hartwell, 10 July 1985, Hoover Institution, Friedman Papers, 200–10.
32. Lenin, *One Step Forward, Two Steps Back* (1904/1947).
33. Friedman, 'The Role of Monetary Policy' (1968).
34. See figure 6.9, below. Kenneth Arrow also overtook Smith for a few years.

and inequalities for most of the population, providing healthcare, education, and protection from life-cycle contingencies by means of progressive taxation. On the other, a neoliberal economic doctrine (neoliberal in doctrine, market-liberal as a wider social movement), committed to undoing these reforms. Over following decades, both neoliberalism (doctrine), and market liberalism (movement) have done much to wrong-side the post-war welfare states, while prosperity and prospects for most people in Western societies have levelled off or fallen. During those same decades, however, and partly as a result of the globalization advocated by neoliberals, prosperity worldwide has actually increased. China, India, and Brazil have penetrated Western markets without submitting to market-liberal dictation, following the earlier lead of Japan, Taiwan, South Korea, and Singapore.[35]

Social Democracy did not have the same intellectual horsepower behind it as economics.[36] Of NPWs, only Gunnar Myrdal (NPW, 1974) can be regarded as a direct advocate (although around half the NPWs in our period inclined towards Social Democracy, and a higher proportion among economists in general).[37] There is not a great deal of doctrine, but the practical achievement is no less formidable than that of market liberalism. As figure I.1 shows, in the leading OECD countries, about 30 percent of national income is devoted to social insurance and social policy, and allocated by central government (bottom curve). In the period 1990–2008, the proportion was still increasing. The element of social insurance was more popular among voters than redistribution.[38] The United States regularly elects conservatives to high office, but the attempt to privatize even a small segment of social security has failed so far. The reason is that, for social insurance, the Social Democratic method is far more efficient.[39] But that does not make it secure. Social Democracy clashes directly with market liberalism in its view of labour. For market liberalism, work is a commodity like any other, to be bought and sold at will. 'At will' is the current doctrine of employment in the United States, which allows workers to be fired at any time with no reasons given (unless protected by contract). For most people, this is a source

---

35. Alpert, *The Age of Oversupply* (2013); Lin, *Demystifying the Chinese Economy* (2011); Wade, *Governing the Market* (1990); and chapter 11, below.
36. Myrdal, *Kris i Befolkningsfrågan* (1934); Crosland, *Future of Socialism* (1936); Korpi and Palme, 'The Paradox of Redistribution' (1988); Esping-Andersson, *Three Worlds of Welfare Capitalism* (1990); Rothstein, *Just Institutions Matter* (1998); Barr, *Economics of the Welfare State* (2012).
37. Below, chapter 5, figure 5.2.
38. Taylor-Gooby, *Double Crisis of the Welfare State* (2013).
39. Offer, 'Economy of Obligation' (2012).

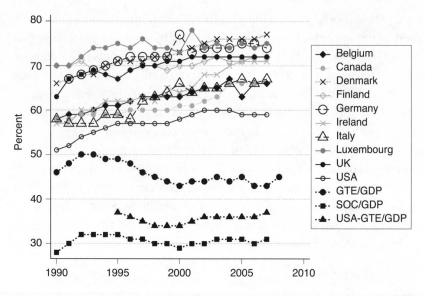

Figure I.1. Social expenditure as percentage of government expenditure and government expenditure as percentage of GDP, 1990–2008.
Source: OECD, 'General Government Spending by Destination' (2014).
Note: GTE denotes government total expenditure; SOC is social expenditure (health, education, and social insurance/welfare).

of intense insecurity, since household obligations (like mortgage payments and children's education) are locked far into the future, and work sustains a sense of dignity and purpose. In the United States at least, healthcare provision is commonly linked to employment. 'Labour market flexibility' is high on the market liberal agenda in Europe today, seeking to converge with the 'at-will' employment doctrine of the United States.

In 2008, the financial markets had to be rescued by governments from their follies; this was a role for welfare which neither Social Democrats nor market liberals had ever envisaged. There was little show of gratitude. Instead, market liberals took the resulting budget deficits as a cue to redouble their attacks on the welfare state, like a drowning man who escapes with his life, leaving the rescuer to drown instead. That story continues beyond this book.

Our subject is not the achievement of individual NPWs, or of Nobel economics as a whole. There are several studies in that vein.[40] It is the worldly

---

40. Grüske, *Die Nobelpreisträger der ökonomischen Wissenschaft* (1994); McCarty, *The Nobel Laureates* (2001); Vane and Mulhearn, *The Nobel Memorial Laureates in Economics* (2006); Breit, *Lives of the Laureates* (2009); Horn, *Roads to Wisdom* (2009); Karier, *Intellectual Capital* (2010); Klein et al., 'Ideological Profiles of the Nobel Laureates' (2013); Ghosh, 'Beautiful Minds' (2015).

power of economics, how and how much a body of doctrine has succeeded in motivating policy. These doctrines are viewed from the outside, as users would see them, not their originators. Those who deploy these doctrines in policy-making are rarely versed in their mysteries. Likewise for those affected, whose viewpoint is the one we adopt here.

GIST OF THE BOOK

Economics works by constructing simple models of economic behaviour which are then mustered to bear on policy. To combine the premises of individual self-seeking and social harmony was an ambitious undertaking, which has to be judged as a qualified failure both analytically and empirically. Disregarding these weaknesses, Chicago economists argued that profit-making firms should replace the welfare state, in line with the objectives of the New Right in politics. For a discipline that celebrates rationality, the Nobel Prize is an anomaly, a form of magic, a one-sided transfer handed down as a gift. Ironically, this magic is transformed into authority for what counts as science. Natural scientists think that theory has to be confronted with evidence. In economics, however, in response to empirical failure, methodologists have waived this requirement. But many practitioners have drawn the opposite conclusion, and turned their backs on the core doctrines: publications of abstract theory peaked in the early 1980s, and there is a new 'empirical turn', of laboratory, field, and natural experiments, with little reference to market-clearing theory. Several Nobel Prize winners have also queried core doctrines.

The Nobel Prize in economics came out of the strife between Social Democracy and business elites in Sweden, a local instance of class conflict in the West more broadly. Sweden, which had been neutral in World War I, and with a rich endowment of abilities and natural resources, made an easy transition to Social Democracy between the wars. In most of Europe, the challenge of debt obligations culminated in domestic and international crises. After 1945, the ruling Social Democratic Party in Sweden prioritized housing and full employment, a policy which was resisted by the central bank on grounds of price stability. The government stifled the bank, which looked for ways to reassert itself. The Nobel Prize in economics was endowed in 1968 by the central bank at the pinnacle of Social Democratic success.

Does economics have a political bias? We examine this by means of NPW citation counts, and opinion surveys within the discipline. The custodians of the prize (a small group of Swedish economists) strove to maintain a mechanical balance between the left and the right, but well to the right of the balance of opinion within the discipline as a whole, which inclined towards Social Democratic values by about two to one. The Nobel Committee achieved credibility by selecting scholars at the top of their game. One exception was Friedrich von Hayek, whose reputation had collapsed, and who received a big citation boost from the award. The committee excluded or held back some highly cited scholars, at least two of them on ideological grounds.

In its first historical phase from the 1870s to the 1950s, market-clearing equilibrium economics accorded with the low-taxation norms of classical liberalism. The post-war success of Social Democracy challenged this model. Economics responded by flipping over; it replaced the premise of harmony with a motivational assumption of bad faith. It challenged Social Democracy on grounds of efficiency, but this reversal carried a cost. Harmony doctrines made it possible to prescribe optimal policies. The assumption of bad faith made outcomes indeterminate. Self-seeking no longer delivered the best outcomes. The authority of economics was undermined. And the assumption of bad faith promoted bad faith.

In Sweden itself, Social Democracy was challenged directly by a group of economists associated with Professor Assar Lindbeck, who also dominated the Nobel awards. Lindbeck's allegations of Social Democratic inefficiency were not well-founded. The economic crisis he warned of eventually arrived, but not for the reasons he expected. It was caused by financial deregulation, which Lindbeck and other market-liberal economists supported. When invited by a centre-right government to lay down policy, Lindbeck was not fazed: he prescribed a contraction of labour entitlements. His reforms were taken up in part, but their relevance is doubtful. Despite market liberalism, Social Democracy in Sweden was adaptable, survived the alternation of parties in government, and also the social change of de-industrialization.

Beyond Scandinavia, market-friendly reforms were imposed by the international financial agencies based in Washington. The 'Washington Consensus' extended credit to developing countries, but on condition of business-friendly deregulation. An unexpected consequence was a tide of corruption which welled up in the borrowing countries, and then spread back into the core Western economies where it has become pervasive. This malaise, we argue, was sanctioned by the ethical neutrality professed by economics. It demonstrated that the ethical indifference of doctrines could have a serious economic and social cost.

In conclusion, the influence of economics is at odds with its shortcomings as a philosophy, as a scientific doctrine, and as a set of policy norms. The invisible hand is magical thinking, and its repeated disconfirmation has had little effect. On the other hand, economics has a set of empirical disciplines and achievements, with enclaves of technical and even scientific credibility. This suggests some downgrading of authority, but not all the way. Economics is not superior to other sources of authority, but is not necessarily inferior to them either; it should be taken as one voice among many. In that respect, it is rather like Social Democracy. The Nobel Prize committee has been able to maintain the credibility of the prize only by acknowledging that economics does not hang together as a single all-encompassing system of thought. Social Democracy provides an alternative that is pragmatically successful, analytically coherent, economically efficient, ethically attractive, and theoretically modest.

CHAPTER 1
IMAGINARY MACHINES

We think of economists as men of the world, but much of their Nobel Prize accomplishment is anything but worldly. 'Economic literature is largely speculative, an apparently inconclusive exploration of possible worlds.'[1] About half of the prize winners have engaged primarily in the building of intellectual constructs, imaginary machines, or simply 'models'. This term should be understood as in 'model aircraft'. Unlike model aircraft, economic models mostly remain on paper, usually in the form of mathematical equations, but mechanical analogues can be constructed: the Phillips MONIAC hydraulic computer simulated the circular flow of money in the economy by means of coloured water in glass pipes, with valves which permitted policy choices to be simulated.[2]

MODEL MAKING

The city of Oxford in England has a vast and beautiful open space called Port Meadow, only a short walk from the centre. It survives undeveloped because it is owned as common property, in defiance of market norms. On weekends, it sometimes attracts a band of model aviators, whose machines buzz overhead all day long. Economic models, however, are rarely taken out to Port Meadow, and are unlikely to fly. It is difficult to know (beyond the claims of their designers) how airworthy they really are.

The environs of Port Meadow also have a poignant memorial to a pair of real flyers, who crashed there in 1912 (figure 1.1). The memorial highlights the difference between models founded on the disciplines of science and

---

1. McCloskey, 'Economics Science: A Search through the Hyperspace of Assumptions' (1991), 11.
2. Morgan, *The World in the Model* (2012), ch. 5.

Figure 1.1. Aviation Memorial in Wolvercote, Oxford.
Source: Photo: Avner Offer.

of economics. Its grasshopper aircraft foreshadows real progress. The first powered flight in Britain took place only four years earlier. The innovation was tested by life-and-death risk-taking, not paper speculations. Motivated by more than money, it required co-operation as well as competition, was undertaken by government, and was embedded in a particular locality. But in the mainstream or orthodox neoclassical tradition, models do not exist in a particular time and place, and if they are rejected, it is not by practical experience, but by other theorists.[3] That is rarely the end of the matter. In the words of Joan Robinson (who deserved the Nobel Prize but did not get it): 'In a subject where there is no agreed procedure for knocking out errors, doctrines have a long life.'[4]

An economic model is not easy to design. It needs to comply with a web of constraints. These include prior convictions (henceforth, 'priors'), policy and political orientations, agreement with some larger theory, internal

3. 'Neoclassical': The economics of Adam Smith, David Ricardo and John Stuart Mill (classical economics, c. 1770–1870) reckoned economic value by the cost of production. Its 'neoclassical' successors (from the 1870s onwards, including W. S. Jevons, Vilfredo Pareto, Alfred Marshall, Paul Samuelson) measured it by willingness to pay.
4. Robinson, *Economic Philosophy* (1962), 79. On her entitlement to the prize, see 136–137, below.

consistency, mathematical technique, stylized facts (for example, producers, consumers, taxes), and analogy with some real-world issue.[5] And it needs to be validated by empirical observation: it needs to fly.[6]

Two particular priors are the core doctrines of economics, 'methodological individualism' and the 'invisible hand.'[7] Economic activity is driven exclusively by private self-interest, and it scales up to an efficient state ('equilibrium') in which supply matches demand, and all markets clear. Adam Smith mentioned the invisible hand only once in an economic context. He did not spell out how it worked, although he did provide an elegant example.[8] But it remained a conjecture, just an article of faith.[9] The quest to demonstrate the validity of equilibrium, that is, to prove its existence mathematically, has a long history.[10] We skip over the century after Smith, and begin with Leon Walras in 1874. He described an economy in which all prices would be brought into equilibrium by an imaginary auction, at the end of which no goods were left unsold. Francis Edgeworth in 1881 and Vilfredo Pareto in 1906, between them, showed that when two traders exchanged one commodity each, they could strike a deal to share all the benefit available (the 'Pareto optimum' already mentioned in the introduction), in proportion to their respective bargaining power. Edgeworth gave reasons to think that with numerous traders, the equilibrium point became unique.[11]

A more encompassing version emerged in the 1930s as 'welfare economics', which specified the conditions for achieving 'efficiency' in market exchange, that is, that no goods should remain unsold. To simplify, these conditions specified an extensive uniformity: that when two inputs were combined in production (say, labour and machinery), all producers delivered the same output, which had a unique value. As prices fell, consumers bought more; as costs increased, producers raised prices, and demand and supply converged on an equilibrium. In other words, the price posted 'at the margin', that is, for the next purchase or sale, would be uniform for all sellers and buyers (as in the initial two-trader example), thus meeting the efficiency requirement that

5. Boumans, 'Built-in Justification' (1999), 93.

6. In substantive agreement with Syll, *On the Use and Misuse of Theories and Models* (2015).

7. Introduction, above, 3.

8. Smith, 'Digression Concerning the Corn Trade', *Wealth of Nations* (1776/1976), IV.5.b 1–9, 524–528.

9. Offer, 'Self-interest, Sympathy and the Invisible Hand' (2012).

10. Precursors, Ingrao and Israel, *The Invisible Hand* (1990), chs. 2–3.

11. Creedy, 'Some Recent Interpretations' (1980); Humphrey, 'Early History of the Box Diagram' (1996).

no output should remain unsold. This marginal pricing norm is sometimes regarded as a third core doctrine of economics. These restrictive assumptions of uniformity (and others not specified here) are at odds with any economy that has ever existed. Indeed, it is not clear how (with no price differences for uniform goods) sellers can even compete with each other.[12] The real world falls short of this ideal, and invites economists to fix it.

In 1954, Kenneth Arrow (NPW, 1972), Gerard Debreu (NPW, 1983), and Lionel Mckenzie, separately showed that the unique equilibrium sought by Walras (and glimpsed by Edgeworth, Pareto, and others) was capable of a mathematical solution. This proof of the existence of 'general equilibrium' (abbreviated as 'Arrow-Debreu') was hailed as the holy grail of economics, which had uncovered the secret of market magic.[13] But it required even more onerous conditions to work: that no single trader could affect prices ('perfect competition') and most importantly, complete markets, namely that every consumer and producer knows all prices of all goods for all time, in all possible states of nature (that is, rain *and* shine), and that all these goods can be traded now, once, and for all. There are no economies of scale: a worker on his own can produce as much as one in a factory. General equilibrium left out government, money, finance, monopoly, co-operation, expectations, and change over time, and had nothing to say about unemployment, distribution, and inequality. It did not say how to get there, or what happens next. This did not resemble any existing world either. The model showed that such an equilibrium was mathematically not impossible (it 'existed'), and was in accord with the full use of available resources ('Pareto efficiency'). But that such equilibria could persist, even in mathematical models (the attribute of 'stability'), remains in doubt.[14] Arrow's co-author Frank Hahn wrote 'the complete market hypothesis is completely falsified', and Arrow added, 'such a system could not exist.'[15] Hahn went further, and said that the conditions for general equilibrium turned out to be so demanding, that Arrow-Debreu was mostly useful as a *refutation* of the 'invisible hand.'[16] Joseph Stiglitz (NPW, 2001) wrote that in the absence of perfect information

12. Blaug, *Economic Theory in Retrospect* (1997), 570–595.
13. Historical survey and analysis, Ingrao and Israel, *The Invisible Hand* (1990).
14. Rizvi, 'The Sonnenschein-Mantel-Debreu Results' (2006); Fisher, 'The Stability of General Equilibrium' (2011).
15. Hahn, 'Reflections on the Invisible Hand' (1982/1984), 121; Arrow, 'Rationality of Self and Others in an Economic-System' (1986), S393.
16. Hahn, 'On the Notion of Equilibrium in Economics' (1973/1984), 52.

and complete markets for all time (both impossible), equilibrium could not be Pareto efficient.[17]

A model aircraft in flight balances precariously between gravity and lift. When it falls to the ground, it achieves a more stable equilibrium. Likewise in economics, equilibrium is almost a truism. It seems to accord with the facts of experience, especially those of being better off. There is food on the table and money in the bank, the shops are full, and the car is in the driveway. Semesters follow in succession and lead into summer holidays and overseas conferences, as things get better all the time. Elsewhere there may be anxiety, unemployment, debt, illness, divorce, long days of dull work, pain, discrimination, mental disorder, prison, war, and death. But if these incentives are needed to make the magic work, then we don't want it disturbed. And if you don't like it, then take yourself off somewhere else. This conception of equilibrium, however, was less compelling to inter-war proletarians seeking for ways out of poverty and insecurity.

When applied in economic modelling, self-interest and equilibrium are priors: they take as given what actually needs to be established. Neither of them is a fact. When Edgeworth and Pareto demonstrated that exchange between two self-interested agents would leave no waste, it was an illuminating analysis of potential market efficiency.[18] But over subsequent decades, the priors of self-interest and equilibrium hardened into rigid requirements, as if possessing some desirable virtue in themselves. Like the Soviet command economy, neoclassical models also embody the dreams and values of their designers. That self-interest is a virtue, as the models posit, is self-evident to the selfish. Within neoclassical models, property owners can gratify themselves with no consideration for those with lesser endowments. If this could be shown (or made) to align with reality by economists, so much the better. And if the model is true, then society is redundant.

HOW MODELS WORK

Economic models are extended to the real world by analogy. Chicago model-maker Robert Lucas (NPW, 1995) explained that the purpose of model-building is to 'argue by analogy from what we know about one situation to what we would like to know about another, quite different situation.'[19] The

---

17. Stiglitz, *Whither Socialism* (1994), ch. 2.
18. Humphrey, 'Early History of the Box Diagram' (1996).
19. Lucas, 'What Economists Do' (1988), 5.

real world is held up to the standard of perfection exemplified in the model. But the model is greatly simplified in comparison with reality. An analogy says that in some essential respect '*x* is like *y*.' It works in one of two ways: either *ceteris paribus* (all other things kept equal), or *mutatis mutandis* (with the necessary modifications). It is not a scale model of reality, but an alternative to it. In analogy, *x* is never *the same* as *y*. Hence, no appeal to reality, no observation or measurement, can show that an analogy is false. Lucas wrote that the analogy that one person finds persuasive, his neighbour might well dismiss,[20] implying the absence of objective criteria for selection.

In economic discourse, a model is only required to demonstrate internal consistency. This theme recurs in Lucas, for example:

> A 'theory' is not a collection of assertions about the behavior of the actual economy but rather an explicit set of instructions for building a parallel or analogue system—a mechanical, imitation economy. A 'good' model, from this point of view, will not be exactly more 'real' than a poor one, but will provide better imitations. Of course, what one means by a 'better imitation' will depend on the particular questions to which one wishes answers.[21]

In other words, the model does not *work* like reality, but seeks to mimic some particular aspect or outcome. This sounds plausible, but even if it works in this single dimension (which it often doesn't), how can it be validated in the complicated richness of an actual, evolving, historical economy?

Analogy is also the method of poetry, and like metaphors in poetry, the model can be beautifully suggestive, without being true.[22] Like a poetic metaphor, an economic model is often surprisingly counter-intuitive, and yet produces the thrill of recognition. That economic models are like model aircraft is a metaphor. An economic model, however, is more than just a mechanical metaphor. When parameters change, it shows (with some probability) what is likely to happen. But it cannot show the effect of what is left out, and which omissions are justified. The policy tools that such models inspire are rarely reliable.[23] In contrast, good science, whatever else it is as intellectual discourse, reliably underpins the daily take-it-for-granted performance

---

20. Ibid., 5.
21. Lucas, 'Methods and Problems in Business Cycle Theory' (1980), 697.
22. McCloskey, 'Economic Science: A Search through the Hyperspace of Assumptions' (1991), 13; King, *The Microfoundations Delusion* (2012), ch. 2.
23. For example, Tovar, 'DSGE Models and Central Banks' (2008), 18.

of the technologies (transport, communication, energy, health) on which society and the economy depend.

Models are constructed by the application of reason. They do not require empirical validity, but they do imply it. The mathematician and game theorist John von Neumann wrote in 1955 that models may exist independently, but can be validated only by observation and empirical performance:

> The sciences do not try to explain, they hardly even try to interpret, they mainly make models. By a model is meant a mathematical construct which, with the addition of certain verbal interpretations, describes observed phenomena. The justification of such a mathematical construct is solely and precisely that it is expected to work.[24]

A good economic model is both counter-intuitive and compelling. The English economist David Ricardo (1776–1823) provided an enduring template for model-making. His theory of comparative advantage postulated two countries each making two goods, to show that trade between them was beneficial even if one country produced both goods more cheaply. Published in 1817, it is still in the textbooks today, underpinning the policy norm of free trade. Such powerful models are not easy to come by. It takes a rare creative talent to take counter-intuitive assumptions and assemble them into a model with meaningful results. This is sufficiently difficult to restrict the pool of potential Nobel candidates. Often the reality check of external validity, the last and most demanding requirement, has to be left out. The difficulty of matching models with observation also has the opposite consequence, namely that no reality can live up to the perfection of the model. The imagined model of perfect competition can never be observed, and so it never fails. This failure to match up to perfection has been called the 'Nirvana fallacy.'[25] But for market liberals, 'Nirvana economics' makes any real economy look bad, especially the high-tax Social Democratic consensus of the post-war years.

THE RICARDIAN VICE

New aircraft models are tested in wind tunnels: calculations alone are not reliable, and hands-on investigation is also required. And from wind tunnel to a working airliner is still a long way. But economic models are rarely rejected

---

24. von Neumann, 'Method in the Physical Sciences' (1955), 492.
25. Demsetz, 'Information and Efficiency' (1969), 1.

merely by testing. Consider Ricardo again, a master of heroic abstraction. In addition to comparative advantage, he devised other compelling models showing that, over the long term, the wages of labour must decline to mere subsistence, and (separately, in another model) that stable prices require a hoard of monetary gold. Given the premises of these models, the conclusions were inescapable. They entered the Victorian worldview, but historical experience has left them behind, and they are no longer regarded as true today. Ricardo's strategy was described by Joseph Schumpeter (a great Austrian economist) as 'the Ricardian Vice':

> His interest was in the clear-cut result of direct, practical significance. In order to get this he cut that general system to pieces, bundled up as large parts of it as possible, and put them in cold storage—so that as many things as possible should be frozen and 'given'. He then piled one simplifying assumption upon another until, having really settled everything by these assumptions ... he set up simple one-way relations so that, in end, the desired results emerged almost as tautologies. For example, a famous Ricardian theory is that profits 'depend upon' the price of wheat. And under his implicit assumptions . . . this is not only true, but undeniably, in fact trivially, so. Profits could not possibly depend upon anything else, since everything else is 'given', that is frozen. It is an excellent theory that can never be refuted and lacks nothing save sense. The habit of applying results of this character to the solution of practical problems we shall call the Ricardian Vice.[26]

Robert Lucas is well-versed in the Ricardian Vice. Between the late 1970s and the 1990s, he held sway as the leading light of neoliberal model-making. He was also unusually clear about how models are made and what they can do. For Lucas, economics is nothing more than the construction of analogue machines: 'Progress in economic thinking means getting better and better abstract, analogue models, not better verbal observations about the world.'[27] A model is typically embodied in a computer program. 'Our task . . . is to write a FORTRAN program that will accept specific economic policy rules as "input" and will generate as "output" statistics describing the operating characteristics of time series we care about, which are predicted to result from these policies.'[28]

26. Schumpeter, *History of Economic Analysis* (1954), 472–473.
27. Lucas, 'Methods and Problems' (1980), 700; Lucas, *Lectures on Economic Growth* (2002), 21.
28. Lucas, 'Methods and Problems' (1980), 709; FORTRAN is a formerly pervasive computer coding language.

The economic golden age of high growth, social insurance, and mass consumption after 1945 was widely attributed to Keynesian policy norms, which allowed government to regulate private and public demand to ensure full employment and low inflation. From the late 1960s, this approach was thrown into question by the combination of falling growth and rising inflation.[29] Lucas's project, the New Classical Macroeconomics (NCM), was one of several emanating from the neoliberal Chicago School and its satellites, which took as their premise the ineffectiveness, indeed the futility, of Keynesian policy interventions. Among the others were Milton Friedman's monetarism, a method of achieving price stability by increasing the money supply at a constant rate to match the expected growth of real GDP. This could not be made to work and can be taken as falsified.[30]

Among other doctrines, the eponymous Coase theorem demonstrated (in the Chicago interpretation) that the initial distribution of assets did not matter, since (in a frictionless world) market exchange would bring them into the most productive hands. In contrast, Ronald Coase himself (NPW, 1991) expected economic frictions to prevent this from happening.[31] George Stigler's doctrine of 'regulatory capture' stated that regulation worked mostly for the regulated industries, and not for the public; and the related 'Public Choice' theory (James Buchanan and others) postulated that public servants were motivated only by self-interest.[32] By 1995, all of these projects had been awarded Nobel Prizes. Edward Prescott, Finn Kydland, and Thomas Sargent, who worked in tandem with Lucas, got their prizes later. Eugene Fama got one in 2013 for the doctrine of efficient markets in finance.[33] The person who hasn't yet is Robert Barro, for his doctrine of 'Ricardian Equivalence', a model attributed to Ricardo which showed that government spending to increase demand would be offset by prudent consumers reducing their outlays in anticipation of future taxation. The policy point was that government could make no difference ('policy ineffectiveness'), implying that Social De-

29. Forder, *Macroeconomics and the Phillips Curve Myth* (2014), argues that neoliberal critics misrepresented Keynesian policies.

30. Modigliani, 'The Monetarist Controversy Revisited' (1988/1997); Mayer, 'The Twilight of the Monetarist Debate' (1990).

31. Coase, 'The Institutional Structure of Production', Nobel Lecture 1991. Nobel Lectures (delivered by NPWs usually a day or two after the prize ceremony) are cited henceforth with title and year. They are available at http://www.nobelprize.org/nobel_prizes/economic -sciences/laureates/index.html, and are mostly reprinted in an irregular series of variously edited volumes entitled *Economic Sciences* with dates.

32. McLean, *Public Choice* (1980); Mueller, *Public Choice III* (2003).

33. Fox, *The Myth of the Rational Market* (2009).

mocracy and Keynesian management were self-defeating and futile. The development economist and historian Albert Hirschman has shown that the futility of reform is one of three enduring tropes of political reactionaries ever since the French Revolution, and places Chicago economics within this lineage.[34]

RATIONAL EXPECTATIONS

Of these components, rational expectations macroeconomics was the most insulated from falsification, the most empirically empty, and in terms of adoption by economists, by far the most successful. This doctrine continues to be influential in macroeconomics, and is practised across ideological and methodological divides by Chicago market fundamentalists and by liberal-minded 'neo-Keynesians'. It is a modelling approach: the assumption is that individual market participants form their expectations of future price levels on the basis of all the public information available. 'Form their expectations' means that in analysing the information available, members of the public are assumed to be applying the economist's own statistical model, regardless of how technically difficult that might be. This enables them to anticipate future prices correctly at least on average. Their self-interested choices then determine the course of the economy as a whole (its 'macroeconomics'). This doctrine is an analytical achievement deemed sufficiently difficult to be worthy of several Nobel Prizes, but its application is nevertheless taken to be within the competence of everybody, even before it had been understood and formulated.

Consider an analogous system: The Antikythera mechanism is a mysterious mechanical device whose corroded remains were found in a Mediterranean shipwreck in 1901. After more than a century of work, it has been decoded and reconstructed as a complex clockwork device with scores of gears that successfully predicted lunar eclipses and the stellar position of five planets.[35] This analogue computer, more sophisticated than anything built before the nineteenth century, was apparently constructed in the second century BC, while the design may date back to Archimedes in Syracuse, a century earlier.

---

34. Hirschman, *Rhetoric of Reaction* (1991), 74.
35. Freeth, *The Antikythera Mechanism* (2008); Freeth et al., 'Calendars with Olympiad Display' (2008); Marchant, *Decoding the Heavens* (2008); Freeth, 'Decoding an Ancient Computer' (2009).

Economists share an assumption with the constructors of the Antikythera computer, namely that the economy has an underlying regularity analogous to that of the heavenly bodies. In his Nobel Lecture, Maurice Allais (NPW, 1988) said,

> Firstly, the prerequisite of any science is the existence of regularities which can be analysed and forecast. This is the case in celestial mechanics. But it is also true of many economic phenomena. Indeed, their thorough analysis displays the existence of regularities which are just as striking as those found in the physical sciences. This is why economics is a science, and why this science rests on the same general principles and methods as the physical sciences.[36]

But unlike the Antikythera mechanism, the economist's machine is not physical. It is an imaginary construction, which never has to roll down a road, land on a runway, or predict a lunar eclipse. Failure is not easy to observe. The machine shimmers in the imagination, but differently so for different scholars. In rational expectations theory, the economist's machine is also present in the mind of every other person in the economy. In the words of Thomas Sargent (one of its originators, and NPW, 2011): 'All agents inside the model, the econometrician, and God share the same model.'[37]

What God and everybody else are all meant to assume is that current prices capture the true value of financial and other assets. Asset prices are present claims on future revenue flows, so a true value implies that these future revenues, and the future course of the economy, are already predetermined, and are thus knowable. There is no uncertainty (there are versions that incorporate uncertainty, but these fall short of the 'rational'). Every individual is in possession of all the data, and uses the best economic model. In consequence, asset prices in the economy are 'correct', and the market price equilibrium represents the best possible allocation of resources; in other words, it is optimal. Any mispricing is random, and the errors cancel each other out. This is a nice 'invisible hand' kind of result.

A justification given for these assumptions is that understanding the economy as a whole (macroeconomics) needs to be based on 'microfoundations', that is, on the self-interest of individuals. This requirement invokes methodological individualism, the doctrine that self-seeking individuals are the

---

36. Allais, 'An Outline of My Main Contributions', Nobel Lecture 1988, 243.
37. Evans and Honkapohja, 'An Interview with Thomas Sargent' (2005), 566.

only drivers of the economy. More instrumentally it allows economists to apply the well-developed microeconomics of individual choice to analysing the economy as a whole. Yet this justification is problematic. First, the so-called microfoundations are not empirical, that is, not what we know for sure, but only what we believe for sure. Behavioural economics shows that real individuals diverge systematically (but not uniformly) from self-interested norms, but this knowledge is ignored. Even if one takes individual choice as foundational, the models do not actually add up all individual choices, let alone the expectations that drive them. That would be difficult, since people differ in their preferences, and nobody knows what goes on in their minds. There is also a theoretical result of the 1970s which shows that such aggregation to a unique general equilibrium is impossible, the 'Sonnenschein-Mantel-Debreu conditions'.[38] Hence the 'microfoundational' approach merely amounts to assuming (or asserting) that all market participants behave as if they are a single individual endowed with uniform assets and preferences, who is designated as the 'representative agent' and is then modelled using microeconomics. But if they were all the same in every respect, why would they want to trade with each other? By now, we have moved a long way from reality.

Microfoundations is taken to be scientifically rigorous, and hence methodologically binding. But the principle is arbitrary: why reduction only to persons, and not to their psychology, biology, chemistry, physics? And why attribute economic aggregates to individual choice? Why not the other way round? Even in microeconomic theory, markets are governed by social rules and conventions, and depend on social media like language and calculation. The principle of microfoundations has been gone over critically several times, and has never been justified with anything approaching rigour.[39] It cannot be taken as a foundational requirement so long as true aggregation from individual choices to macroeconomics remains impracticable;[40] it is no more than a slogan to browbeat (and sometimes to lock out) alternative practice. But it was necessary for Lucas's models to work.

---

38. Kirman, 'Whom and What Does the Representative Individual Represent?' (1992); Rizvi, 'The Sonnenschein-Mantel-Debreu Results after Thirty Years' (2006).
39. Kirman, 'Whom or What Does the Representative Individual Represent?' (1992); Hartley, *The Representative Agent* (1997); Kincaid, *Individualism and the Unity of Science* (1997); Hoover, *Methodology of Empirical Macroeconomics* (2001), ch. 3; Duarte, *Microfoundations Considered* (2012); Janssen, *Microfoundations* (2012); King, *The Microfoundations Delusion* (2012); Syll, *Use and Misuse of Theories and Models* (2015), ch. 3.
40. Hoover, *The New Classical Microeconomics* (1998), 224–230, 241–244.

The demand for microfoundations can also be construed differently, namely that macroeconomic aggregates should be analysed using the economics devised for individual behaviour. That is the sense in which the requirement for microfoundations is really understood. It amounts to imputing intentionality and rationality to economic aggregates (for example, a 'representative consumer') and assuming that this imaginary person's choices deliver the best possible (equilibrium) outcome over the whole of time. If the world was really like that, then this would be a good method to study it.[41] To imagine that it is, is surreal. It is only a 'pretense of knowledge.'[42]

In the early 1980s, it was also shown mathematically that rational expectations with more than one person was internally inconsistent—that for rational individuals to converge on the right expectations they would need to know what other individuals were expecting. As the critics (one a future NPW) put it: 'The "hypothesis" of rational expectations is like the "hypothesis" of the knowability of God.' There is hardly any point in looking for evidence.[43]

Despite all these problems, the models remain attractive for two reasons. First, they are orthodox: they deploy the standard motivational assumptions of economics. They make it possible to model macroeconomic reality, seemingly from the bottom up. Paul Krugman (NPW, 2008) explained that: 'While there is only one way to be perfectly rational, there are an infinite number of ways to be irrational, and how do you choose?'[44] That is not strictly true: this perfect rationality will work only if the world is stable and knowable. Some assumptions can be relaxed, but not that people work to discover a future that already exists (the assumption of 'ergodicity').[45] Without the assumption that expectations turn out to be right, modelling becomes very difficult, and macroeconomists are reduced to generalizing from observed regularities (for ourselves, that is actually the correct procedure). Lucas famously criticized empirical Keynesian models of the economy (associated with Lawrence Klein, NPW, 1980) for extrapolating from the past into the future, without taking account of their potential subversion by self-seeking agents acting on rational expectations (the 'Lucas critique'). But no

41. Hahn, 'Macroeconomics and General Equilibrium' (2003), 206.
42. Caballero, 'Macroeconomics after the Crisis' (2010), 89.
43. Frydman and Phelps, 'Introduction' (1983), 26; Frydman, 'Towards an Understanding of Market Processes' (1982); Arrow, 'Rationality of Self and Others' (1986), S393.
44. Macfarquar, 'The Deflationist' (2010).
45. Davidson, 'Reality and Economic Theory' (1996).

information can come out of the future. Rational expectations rely on past and current information. The assumption that everyone can reliably use this knowledge is far-fetched, and (as shown in the next section) has been falsified repeatedly. The Lucas critique is valid in principle (though anticipated by some of the very model-builders whom Lucas criticized). If everyone was perfectly informed and relentlessly acquisitive, it would have to be heeded. But the empirical effect of the Lucas critique has been found to be weak or non-existent, which is not surprising given how far people diverge from the ideal.[46] It has nevertheless become a pillar of macroeconomics.

The assumption of rational expectations provided a role for policy. Government commitment to stable prices could not be relied on. To overcome this problem, monetary policy has been relegated to central banks, who were cut loose from mere politics and set the technocratic task of keeping inflation within a narrow range (typically around 2 percent). As soon as inflation began to rise, the central bank reined in the economy with higher interest rates, thus keeping wages in check by means of unemployment.[47] Rational expectations is an 'invisible hand' theory that implies that markets cannot be improved upon. Any government intervention is likely to be anticipated and offset by market participants. If an intervention is effective, it 'distorts' the economy away from its natural and optimal configuration. Intervention is therefore futile, indeed harmful, except, oddly, for inflation targeting. This doctrine is conveniently aligned with the interests of business and the wealthy in stable prices, lower taxes and freedom from regulation. Rational expectations is a conservative doctrine: its application by central banks required wages to be regulated, but not the prices of housing and securities.

It is easy to forget that, in the words of Joseph Stiglitz (NPW, 2001), 'the invisible hand must be taken as an article of faith, not a scientifically established proposition'.[48] Rational expectation policy norms (like most invisible hand discourse) are not founded on justified knowledge: they merely reflect the theorist's preferences and priors. They are written into the premises. This is not an argument against abstract economic reasoning, but against the claims made for its authority in policy-making.

---

46. Favero and Hendry, 'Testing the Lucas Critique' (1992); Ericsson and Irons, 'The Lucas Critique in Practice' (1995); Linde, 'Testing for the Lucas Critique' (2001); Hendry, 'Forecast Failures, Expectations Formation and the Lucas Critique' (2002).
47. Grimes, 'Four Lectures on Central Banking' (2014), 4–37.
48. Stiglitz, 'The Invisible Hand and Modern Welfare Economics' (1991), 35.

IS IT TRUE?

Lucas was asked in the early 1980s, 'Are you after truth?', and replied, 'Yeah. But I don't know what we mean by truth in our business. . . . We're programming robot imitations of people, and there are real limits on what you can get out of that.'[49] Such flimsy constructions are vulnerable to close examination even by their creators. This model of godlike knowledge and eternal stability is undermined by the constant need to fix it, mostly in order to take account of its poor fit with reality. Lucas abandoned his efforts to drive his business-cycle models with monetary shocks. Thomas Sargent (NPW, 2011) is one of the originators of rational expectations. One of his students has listed 'ten stories about the rise of rational expectations' in Sargent's own work. Every formulation is intended to overcome some difficulty in a previous one.[50]

These 'stories' are not always consistent with each other, and they illustrate an improvised quality in the doctrine. Sargent is known for his analytical rigour. What is lacking in this paradigm is respect for reality. He is candid about this. Empirical testing does not confirm the existence of rational expectations, so the empirical parameters are aligned with the model in a process called 'calibration'. Cycles generated within the model are kitted out with real-world parameters obtained from what are purported to be stable 'deep' microeconomic preferences (for example, between work and leisure), technological variables, and the very empirical macroeconomics whose validity Lucas has denied. It counts as an achievement if these cycles can match, not any particular historical cycle, but the 'second moments' of real historical cycles, that is, their general shape, often de-trended and plucked out of stable periods. Even that is not easily managed, and can be judged to have failed.[51] This should not be surprising—for example, neither tastes nor technology are truly invariant, or even easy to identify except by assumption. Sargent has divulged that

> Calibration is less optimistic about what your theory can accomplish because you'd only use it if you didn't fully trust your entire model, meaning that you think your model is partly misspecified or incompletely speci-

---

49. Klamer, *The New Classical Macroeconomics* (1984), 49.
50. Sent, *Evolving Rationality of Rational Expectations* (1998), 1–11.
51. Watson, 'Measures of Fit for Calibrated Models' (1993); Hoover, 'Facts and Artifacts' (1995); Hansen and Heckman, 'Empirical Foundations of Calibration' (1996); Carlaw and Lipsey, 'Does History Matter?' (2012).

fied, or if you trusted someone else's model and data set more than your own. My recollection is that Bob Lucas and Ed Prescott [NPW, 2004] were initially very enthusiastic about rational expectations econometrics. After all, it simply involved imposing on ourselves the same high standards we had criticized the Keynesians for failing to live up to. But after about five years of doing likelihood ratio tests on rational expectations models, I recall Bob Lucas and Ed Prescott both telling me that those tests were rejecting too many good models. The idea of calibration is to ignore some of the probabilistic implications of your model but to retain others. Somehow, calibration was intended as a balanced response to professing that your model, though not correct, is still worthy as a vehicle for quantitative policy analysis.[52]

In contrast, when Sargent wrote economic history he largely dispensed with the modelling apparatus.[53]

For Lucas, the cycles of prosperity and depression, of unemployment and boom, which presented such a challenge to Keynes and which drove Social Democracy, were not policy challenges at all, only wobbles in equilibrium. In Lucasian models, policy interventions are defeated because individuals know how the economy works ('rational expectations'), and will use this knowledge to avoid adverse effects on their own interests. Only individuals can have expectations, and selves to be interested in. A true microfoundational explanation would extrapolate from individual choices, but the NCM knows nothing about actual choices. It deals in 'representative agents', that is, the economy as a whole is modelled as consisting of only one or two individuals. Once this leap is made, it is possible to construct a model in equilibrium over time, a 'real business cycle' in which the fluctuations arise from external surprises (or 'shocks'). The 'equilibrium' consists of a single 'representative' consumer buying from and working for a single 'representative' firm. The Arrow-Debreu general equilibrium result is invoked to claim economic efficiency, despite its own lack of realism.[54] Arrow-Debreu can apply only to large economies with many agents; and it is a static result, once and for all, with no room for either shocks or wobbles.[55] Even when converted to a succession of equilibria, it still requires markets for all

52. Evans and Honkapohja, 'Interview with Thomas Sargent', 568–569.
53. Sargent and Velde, *The Big Problem of Small Change* (2002).
54. Lucas, 'Methods and Problems in Business Cycle Theory' (1980), 701.
55. Hahn, 'General Equilibrium Theory' (1981/1984), 79.

contingencies ('complete markets'). And with two agents, it is hardly a 'general' equilibrium.

Another set of rational-expectations economists associated with top academic departments at MIT, Harvard, Berkeley and Stanford ('saltwater economists' as opposed to the 'freshwater' ones of Chicago and Minnesota) modified the Lucas-Sargent approach by injecting frictions and disturbances into the models. These 'neo-Keynesian' models became increasingly elaborate. Eventually during the 2000s, the NCM and neo-Keynesian tributaries converged, to construct dynamic stochastic general equilibrium models (DSGE), which attempted to incorporate more reality into inter-temporal equilibrium models. These models went beyond calibration to apply more orthodox methods of statistical inference and to derive parameters from real data ('estimation'). The resulting models were run with increasingly large amounts of empirical data, and such use of real data did something to improve their forecasting accuracy.[56] DSGE came to dominate academic macroeconomics, and was implemented and consulted by central banks all over the world.[57] The attraction is the orthodox premises of rationality and equilibrium, but these unrealistic premises limit their reliability and accuracy. They also imply, for the most part, a preference for markets over policy. At best, the quality of their forecasts could be compared with results from statistical extrapolation techniques (VAR), which imposed no economic-theory assumptions at all, and indeed the two methods are now frequently combined.[58] After three decades of effort, these models continue to perform poorly empirically. Practitioners concede this. Despite being widely deployed in central banks, they 'are not yet part of the core decision making framework', and 'are not fully ready for "prime time".'[59] They failed to anticipate the 2008 financial crisis, not least because they typically left out the financial sector. 'Modern macroeconomics tortures data to demonstrate consistency with an *a priori* world view.'[60] Despite falling in wholesale for DSGE, central banks have not discarded the large statistical models of Keynesian origin, whose alleged shortcomings helped to instigate the Lucas revolution.

---

56. Woodford, *Interest and Prices* (2003); Smets and Wouters, 'Estimated Dynamic Stochastic General Equilibrium' (2003).

57. Chari, 'Statement of V. V. Chari' (2010), 32.

58. Gürkaynak et al., 'Do DSGE Forecast More Accurately' (2013).

59. Tovar, 'DSGE Models and Central Banks' (2008), quotes, 2, 18; Schorfheide, 'Estimation and Evaluation of DSGE Models' (2011).

60. Marchionatti and Sella, 'Is Neo-Walrasian Macroeconomics a Dead End?' (2015), 27.

In contrast, where private money is at stake, business relies almost exclusively on descriptive statistical models for its forecasting, and has no use at all for DSGE, except sometimes to try to mimic central bank thinking.[61]

The exponents of rational expectations can fall back on a methodological statement by Milton Friedman (NPW, 1976), which argues that the realism of premises does not matter so long as the model delivers good predictions.[62] Good predictions, however, cannot be claimed for rational expectations. Its empirical record is poor, and complicated contortions are required in order to bring it into any sort of alignment with empirical evidence.[63] Here the comparison with Antikythera ends. The ancient Greek mechanism was based on faulty earth-centred cosmology (not a problem for Milton Friedman), but it delivered respectable predictions, given the magnitude of the task and the unreality of the premises. Rational expectations shares the attribute of unrealism with Antikythera, but unlike the ancient Greek mechanism, it predicts poorly.

NEW CLASSICAL MACROECONOMICS AGAINST SOCIAL DEMOCRACY

With (say) two active agents, almost perfect foresight, and immortal (or dynastic) lives, the new classical economics has no need for social insurance. It is an economy without government, money, or society. With no public, there is no conception of a public good. Perhaps that is why it caught on so well. This was partly anticipated in Milton Friedman's 1957 'permanent income' hypothesis, which assumed that consumers adjusted for fluctuations in income by borrowing and saving. With infinite lives, there was no need for retirement. Two years earlier, a more realistic life-cycle version by the Keynesian Franco Modigliani (NPW, 1985) acknowledged at least that retirement would occur.[64] At the same time, and with somewhat different assumptions ('overlapping generations' of workers and retired), Paul Samuelson

---

61.   Bachman, 'What Economic Forecasters Really Do' (1996); Smith, 'The Most Damning Criticism of DSGE' (2014), including comments by Daniel Bachman; Dou, 'Macroeconomic Models' (2015).

62.   Friedman, 'The Methodology of Positive Economics' (1953).

63.   Ball, 'Intertemporal Substitutions' (1990), 706, lists several earlier empirical failures; Pollock and Suyderhoud, 'An Empirical Window on Rational Expectation Formation' (1992); Carter and Maddock, *Rational Expectations* (1984), 141–143; Lovell, 'Tests of the Rational Expectations Hypothesis' (1986); Obstfeld and Rogoff, *Foundations of International Macroeconomics* (1996), 625, cited in Frydman and Goldberg (below), 28–29; Estrella and Fuhrer, 'Dynamic Inconsistencies' (2002); Frydman and Goldberg, *Beyond Mechanical Markets* (2005), ch. 5.

64.   Modigliani, 'Life-Cycle, Individual Thrift and the Wealth of Nations', Nobel Lecture 1985.

(NPW, 1970) was able to construct a model in which social insurance was necessary or at least useful. All three models derived the results (cleverly) out of the premises, and highlighted the bearing of models on the (still nascent) contest between Social Democracy and market liberalism. All were acknowledged by Nobel Prizes.

Lucas's New Classical Macroeconomics (NCM) satisfied the modelling requirements of counter-intuitional cleverness, theoretical coherence, arresting metaphor, plausible analogy, mathematical technique, stylized facts, and policy/political correctness. Lucas gloated in 1981: 'In general, I believe that one who claims to understand the principles of flight can reasonably be expected to be able to make a flying machine, and that understanding business cycles means the ability to make them too, in roughly the same sense.'[65] Those aircraft again. Note, however, that this is not a claim about controlling the business cycle (this was not regarded as necessary), but of constructing a plausible mock-up.

It is an achievement to have come so far against the grain of reality. After all the other requirements are satisfied, the final one, the test of empirical validity, could be an embarrassment. In standard econometrics, a causal model seeks to include all relevant variables, and the estimation procedure uses real-life raw data to discover their magnitudes and relative importance. This procedure is essentially descriptive. If the match is poor, the model is rejected. It still encounters serious problems (see chapter 2). The NCM procedure of 'calibration' does not have to meet such a test: it pre-selects data that fit, and estimation results are still poor.

Frank Hahn, himself an esteemed model-builder, wrote of the New Classical Macroeconomics in the early 1980s,

> I have always regarded Competitive General Equilibrium analysis as akin to the mock-up an aircraft engineer might build. My amazement in recent years has accordingly been very great to find that many economists are passing the mock-up off as an airworthy plane, and that politicians, bankers, and commentators are scrambling to get seats. This at a time when theorists all over the world have become aware that anything based on this mock-up is unlikely to fly, since it neglects some crucial aspects of the world, the recognition of which will force some drastic redesigning. Moreover, at no stage was the mock-up complete.[66]

---

65. Lucas, *Studies in Business-Cycle Theory* (1981), 8.
66. Hahn, 'Review of Beenstock' (1981), 1036.

Lucas was undeterred. Speaking *ex cathedra*, he addressed departing Chicago graduates in 1988. Starting with an imaginary problem, he told them that we need to

> free ourselves from the limits of historical experience so as to discover ways in which our society can operate better than it has in the past. . . . We do not find that the realm of imagination and ideas is an alternative to, or a retreat from, practical reality. On the contrary, it is the only way we have found to think seriously about reality.[67]

This imaginary-reality principle was also held out as a guide to policy. Here is Lucas again in 2003, now delivering the presidential address to the American Economic Association. It is an 'end of history' speech, or rather, the end of macroeconomics: 'The central problem of depression prevention has been solved.'[68] It was a tenet of his approach that recessions did not matter: the ups and downs of the business cycle followed the best path for the economy. Hence, there was nothing to be gained from seeking stability, but more competitive markets (especially for labour) could raise consumption substantially.

Only five years later, the economy crashed. Lucas had previously predicted 3 percent growth forever.[69] Where did his confidence come from? It was based on several models, all of which were 'variations on a one-good growth model in which consumers (either an infinitely lived dynasty, or a succession of generations) maximize the utility of consumption and leisure over time, firms maximize profit, and markets are continuously cleared.'[70] In other words, a one-good, one-consumer, one-firm model. Such models are hard to construct, and not easy to understand. It may not really matter—they are only models. In a Ricardian leap, Lucas casts aside the argument that these are only toys. That policy is inherently ineffective (the core of his own creed) is forgotten here.

For Lucas at his pulpit, NCM models provided intellectual cover for a radical market-liberal agenda of upwards redistribution: repeal taxes on capital, a flat tax on income, privatize the welfare state. Cutting capital income taxation to zero (and covering expenditure with other taxes) was a favourite NCM result from the mid-1980s which has provided the justification for

---

67. Lucas, 'What Economists Do' (1988).
68. Lucas, 'Macroeconomic Priorities' (2003).
69. Klamer, *The New Classical Macroeconomics* (1984), 52.
70. Lucas, 'Macroeconomic Priorities' (2003), 2.

de-taxing income from capital in the United States and Britain in subsequent decades (the theory has since been challenged).[71] Economic growth from the trickle-down effect would provide an increase in consumption of 7.5 to 15 percent. In another example, higher taxes in France accounted for shorter working hours. The 'steady-state welfare gain' to French households of adopting lower American tax rates on labour and consumption (and longer hours at work) would be the equivalent of a consumption increase of about 20 percent. This all comes out of dubious leisure/work trade-offs in single-person models.[72]

With this extra income, the French would be able to buy what the government currently provides. 'Think,' he says, 'of elementary schooling or day care', currently financed by 'distorting taxes'.[73] Listeners are tacitly invited to concur that efficient markets are not an assumption but established fact, although no such markets exist. Another assumption was that the French workers got nothing in return for their taxes that they could not purchase over the counter in private markets. Against Lucas, one can point out that the pensions, healthcare, social insurance, and free education provided by French taxation was worth (even in financial terms) more than a market consumption increase of 20 percent, and more to those with lower incomes. American market health services are twice as expensive, and less effective than those provided in European Social Democracy. European pensions are much more generous.[74] In the sweep of rhetoric, Lucas forgets that the French would also have to work longer hours to replace what the state provides already. Later, he expressed revulsion for downwards distribution: 'Of the tendencies that are harmful to sound economics, the most seductive, and in my opinion the most poisonous, is to focus on questions of distribution'.[75] The irrelevance of distribution for growth has been shown to be wrong for the United States even using Lucas's own method, not surprisingly in a country in which the vast majority had derived no benefit from economic growth for the previous three decades.[76] To repeat ourselves, 'representative agent' models provide a poor warrant for policy.

---

71. Straub and Werning, 'Positive Long Run Capital Taxation: Chamley-Judd Revisited' (2014).
72. Lucas, 'Macroeconomic Priorities' (2003), 1–2; 'Dubious', see Hansen and Heckman, 'Empirical Foundations of Calibration' (1996), 100.
73. Lucas, 'Macroeconomic Priorities' (2003), 1–2.
74. Offer, 'Economy of Obligation' (2012); Offer, 'A Warrant for Pain' (2012).
75. Lucas, 'The Industrial Revolution—Past and Future' (2014).
76. Córdoba and Verdier, 'Lucas vs. Lucas: On Inequality and Growth' (2007).

WHAT IS IT ABOUT?

The New Classical Macroeconomics coincides historically with the post-modernist movement in the humanities.[77] Post-modernism is not easy to pin down. Its core, if it has one, is to reject observation and measurement, the analysis of cause and effect, as criteria of validity. The connection with economics has been made before. It has focused on eddies of indeterminism in fields such as game theory, asymmetric information, behavioural and feminist economics.[78] From the point of view of post-modernism, what is at fault in economics is its 'modernist meta-narrative' of rationality and equilibrium, the Enlightenment belief in a logic of scientific explanation. In a series of wonderfully learned and entertaining books, the economist and historian Deirdre McCloskey draws on the classic literary tradition to depict economic discourse as an indeterminate but stimulating conversation, an endless quest for persuasion. This is exemplified in her own dazzling eloquence.[79] The notion of persuasion as the purpose of economic argument appealed to NCM macroeconomists. But, in the words of Christopher Sims (NPW, 2011), there is a risk that 'it makes us soft on quackery.'[80] Without some notion of truth, how can persuasion come about? What is there to talk about? Persuasion is presumably an effort to show that you are right. A notion of truth is necessary for inference, for learning, for co-operation, for contract. Truth is not for all time, but in its absence all we have is arousal.

The real similarities with post-modernism are not on the fringes of the discipline but at the heart of the New Classical project. Like post-modernism, NCM reduces reality to individual whim, and is comfortable with the post-modern levelling of high and low culture. It goes further than post-modernism in having no room for society or a common good. Like post-modernism, it is indifferent to the collective aspirations that have driven Social Democracy, to the existence of others and their special needs, to the reciprocity of mutual obligation.

----

77. Rosenau, *Post-Modernism and the Social Sciences* (1992); Blaug, 'Why I Am Not a Constructivist' (1994), 130.
78. Heap, 'Post-Modernity and New Conceptions of Rationality' (1993); Cullenberg et al., *Postmodernism, Economics and Knowledge* (2001); Amariglio and Ruccio, *Postmodern Moments in Modern Economics* (2003).
79. McCloskey, *The Rhetoric of Economics* (1985); *Knowledge and Persuasion in Economics* (1994).
80. Sims, 'Macroeconomics and Methodology' (1996), 110; Athreya, *Big Ideas in Macroeconomics* (2015), 13–14.

NCM is anti-realist: 'Social theory, unlike thermodynamics, is condemned to remain untestable, and stuck in the realm of opinion.'[81] Immunity from the disciplines of reality allowed Lucas to befuddle his readers: On the one hand, the thought experiment (there are no other experiments in the NCM) that unemployment was a voluntary choice.[82] On the other, a scattering of seemingly approving references to social insurance.[83] On balance, his own guess was that 'efficiency requires subsidizing unemployment and hence increasing its average level' (his lectures were given in Finland, a Nordic welfare state).[84] The reader scratches his head in an effort to reconcile these contradictions, and to penetrate abstruse models which endorse radical social transformations, most of them (on the face of it) in favour of the rich.

But one might also withhold the benefit of doubt. The preconditions of the models are never satisfied, and there is no reason to believe that other things can be kept equal (*ceteris paribus*), or that the necessary changes (*mutatis mutandis*) will be made. The conventions of causation and inference are suspended.[85] It makes for a stimulating spectacle, but when pronouncing on policy, Lucas is just pulling rank. An economy of two 'representative agents' is not built on microfoundations. Even within the model, a competitive economy which falls short of the stringent Arrow-Debreu conditions (impossible to satisfy in the real world) is not known to be more efficient than any other, even in the limited sense of Pareto.[86]

But it is futile to argue back, and as a rule, NCM, like economics more generally, does not engage with its critics, even those within the discipline.[87] Lucas has been uncivil to critics, for example, describing the rival Keynesian scholarship as forlorn 'skeleton rattling'.[88] Economists in general are seen in other disciplines (and by heterodox practitioners) as condescending and remote. This is confirmed in citation patterns—in comparison with other

81. Varoufakis, 'Deconstructing *Homo Economicus?*' (2012), 393.
82. Lucas, *Models of Business Cycles* (1987), section V.
83. For example, Lucas, ibid., 31, 61, 105.
84. Ibid., 69.
85. See also Arrow, 'Rationality of Self and Others' (1986), S390.
86. Lipsey and Lancaster, 'The General Theory of Second Best' (1956); Buiter, 'The Economics of Dr Pangloss' (1980), 45.
87. Kapeller, 'Some Critical Notes' (2010), 332–334; Francis, 'The Rise and Fall of Debate in Economics' (2014); Fourcade et al., 'The Superiority of Economists' (2015).
88. Lucas, 'Methods and Problems' (1980), 698; Lucas, 'Macroeconomic Priorities' (2003), 1; also Klamer, *The New Classical Macroeconomics* (1984), 50–51; Mankiw, 'The Reincarnation of Keynesian Economics' (1991), 1.

disciplines, economists cite little from the outside, and when they do, they mostly draw on the kindred fields of finance, statistics and business, and on people who agree with them.[89] This is unlikely to be mere defensiveness. The view is that outsiders are not qualified to judge, even when their own interests are at stake (often true, but at odds with standard economic assumptions). While it may be tempting to take offence at what seems to be unwarranted pretension, this would be falling into the common error of attributing behaviour to dispositions rather than situations.[90] Stand-offishness in this case is not a collective personality defect, but is more likely to rise out of a doctrinal worldview. Economic doctrines are 'rationalist'. They are derived logically from what is taken to be self-evident. Hence, they are resistant to evidence, and so (for the economist) it does not matter that they violate common sense or do not accord with reality.[91] And if the premises are not shared, there is not much point in conversation.

Disrespect for reality and the conventions of inference is also part of the right-wing temper of the times. It is tempting to regard Lucas's performance (and the rational expectations/representative agent strategy when applied to discredit Social Democracy) as an exercise in 'agnotology'—the term was originally coined for deniers of the link between tobacco and cancer, of global warming, for drug trial manipulation, and for 'business as usual' after the financial crisis of 2008.[92] It denotes arguments made in what looks like good faith, but lacking in credible evidence, and intended to sow confusion and doubt.[93] Incoherence makes sense if the intention is not to arrive at the truth, but to pursue a cause. Like Bush marching into Iraq, NCM economists seem to 'create their own reality'.[94] This can be effective for a while. We confess to our own confusion and doubt, in view of massive professional acceptance well beyond Chicago, even by opponents of its political ideology. Leading economists share our bewilderment.[95]

---

89. Fourcade et al., 'The Superiority of Economics' (2015).
90. Nisbett and Ross, *Human Inference* (1980), 30–32.
91. Carter and Maddox, *Rational Choice* (1984), 142.
92. Proctor, *Cancer Wars* (1995), 8; Proctor and Schiebinger, *Agnotology: The Making and Unmaking of Ignorance* (2008); Pinto, 'Tensions in Agnotology' (2015).
93. Mirowski, *Never Let a Serious Crisis Go to Waste* (2013), ch. 4; Krugman, 'What They Say versus What They Mean' (2013).
94. Suskind, 'Faith, Certainty and the Presidency of George W. Bush' (2004).
95. For example, Robert Clower and David Colander, in Snowdon and Vane, *Conversations with Leading Economists* (1999), 188–189, 212, 214–215; Caballero, 'Macroeconomics after the Crisis' (2010).

There cannot be any objection to theorizing. If scholars wish to investigate the mathematical implications of an immortal, consistent, prescient, one-person economy, then why not? John Hicks (NPW, 1972) has written:

> There is much of economic theory which is pursued for no better reason that its intellectual attraction: it is a good game. We have no reason to be ashamed of that, since the same would hold for many branches of pure mathematics.[96]

Granted. And long may it thrive. But such models provide no warrant to rule out collective action, or indeed (on their own) for any other policy.

DISSENSION WITHIN ECONOMICS

NPW economists are far from being aligned behind the NCM. Indeed (as shown in chapter 5), the opposite is closer to the truth. The Nobel Committee has also dithered. Among NPWs, NCM has been rejected explicitly by Kenneth Arrow (NPW, 1972), James Tobin (NPW, 1981), Franco Modigliani (NPW, 1985), Robert Solow (NPW, 1987), Vernon Smith (NPW, 2002, in his Nobel Lecture), Edmund Phelps (NPW, 2007), Paul Krugman (NPW, 2008), Christopher Sims (NPW, 2011), and possibly by others.[97] Solow has written that 'the macro community has perpetrated a rhetorical swindle on itself, and on its students.'[98] At a congressional hearing on the crisis of 2008, this Keynesian macroeconomist was rude in return about NCM:

> They take it for granted that the whole economy can be thought of as if it were a single, consistent person or dynasty carrying out a rationally designed, long-term plan, occasionally disturbed by unexpected shocks but adapting to them in a rational, consistent way. I don't think that that picture passes the smell test. And the protagonists of this idea make a claim to respectability by asserting that it is founded on what we know about

96.   Hicks, *Causality in Economics* (1979), viii.

97.   Phelps, Frydman and Phelps, 'Introduction' (1983); Tobin, see Klamer, *Conversations with Economists* (1984), 110–111; Arrow, 'Rationality of Self and Others' (1986), S393; Modigliani, see Hirschman, *Rhetoric of Reaction* (1991), 74; Hahn and Solow, *A Critical Essay on Modern Macroeconomic Theory* (1995); Sims, 'Macroeconomics and Methodology' (1996); Sims, 'Comment on Del Negro, Schorfheide, Smets and Wouters' (2006), 2; Krugman, 'How Did Economists Get It So Wrong?' (2009).

98.   Solow, 'Reflections on the Survey' (2007), 235; also Solow, 'The State of Macroeconomics' (2008).

microeconomic behavior; but I really think that this claim is generally phony.[99]

Modelling is inescapable, in economics as in aviation. We use a mathematical model ourselves in chapter 6, to describe and explain the reputational trajectories of Nobel Prize winners. Solow's own NPW growth model with its dual-factor economy (capital and labour) is close to a representative agent model, although it does not assume that the aggregates of capital and labour have minds of their own. But models have no independent authority. To justify policy, a model must have some real purchase. The mathematician, physicist and polymath John von Neumann is reputed to have said: 'There is no sense in being precise when you don't even know what you're talking about.'[100]

Decision-makers, just like the present authors, have to take their experts partly on trust. They are not model-makers themselves. How to decide which one to listen to? Policy does not rely on models alone. It is not designed with the same rigour as a jetliner, and its performance is not so easily measured. Information is collected, studies are carried out, papers written, intuitions consulted, as well as prejudices, biases, loyalties, and spouses. Models are only part of the mix. The most successful ones enter policy-making as 'meta-models', essentially as articles of faith, which policy-makers think they know, without being quite sure of how and why. Those who apply policy norms would rarely be able to take a model apart, or pull its levers themselves. The mere existence of powerful models has some probative value, independently of their confirmation. Models are difficult to test, and disconfirmations are ignored. Hence the importance of the authoritative quality hallmark of the Nobel Prize. The magic of the prize and the validity of its authority are the subject of the next chapter.

---

99.   Solow, in US Congress, 'Building a Science of Economics for the Real World' (2010), 12; also Solow, 'Dumb and Dumber in Macroeconomics' (2003/2009).
100.   Wikiquotes, 'Talk: John von Neumann' (2015).

CHAPTER 2
A PRIZE IN 'ECONOMIC SCIENCES'

In a turbulent world, the prizes that Alfred Nobel endowed in 1895 shine as beacons of enduring value. They signal that effort, integrity, and success in pursuit of truth can earn mighty acclaim. In 1968, the Swedish central bank persuaded the Nobel Foundation to add a prize in economics, identical in all but name to those in science, literature, and peace. For a paltry investment, it extended the aura of Nobel authority to the discipline of economics. It was an entrepreneurial move worthy of Alfred Nobel himself. Like Nobel's invention of dynamite, the economic prize was a force with potential for good but also for harm. How to think of economics as science? Specialists in scientific method, practising economists, and Nobel Prize winners tell different stories. This matters when we look to economics for policy advice.

PRIZES AS SYMBOL AND RITUAL

In the natural sciences, the Nobel Prize is the pinnacle of reputation. It stands above money because it is founded so solidly on money. Part of its credibility is the financial windfall it confers, a tiny outlay for a central bank, but large even for worldly scholars.[1] But money alone is not sufficient. The Cato Institute's Milton Friedman Prize ($500,000 in 2002) does not carry the same cachet, nor do the Wolf or Balzan prizes, which give out similar amounts. Ironically for a prize that (mostly) celebrates the application of reason, it is in itself an archaic ritual, with a calculated magic that confers an almost transcendent halo. An admirer wrote to Milton Friedman in 1976: 'I

---

1. Cash values in http://www.nobelprize.org/nobel_prizes/about/amounts/prize_amounts_13.pdf.

rejoice in your award for the simple and selfish reason I can tell my kids that I once shook the hand of a Nobel laureate.[2] Friedman himself recalled that

> the announcement of [a Nobel] award converts its recipients into an instant expert on all and sundry, and unleashes hordes of ravenous newsmen and photographers from journals and TV stations around the world. I myself have been asked my opinion on everything from a cure for the common cold to the market value of a letter signed by John F. Kennedy. Needless to say the attention is flattering, but also corrupting.[3]

The magic works the other way too: the Swedish royal court (another archaic relic) basks in the radiance of the prize.

The prize celebrates the power of mind. There is an ambiguity about this power, between the insight that knowledge confers, and the mastery that it makes possible. Command over nature is what created the Nobel fortune in the first place. Alfred Nobel converted the unstable explosive nitro-glycerine to dynamite, which could be stored, transported, and handled safely. His smokeless gunpowder ballistite aggravated the dangers of battle by hiding the sources of gunfire. Developed in Britain into cordite, it provided firepower for two world wars, and for endless lesser violence. Had it not been for Nobel, others would have come up with an inert explosive, but not with his prizes. Nobel's innovations needed no authentication: they worked with a bang, and the profits rolled in. Scientific success rarely has such finality and clarity, and is usually beyond the grasp of the ordinary person. The Nobel Prizes have turned the spotlight on some less transparent achievement, and endowed it with money and fame.

The intellectual prize is an Enlightenment device with a fractal structure, in which every level in the hierarchy replicates the lower ones. Each step on the ladder of learning, from grade school onwards, is punctuated with ceremonials of recognition and selection. Examinations, graduations, gowns, and degrees mark the stages of academic progress, and scholars dress up for these occasions. The path narrows as it rises. Every university has its elite of professors, every nation its academies of science and letters. Venerable libraries are replete with thousands of essays, some as old as three centuries, submitted as bids for the prizes given out by sovereigns and learned societies.

---

2. Gerald T. Dunne to Milton Friedman, 16 October 1976, Hoover Institution, Friedman Papers Box 6/4.
3. Friedman and Friedman, *Two Lucky People* (1998), 453.

When founded, the Nobel Prize was the latest and most exalted of a pre-existing hierarchy.[4] Great international exhibitions gave out a profusion of medals. The late-Victorian period was a time of intense patriotism, and the prizes honoured not only individuals, but also the nations they belonged to and those that conferred them. In the new Olympic Games at Athens (1896), one-tenth of a second could separate gold, silver, and bronze. It is tempting to think of the Nobel Prizes, which also confer a gold medal, as providing a similar precision of ranking.

Friedrich von Hayek received notification that he had won the prize on 14 October 1974. Two months later, on 6 December, he arrived in Stockholm with an entourage made up of his children, a son-in-law, and his wife. An official of the foreign ministry remained at his side for the following week. The next three days were a whirlwind of receptions, official lunches and dinners, with a morning rehearsal for the prize ceremony on the 10th.[5] The Nobel Festival (so-called) began on the same day at 4.00 p.m. In the dark and cold Nordic midwinter, it was 'the Swedish social event of the year', a dazzling anticipation of Christmas.[6]

Nobel Prize winners of all disciplines, each wearing a black *frack* ('swallowtail, tailcoat, evening coat with tails') and white tie if they were men, marched in a procession of students preceded by banners into the grand space of the Stockholm Concert Hall. The students wore dinner jackets (dark gowns for the women), with a white naval peaked cap sporting a yellow circle on blue, and also sashes in blue and yellow, the Swedish flag colours. Trumpets blazed as the king handed out gold medals and diplomas. The dignitaries in their hundreds then moved over to the Blue Hall of Stockholm City Hall, where for three hours they shared in 'a festive mixture of royal banquet, family gathering, and student celebration'.[7] The food was chosen in secret by the Chef of the Year Association, and a test meal was sampled a month in advance. In keeping with a sweet Swedish banqueting custom, a student choir punctuated the dinner with song. In later years, an orchestra played, and by the 1990s, the entertainment had become a 'mini-opera', with the whole country watching on television. The occasion was punctuated by toasts and short speeches, and ended with dancing to the strains of Viennese

---

4. English, *Economy of Prestige* (2005), chs. 1–3.
5. Documents in Hoover Institution, Hayek Papers 4/10.
6. Friedman, *Politics of Excellence* (2001), 272.
7. De Champs, 'Organizing the Nobel Festival Day' (2000).

waltz.[8] The next day, Hayek delivered the customary Nobel Lecture. Two weeks later he wrote to the Nobel Foundation director: 'We are slowly awakening from the beautiful dream of Stockholm and returning to ordinary life ... ?[9] His Social Democrat co-winner Gunnar Myrdal donated the money to good causes, but it relieved Hayek of his dependence (for costly medical treatment) on the welfare state he hated.[10]

For Milton Friedman, the prize released a huge flow of congratulations, each one of which he acknowledged personally. They included messages from three distinguished Israeli Social Democrats, the first of them a kibbutznik (Ehud Avriel, Sholomo Avineri, Michael Bruno).[11] Ralph Harris and Arthur Seldon from the Institute of Economic Affairs (the British neoliberal think tank) sent a telegram, 'WE ARE DELIGHTED YOU DO NOT SHARE THE AWARD WITH GALBRAITH AS HEYAC DID WITH MYRDAL' [sic]. Samuel Brittan, a prominent British economic journalist, wrote ambivalently that the prize 'has given us heart to do what we can to see that the UK does not go the way of Chile.' (In May 1975 Friedman had written to Harris: 'Rose and I had a fabulous week in Chile ... Chile is the shape of things to come in Britain I fear.')[12] Kenneth Arrow (NPW, 1972), an ideological opponent, sent some qualified reassurance that the prize had been earned.[13] Edward Crane III, chairman of the 'Libertarian Party', wrote as a familiar: 'What with you and Hayek within three years the free market may become respectable after all.'[14] The philosopher Karl Popper wrote to Friedman: 'what wonderful news for the Mont Pèlerin Society! two of its Presidents Nobel Prize Laureates!'[15]

The procedure was well established.[16] The authority to make an award was vested in prestigious academic bodies: the Royal Swedish Academy of Sciences, the Swedish Academy and the Karolinska Institute. The exception was the peace prize, which was given by the Norwegian Parliament. The literature prize was awarded by the second of Sweden's academies. The Royal Swedish Academy of Sciences, custodian of the economics prize, has a

---

8. Friedman, *Two Lucky People* (1998), 451.
9. Hayek to Stig Ramel, 24 December 1974, Hoover Institution, Hayek Papers 47/10.
10. Levine and Ames, 'Charles Koch to Friedrich Hayek: Use Social Security!' (2011).
11. Distinguished diplomat, scholar and economist, respectively.
12. Friedman to Ralph Harris, 6 May 1975, Hoover Institution, Friedman Papers Box 85/7.
13. Arrow to Friedman, 14 October 1976, Friedman Papers Box 6/3.
14. Crane to Friedman, 14 October 1976, Friedman Papers Box 6/4.
15. Popper to Friedman, 16 October 1976, Friedman Papers Box 6/9.
16. Friedman, *The Politics of Excellence* (2001); Feldman, *The Nobel Prize* (2000).

fifty-year embargo on the records but three published accounts, an archival source, and three interviews provide some information.[17] As in the case of other Nobel Prizes, a permanent committee made up of five specialists was tasked with ranking and recommending candidates. Nominations were invited each autumn (with a deadline on 1 February), from among Academy members, Nordic professors, former NPWs, and a global sample of economists which changed every year. Shortlists were selected, overseas referees were commissioned, and recommendations were written over the summer. The names of the final candidates were taken to the appropriate disciplinary sections (called classes), and then to a plenary of all academy members. There was no election without nomination, and sometimes it was a struggle to get one. Leo Tolstoy was not nominated for the literature prize in 1901, and refused to be considered thereafter.[18] Also missing are Anton Chekhov, Joseph Conrad, Thomas Hardy, Henrik Ibsen, Henry James, James Joyce, Marcel Proust, August Strindberg, Virginia Wolf, and Emile Zola, while many of the winners are obscure or quite forgotten.

National academies typically consist of senior and older scholars. Hierarchy sits uneasily with the disruptive potential of innovation. The Republic of Science has a convention that substance counts for more than status, and that everybody gets a hearing. This was a challenge for Nobel Committees in natural science.[19] Sweden was rarely at the very forefront, and academicians sometimes found it difficult to keep up. They were not above supporting favourites, or even each other. Powerful individuals like the chemist Svante Arrhenius and the physicist Carl Wilhelm Oseen came to dominate committees. One irregularity was to withhold an award for the year, whose financial value was then diverted into a fund for Swedish research, sometimes to the indirect benefit of committee members. A single solicited nomination could overcome candidates with many external nominations. Albert Einstein had published three epochal papers in 1905, and was world-famous by the end of World War I, but was passed over several times and received the prize as late as 1922 for a paper which may not have been his most important, but which was easier to reconcile with the committee's aversion to relativity.

---

17. Myrdal, 'The Nobel Prize in Economics' (1977); Lindbeck, 'The Prize in Economic Science' (1985); Ingemar Ståhl, 'The Prize in Economic Science and Maurice Allais' (1990); Nasar, *A Beautiful Mind* (1998), ch. 48. We have interviewed three former members of the economics committee, including two former chairmen.

18. Feldman, *Nobel Prize* (2000), 69–70.

19. What follows is from Friedman, *Politics of Excellence* (2001).

Other giants were also slow to be recognized, some died before their turn arrived, while a few were passed over for joint discoveries. Nordic candidates may have faced lower hurdles. The decision of the nominating committee (which did most of the work) could still be overturned in the natural or social science classes, or in the full academy. Despite some flaws and recurrent doubts and queries, the awards retain a high standing. The world appreciates the difficulties, and there is always another day. The prizes were founded at a high point of personal and institutional integrity in northwestern Europe, virtues that were manifest in the institutions of science.[20] Swedish academicians are credible adjudicators: respected but not numerous, they have had little opportunity to swamp the prize with their own numbers.

The Nobel archival record for economics will be opened in 2019, initially for one year only. The principles of selection, published in 1985, were broadminded, and on the face of it, largely borne out in practice.[21] One member of the academy did break ranks. In response to Friedman's award in 1976, Gunnar Myrdal (NPW, 1974) suggested that the procedure in economics was less proper than in other disciplines. His main complaint was that the economics committee prevented independent judgment by higher academy jurisdictions: 'By presenting its proposal and supporting documentation so late in the year, without any prior consultation, it precluded any different proposal from having a chance.' The procedure was amended subsequently, maybe in response.[22] Rebellions and protests against academy procedures had occurred in the past. Indeed, disdain for prizes is an established element of their culture.[23]

The same problems of identifying distinction occur at every level of prizegiving. At the British Academy, for example, which elects a few economists every year, the process involves successive rounds of deliberation and voting, and yet the outcome remains something of a mystery. The winners emerge by an elaborate process of discussion and votes that is not capable of precise reconstruction. Initial favourites drop by the wayside, or recover suddenly after a well-timed intervention. Delicate webs of mutual obligation can sometimes hinder candid discourse.[24] Experience on academic appointment

---

20. Neild, *Public Corruption* (2002), chs. 3–4, 6–8; chapter 11, below.
21. Lindbeck, 'The Prize in Economic Science' (1985).
22. Myrdal, 'The Nobel Prize in Economic Science' (1977), 50; Ståhl, 'The Prize in Economic Science' (1990), 6.
23. English, *Economy of Prestige* (2005), ch. 8.
24. Personal experience.

committees suggests a similar qualified indeterminacy, where outcomes are sometimes difficult to predict. That is only to be expected. To think otherwise requires two assumptions: that there is an objective ranking of merit which is there to be revealed, and that selection committees can achieve this reliably.

Alfred Nobel had specified that his prize should be given to individuals who in the previous year 'had conferred the greatest benefit on mankind.' The prize is a social act: a thanks-offering to the beneficiary from a grateful community. The existence of the prize implies a role for economics as a social benefactor. Its existence endorses a core doctrine of economics, the invisible hand, which implies that the pursuit of self-interest is socially beneficial. This doctrine, it is worth repeating, has never been proven, except in an abstract and exotic form.[25]

The prize looks like a one-way transfer, a free lunch. The economics of self-interest for which the prize is given would find it difficult to explain it. The most sustained attempt to do so (in economics) is mostly about costless distinctions, not large windfalls like the Nobel.[26] On the face of it, the prize is not consistent with methodological individualism, the doctrine that everything should be explained in terms of individual choice. By 1969, when the economics prize was first given, methodological individualism had congealed around 'rational choice', a model of a single actor constrained by a 'budget' of resources, doing the best for themselves in market exchange. But lotteries can be reconciled with rationality. Adam Smith had already recognized that people could also be paid by the mere chance of a payoff, as in winning a lottery; the fewer the winners, the higher the payoff.[27] A lottery incentive was particularly suited for activities in which many are called but few are chosen, such as rising through the ranks in wartime, or success at the English bar. People are willing to work hard for the chance of a prize, and conversely, the chance of a prize can be seen as an alternative to being paid.

WHAT COUNTS AS SCIENCE?

The Riksbank Prize invites us to assume that economics is a science like physics, chemistry, and medicine. That is how the Bank's Governor Per Åsbrink justified it in 1969:

25. Above, 18–20; below, 243; Hutchison, 'From *The Wealth of Nations* to Modern General Equilibrium Theory' (2000).
26. Brennan and Pettit, *Economy of Esteem* (2004).
27. Smith, *Wealth of Nations* (1776/1976), bk. 1, ch.10.

I do not find it particularly difficult to motivate the new prize. The domain that is the object of the economic science, is if anything central and important for all people and all societies around the world. Would anyone claim, that advances in this area are less important or less pressing than advances for instance in medicine, physics or chemistry? I can certainly understand if anyone thinks that these things cannot be compared, or even if someone finds that other circumstances, for instance the difficulties in separating politics and science in this particular area, makes it problematic to award a prize in economics. But I would still like to believe that the economic science today is so developed and established as a scientific discipline, that such caveats cannot be decisive ... putting the prize decision and prize award in the hands of the institutions that have already proven themselves capable of carrying out the equivalent tasks for the already existing Nobel Prizes in a way that has given them their present prestige and status, will give the best guarantees for a fortunate result .... [28]

This was circular: scientific validity was guaranteed by the reputation of the Swedish Academy, but the task of validation was allocated to members of the very discipline which was meant to be scrutinized. A priori economic principles also suggest that the transaction may not be as disinterested as it seems, and that benefactors were getting in return at least as much as they gave.

In Swedish, the term 'science' (*vetenskap*, like the German *Wissenschaft*) means scholarship more broadly. But the English-speaking layperson's idea of science up to the 1960s, and indeed up to the present day, is that it reliably identifies and explains natural regularities. That is exemplified in a lecture delivered by the physicist Richard Feynman in 1964 (he won the Nobel Prize one year later):

Now I am going to discuss how we would look for a new law. In general, we look for a new law by the following process. First, we guess it, then we compute the consequences of the guess, to see what it is if this law is right it would imply, and then we compare these computation results to nature, or to experiment, or to experience. Compare it directly with observation to see if it works. If it disagrees with experiment, it's wrong. In that simple statement is the key to science. It doesn't make a difference how beautiful your guess is, it doesn't make a difference how smart you are who made the

---

28. Per Åsbrink to Gez. Hölzer, 27 May 1968, Bank of Sweden Archives, P. Åsbrinks Korrespondens 1968.

guess, or what his name is, if it disagrees with experiment, it's wrong, that's all there is to it.[29]

This is the 'hypothetico-deductive method' widely held from World War I and up to the 1960s. Scientific theory was justified by the extent to which it agreed with observation. Ideally, theory issues a precise prediction, which can be matched with empirical measurements. To evaluate the fit may be difficult, but the match underpins theoretical authority.

Cognoscenti will recognize this as a version of logical positivism (or logical empiricism), in which a theory or model specifies the relevant aspects of a causal mechanism or regularity, while observation and measurement validate the theory. This approach was already going out of fashion when Feynman expressed it, due to ambiguities in observation and validation. By the 1960s, it was understood (by philosophers of science) that finality of verification (or colloquially, 'proof') was beyond reach, and that measurement and observation could only provide corroboration or 'confirmation', that is, raise the truth-value of a theoretical proposition. In the 1960s and 1970s, some respite was provided by Karl Popper, with his immensely popular concept of falsification, which was supposed to provide finality for refutations at least. And persisting non-falsification was not very different from confirmation. What all these doctrines (which originated in Vienna in the 1920s and 1930s) implied was that observation was the arbiter of knowledge, although perhaps not a sufficiently powerful one.[30]

The mathematician John Von Neumann expressed himself in the same vein as Feynman,[31] and Nobel Prizes in the natural sciences continue to be awarded in this spirit. Most of the prizes in physics, for example, invoke empirical discoveries and all of them established some empirical correspondence. Paul Higgs, who theorized the existence of the Higgs boson in 1964, received the Nobel Prize only in 2013, after evidence of the particle was found. Edward Witten, a celebrated mathematical physicist at the Institute for Advanced Study in Princeton, is not a Nobel candidate because the string theory he works on has no empirically testable correlates.[32]

Feynman began by 'looking for a new law.' But after three centuries, economics has yet to come up with a single non-obvious 'law', or universal reg-

---

29. Available at https://www.youtube.com/watch?v=EYPapE-3FRw.
30. Friedman, *Reconsidering Logical Positivism* (1999); Backhouse, 'The Rise and Fall of Popper and Lakatos in Economics' (2012).
31. Above, 22.
32. Dawid, *String Theory and the Scientific Method* (2013).

ularity. Economic sophistication takes the form of an elaborate transformation of initial premises about human behaviour (like 'rationality') which are known to be invalid for much of the time. This feature of economics cannot be attributed to Adam Smith, who told a rich empirical story. But less than a century later, it was already evident to John Stuart Mill, who maintained that political economy was inexact, a science of 'tendencies' whose claims were 'truly in the abstract', which could not be fulfilled in practice owing to disturbing causes. Skip a century, and a notable methodological tract, Daniel Hausman's *The Inexact and Separate Science of Economics* (1992), repeated Mill's argument. In the same year, another significant study (by Alexander Rosenberg) concurred, and described economic predictions as merely 'generic', that is, not precise.[33] A Finnish authority, Uskali Mäki, has long conceded that economics is only 'realist' in the sense that it is imaginably true, that 'if we opt for radical physicalist scientific realism, current economics will not fit.'[34]

The most widely read text in this vein is Milton Friedman's 'The Methodology of Positive Economics' (1953).[35] It concedes that the assumptions of economics are unrealistic, but makes a virtue of it. Science proceeds by making counterintuitive discoveries; by abstracting from experience, not by describing it. Lack of realism in assumptions does not matter. The bolder the departure from convention, the greater its value when it is sustained. What justifies economics is that its postulates are not falsified. It had been pointed out that businessmen did not consciously and explicitly always maximize profits. That evidence did not falsify the theoretical assumption that profit was always maximized:

> An even more important body of evidence for the maximization-of-returns hypothesis is experience from countless applications of the hypothesis to specific problems and the repeated failure of its implications to be contradicted. This evidence is extremely hard to document; it is scattered in numerous memorandums, articles, and monographs concerned primarily with specific concrete problems rather than with submitting the hypothesis to test. Yet the continued use and acceptance of the hypothesis over a long period, and the failure of any coherent, self-consistent alternative to be developed and be widely accepted, is strong indirect testimony to its worth.

33. Hausman, *The Inexact and Separate Science of Economics* (1992), 125; Rosenberg, *Economics: Mathematical Politics or Science of Diminishing Returns?* (1992).
34. Mäki, 'Realism' (2008), 437.
35. Friedman, 'The Methodology of Positive Economics' (1953).

The evidence for a hypothesis always consists of its repeated failure to be contradicted, continues to accumulate so long as the hypothesis is used, and by its very nature is difficult to document at all comprehensively.[36]

This is not a high hurdle for any theory to jump, and there is plenty of disconfirming evidence of the same and much better quality. When challenged by a critic, Friedman responded privately at length giving a single example, of the Rockefeller Standard Oil Monopoly, which his Chicago colleague John McGee had argued did not engage in predatory pricing. But Friedman did not take up an invitation (by the philosopher Imre Lakatos) to publish this response.[37] Since then, McGee's Standard Oil example has been discredited in three articles as being based on deduction (his argument was from theory, not empirical), and that his use of evidence was selective and distorted.[38] Paul Samuelson and Herbert Simon (NPWs, 1970 and 1978) rejected out of hand the so-called F-Twist that assumptions did not matter.[39]

From the 1960s onwards, writers in history and philosophy of science began to reject the confrontation of theory with observation as expounded by Feynman. Starting from Thomas Kuhn's *Structure of Scientific Revolutions* (1962), they argued increasingly that there was no canonical logic of scientific discovery—that science was what scientists did.[40] Influential in the 1970s was Paul Feyerabend's *Against Method* with its message of 'anything goes'.[41] Within the natural sciences this was not much of an issue, since scientists themselves continued to insist on empirical validation. Methodologists in economics, however, took it as a licence for anti-realist, non-empirical economics, thus accommodating the anti-realist macroeconomics of Lucas and Sargent described in the previous chapter.[42] The Popperian window for falsification in economics did not remain open for long. By the mid-1980s, falsifi-

36. Ibid., 14.
37. This episode is described in Anon., 'Imre Lakatos', *World Heritage Encyclopaedia* (n.d., but after 2012). The relevant letters cited are Friedman to Spiro Latsis, 6 December 1972, and Latsis to Friedman, 27 January 1973, Hoover Institution, Friedman Papers Box 29/36, and Lakatos to Friedman, 2 February 1973, Friedman Papers Box 29/32. Also personal communication, John Latsis. Thanks to Carol A. Leadenham for providing copies.
38. Anon., 'Imre Lakatos' (n.d.); Leslie, 'Revisiting the Revisionist History of Standard Oil' (2012).
39. 'F' for Friedman. Archibald, Samuelson and Simon, 'Problems of Methodology' (1963); See Mäki, 'The Methodology of Positive Economics' (2009).
40. Arguably, the logical positivists had been no different in that respect (Friedman, 'The Re-Evaluation of Logical Positivism' [1991]).
41. Feyerabend, *Against Method: Outline of an Anarchistic Theory of Knowledge* (1975).
42. Klamer, *Conversations with the New Classical Economists* (1985); McCloskey, *Knowledge and Persuasion in Economics* (1994).

cation was an embattled position among methodologists.[43] Economics, said McCloskey, was what economists did. And most other methodologists (a small and tightly knit group) concurred with variants of their own.[44]

FROM THEORY BACK TO REALITY

Evidence is at odds with theory in economics: the fit is poor. Economic evidence is not well behaved. This suggests a disparity between the premises of theory and the way the world really is.[45] Economists are happy to postulate non-observables in their theories, entities like expectations, preferences, utility, taste, and representative agents. In their approach to evidence, however, they ignore the individual intentionality that they postulate. Only price and quantity count. They reject the testimony of texts, and of attitude and opinion surveys. But to validate economics, numerical evidence has to accord with two different theoretical frameworks, those of economics and of statistics.

Evidence has to be squeezed into the boxes of economic theory—supply, demand, elasticity, rationality, equilibrium. This is mediated by statistical theory. Raw numbers are merely 'descriptive statistics'; the real action is detecting regularity in messy ('stochastic') clusters of numbers, by means of sampling and manipulation. In its crudest form, this involves some kind of 'curve-fitting', in which the curve describes the phenomenon (for example, y causes x) and the actual observations (mostly off the curve) measure deviations, systematic and random. The signal (or 'curve') can be regarded as providing a valid inference (for example, y causes x) only if it satisfies stringent statistical constraints (normality, linearity, homoscedasticity, independence, t-homogeneity, stationarity).[46] In a more elaborate form ('regression analysis'), the separate effect of several 'independent variables' jointly is estimated on the variable of interest (for example, the joint effect of urbanization and tariffs on economic growth). Econometrics is statistical theory applied to economics. It sets out how methodological constraints can be managed. The

43. De Marchi, *The Popperian Legacy in Economics* (1988); Backhouse, 'The Rise and Fall of Popper and Lakatos in Economics' (2012).
44. As reflected in the collected volumes, Backhouse, *New Directions in Economic Methodology* (1994) and Mäki, *Philosophy of Economics* (2012). The most notable (and distinguished) exceptions were Mark Blaug, *Methodology of Economics* (1992), and Kevin Hoover (for example, *The New Classical Macroeconomics* [1988]). Also Mayer, *Truth versus Precision in Economics* (1993), and T. W. Hutchison in several works.
45. Haavelmo, 'Econometrics and the Welfare State', Nobel Lecture 1989.
46. Spanos, 'Philosophy of Econometrics' (2012).

sad reality known to every empirical investigator is that conformity is rare. Most data are 'badly behaved'. Wassily Leontief (NPW, 1973) said this in his presidential address to the American Economic Association:

> Like the economic models they are supposed to implement, the validity of these statistical tools depends itself on the acceptance of certain convenient assumptions pertaining to stochastic properties of the phenomena which the particular models are intended to explain; assumptions that can be seldom verified.
>
> In no other field of empirical inquiry has so massive and sophisticated a statistical machinery been used with such indifferent results.[47]

In the late 1970s and early 1980s, critics exposed the practice of extensive off-the-record searches for the 'correct' results, and withholding of negative findings, which invalidated standard data-selection assumptions. These writers mostly admonished practitioners for not trying hard enough, or in David Hendry's words, failing to 'test, test, test'.[48] In 1980, Christopher Sims (NPW, 2011) led the way towards statistical techniques ('vector autoregression', VAR in short) that eschewed economic theory altogether.[49] The work of Granger and Engle in the 1980s on spurious correlation and co-integration (NPW for both, 2003) invalidated a good deal of previous econometric estimation.[50] After a hundred years of econometrics, wrote a more recent critic, 'the overwhelming majority of published applied papers ... are unlikely to pass [a simple] statistical adequacy test'.[51] Two decades after the soul-searching of the 1980s, Ed Leamer, one of the critics, still writes: 'Econometric theory promises more than it can deliver, because it requires a complete commitment to assumptions that are actually only half-heartedly maintained'.[52] Attempts to replicate empirical findings in economics are not frequent, and when carried out, 'over three-fourths of replication studies report failing to confirm one or more major findings from the original research'.[53] All of this suggests that

---

47. Leontief, 'Theoretical Assumptions and Non-observed Facts' (1971), 3.
48. Leamer, 'Let's Take the Con Out of Econometrics' (1983); Hendry, 'Econometrics: Alchemy or Science?' (1980); Spanos, 'Econometrics in Retrospect and Prospect' (2006), 32–34.
49. Sims, 'Macroeconomics and Reality' (1980).
50. Hendry, 'The Nobel Memorial Prize for Clive W. J. Granger' (2004).
51. Spanos, 'Econometrics in Retrospect and Prospect' (2006), 18; Qin, *History of Econometrics* (2013), ch. 1.
52. Leamer, 'Tantalus on the Road to Asymptotia' (2010), 36.
53. Duvendack et al., 'Replications in Economics: A Progress Report' (2014), 22.

the empirical validity of theory in economics should not be taken as compelling. This situation is not peculiar to economics: empirical validity is elusive in some fields of natural sciences as well, and for similar reasons. It has been argued that in bio-medical science, 'most research findings are false for most research designs and for most fields'.[54]

The trouble with the quest for the perfect model is that, if pursued rigorously enough, it will exclude all the evidence. Despite the range of statistical recipes for bringing data into line, one expert writes, 'severely probed statistically adequate regularities are very rare indeed'.[55] The problem then is not incompetent statisticians. It is reality which refuses to co-operate. Which is another way of saying that, empirically at least, much of economic theory appears to be wrong, even when it has internal validity.[56]

The consequent temptation for methodologists (often themselves embattled within economics departments) was to turn their back on empirics. But they got their timing wrong, and were left behind by changes in practice. Within the discipline, the retreat from reality was already being reversed. In the 1970s, computer power reached into every department, and by the 1980s, it was on every desk. Econometrics was positioned to apply Popperian falsificationist discipline to economic models, and in fact econometric 'testing' proliferated, but not in the form of falsification. Instead, it largely consisted of the methodologically discredited method of confirmation—searching for evidence consistent with the model.[57] Twenty of the Nobel Lectures up to 2005 invoked confirmation in some form, twelve used the stronger positivist test of verification, and only five invoked falsification. In econometrics, the quest for confirmation could involve 'fitting maybe, perhaps thousands, of statistical models. One or several that the researcher finds pleasing are selected for reporting.' The resulting models are typically whimsical (that is, arbitrary) and fragile, and hence not to be taken entirely seriously, except in the case of one's own.[58] The precision of coefficients had to be taken with a pinch of salt—although not discarded altogether. If every investigator follows the same questionable practices, some results are still better than others,

54. Ioannidis, 'Why Most Published Research Findings Are False' (2005), e124.
55. Spanos, 'Econometrics in Retrospect and Prospect' (2006), 44.
56. Mayer, *Truth Versus Precision in Economics* (1993), ch. 10.
57. Canterbury and Burkhardt, 'What Do We Mean by Asking Whether Economics Is a Science?' (1983), 31; Caldwell, *Beyond Positivism* (1982), 231.
58. All this in Leamer, 'Let's Take the Con Out of Econometrics' (1983).

in the direction of the signs and the magnitude of effects. They were just not precise—which takes us back to 'tendencies' again, as being possibly all that economics can provide.

The new empirical turn after the 1980s was reflected in publication trends. Taking the three top journals at ten-year intervals since 1963, theory articles peaked at 57.6 percent of the total in 1983 (plus 4.0 percent theory with simulation), and have subsequently declined to 19.1 percent in 2011 (plus 8.8 percent theory with simulation). Experimental and own-data articles rose from 3.2 percent in 1983 to 42.2 percent in 2011.[59] This 'empirical turn' is recent. In 1993 and 2003, theory (including simulation) still accounted for 40 percent of all articles. In 1947, the econometric guru Tjalling Koopmans (NPW, 1975) castigated the dominance in his day of 'measurement without theory.'[60] So just as methodologists were turning their back on reality, practical economists re-discovered it, and when in doubt, have often preferred evidence to theory.[61]

Many reverted to experimental methods which antedated econometrics. A policy (or 'treatment') was administered to one group of subjects, and withheld from a control group, either in the field or in the lab. It could also be used for 'natural experiments' in history when sharp breaks allowed comparison of different experiences in comparable circumstances, or to predict policy effects on the basis of past consumer choices. This 'credibility revolution' in empirical economics was not dependent on prior economic theory.[62] It was recognized only once by the Nobel Committee before 2005, in the work of McFadden and Heckman (NPWs, 2000), a belated one for Heckman to judge by his citation record, with the most rapid and sustained acceleration of citation of any NPW and by far the highest one-year peak.[63] To the extent that this new empiricism in economics seeks to generalize, it is inductive, that is, extrapolating from the particular to the general. Ever since David Hume, it has been understood that induction cannot claim general validity: a counter-example might always turn up, a white raven, or a black swan. So the gain in empirical credibility has been achieved at a big cost in generality.

---

59. Hamermesh, 'Six Decades of Top Economics Publishing: Who and How?' (2013).

60. Koopmans, 'Measurement without Theory' (1947).

61. Backhouse and Cherrier, 'Becoming Applied: The Transformation of Economics after 1970' (2014).

62. Angrist and Pischke, 'The Credibility Revolution in Empirical Economics' (2010); Card et al., 'The Role of Theory in Field Experiments' (2011).

63. Chapter 6, below, 147.

Our own sub-discipline of economic history is by its nature empirical, and might have been designed to provide reality-checks to theory. Arthur Lewis (NPW, 1978) worked in that spirit; two other Nobels were awarded for historical work in 1993 (Fogel and North), while Mundell (NPW, 1999) used economic history to frame policy analysis in his Nobel Lecture. These narrative efforts lent little support to the models of general equilibrium microeconomics at the heart of the discipline.

Some of the earlier Nobel Prizes were given for an older macroeconomic empiricism of the 1930s and 1940s. The massive double-entry bookkeeping enterprise of the National Accounts created the ubiquitous measures of national income and product (for example, GDP) which allow the precise monitoring of economic performance from one quarter to the next.[64] It was recognized in the prizes to Kuznets (NPW, 1971) and Stone (NPW, 1984), while Leontief (NPW, 1973) and Klein (NPW, 1980) enhanced and exploited this breakthrough.

In a new departure (with some antecedents), behavioural economics produced an overall finding that was not consistent with the foundational microeconomic premise of self-interested, consistent, and well-informed individuals. On the contrary, in experimental settings and in the field, people were found to be predictably biased, myopic, inconsistent, and altruistic, concerned as much about the opinion and welfare of others as about maximizing their own market advantage. This behavioural strand in economics was acknowledged early on in the prize for Herbert Simon (NPW, 1978) and in later prizes for Daniel Kahneman and Vernon Smith (both NPW, 2002). Smith said in his Nobel Lecture: 'Good theory must be an engine for generating testable hypotheses, and utility theory runs out of fuel quickly.'[65]

Computing made it possible, from the 1970s onwards, to collect and analyze large datasets, often combined from many countries, to investigate the efficacy of policy. In contrast to the New Classical Macroeconomics, when findings and theory diverged, investigators often set theory aside. In these applications, it was usually regarded as sufficient to demonstrate that some policy or other accorded with the experimenter's intuitions, without rigorous grounding in theory. Especially popular have been cross-country regressions, in which the impact of some implemented policy measure (the independent

---

64. More detail, chapter 7, below, 153–157.
65. Smith, 'Constructivist and Ecological Rationality in Economics', Nobel Lecture 2002, 505, n. 11.

variable, for example, protective tariffs) was estimated ('regressed') on economic growth, in large heterogeneous clusters of countries. One notorious example was a purported empirical regularity that public debt beyond 90 percent of GDP was inimical to growth (this was later shown to be the result of a miscalculation). These loose empirical exercises supported policy priors, often side-stepping the theoretical straitjacket of post-war microeconomics, and indeed some of the statistical constraints as well.[66] These are also exercises in induction which lack a more general validity, but that is often ignored in discussing their policy implications.

IS ECONOMICS A SCIENCE? THE VIEW FROM STOCKHOLM

What did economics NPWs think of their own science? In the first decade or so, their Stockholm lectures provide a commentary, much of it critical. To simplify, orthodox microeconomic theory assumes perfect knowledge: the future is knowable (and hence fixed, or 'ergodic'), and everybody acts on that knowledge.[67] The debate mostly revolved around this perfect-knowledge assumption.

Young communist leaders in Czechoslovakia in the 1940s had mastered Marxist theory and believed they had mastered the world.[68] This might be said of post-war economic theory with even greater truth. At the first award ceremony in 1969, Erik Lundberg, economics committee chairman, stated that constructing mathematical models and specifying them empirically was evidence of scientific maturity.[69]

The first three Nobel Prize winners were flattered to think of themselves as being on a par with the Nobel Prize winners in the natural sciences, although each one of them had a different idea of what that implied. Ragnar Frisch (NPW, 1969) aspired to the same precision as the physical sciences, and also argued that economics had a working technology to apply. Politicians could be asked by economists about their policy preferences, which would be fed into a valid pre-existing computer model of the economy: 'From this will come out a solution, in the form of an optimal development path of the economy.' Parliaments could concentrate on really important

66. Rodrik, 'Why We Learn Nothing from Regressing Economic Growth on Policies' (2012); Égert, 'The 90% Public Debt Threshold' (2013).
67. Davidson, 'Reality and Economic Theory' (1996).
68. Mlynar, *Night Frost in Prague* (1978/1980), 2–3.
69. Lundberg, 'Award Ceremony Speech' (1969).

things and leave the details to economists.[70] A good deal of this has come to pass, especially in the form of independent central banks (although their New Classical models are impossible to validate, and have not passed even the conventional weak tests of econometric validity).[71]

The other NPW of the first year, Jan Tinbergen (NPW, 1969), accepted empirical verification (the Feynman criterion) as an objective. His idea of a science of economics was to identify the best institutions capable of achieving the social optimum. This was the opposite of Frisch's notion that the economist's job was simply to execute politicians' preferences. He was also sceptical of the 'scientific strategy of official welfare economics', that is, standard microeconomic theory.[72]

Not so Paul Samuelson (NPW, 1970) the following year, who was praised by the Nobel Committee in these terms: 'More than any other contemporary economist he has contributed to raising the general analytical and methodological level of scientific analysis in economic science.'[73] His Nobel Lecture set out to show what this meant. Newton was invoked three times, Galileo twice. No mention however of the Feynman criterion of empirical validity, rather the opposite. Samuelson invoked a model which allowed prediction without observation: for an imaginary firm with 99 inputs, if an increase in the price of fertilizer always increases the amount the firm buys of caviar, then 'an increase in the price of caviar alone will increase the amount the firm buys of fertilizer.' This was a counter-intuitive, but also a safe, prediction to make. It was not meant to be tested.[74] A second model in his lecture had come out of physics. Samuelson handed back an improved version to the discipline of origin. Unlike either Newton or Galileo, his concept of science required no observation: 'Pressure and volume, and for that matter absolute temperature and entropy, have to each other the same conjugate or dualistic relation that the wage rate has to labour or the land rent has to acres of land.'[75] The physical ratios, Feynman might have pointed out, were stable, testable constants; the economic ones were not.

70. Frisch, 'The Use of Models: Experience and Prospects', Nobel Lecture 1969 (delivered 17 June 1970).
71. Tovar, 'DSGE Models and Central Banks' (2008).
72. Tinbergen, 'From Utopian Theory to Practical Applications: The Case of Econometrics', Nobel Lecture 1969, 6.
73. Assar Lindbeck, Nobel Award Ceremony Speech 1970.
74. Samuelson, 'Maximum Principles in Analytical Economics', Nobel Lecture 1970, 67.
75. Ibid., 69.

Arrow (NPW, 1972), another high theorist, presented a wonderfully clear account of the general equilibrium existence result mentioned in chapter 1. It was a normative ideal (of Pareto efficiency, admittedly a weak norm) and an empirical one. Although inconceivable in any real world, it indicated the direction in which social policy could move.[76] But already in 1956, Lipsey and Lancaster had shown that gradual movement towards general equilibrium was not necessarily more efficient.[77] Arrow drifted in and out of realism with regard to his invisible hand model, at one point idealizing the market to such an extent as to criticize the use of economic controls even in wartime: 'There is no reason to believe that the same forces that work in peacetime would not produce a working system in time of war or other considerable shifts in demand.'[78] As in the case of Frisch, these musings were soon acted on. In 1976, soon after losing its conscript war in Vietnam, the United States abolished the draft, and began to pay market wages for soldiers and war contractors (also urged by Milton Friedman, NPW, 1976).

What Arrow and Friedman overlooked is that war traded in violence, not commodities. For all its preponderance in wealth and population, the US free-enterprise war machine could not prevail in the many wars and conflicts it initiated thereafter (assuming that the purpose was to prevail—an enduring war may have other uses). For the United States, it turned out that the scarce factor was the willingness of market-wage warriors to risk their lives. A subtle mind like Arrow's may have meant to convey that market war was impossible, just as general equilibrium was impossible in reality. Nothing in Arrow's general equilibrium model could warrant his statement: it has no role for government.

In contrast, at the Nobel banquet earlier, Arrow's prize-partner John Hicks (another high theorist) dismissed the idea of economics as a science: 'Our science colleagues find permanent truths; economists, who deal with the daily actions of men and the consequences of these, can rarely hope to find the same permanency.'[79] In his 1974 Nobel Lecture, Friedrich von Hayek denied that economics could meet the standards of science.[80] 'As a

76. Arrow, 'General Economic Equilibrium: Purpose, Analytical Techniques, Collective Choice', Nobel Lecture 1972, 127.
77. Lipsey and Lancaster, 'General Theory of the Second Best' (1956).
78. Arrow, 'General Economic Equilibrium: Purpose, Analytical Techniques, Collective Choice', Nobel Lecture 1972, 109.
79. Hicks, Nobel Banquet Speech, 10 December 1972.
80. Hayek, 'The Pretence of Knowledge', Nobel Lecture 1974.

profession we have made a mess of things', he said, alluding to the dominant Keynesian macroeconomics. His criterion of scientific validity was Popper's falsification. The Nobel Prize for economic science did not live up to it, and risked a descent into 'scientism', the mere pretence of scientific certainty.[81] Hayek did not advocate better science—economics could never be a science, because its core variables could not be observed. It was better to be vaguely right than precisely wrong, he stated (although in different words), a view often attributed to his rival Keynes.[82] Economics was indeterminate, like biology or gardening. True knowledge was innate, and could not be confirmed scientifically by observation.

Milton Friedman (1976) also endorsed reality-testing in its Popperian form, but drew a different conclusion. Knowledge was fallible, but that was the nature of science. His lecture was meant 'primarily to make the point that economics was or could be a positive science like physics and chemistry.'[83] No mention here of enduring laws:

> there is no 'certain' substantive knowledge; only tentative hypotheses that can never be 'proved', but can only fail to be rejected, hypotheses in which we may have more or less confidence.... In both social and natural sciences, the body of positive knowledge grows by the failure of a tentative hypothesis to predict phenomena the hypothesis professes to explain; by the patching up of that hypothesis until someone suggest a new hypothesis that more elegantly or simply embodies the troublesome phenomena, and so on ad infinitum.

Unlike high theorists, Friedman invoked uncertainty and cognitive error.[84] Nevertheless, (like Frisch and Arrow on the left) he suggested (half-jokingly) that technology could replace political discretion: 'My monetary studies have led me to the conclusion that central banks could profitably be replaced by computers geared to provide a steady rate of growth in the quantity of money.'[85] True to his method, this notion could be falsified—and it eventually was: the relation between central bank money and broader measures of money turned out to be unstable, and could not be used to control inflation.[86]

---

81. Hayek, 'The Pretence of Knowledge', Nobel Lecture 1974; Hayek, 'Scientism and the Study of Society' (1942).
82. Hayek, 'Pretence of Knowledge', Nobel Lecture 1974, 4.
83. Friedman, *Two Lucky People* (1998), 457.
84. Friedman, 'Inflation and Unemployment', Nobel Lecture 1976.
85. Friedman, *Two Lucky People* (1998), 453–454.
86. Mayer, 'The Twilight of the Monetarism Debate' (1990).

Friedman's award provoked Gunnar Myrdal (NPW, 1974) to suggest the abolition of the prize. Rather like Hayek (his ideological opponent) he stated that economics could not be a science, since its data were human attitudes and behaviour, whose causes are evolving and inaccessible. Economics could never identify constants or what in former times were called 'laws of nature'.[87] Economists were as unlike astronomers as was possible. The other reason to distrust economics (on which Myrdal had written with authority some decades before) was that it was shot through with values, and could not avoid taking a view about proper ends.[88] '[Economists] keep silent about the role of values in research. They regularly assume that there is a solid body of theories and facts, established without implying value premises, from which policy conclusions can then also be drawn'.[89]

Herbert Simon (NPW, 1978) in his Nobel Lecture presented the most acute challenge for the self-interest/invisible hand model of economics, aggressively judging the discipline by the demanding criterion of 'verification' (that is, finality of explanation by means of observation). Contrary to Friedman's assertions, empirical research on business decisions over many years had shown that both the premises and the conclusions of the neoclassical theory of a profit-maximizing firm were empirically false, and constituted 'a direct refutation of the neoclassical assumptions'. The word 'refutation' or its variants was repeated six times. At stake was the perfect information assumption in neoclassical analysis. An alternative and successful economics of imperfect cognition was already being widely applied by management scholars and psychologists. Unlike Hayek, Simon did not expect that cognitive limitations ('bounded rationality') would give rise to a benign spontaneous order. Like Hayek, however, he pointed to biology as a better model than physics. If the Nobel Committee took notice of these challenges to microeconomics, it shrugged them off and continued to award prizes to neoclassical theorists.[90]

After Simon, references to reality-disciplined science began to drop away, with two notable exceptions, both of them, like Friedman, members of the Mont Pèlerin Society (figure 2.1). For the objective of rolling back Social Democracy, the sanction of science counted for a great deal. George Stigler (NPW, 1982) referred to science more than seventy times in his Nobel Lec-

87. Myrdal, 'The Nobel Prize in Economic Science' (1977), 51.
88. Myrdal, *Political Element* (1930/1990).
89. Myrdal, 'The Nobel Prize in Economic Science' (1977), 51.
90. Chapter 5, below.

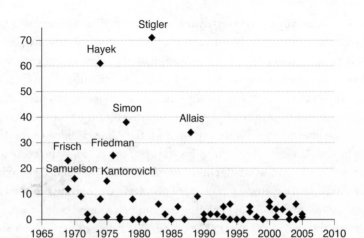

Figure 2.1. References to 'science' in NPW Nobel Lectures, 1969–2005.
Source: Nobel Lectures (delivered by NPWs usually a day or two after the prize ceremony), available at
http://www.nobelprize.org/nobel_prizes/economic-sciences/laureates/index.html.
Note: 'Science' and its derivatives, excluding publication references and institutions.

ture. He acknowledged reality, though a lawyer might note that testing was
not mentioned:

> The central task of an empirical science such as economics is to provide
> general understanding of events in the real world, and ultimately all of its
> theories and techniques must be instrumental to that task.[91]

He likened science itself to a marketplace. What he neglected to say, was that
if science was like a market, then everything was up for sale; and for economics, there were plenty of customers if the message was right. Economics
was more of a seller's market, dominated by a coterie of North American
departments, and even fewer journals, 'We Happy Few', in which the producers themselves, not the 'market', certified their own output as the hallmark
of quality.[92] As Paul Samuelson (NPW, 1970) put it, 'the economic scholar
works for the only coin worth having—our own applause.' In a footnote, he
immediately retracted, saying that he did not mean leaving the real-world
problems of political economy to non-economists.[93]

---

91. Stigler, The Process and Progress of Economics', Nobel Lecture 1982, 60.
92. Canterbery and Burkhardt, 'What Do We Mean by Asking Whether Economics Is a
Science' (1983); Samuelson, 'Economists and the History of Ideas' (1962), 17.
93. Ibid., 18.

The last grand appeal to positivism among Nobel Prize winners was made by the French economist Maurice Allais (NPW, 1988). Allais invoked the Feynman criterion in elevated tones: 'Submission to observed or experimental data is the golden rule which dominates any scientific discipline. Any theory whatever, if it is not verified by empirical evidence, has no scientific value and should be rejected.'[94] Allais himself received the prize for theoretical work on general equilibrium, and not for the Allais paradox of the 1950s which he did, however, mention in his lecture. That paradox showed experimentally that when individuals chose among lotteries, they defied the axioms of rationality. This devastating critique of neoclassical economics in the 1950s anticipated the emergence of experimental and behavioural economics.

Towards the end of our period, the experimental economist Vernon Smith (NPW, 2002) revisited the relation between theory and evidence. He made a distinction between 'constructive rationality', the prescriptive model of rational choice, and 'ecological rationality', the way that choice is actually made, much of it unconscious, due to the confrontation of limited brainpower with hyper-abundant information.

> A theorem is a mapping from assumptions into testable or observable implications. The demands of tractability loom large in this exercise. . . . But the temptation is to believe that our 'castles in the sky' (as W. Brock would say) have direct meaning in our world of experience and to proceed to impose them where it may not be ecologically rational to do so.[95]

WHAT AUTHORITY DOES SCIENCE CONFER?

Does it matter if economics is science or not? If science is what scientists do, then perhaps we can leave it to economists to decide. But once economists begin to lay down policy, that autonomy is no longer tenable. The endowment of the prize by a central bank signals that economics is of wider social interest. In natural science, the primacy of reality is secure, even if there is no finality of explanation. Theory can be shown to be wrong by empirical observation and measurement.

In addition to theory and evidence, economics is also a normative discipline, and often claims that one policy is better than another. Implicit in the

---

94. Allais, 'An Outline of My Main Contributions to Economic Science' Nobel Lecture 1988.
95. Smith, 'Constructivist and Ecological Rationality in the Economics', Nobel Lecture 2002, 511.

discipline's policy norms are its norms of validity. Taking economics at face value, it privileges the value of efficiency, defined as satisfaction of individual preferences at the lowest cost. Now efficiency is worth having, but so are other values, such as truth, justice, beauty, freedom, loyalty, or obligation. To privilege efficiency is a value choice, which is not independent of the state of the world, and of the prevalence of other desirables. And the aggregation of individual preferences under standard assumptions, even assuming this was the only proper objective, cannot be made to work analytically. The ultimate economic efficiency criterion, 'Pareto efficiency', is not even a pure efficiency criterion of 'more for less', since it does not question pre-existing endowments (inherited or otherwise unearned), which is itself a value choice.[96]

When economists lay down policy, it needs to be possible to query their authority, and to ask whether they might be wrong. That is why Mark Blaug, the outstanding economic methodologist of our period, remained 'an unrepentant Popperian'. Not because Popper's falsification criterion reliably separated science from non-science, but for its insistence on empirical testing as the arbiter of knowledge.

> If we accept and even welcome the inevitable policy implications of much even seemingly abstract economic theory, we cannot at the same time pour cold water on the predictability of economic theories, sometimes going so far as to suggest that the very character of economics as a social science necessarily robs the subject of any capacity to predict ... if economics is to be practically relevant, there must be some concrete truths in which we can place confidence.[97]

In the absence of measuring up against reality, how to choose between competing economic doctrines apart from prior convictions?

In their Nobel Lectures, several NPWs stated, with all the authority of a newly minted NPW, that orthodox neoclassical theory was actually wrong, in whole or in part, on either empirical or theoretical grounds. Hayek, Simon, Solow, Haavelmo, Coase, North, Sen, Kahneman: all of them said that the theory could not be true. Another three (Kuznets, Leontief, and Stone) explicitly distanced themselves from the North American neoclassical consensus

---

96. Little, *Critique of Welfare Economics* (1957), ch. 6; Atkinson, 'The Mirrlees Review' (2012), 799.
97. Blaug, 'Confessions of an Unrepentant Popperian' (1994), 118–119.

on other occasions, one of them (Leontief) at a presidential address to the American Economic Association.[98]

If economics was a science and falsification was its touchstone, these Nobel falsifications achieved no finality: falsification was itself falsified, on its own criterion. In an earlier debate on method, Samuelson had bluntly said that 'if the models contain empirical falsities, we must jettison the models, not gloss over their inadequacies.'[99] Apparently not so. It is to the Nobel Committee's credit that it provided a platform for these acute and mutually inconsistent criticisms. It did not apply the Samuelson (or Feynman, or Popperian) razor of positive, confirmable or falsifiable 'science', but followed the pluralist line that economics was what economists did. Had it gone any other way, it would have had to exclude many eminent candidates. It declined to take any position on what science was, except to reject the criterion of empirical validity. Its practice proclaimed that there were different ways to the truth. It could hardly act any differently and maintain the credibility of the prize.

But pluralism has a price. Some economic doctrines were empirically validated, others were not, and empirical validation, although there was a good deal of it, was not compelling. In the absence of empirical constraint, the rationalist, deductive, non-empirical doctrines tended to be more strongly prescriptive than those that were empirically validated. Hayek had it right: 'to entrust to science ... more than scientific method can achieve may have deplorable effects.'[100] Joseph Schumpeter (an NPW-level economist born too soon), wrote,

> Unsatisfactory [empirical] performance has always been and still is accompanied [in economics] by unjustified claims, and especially by irresponsible applications to practical problems that were and are beyond the powers of the contemporaneous analytic apparatus.[101]

This was also the view of Hjalmar Branting, the first Swedish Social Democratic prime minister, who was an astronomer by training:

> Economics is not like the natural sciences, in which what one investigator has demonstrated to be true cannot be questioned by another authority,

98.   Offer, 'Charles Hilliard Feinstein 1932–2004' (2008), 197–198; Leontief, 'Theoretical Assumptions and Nonobserved Facts' (1971); Foley, 'An Interview with Wassily Leontief' (1998), 117–118, 125–128.

99.   Archibald et al. 'Problems of Methodology: Discussion' (1963), 236.

100.   Hayek, 'Pretence of Knowledge', Nobel Lecture 1974, 5.

101.   Schumpeter, *History of Economic Analysis* (1954), 19.

since the critic would then simply show that he is ignorant of the facts. In the field of economic science we still see school ranged against school; while the number of authentically recognised general truths is, unfortunately, still very small.[102]

Methodologists hardly mention the normative claims of economics. They discuss knowledge and persuasion in economics as if it was largely a matter for seminars, conferences, and journals.

Academic evidence might be inconclusive, but reality is not. As Gunnar Myrdal said, 'facts kick'.[103] Bad theory makes bad policy, and when reality does not comply, it often has to be coerced. Bad theory is itself a means of coercion: In the Soviet Union, it provided justification for the gulag; in the 'free market' United States, for its own massive gulag, a prison system larger in proportion than in any other country, fed by a labour market with frayed safety nets, and managed for profit.[104] The Nobel Prize in economics (as we shall see) was an afterthought, a whimsy almost, of a modern central bank. Monetary doctrine between the wars, which gave rise to modern central banking, also gave rise to depression, unemployment, inequality, and ultimately to a second world war. Good economic theory (in the same years), went some way to fix the harm. This leads into the next chapter.

---

102. Quoted by Myrdal, *Political Element* (1930/1990), Swedish preface, xiii.
103. Myrdal, 'Asian Drama' (1968), 46.
104. Selman and Leighton, *Punishment for Sale* (2010).

CHAPTER 3

BITTER ROOTS: FINANCE AND SOCIAL DEMOCRACY BETWEEN THE WARS

The Nobel Prizes, like opera houses and museums in North America, signify the power of finance. As in opera, the plot is not always easy to follow. But when the prizes are given out, librettos do not matter: the spectacle sings the abundance of capitalism, applauded by well-dressed patrons in good seats. When founded in 1968, the Nobel Prize in economics was a delayed artefact of the quest to understand and control financial and business cycles in the twentieth century. Like the original Nobel Prizes, it was endowed from the bounty of a single benefactor, in this case the governor of the Riksbank, Sweden's central bank. Alfred Nobel's motivation was sublime, and the money came out of his will; the chain of causes for the economics prize was something of a farce, and was paid for by Swedish taxpayers. How it came about cannot be separated from what it is about, and the context is more telling than the prize itself. It was a belated incident in one of the central plots of modern history, the distributional struggle between the owners of wealth and the rest of society. In an ironic twist, this late-coming Nobel was authorized by Swedish Social Democracy in the course of its long stand-off with Swedish capitalism, in the belief that it didn't matter. But it did.

MONEY AND GOLD

The story comes out of the eighteenth century, from the interaction of commercial enterprise and Enlightenment thinking. Gold and silver coins had been minted by monarchs for centuries to pay for provisions, courtiers, and soldiers, and were now required for overseas colonization and commerce. Fortunately, colonies and commerce paid off, first in the form of gold and silver flows from Spanish America, and then, in the eighteenth century, as paper money and promises to pay, devised by merchants and bankers to expand the currency. Gold is scarce and hard to produce, but paper is cheap, sometimes too cheap. Regulating paper money has not been mastered even today.

In a brilliant example of model-making which still retains its grip, the eighteenth-century philosopher David Hume worked out the relation between money and prices in trading economies. He began with a thought experiment: 'Suppose four fifths of all the money in Great Britain to be annihilated in one night ... what would be the consequences?' Prices would fall to one-fifth of their previous level. But in the rush to acquire cheap British goods, foreign gold would flow back into the country, until prices rose back to their previous levels. If in contrast the quantity of British gold increased fivefold overnight, the opposite would happen: prices would shoot up. The quantity of money in circulation was, therefore, 'nearly proportional to the art and industry of each nation. All water, wherever it communicates, remains always at a level.'[1] In other words, the quantity of money was in a self-adjusting equilibrium with the volume of trade. It required no deliberate oversight. The vision is dazzling and, despite the experience of almost three centuries, many still find it compelling: an automatic self-regulating system which requires no human intervention to keep commerce flowing and prices at a level. It is at once a quantity theory of money and a model of international trade, in the true spirit of the invisible hand of which it is a precursor.

In this model, money doesn't really matter. Assume that only gold is money, and that its quantity is fixed. If art and industry improve, still no problem: prices will fall, wages may rise, but business will continue as usual. But there is a flaw in this model, which is not immediately obvious. Money is used for transactions and exchange, but also as a store of value and a unit of account. Hume's model takes no account of money as debt.[2] But one purpose of money is to discharge debt obligations. And money itself is a debt, namely a promise to pay, which is actually inscribed on some banknotes. Money is

1. Hume, 'On the Balance of Trade', *Essays Moral, Political and Literary* (1742/1994).
2. Another of Hume's essays, 'Of Public Credit', was violently opposed to public debt. Ibid., 349–365.

legal tender, that is, cannot be refused in payment for debt. Contracts, obligations, and debts persist over time. If prices change between promise and fulfilment, between contract and delivery, between borrowing and repayment, then there will be winners and losers. If prices fall, creditors will receive more in terms of goods than they lent out. If prices rise, then creditors will lose. Hume treated money as a medium of exchange, but money is also value stored. Exchange is more predictable, efficient, and rational if prices do not vary. Hume's specie-flow mechanism on its own cannot do this.

Historically, the quantity of minted money was likely to diverge from the amount of money needed in two particular circumstances. One was war, with its urgent demands for materials and men. The resources invested did not produce anything to sell. On the contrary—the higher the spending, the greater the loss. The second circumstance was the opposite, those very improvements in art and industry, namely sustained economic growth, in which the supply of new precious metal could not keep up with the expansion of production, and the shortage of money might hold it back. War and economic growth have both motivated the use of paper money and paper credit. War and economic cycles repeatedly threw the economy into excess and shortfall of supply. In modern history, and especially since World War I, such departures from the Humean model have become the rule, not the exception. But even before World War I, the two objectives of price stability and prosperity were in conflict. If international trade was to adjust smoothly, then prices had to reflect the changing cost of production in different countries. But if prices varied, they lost the stability which made money useful as a store of value and a unit of account.

Time and debt undermined the automatic operation of Hume's apparatus. It could not be left to work unattended. It required a deliberate effort for a difficult task, to keep the commodity purchasing power of a unit of money stable over time. That way, neither creditors nor debtors would lose. That is the doctrine of 'sound money'. In the nineteenth century, this was achieved by giving all the main currencies a fixed value in gold, thus making them interchangeable. That did not solve the problem entirely, since the commodity value of gold is not itself stable. The task is hard, since there are so many variables involved, many of them beyond control: the supply of commodities and the introduction of new ones, their desirability and cost in relation to each other, the supply of gold and silver, the demands of government in war and peace, the volume of employment and trade, the balance of trade and migration, indeed, the weather and the harvest, always moving in unpredicted ways and threatening to alter the purchasing power of money. Instead, in order to keep money values stable, it might be possible to affect the cycles and trends of the real economy. A hopeless task on the face of it, but whether due to skill or good fortune, largely achieved during the nineteenth century.

In the eighteenth century, the Bank of England guaranteed the redemption of its banknotes in gold. The cost of fighting Napoleon on the Continent drained away British gold, and the Bank of England was authorized to suspend the convertibility of its banknotes in 1797. Without the discipline of gold on demand, how many banknotes should the Bank of England issue, and how much credit should it advance? One set of financial writers said that the bank should lend against any good commercial security, to maintain the flow of business. And that is mostly what it did. Others wanted the bank to keep the pound stable against gold-based currencies by rationing credit to merchants and other bankers. In other words, that the bank should continue to accept the discipline of gold even while keeping it out of circulation. The first policy was discretionary and accommodating to business needs, the second was rigid: it was rule-based, and was meant to be automatic, but in fact it required constant management, and tended to quench economic activity.[3]

This debate during the first two decades of the nineteenth century has defined the policy issues ever since: on the one side, the view that money supply should stretch in order to accommodate employment, production, and trade; on the other, that price stability should be paramount, by anchoring money to gold or to another currency. Sound money won the day, and several others afterwards in the course of the nineteenth century. The return to gold in Britain in 1821 drove prices downwards, with economic depression and financial crises. But this was also a time of innovation, of steam engines, textile factories, and growing cities. Coal and railways unlocked the bounty of nature, in Britain and overseas, and released a flow of ever-cheaper manufactures. That is what kept Victorian prices low and stable, not the gold standard (like the inflow of Chinese manufactures from the 1990s onwards which kept prices low in the West). In the nineteenth century, business demand for money eventually outstripped the supply of gold coin and Bank of England notes. Most money took the form of credits in bank ledgers, moved around by cheques and bills of exchange. The Bank of England, learning to act as a central bank, regulated the price level by setting an interest rate

---

3. Viner, *Studies in the Theory of International Trade* (1937), ch. 3.

that would keep enough gold in the country and no more than required to ensure convertibility of its banknotes. This might appear to be automatic and rule-based, but actually required vigilance and effort.[4] Towards the end of the Victorian period, commodity scarcities and intensifying Great Power competition for resources eventually spiralled into global conflict, a convulsion of economic and military effort which gold was utterly inadequate to support.[5]

World War I shattered the gold standard mechanism, which was already quite fragile. For prices, the war was a short episode of violent inflation, followed (within three years) by an equally sharp deflation in most of the former allied and neutral countries. Purchasing power and the value of money fluctuated, and bankers everywhere hankered for the simplicity of gold. This resonated more widely in society, where inflation had squeezed the standard of living, and the subsequent deflation pushed wages down. But the war also left behind it, among other forms of destruction, a legacy of debt. Every combatant nation had incurred mountains of domestic debt to fight the war, which it mostly owed to its own rich. They expected to get back money as good as they had lent. To service this debt, taxation had to remain high, so wages and business were squeezed. But the non-rich had sacrificed effort and blood, and now also expected something in return. Revolution in Russia, and riots in the West, made this demand no idle threat. In response, the parliamentary vote was extended to all males, and eventually to women as well. The other debt overhang was *between* nations, the reparations demanded from Germany, the defaults of Bolshevik Russia, the debts owed by the Allies to the UK, and by the UK to the United States. Such magnitudes of debt could not be treated like ordinary trade contracts. To service and repay them required a brutal re-distribution to follow the massive destruction and slaughter of the war. Little room here for Hume's hydraulic level. Debt hung over Europe like a black cloud. It was a moral cloud as well. The war had been a monstrous moral transgression, a whole continent flouting the imperative of 'thou shalt not kill' over four years. A pervasive doubt persisted whether international obligations were legitimate and truly owed. Mass killing had been normalized by patriotism and the rigidities of military organization. After the war, the financial system endeavoured to normalize the outcome and to transform it into a stock of ordinary debt contracts. But Germany, which had brushed aside its treaty obligations as a 'scrap of paper'

---

4. Dimsdale, 'The Bank of England and the British Economy, 1890–1913' (2013).
5. Offer, *The First World War* (1989).

to embark on the war, found it hard to submit to another set of treaty obligations. Normalization could not contain the sense of grievance, outrage, and
fear, both within nations and among them.

Initially, creditors and bankers tried to have their way, and returned their
countries to gold during the 1920s. But managing the debt obligations of
most countries gave rise to new and difficult challenges. Central bankers
suddenly became national figures in their own right, acting as oracles of fiscal virtue and as arbiters of national destiny. Foremost among them was the
enigmatic and neurotic Montagu Norman, a former international merchant
banker who was the governor of the Bank of England from 1920 to 1944.
For him, the central banker's loyalty was to something higher than mere
country, it was to the financial order as a whole, as embodied in Hume's
imaginary machine. Norman was intelligent, a romantic and something of a
mystic, and held economists in disdain:

> To Norman personally, according to his closest colleagues, the gold standard
> represented something more than a gloriously simple yardstick by which the
> nation's financial strength at any given moment could be measured. Though
> he could not have expressed it adequately in words, it was also a mystical sym-
> bol of all that was finest in the struggle of mankind to better its lot on earth.[6]

Debt for Norman had the force of ethical obligation, which politics could
only debase.[7] Norman was not articulate, and would have been hard pressed
to spell out the logic of his position. But he had a vision of Hume's machine,
in the form of a restored international gold standard, to be co-ordinated by
central bankers outside and above politics. The mystery that central bankers alone possessed was the co-ordinated self-adjustment of Hume's gold-
flow mechanism. 'Strong-willed, tireless, and ruthless, he viewed his life as a
kind of cloak-and-dagger struggle with the forces of unsound money which
were in league with anarchy and Communism.'[8] In 1921, he drafted a reso-
lution for a prospective conference of central bankers, in which the first and
leading item was 'autonomy and freedom from political control.'[9] By 1925,

---

6. Boyle, *Montagu Norman* (1967), 128.
7. For example, in a letter to the American banker Thomas W. Lamont, July 1938, Clay, *Lord Norman* (1957), 453.
8. Quigley, *Tragedy and Hope* (1966), 326.
9. Montagu Norman, 'Resolutions Proposed for Adoption by the Central and Reserve Banks Represented at Meetings to Be Held at the Bank of England' [early 1921], Sayers, *Bank of England* (1976), vol. 3 (appendices), 75.

Britain was back on the gold standard, at the pre-war exchange rate parity with the dollar, which overvalued the currency, and made it vulnerable to foreign drains of gold.

Within two years, Norman had realized that resuming the gold standard was a mistake.[10] The equilibrium he found was that of the tightrope. For Norman, who had to defend an overvalued pound sterling with limited stocks of gold, this was a cause of intense stress, which brought about frequent and prolonged personal breakdowns. The solution that he reached for was intuitive and consistent with his personality. It was to harness the power of face-to-face reciprocity and regard. Personal interactions among status equals gives rise to a web of reciprocal obligation, an 'economy of regard'.[11] Norman set out to offset the failure of the Humean apparatus with a system of reciprocal personal obligation. He had little or no theory, only a bundle of intuitions and an agile intelligence. Although far from gregarious, he could switch on a beam of personal charm, and was difficult to resist face-to-face. He had to work with what he had, and extrapolated these personality traits into a system for managing the international monetary system. He cultivated a personal acquaintance with everybody that mattered, both domestically and internationally. A stream of people went through his office every day. When they did not come to him, he went to visit them, and made friends with the top officials of European central banks. Occasionally this misfired, especially in his relations with Émile Moreau, governor of the Bank of France; but he established a firm bond with Benjamin Strong, the head of the Federal Reserve Bank of New York, and their personal friendship kept the gold standard co-ordinated until Strong's death in 1928.[12] Within this web of personal relations, the top central bankers strove to help each other within the constraints of national governments and policy objectives. Their banks were constantly on the telephone to each other. Consultations, timely loans and other interventions made sure that obligations were met, and that central banks remained solvent. For their own sakes, they had to make the system work. This intimacy had not existed before the war. It was the very opposite of Hume's impersonal mechanism, a bond of reciprocal obligation more like Chinese *guanxi* than *homo economicus*. In the absence of a valid working theory of financial reality, this was an astute approach, and

10. Sayers, *Bank of England* (1976), vol. 1, 334.
11. Offer, 'Economy of Regard' (1997).
12. Best captured by Boyle, *Montagu Norman* (1967), esp. chs. 6–8; Ahamed, *Lords of Finance* (2009).

the system of frequent personal interaction has endured among the custodians of the world's monetary system up to the present day.

Norman's bankers' cabal was a challenge to the new democracy, and Norman was a class warrior. The bankers aspired to override democracy and sovereign states, and to manage the monetary system by self-regulation. Their main priority (sound money) was the financial sector. The Bank of England was still a private corporation, and in peacetime Norman was accountable only to the so-called court of shareholders, the merchants and bankers who had elected him. His ascendancy was so compelling that he remained for twenty-four years in what had normally been a two-year post. Likewise, the Federal Reserve Bank of New York, his main partner in the 1920s, was privately owned, and Benjamin Strong was a former executive of J. P. Morgan. Norman acted as custodian of high finance, not of the interests of the UK. He was hostile to labour, and largely indifferent to the domestic consequences of monetary policy. Unemployment he saw as part of the natural order, and the unemployed as in most part unemployable.[13] His posture implied that governments had fallen under the sway of the masses, and that politicians could no longer be trusted by other elites to look out for their interests. Britain's grip on gold, however, was not loosened by the labour movement, but by capitalism itself, from a quarter which no one had anticipated. Frenzied speculation on the New York stock exchange from 1927 onwards raised interest rates in the United States to levels so high that they drained Britain of gold. Gold also flowed out of Europe, and especially Germany, which made reparations payments difficult for that country to sustain. Hanging on to the gold standard became self-defeating. The stock market bubble burst in the autumn of 1929, and started off the Great Depression.

What actually pushed Britain off the gold standard was a particular stand-off between capital and labour. In 1929, Britain elected a Labour government. Throughout 1930 and 1931, pressure on the pound continued. The Liberal Party and Keynes were advocating public works to relieve unemployment, at the cost of further borrowing if necessary. But orthodoxy within the Labour Party itself, influenced by wartime and post-war inflation, was that there was no money available: budgets had to be balanced or prices would soar. In August 1931, financial market opinion insisted that the British budget deficit had to be closed, and most politicians concurred. But on 23 August, nine out of twenty Labour cabinet members would not

---

13. Boyle, *Montagu Norman* (1967), 68.

countenance large cuts in unemployment benefit (the cabinet split on lines of class origin, with working-class ministers opposed to the cuts). Labour Prime Minister Ramsay MacDonald and his chancellor Philip Snowden left their party and formed a government with the Conservatives and Liberals, taking a few MPs and cabinet ministers with them. Neither balanced budgets nor defection sufficed: Britain had to take the pound off gold less than a month later. When it happened, a former Labour minister lamented, 'Nobody told us we could do this!'[14] The American departure from gold two years later, more gradual and less complete, also arose from the struggles of a reforming government against the banking orthodoxy, in this case Franklin Delano Roosevelt and the Democrats.

Most countries followed Britain off gold. Sweden hung on for another week and then capitulated. But its central bank, the Riksbank, continued to do what it knew best: it replaced gold with the pound sterling, which it simply pegged to the krona throughout the 1930s, at a rate which undervalued the local currency, and thus encouraged exports and import substitution. Sweden, as a neutral, had an easy war, did not incur any great debts, and actually had to stem an inflow of gold. Its labour movement was not split by the 1931 crisis as in Britain, and Sweden led the world in electing the first enduring Social Democratic government in 1932. The Social Democratic Party (SAP) remained in power for more than forty years.

THE STOCKHOLM SCHOOL OF ECONOMISTS

Sooner or later, Swedish Social Democracy was bound to clash with the orthodoxy of sound money.[15] Sweden had a strong indigenous tradition of economics, but its senior figures, Knut Wicksell, Gustav Cassel, Eli Heckscher, and David Davidson, despite some notable innovations, were committed to sound money and balanced budgets. Like economists elsewhere, they were thrown off by the large events of the war, advocated a quick removal of wartime controls and a return to the normality of gold exchange and price stability. Unburdened by large war debts, and with a large stock of foreign currency, Sweden in 1922 was the first country to return to gold.

A new generation of young and able economists was emerging in Sweden, and the discipline no longer spoke with a single voice. They had recently

---

14. Attributed to Sidney Webb, Lord Passfield. Taylor, *English History* (1975), 297.
15. The rest of this chapter draws on Söderberg, *Constructing Invisible Hands* (2013).

completed doctorates, or in some cases were still writing them, and came up with some remarkable innovations. Erik Lindahl, Gunnar Myrdal, Bertil Ohlin, and Erik Lundberg, the main figures of the 'Stockholm School', have acquired some renown as precursors of Keynesian economics.[16] This was never fully conceded, and most of what they wrote remained locked up in Swedish. Like Keynes (and like their predecessors in Sweden), they mostly wrote theory at a high level of abstraction, and dealt with the economy as a whole. They mostly lacked the precision of mathematics and used ordinary language, rather like their Austrian contemporaries, Ludwig von Mises and Friedrich von Hayek, which made them possible to read, though still not easy to follow. Their big novelty was to incorporate the element of time, which was absent in the Humean gold standard mechanism. The implication was that economic equilibrium was not a matter of supply and demand coming instantaneously into balance, but a process unfolding over years, which involved choices informed by expectations, constantly revised by the experience of the past, a matter of anticipation and uncertainty. In principle, this was a step towards realism, which helped to make it plausible despite the absence of specifics.

But these clever, subtle insights gave no handles for policy. Their value was negative: they challenged the old guard, and pointed towards a plausible alternative, a new option for policy, namely temporary borrowing for public works in order to reduce unemployment. This had already been advocated and implemented in British cities before World War I, and was supported as expedient by otherwise orthodox economists like Arthur Pigou in Britain and Gösta Bagge in Sweden. It was also a staple of left-wing writing in the 1920s, both in Britain and in Sweden. It was only new in its defiance of economic orthodoxy. Between 1927 and 1935, most of the younger Swedish economists contributed theoretical and empirical studies to a massive government-sponsored study of unemployment, and wrote papers in support of a new policy objective, of reducing unemployment instead of tracking gold. These initiatives were resisted fiercely by the leading orthodox economists Cassel and Heckscher, as being inconsistent with their assumption of market-clearing equilibrium, which they clung to in defiance of evidence.[17]

---

16. Jonung, *Stockholm School* (1991); Jonung, 'Knut Wicksell's Norm of Price Stabilization' (1979).
17. Carlson, *The State as a Monster* (1994), ch. 12.

The Social Democrats who came to power in 1932 could begin to sense that economic science was moving to their side. Their intuition that there was something wrong with government by markets had found a theoretical articulation. A new role for economics was to make sure that the wealth of society increased, while unemployment was kept in check. Tage Erlander, the Social Democratic prime minister from 1946 to 1969, later recalled: 'We thought that the large number of unemployed was proof of the appalling organization of society. . . . At least it should be possible, through greater understanding of economic contexts, to abolish the part of unemployment that is dependent on business cycles.'[18]

Erlander had read some economics himself at university in the 1920s, and wrote in retrospect, 'Social Democracy here experienced a troubling conflict between the scientists' theoretical analysis of reality, and the revolt of the feeling of righteousness against this reality. This conflict was experienced by us young as a feeling of helplessness in creating a theory that was both rational and righteous for employment policy.'[19] Ernst Wigforss, the party's long-serving minister of finance, took a sustained interest in economic theory, was welcomed by Stockholm economists to their debating club, and sat in as a member on almost 150 sessions of the Unemployment Inquiry. He acknowledged the support of Stockholm School economists for his policies, but claimed that neither they nor Keynes had offered anything really new. Writing in retrospect in 1960, he quoted chapter and verse from his own party's programme of 1919, and from G.D.H. Cole in the early 1920s, to argue that the Social Democratic insight was not to support the unemployed, but to make physical and social investments to prevent unemployment in the first place.[20] Like the Swedes, in the 1920s, Keynes had been groping in the dark, and knew what had to be done before he could adequately theorize it. *Britain's Industrial Future* (1928), also known as 'The Yellow Book', was published for the Liberal Party, inspired and partly written by Keynes, who followed soon afterwards with *Can Lloyd George Do It?* (1929). Its forceful language, passion, and authority were as compelling as the young Swedish theorists.[21] Erlander recalled: '[The Yellow Book] became for us a means to rediscover our path. In it some

18. Erlander, *Tage Erlander* (1976), 173.
19. Ibid., 172–173.
20. Wigforss, 'Den Nya Ekonomiska Politiken' (1960).
21. Landgren, *Den 'Nya Ekonomien' i Sverige* (1960); Jonung, 'Knut Wicksell's Norm of Price Stabilization' (1979), 484–485.

of England's, not to mention the world's, greatest economists, among them J. M. Keynes, wrote that unemployment could be fought through expansion of the public sector.[22] Expansion of employment at public expense was not only compassionate but also prudent. This had important consequences:

> A bridge had been built over the gap between Socialism's will to act and its demand that its policies should rest on a solid theoretical ground. In *The Yellow Book* we read that the demand that the public sector should play a large role in employment policy was incompatible with earlier Liberal views. But that did not matter, according to the authors of the *Yellow Book* .... The battle between Liberalism and Socialism belonged to the past.... *The Yellow Book* did not contain anything new to us Social Democrats. It reconnected to thoughts, which had been present earlier in the worker's movement, but it filled us with self-consciousness. It was we who had the real theory, not our opponents. Our satisfaction became even greater, when during the 1930s the young Swedish economists Gunnar Myrdal and Bertil Ohlin supported the theory of active employment policy. The era of ideological perplexity was over.[23]

These words were written by Erlander in the 1970s, and their historical accuracy is not critical here. What matters is that the longest-serving Swedish prime minister felt that the party's doctrines were supported by scientific economics, and that the sound money orthodoxy had become obsolete.

'In Sweden,' wrote a visiting British economist in 1936, 'great respect is paid to the professional economist. He commands an honoured place in the scheme of things, in marked contrast to the skepticism or the polite indifference with which he is regarded in this country and the United States.'[24] Professor Gustav Cassel, a world-famous Swedish monetary economist, wrote more than 1,500 popular articles on economic matters, and also advised several Swedish governments. He presented the economist as a neutral observer, capable of rising above party politics and special interests. The scientific economist's task was to offer rational solutions to economic problems.[25]

---

22. Erlander, *Tage Erlander* (1976), 177.
23. Ibid., 177–178.
24. Quote from Thomas, *Monetary Policy & Crises* (1936), xx; Berg and Jonung, 'Pioneering Price Level Targetting' (1999), 528; Carlson and Jonung, 'Knut Wicksell' (2006); Magnusson, 'Economists as Popularizers' (1993).
25. Magnusson, 'Economists as Popularizers' (1993), 95.

Economists were active in public debate, 'serving as journalists-lecturers-debaters-opinion makers and as members of parliamentary committees'.[26]

The economist's posture of disinterested reason was questionable, and there was plenty of evidence to the contrary. Cassel's own popular writings attacked socialism and the labour movement; the other leading economist, Eli Heckscher, had similar political views and also wrote in the anti-socialist press.[27] The economist Gösta Bagge was chairman of the right-wing Conservative Party for almost a decade. Of the two future NPWs, Gunnar Myrdal and Bertil Ohlin, the first became a member of Parliament for the Social Democratic Party in the 1930s, and a cabinet minister in the 1940s. The second, Ohlin, became a Liberal politician (somewhat to the right of the Social Democrats' Agrarian coalition allies). He had a stint as cabinet minister in the 1940s, was a member of Parliament and the chairman of the Liberal Party for several decades, and wrote some 2,000 newspaper articles over his lifetime. The Social Democrat Myrdal, who was Cassel's favourite student and later succeeded to his chair, showed in a classic book (published 1930) that political bias in economics was inescapable.[28] The economist Dag Hammarskjöld (later secretary-general of the United Nations), another young economist who advised the Bank of Sweden and later the minister of finance, argued that without the constraint of gold, the bank required expert economic analysis, and that no monetary policy could now 'be viewed as given independently of the political values of its economic and political consequences'.[29]

Gunnar Myrdal, whose initial contribution to economics was in abstract theory, also provided Swedish Social Democracy with its distinctive outlook. From 1934, he was a Social Democratic member of Parliament, and later a cabinet minister. 'Do social reforms cost money?' he asked in a seminal article of 1932. No—social insurance would pay for itself in a more secure, educated, healthy, capable workforce.[30] So the objective of Social Democracy was not merely a matter of equitable redistribution, not only a matter of fairness, not only prudential provision: it would not only re-divide the pie, but would also increase its size. This was already manifest in a variety of co-operative production, housing, and retail ventures, and in technologically progressive

26. Jonung, 'Introduction', in *Stockholm School* (1991), 3.
27. Cassel, *Socialism eller Framåtskridande* (1928); Carlson, *The State as Monster* (1994); Jonung, 'Introduction', Jonung, *Stockholm School* (1991), 3.
28. Myrdal, *The Political Element* (1930/1990).
29. Hammarskjöld, 'Centralbankerna i Nutidens Ekonomiska Liv' (1935), 7.
30. Andersson, *Between Growth and Security* (2006), ch. 2; ibid., nn. 8, 24.

state enterprises in hydroelectricity, air transport, and telecommunications. Myrdal provided a professional economist's blessing for a productivist orientation which was already forming as a distinctive 'Swedish model.'[31]

SAFEGUARDING CAPITALISM: THE BANK OF INTERNATIONAL SETTLEMENTS

Capital was embattled between the wars. The share of wealth of the top one percent in Britain declined from about 70 percent of all wealth in 1910, down to about 55 percent in 1930 (despite a killing made in war bonds), a decline that was not arrested until it reached little more than 20 percent in 1970. This was largely the consequence of creeping Social Democracy, and of heavy taxation to pay for war and welfare. The pattern in the rest of Europe was similar.[32] The task of standing up for sound money and the rights of property fell to central bankers.

The automatic role of the gold standard, which lapsed in 1931, was taken up informally in the Bank of International Settlements (BIS), established in Basel the year before. The bank was an international institution, founded after a long gestation in the 1920s, which realized Montagu Norman's vision and advocacy of an 'economy of regard' of central bankers. Its function was to deal with the legacy of war debt and reparations by transforming and 'normalizing' the debt overhang of war into de-moralized and de-politicized commercial obligations. Quite apart from the problematic ethical legacy of reparations and war debts, in the first part of the 1920s it became clear that Germany could/would pay reparations only if it were lent the money to do so. Under the Dawes Plan of 1924, Germany was lent the money (mostly by American banks) and used it partly to rebuild, and partly to transfer reparations in dollars, without exporting goods (which recipient countries were reluctant to take). German reparations ultimately found their way back to the United States as repayments of allied war debts. Towards the end of the 1920s, as the flow of American loans subsided, a further bid to keep the show on the road was the Young Plan, and the BIS found its first large assignment in bringing together the loans for Germany raised in twenty different countries, and allocating reparation payments among them.

---

31. Childs, *Sweden: The Middle Way* (1936); Andersson, *Between Growth and Security* (2006), ch. 1.
32. Piketty, *Capital* (2014), ch. 10.

What soon became its most important task, however, was to act as an informal headquarters and a formal clearing house for central banks. BIS members could cancel out offsetting obligations without shipping gold. BIS headquarters in Basel became a club where central bankers from different countries assembled every second weekend of the month, for up to ten weekends a year. Most of their time there was spent in informal discussion and in forging a common outlook, a function which continues to the present day.[33] The board of directors consisted of national central bank governors. No sooner had it been set up than reparations were suspended by the Hoover Moratorium of 1931. They were never resumed (although Germany continued to service the Dawes and Young loans). But the bank soon found a new role for itself. As the currencies cast off their link to gold, the new challenge was to try to co-ordinate the new regime of floating exchange rates. The meetings in Basel allowed central bankers to confer frequently without drawing attention or alerting the press, as Norman testified, 'a method of conference, or a club ... which has become regular and useful and, without comment from outside', to discuss the pressing issues of the moment.[34]

It was remarkably successful. Despite the manifest failure of 'golden fetters', the doctrine of sound money still prevailed, and prices remained stable. So powerful was the attachment to fixed exchange rates, that central banks managed to keep this objective in focus even in the absence of gold, by pegging their currencies to those of sterling, dollar, or gold, depending on which block they aligned with.[35] The deficits were offset by increasing the money supply (rather than reducing them, as orthodoxy required).[36] Commentators have wondered why the attendance of central bankers at these monthly meetings, before air travel, was so regular and complete. Here is a role which may have escaped their eye. Increasingly, they saw themselves as an international brotherhood with a common vision and shared expertise, above national politics.[37] Ironically, however, their fondest wish was to return to the gold standard and its perverse disciplines.

---

33. LeBor, *Tower of Basel* (2013).
34. Sayers, *Bank of England* (1976), vol. I, 358. On the BIS, Toniolo, *Central Bank Cooperation* (2005); LeBor, *Tower of Basel* (2013).
35. Urban, 'Gold in the Interwar Monetary System' (2012); League of Nations, *International Currency Experience* (1944).
36. Nurkse, 'Conditions of International Monetary Equilibrium' (1945), 12–13.
37. Toniolo, *Central Bank Co-operation* (2005), 195–200.

The BIS was dominated by Montagu Norman. His 'far-reaching aim' (as described by the American conspiracy historian Carroll Quigley), was defensive:

> Nothing less than to create a world system of financial control in private hands able to dominate the political system of each country and the economy of the world as a whole. This system was to be controlled in a feudalist fashion by the central banks of the world acting in concert, by secret agreements arrived at in frequent private meetings and conferences. The apex of the system was to be the Bank for International Settlements in Basel, Switzerland, a private bank owned and controlled by the world's central banks which were themselves private corporations. Each central bank, in the hands of men like Montagu Norman of the Bank of England, Benjamin Strong of the New York Federal Reserve Bank, Charles Rist of the Bank of France, and Hjalmar Schacht of the Reichsbank, sought to dominate its government by its ability to control Treasury loans, to manipulate foreign exchanges, to influence the level of economic activity in the country, and to influence cooperative politicians by subsequent economic rewards in the business world.[38]

In Norman's manifesto of 1921 for an international club of central bankers, he had envisaged an absolute right of withdrawal and transfer of all gold, monies and securities held on behalf of other central banks, free from political restrictions.[39]

Norman's intimate friend Schacht was a Nazi supporter, became president of Hitler's central bank and minister of economics in the Nazi government, and was one of the Nuremburg war trial defendants. Norman sent him food parcels to prison.[40] In March 1939, after the German occupation of Prague, Norman authorized the transfer of a large quantity of Czech gold held for the BIS at the Bank of England to Nazi Germany, in defiance of a government freeze on Czech assets. In November 1939, two months after the outbreak of World War II, the British directors of the BIS were still reluctant to block transfers of Czech gold held by the BIS in Amsterdam to Hitler's Germany.[41] Norman was not acting in ignorance; he treated the Nazi

---

38. Quigley, *Tragedy and Hope* (1966), 324; also Ahamed, *Lords of Finance* (2009).
39. Montagu Norman memorandum, early 1921, printed in Sayers, *The Bank of England* (1976), vol. 3, 75.
40. Ahamed, *Lords of Finance* (2009), 403, 479–483, 488; Lebor, *Tower of Basel* (2013), 44–48.
41. Blaazer, 'Finance and the End of Appeasement' (2005).

occupation of Prague as not affecting the supra-national obligations of the BIS. In doing so, he effectively endorsed that occupation as legitimate. 'This was little short of treason.'[42] During the war, Nazi bankers and industrialists remained on the BIS board, its officials went regularly to Nazi Germany, and received German officials in Switzerland. The bank stored looted Belgian and Dutch gold for the Reichsbank, and also other 'victim gold'. For its income, it depended almost entirely on German bonds, whose interest made up some 80 percent of its revenues (some of that even went back to Germany in the form of BIS share dividends). At the Bretton Woods Conference in 1944, Norway (then still occupied) proposed the liquidation of the bank, and this was approved, but never carried out. The bank and its ideology survived the war.[43]

The bank's sound money doctrine was a warrant for pain, or in the language of today, for 'austerity'. It continued to support convertibility to gold throughout the 1930s, and indeed during the early post-war years. It insisted on balanced budgets. It decried economic controls and interventions. The rise of the labour and socialist movements in Europe, the first Social Democratic and Labour governments, the emergence of the Stockholm School and Keynesian deficit economics should all be seen as a rebellion and rejection of the dictates of sound money, and the social havoc that they caused. In the United States, convertibility had led to the Great Depression, in Europe, even worse, to the rise of the Nazis, and eventually to World War. As the custodian of sound money, the bank was opposed to re-distributive social movements. Its economic director, the influential Swede Per Jacobsson, was bitterly opposed to Keynesian economics of deficit, and regarded welfare states with distrust. He wanted a public sector at no more than one-fifth of the economy. His views anticipated the 'Washington Consensus' of the 1980s, and he became the director of the IMF in 1956.

World War II again required the suspension of normality, as governments stepped in to allocate resources and regulate markets. This time inflation was kept in check. Even more important, the curse of debt was avoided. Germany did not pay reparations, and the flow of Marshall Plan grants and loans drove European recovery. Managing and winning the war reflected well on the capacity of government in general. The electorates expected a respite from the insecurity and hardships of more than two decades, and

---

42. Lebor, *Tower of Basel* (2013), 63.
43. Toniolo, *Central Bank Co-operation* (2005), ch. 7.

Social Democratic governments everywhere stepped forward to satisfy those yearnings, by stifling their central bankers if necessary. Inflation this time had not been such a traumatic experience, but the memory of inter-war unemployment continued to burn. In most countries, housing squalor was high on the social agenda. Governments were mindful of the risk of inflation, and their solution was to allocate and ration credit. The central banks were required to play this part in the managed economy.

In Sweden, the Riksbank governor, Ivar Rooth, had been appointed in 1929, before the Social Democrats came to power. He was an associate of the megalomaniac con-man entrepreneur Ivar Krueger, and when the latter's empire collapsed in 1932, Rooth survived the discovery that the Riksbank had placed much of its foreign exchange in Krueger dollar securities.[44] Rooth joined the board of the BIS, he visited Basel at the 'very least two times a year, and felt very much at home there.'[45] After World War II, when the Social Democrats set out to re-shape Swedish society, their political vision clashed with Rooth's attachment to sound money.[46] In 1944, Parliament set the bank three goals: a stable level of interest rates, prices, and exchange rates, without an explicit ranking. Considered in retrospect, this was a 'trilemma' which was impossible to solve: any two might be achieved, but not all three. When inflation began to rise in 1947, the bank demanded higher interest rates, and the government resisted. It was a harbinger of future tensions, and Rooth finally resigned in 1948. His connections in international finance served him well. Within three years, he became the second head of the International Monetary Fund, where he continued to argue for sound money, and against the folly of full employment.

After World War II, the Bank of International Settlements remained a defiant island in a Keynesian sea. Its ideals of the gold standard, independent central banks, balanced budgets and free markets were expounded by Per Jacobsson, who was the head of the Monetary and Economic Department, and also 'the tireless preacher of BIS economic philosophy'[47] and 'the intellectual driving force of the bank.'[48] Jacobsson's biography was aptly called *A Life for Sound Money*. He is significant for articulating the ideology of international central banking, most exhaustively as the main author of the BIS's

---

44. Jonung, 'Knut Wicksell's Norm of Price Stabilization' (1979), 478–479.
45. Rooth, *Ivar Rooth* (1988), 57.
46. Ibid., p. 68.
47. Toniolo, *Central Bank Cooperation* (2005), 333.
48. Ibid., 287.

annual reports, as a personal focal point for sound money doctrine, and also as a Swede.

Jacobsson was an articulate and gregarious policy analyst, but not a profound thinker, a failing of which he was acutely aware. His degree was in law, although he took courses in economics. He never wrote a doctorate or even a book expounding his views. His views, as quoted verbatim at length in his biography, tend towards the oracular and mushy, at least in English. But his convictions were crisp. His fundamentalist commitment to sound money was an article of faith, partly arising from laissez-faire political convictions, partly the conventional wisdom of policy-makers at the time.[49] He would not have been able to ground them in rigorous analysis, and he never tried.

His formative experience was in 1920, when as a League of Nations official he participated in imposing a brutal austerity programme in Austria. His committee took a stand 'against all expansion and for the fastest possible retrenchment of government activity, whether the latter applies to the actual administration or to government subsidies irrespective of their compassionate purpose'. For Jacobsson, who was a clever man but thoroughly conventional, it was markets free from government control, and not human suffering, that were the moral imperative.[50] Throughout the 1930s and the 1940s, he became a voice crying in the wilderness, castigating government intervention, whatever the human cost. Deficit spending, he wrote in his diary in 1942, 'is dangerous. . . . It provides, so to say, an easy way out, palatable to the politicians; it is the duty of the economist to emphasize the sterner measures that have to be taken to attain full employment.'[51] In the 1930s, he was an enemy of public works; in the 1940s, of nationalization and the British Labour government. He thought that his countryman Dag Hammarskjöld, managing the Swedish Treasury and chairing the central bank board, had effectively gone native.[52] Among the few economists whose company he found congenial were Mont Pèlerin Society members Fritz Machlup, Gottfried Haberler, Ludwig von Mises, Wilhelm Roepke, Lionel Robbins, John Jewkes, and Hayek.[53] His views would have placed him squarely among

49. Blyth, *Austerity* (2013), 118–125; Jacobsson, *A Life for Sound Money* (1979), pt. VI, ch. 10.
50. Jacobsson, *A Life for Sound Money* (1979), 40–42; quote ibid., 40–41, from a contemporary article by Jacobsson in a Swedish business magazine.
51. Jacobsson, diary 23 February 1942, ibid.,160.
52. Ibid., 166, 212.
53. Ibid., 161, 214.

them, although we have found no trace of him in society records, or in Hayek's voluminous correspondence.

For a cultured and civilized man, as Jacobsson was, it was necessary to believe that sound money was not only efficient, but also benign, that is, to believe in the privileges of management and capital, and of the workings of a benign invisible hand. The winning formula for Jacobsson, as for the economic right more generally, was that freedom came before compassion. But sound money was moral too—it was the morality of contracts and debt—promises must be kept, however extracted: 'sound monetary relations with a return to freedom in payments, which is a prerequisite for freedom of trade, and, maybe, for freedom also in a more spiritual sense.'[54] He spent much energy in debating academic Keynesian economists, and roundly criticized Social Democratic cheap-money policies within Sweden.[55] In the 1950s, he wrote: 'I must emphasise once again how dangerous it is if the welfare system is such that it is allowed to impede the adjustments needed for continued economic progress.... Improved standards for the many can be obtained in a wide field by the operation of the market system ... without direct intervention by government.'[56]

AFTER THE WAR: CENTRAL BANKS RECLAIM AUTONOMY

Ever since World War I, the main focus of economic policy had been macroeconomics, with the Humean gold standard orthodoxy fighting to maintain its position in a world economy which no longer conformed to its model, against the challenge of Social Democratic politics and of Keynesian economics. Its loyalists hunkered down within the central banks and the Bank of International Settlement.

In the late 1940s, central banks began to reassert themselves. Their governors came more frequently to Basel. The BIS had carved itself a niche in the Bretton Woods system, by facilitating inter-bank payments.[57] The BIS opposed the low interest rate policy and the political subordination of national central banks that went with it.[58] During the 1930s, the BIS had advocated

---

54. Ibid., 221.
55. Ibid., 208–213.
56. Ibid., 402.
57. Deane and Pringle, *Central Banks* (1994), 277; Toniolo, *Central Bank Cooperation* (2005), 317.
58. Endres and Fleming, *International Organizations* (2002), 324.

lower interest rates, to stimulate economic activity. In the 1940s and 1950s, it took the opposite position. It was suspicious of full employment ('over-full', as Jacobsson thought of it), and wanted interest rates increased, to prevent inflation.

The president of the New York Federal Reserve Bank wrote that since the 1930s, 'the Treasury had decided what it was going to do and had then informed the Federal Reserve.'[59] In August 1950, the central bank challenged its subordination. A public conflict with the Treasury ended in an accord in 1951 which recognized that the 'Treasury and the Federal Reserve are coequals in the area of their overlapping responsibilities.'[60]

In West Germany in 1956, Chancellor Konrad Adenauer attempted to stop the central bank from raising the interest rate, in what became known as the 'guillotine affair.' The bank, which had constitutional autonomy, resisted. In response, Adenauer complained: 'what we have here is an organ responsible to no one, neither to parliament nor to any government.' The bank had dealt a blow to the German economy, and 'the guillotine falls on the man on the street.'[61] The bank defended itself in the media, and won over the public, at some damage to Adenauer. No German government ever interfered again in the Bundesbank's interest rate decisions. In Britain as well, in response to a run on sterling, the governor of the Bank of England proposed a steep increase in the bank rate in September 1957. The government tried to face him down, but Cabinet gave way eventually and the rate rose from 5 to 7 percent in one step. It was a 'thunderbolt', and accusations of insider trading soon required an official inquiry, which cleared the bank without persuading everybody.[62] These international reverberations eventually reached Sweden as well, and launched it on the road to the Nobel Prize in economics.

---

59. Sproul, 'The "Accord"' (1964), 230.
60. Ibid., 231, 236.
61. Baltensperger, *Fifty Years of the Deutsche Mark* (1999), 291.
62. Capie, *Bank of England* (2010), 90–99.

CHAPTER 4

THE RIKSBANK ENDOWS
A NOBEL PRIZE

During the 1950s, the forces of sound money in Sweden became restive.[1] When inflation began to rise, the choice appeared to be between full employment and housebuilding on the one side, or price stability on the other. The Nobel Prize was an indirect and unintended outcome of this dilemma.

SOCIAL DEMOCRACY AND THE BANKS

Swedish Social Democrats did not trust the banks. In 1944, they envisaged that: 'The whole system of credits should be arranged from the point of view of the community so that production develops systematically according to national needs and all productive resources are utilized in the most efficient manner. The policy of the Bank of Sweden must further this aim.'[2]

Unlike most central banks between the wars, the Riksbank was the bank of Parliament and belonged to the nation. After the war, low interest rates were imposed by government on the bank (as in the United States and Britain). In Sweden, the main reason was to keep housing credit cheap. The central bank was made to purchase government and mortgage bonds. At one point, a top capitalist, Jacob Wallenberg, told the governor, Ivar Rooth: 'The problem with you is that you let the central bank print way too much money.' He replied: 'Of course we do, but remember that it is not my fault and that I have orders to act in this way and that it is against my wish.'[3]

---

1. Draws on Söderberg, *Constructing Invisible Hands* (2013).
2. Landsorganisationen, *Postwar Programme of Swedish Labour* (1946), 22.
3. Rooth, *Ivar Rooth* (1988), 68–69.

The prospect of work and good housing bound the Social Democratic Party to its voters.[4] The inter-war years had left a legacy of housing neglect. Bright, modern apartment blocks, set in communal gardens, held out a foretaste of the future, as in Britain and the rest of northwestern Europe. Construction also employed large numbers. In 1945, a Royal Commission on Housing set out a target to eliminate shortages in fifteen years and to end overcrowding, at a cost that workers could afford. The report was co-written by Gunnar Myrdal. It proposed finance for all builders (municipal, co-operative, private) at subsidized low interest rates.[5] But cheap money threatened to stoke inflation, so the central bank pressed to curtail it. In one final stand-off in 1948, the governor resigned.

In December 1950, the central bank again wanted to raise the interest rate but was told to keep it low. It requested powers to regulate lending and deposit rates directly. Armed with this authority, the Riksbank implemented 'voluntary agreements' with the commercial banks. Every month, their executives assembled at the Riksbank: those who didn't come received the minutes. The governor reviewed performance and handed out instructions. Stepping out of line was reprimanded, sometimes quite brutally. Occasionally, credit was made available only to the government, and for housing.[6]

The governor's role did not fit the norm of market allocation, and gave him disagreeable work to do. Business and finance did not like it, since it tied their hands. Laissez-faire economists disliked it, since it violated their ideal of a self-regulating market. Conservative parties did not like it, since it restricted business freedom, and benefited workers, whose bargaining power it increased. These views were played out in a large and influential press, mostly partial to the businessmen who owned it. An exhaustive official inquiry in Britain around the same time (the Radcliffe Commission) concluded that controlling credit directly was the best way to maximize investment and keep inflation in check. Arguably, this was the correct policy, which served both Britain and Sweden well so long as it lasted. In Sweden, it continued up to 1985, and financed the growth that made it one of the richest and most equitable countries in the world. When it was abandoned (much earlier in Britain and the United States), monetary disorder quickly followed.[7]

4.   Landsorganisationen, *Postwar Programme of Swedish Labour* (1946), 8–9, 25–26, 82–87, 128–131.
5.   Headey, *Housing Policy in the Developed Economy* (1978), ch. 4.
6.   Jonung, 'Rise and Fall of Credit Controls' (1993), 351; Haavisto and Jonung, 'Central Banking in Sweden and Finland' (1999), 116–117; Lindbeck, *Ekonomi* (2012), 109.
7.   Offer, 'Narrow Banking' (2014).

The Riksbank governor was appointed by the party in power and its board consisted of MPs in proportion to party strength in Parliament.[8] After Rooth (and a short interlude), the governor was a party man. His idea of independence was to anticipate government policy and to implement it in advance. In 1955, a new governor was needed. Several candidates refused, one of them because the post was too subordinate.[9] It went to Per Åsbrink, a bright party operative with experience of official inquiries and party media. Prime Minister Tage Erlander had noted his ability, which stood out in a dull party.[10]

Åsbrink is important here: he conjured up the Nobel Prize and pushed it through, and the chain of events began soon after his appointment in 1955. He was 'a highly talented person, with a lot of common sense and vigour',[11] but with no experience of banking. As governor of the Riksbank, a post he filled until 1973, he sprang a sequence of policy surprises which cut against the grain of party and government policy. These were not purely erratic, but were harbingers of deep underlying social trends away from Social Democracy, which would come to the fore in Sweden only after his retirement. But Åsbrink was appointed to implement Social Democratic policy. Once appointed, however, the central bank community drew him to its bosom. Ivar Rooth, now head of the IMF, wrote to commend the 'important role in most countries of personal, international contacts between governors, ministers of finance and other leading men of finance'.[12] He advised Åsbrink to get to know them. Per Jacobsson wrote from the BIS in Basel to invite him to the upcoming monthly meeting.[13] Jacobsson, a Swede who soon followed Rooth at the IMF, had criticized the Swedish practice of housing bond purchases by the central bank.[14]

Åsbrink soon began to assert independence. Throughout the summer of 1955, he annoyed the prime minister by demanding tighter credit for housebuilding, a 'time bomb' that threatened the party's highest priorities.[15] At the annual gathering of politicians, labour unions, and business associations

8. Haavisto and Jonung, 'Central Banking in Sweden and Finland' (1999), 121.
9. Erlander, *Dagböcker* (2005), 16.
10. Erlander, *Dagböcker* (2001), 110–111.
11. Lindbeck, *Ekonomi* (2012), 109.
12. Ivar Rooth to Per Åsbrink, 3 April 1955, Swedish Central Bank Archive: P. Åsbrink Korrespondens 1955–1956.
13. Per Jacobsson to Per Åsbrink, 18 April 1955, Swedish Central Bank Archive: P. Åsbrink Korrespondens 1955–1956.
14. Jacobsson, *A Life for Sound Money* (1979), 213.
15. Erlander, *Dagböcker* (2005), 90–91, 109 (quote), 110, 114–15, 127.

in November, he attacked the national wage bargain as being conducive to inflation. The Riksbank stood above sectional bargaining, he said, and was independent of the government, with whom he did not 'have too many children together'. As governor, he needed to 'say what I think'.[16]

The annual wage bargain was the cornerstone Social Democratic policy. Gösta Rehn and Rudolf Meidner were economists for the Trade Union Federation. Their so-called Rehn-Meidner plan (adopted in 1951) was one of wage compression, which, together with the annual wage bargain, limited the scope for wage flexibility. In this annual consensus-building conference, Åsbrink deliberately stepped out of line, to sound an austerian warning of imminent collapse: 'Now is the time again to decide about wages. . . . What we have been doing is a childish game in driving up the incomes and driving up an inflation that we at the same time lament'.[17]

The speech was widely reported, and Åsbrink received an admiring letter from the German Bundesbank president (who had recently prevailed over Chancellor Adenauer in a dispute over interest rates). In reply, he wrote: 'I would like to hope that my work will have the same opportunity to influence the domestic economic development that you have, Mr. President'.[18] Another letter of commendation for his 'wise and forceful speech' came from the governor of the Bank of England. Åsbrink joined the governing board of the BIS in Basel in 1955. He was 'not only prepared but also eager to take part in and learn from the work of the board'[19] and developed 'very intimate relations to BIS'.[20] In Basel, he would have absorbed anti-Keynesian sentiments. He was co-opted into the central banking cabal.

To justify his quest for independence, the governor reached out to economics. The veteran economist Erik Lindahl had long advocated an independent central bank.[21] He became the governor's 'private tutor' in economics.[22] In the first part of 1957, Lindahl published a series of newspaper

16. 'Åsbrink till Attack: "Tio Års Lättsinne"', *Dagens Nyheter*, 6 November 1955.
17. Ibid.
18. Per Åsbrink to Wilhelm Vocke, 11 November 1955, Swedish Central Bank Archive: P. Åsbrink Korrespondens 1955–1956.
19. Per Åsbrink to Maurice Frère, 2 December 1955, Swedish Central Bank Archive: P. Åsbrink Korrespondens 1955–1956.
20. Rooth, *Ivar Rooth* (1988), 57.
21. Lindahl, *Penningpolitikens Mål* (1929); Lindahl, *Penningpolitikens Medel* (1930); Jonung, *Stockholm School* (1991), xix.
22. Per Åsbrink to Erik Lindahl, undated, Lund University Library: Lindahl Papers (Erik Lindahls efterlämnade papper), vol. 9: Brev, nyare (ca 1950–), Q–Ö.

articles in support of price stability.[23] Other well-known economists joined in.[24] 'During the gold standard,' wrote Lindahl, 'monetary policy was not subject to any party conflicts to speak of.'[25] The central bank ought to 'perform its monetary policy above the party trenches.'[26] Without the anchor of gold, interest rates had become politicized, due to the Social Democratic policy of full employment, at some cost in inflation.[27] Economic experts should join the board, with more discretion for the governor. Full employment should rank lower than stable prices.[28] This was Hume's old doctrine of automatic equilibrium. It was in line with thinking at the BIS, and also in the United States and Germany.

A 'ONE-PERCENT REVOLUTION'

In January and February 1957, the Social Democratic government struggled to finance its housing programme in the face of credit rationing by commercial banks. A higher interest rate would have pacified the banks, but housing would cost more. In the stand-off, the bankers seemed to be getting the upper hand. A credit squeeze could split the governing coalition and divide the Social Democratic Party. The prime minister was determined to fight. Åsbrink gave way and purchased the government's housing loan.[29]

But on 10 July 1957, he sprang a 'coup'. Without consulting ministers, he persuaded the Riksbank board to curtail government borrowing and to raise the discount rate by one percent.[30] This kicked off an acute political crisis. It was badly timed: the coalition with the Agrarian Party was fragile, and that party's delegate on the Riksbank board had opposed the hike. Furthermore, the government was planning a new tier of occupational pension funds, to be financed by a new tax. The money could be invested in housing, which would relax the credit constraint. This proved to be the case when the proposal was approved two years later.[31]

23. For example, Lindahl, 'Riksbanken och Regeringen', *Stockholmstidningen*, 13 May 1957.
24. Carlson, 'Den Enprocentiga Revolutionen' (1993), 7–10.
25. Lindahl, 'Riksbanken och Regeringen', *Stockholmstidningen*, 13 May 1957.
26. Ibid.
27. Ibid.
28. Lindahl, 'Riksbankens Avpolitisering', *Stockholmstidningen*, 17 May 1957.
29. Erlander, *Dagböcker* (2007), 23 January 1957, 21; 24 January 1957, 23.
30. Carlson, 'Den Enprocentiga Revolutionen' (1993).
31. Jonung, 'Riksbankens Politik 1945–1990' (1993), 300.

The prime minister was livid at Åsbrink's 'stupidity'; the government had 'suffered a very serious loss of prestige.'[32] His advisor Per Edvin Sköld, who had pushed for Åsbrink's appointment, was enraged. He felt cheated, since he and the governor had 'agreed that Åsbrink was to function as a representative of the party.' If Åsbrink failed to do this, the party had to go to the Riksbank board directly and explain what 'party loyalty demanded.' In his diary, Erlander conceded that the leadership had taken their eye off the ball. The board chairman had assumed that he was acting on party instructions.[33] Nobody had thought to monitor Åsbrink, despite the warning signs. Their own negligence acted only to stoke the politicians' anger.

The finance minister Gunnar Sträng demanded explanation. The governor flew into a rage and shouted that he 'did what he pleased.'[34] Sträng called him a 'damn cunt' and a 'political infant.'[35] The governor replied that the government ought to be grateful for his independence, because it shielded them from responsibility. Leave political judgments to the party, said Sträng.[36] The prime minister was devastated. In his diary, he wrote: 'Yesterday is one of the darkest days in my political life. I had bet everything that it would be possible to lead our huge party without large gestures and without other party discipline than the one that loyalty to the party demands of all of us. The decision of the board of the Riksbank this Wednesday crushed this main thesis.' He considered resignation.[37]

Several members of the party executive met to discuss the 'dangerous situation' that Åsbrink had created, and agreed that a 'sharp reaction' was inevitable both for 'psychological and practical reasons.'[38] But dismissal was dangerous: 'Åsbrink will not step down without a fight,' Erlander noted. 'He will ruthlessly attack the government's mistakes.'[39] Instead, the chairman of the board, an old party loyalist, was dismissed. Erlander felt remorse. The remaining board would need to take an 'oath of loyalty.'[40]

In Britain during World War I, the governor of the Bank of England Lord Cunliffe had asserted policy independence against the Treasury, and trans-

---

32. Erlander, *Dagböcker* (2007), 10 July 1957, 121.
33. Ibid., 11 July 1957, 122.
34. Lindström, *I Regeringen* (1969), 165.
35. Erlander, *Dagböcker* (2007), 13 July 1957, 124.
36. Ibid.
37. Ibid., 16 July 1957, 126.
38. Ibid., 13 July 1957, 123.
39. Ibid., 124.
40. Ibid., 13 July, 14 July 1957, 124, 125.

ferred some overseas gold deposits from Canada to the United States without permission from the government or his own board. In response, the chancellor of the Exchequer (Bonar Law) made it clear that the governor held his post at the government's pleasure. Appearances were preserved, but Cunliffe was ejected in due course.[41] Åsbrink's defiance of government was equally blatant.

Åsbrink's coup topped the headlines for several days, and delighted the opposition. The coalition partner (the Agrarian Party) feared it would hurt its constituents. Opposition newspapers wrote that government had itself to blame for creating a 'sick economy' that needed this medicine. The socialist dream of low interest rates had gone up in smoke. Another wrote that Åsbrink had 'proven his mettle' and had shown 'that the central bank is not some annexe' to the Ministry of Finance.[42]

The outcome seemed good. The bank had defied the government and was not punished. Its power and status had risen. The parliamentary oversight committee for the central bank launched an investigation. When Åsbrink testified, according to an opposition newspaper, he did 'so well and powerfully that his opponents lost initiative.' The result was a 'victory for Åsbrink.'[43] A few days later, at the annual meeting of the Swedish Bankers' Society, the economist Erik Lindahl again made a case for central bank independence, and the bankers endorsed it.[44] The powerful banker Jacob Wallenberg said that the central bank 'should be free from paying any concern to full employment.' Low inflation on its own would secure it.[45]

Behind the scenes, however, the balance of power was quickly restored. The prime minister was determined to restore order.[46] In November, he overcame his revulsion, and they finally spoke. Erlander stated that government had complete responsibility and authority over taxation and interest rates. Åsbrink conceded the fact, but not the principle: 'Unfortunately that is true,' he said, 'but it is not certain that this division of responsibility is best.' An agreement was dictated:

> 1) Cooperation concerning more important issues. 2) The government must have the responsibility; the Governor of the central bank must assert

41. Sayers, *Bank of England* (1976), vol. 1, 99–109; Clay, *Lord Norman* (1957), ch. 3; Boyle, *Montagu Norman* (1967), ch. 5.
42. Carlson, 'Den Enprocentiga Revolutionen' (1993), 12–13.
43. Ibid. 25.
44. 'Ökad Frihet för Riksbanken Enigt Krav Från Bankföreningen', *Dagens Nyheter*, 26 October 1957.
45. Svenska Bankföreningen, 'Riksbankens Ställning och Uppgifter '(1957).
46. Erlander, *Dagböcker* (2007), 11 July 1957, 122; 12 November 1957, 205.

himself through the strength of his arguments or by threatening to resign just as any other head of a department in a government. 3) No election coups just before an election, such as the one [carried out by] the Danish central bank Governor.

'Much more was said over the 65 minutes the meeting lasted. It gave glimpses into Åsbrink's psyche—he seemed surprised that I counted him [Åsbrink] as one of us, refused to be described as greedy for power, but accepted responsibility for the event.'[47]

That was not the end of the matter. In March 1958, the parliamentary oversight committee reported, and its socialist majority rejected the bank's stated motives.[48] Lindahl once again defended the governor,[49] but other economists (Bent Hansen and Erik Lundberg) thought there had been no urgent call for the 'coup', although they still supported it for restoring interest rates as a policy instrument.[50] The episode culminated with debates in both houses of Parliament on party lines. For the Social Democrats, it was a transgression not to be repeated.[51]

THE CENTRAL BANK HUMBLED

For several years afterwards, interest rates did not rise, and never again would this governor step out of line. Further retribution followed. The central bank derived its income from seigniorage, the interest on the bonds that it purchased from the government with the money it created. Higher interest rates meant that the bank's profits from government borrowing were paid for by Swedish taxpayers. The bank handed over a small amount to the Treasury every year, and kept the rest in a special account, which built up into a large stock of capital. The one percent coup had produced an infusion of revenue, but the Treasury moved quickly to cut it off, by raising its share of the take fivefold.

By 1961, the new pension funds opened up large new sources of credit, and the government was no longer so dependent on the governor's amour-propre. Its first shot was a parliamentary inquiry early in 1962. By the end of 1961, the profit account had grown to almost 700 million kronor, which

47. Ibid., 12 November 1957, 225.
48. 'Bankoutskottet Prickar Riksbankens Chef' (1958), *Svenska Dagbladet*, 11 March 1958.
49. Lindahl, 'Bankoutskottets Dom', *Stockholmstidningen*, 16 March 1958.
50. Carlson, 'Den Enprocentiga Revolutionen' (1993), 37.
51. Ibid., 32–34.

meant that 'the Riksbank's wealth [had] reached a size that requires an over-view over the disposition of profits and wealth.'[52] On 6 February 1962, the committee asked the bank about the disposition of its surplus. It recom-mended transfer to the Treasury.[53] In response, the bank acknowledged a one-time interest rate windfall, but denied that this had influenced its de-cision. It needed its own capital for trading and lending ('open market op-erations'). Handing over profits could be harmful if it raised government expenditure.

The bank conceded the surrender of two-thirds of its profit account to the Treasury, but wanted to keep something for itself. It would set up a scientific research foundation.[54] The income would be spent, and the capital would be held in reserve for open market operations.[55] The justification given was the bank's forthcoming tercentenary in 1968. Such 'a special jubilee' should be 'commemorated and celebrated in a way that is worthy of the position and long history of the Bank of Sweden.' A research fund would mark the event and also address a pressing national need (namely support for research).[56] The loss of its discretionary capital was a blow for the bank. The foundation proposal can be seen as a bid to transform one form of social power, its au-thority over interest rates, into another, as a patron of the sciences.

There is a question as to why the Bank of Sweden required a lavish jubilee, and what purpose it was meant to achieve. The jubilee itself was spurious: The institution established in 1668 (to replace another defunct one) was worlds away in structure and function from the modern one. For exam-ple, the bank had attained a monopoly of note issue only at the end of the nineteenth century, and was still much concerned about its profits into the 1930s.[57] For the bank, however, a 'jubilee' provided a way of spending taxpay-ers' money to exalt itself, and to underpin future bids for independence. The research fund would salvage something from the bank's lost balances.

The committee accepted this compromise, and the matter was referred to Parliament, where it was not well received. Some MPs questioned the pro-fessed lack of interest in profits. One of them asked whether the 'balancing

52. 'Bankoutskottets Utlåtande Nr 13 År 1962', 3.
53. Ibid.
54. Riksbankens Jubileumsfond, *Hinc Robur et Securitas* (2004), 19.
55. 'Bankoutskottets Utlåtande Nr 13 År 1962', 17.
56. 'Bankoutskottets Utlåtande Nr 13 År 1962', 16–17; Söderberg, *Constructing Invisible Hands* (2013), 142.
57. Jonung, 'Knut Wicksell's Norm of Price Stabilization' (1979), 474–475.

between interests of the Bank of Sweden and the state has been done properly.' By keeping funds and allocating them to research, the bank acted 'as a kind of state within the state', which was inconsistent with principle.[58] The bank's profits were no different from other state revenues, and research funds should be distributed through universities, institutes, and research councils. Another MP found the proposition 'one of the strangest' in a very long time. Research funding was not within the scope of the central bank.[59] Setting themselves up as benefactors was the usual way for persons and 'organizations which dispose over large resources . . . to acquire a halo' which the money alone could not give them.[60] The speaker did not object to the bank's need for reserves, or to a celebration of its jubilee, but pointed out that no other state institution could distribute such largesse 'since none other can accumulate funds like the central bank'.[61] The speaker understood, if only intuitively, that a gift gives rise to an obligation, and that the bank intended to build up a dependency on its largesse among scientists and scholars.

But Parliament signed on.[62] The bank kept some money and prestige. It created the Jubilee Research Fund, and began to construct a new headquarters. Described as a 'house for eternity', this massive building on a prime site, with its imperious design (a lattice of rough slabs of black granite) would not be completed until 1976. The jubilee fund is still an important resource for research in Sweden today. These consolation prizes also provided the spur for a more ambitious move: the Nobel Memorial Prize in Economic Sciences.

REACHING FOR THE NOBEL

Åsbrink decided to use the jubilee occasion for a great international splash. Around a hundred central bankers would be invited. The date would come forward from the actual anniversary in the autumn, to avoid a clash with the annual meeting of the IMF.[63] A large gesture was called for, but Åsbrink was not sure what it should be. He consulted his young economic advisor, Assar Lindbeck.

58. Swedish Parliament, *Andra Kammarens Protokoll* Nr 11–15 [Second Chamber Debates], no. 15, 11 April 1962, 134.
59. Ibid, 130–131.
60. Swedish Parliament, *Första Kammarens Protokoll* Nr 14–19 [First Chamber Debates], no. 15, 11 April 1962, 108.
61. Ibid.
62. Riksbankens Jubileumsfond, *Hinc Robur et Securitas* (2004), 20.
63. Anon., 'Riksbankens Jubileum' (1968), 3.

Lindbeck is making his first appearance here, and will loom large in subsequent chapters. The two had known each other since the second half of the 1950s, when Lindbeck, a recent economics graduate and already an occasional advisor to ministers, was in his late twenties and on the way up. When he went to visit the United States, Åsbrink provided references. Lindbeck was a nominally a Social Democrat and close to the party elite, but already inclined towards heresy. In the 1960s, he undertook research for the business-funded Industrial Institute for Economic and Social Research (IUI). Lindbeck was in the Swedish mould of the economist as a policy intellectual (though not, in his case, in pursuit of political office). In 1964, at Åsbrink's request, Lindbeck began to advise him by means of late-night telephone calls a few times every month. Lindbeck tried 'to convince him that much was to be gained by conducting a more market-oriented monetary policy, with ... greater emphasis on market operations instead of admonitions and threats'.[64]

The first idea for marking the jubilee was to commission a series of scholarly books by famous economists. Lindbeck came up with a list of Swedish and foreign names. Money was no object, but a more experienced academic would have realized that the deadline was too short and that the payoff for the bank would be limited. Åsbrink worked this out for himself in correspondence with the prospective editor, the economist Bent Hansen.[65]

The jubilee date was fast approaching. Åsbrink had been a journal editor, and his next idea was truly inspired: to create a new Nobel Prize in economics. Deadlines would no longer matter. A new Nobel Prize was sure to attract more acclaim than any scholarly publication. Instead of risky investment in new scholarship, Åsbrink could appropriate the achievements of the past. He put the idea to Lindbeck in one of their late-night conversations in 1967. Åsbrink was a man of wayward brilliance and impulsive coups. He disliked handing back so much money. Would it be possible to use it for a Nobel Prize in economics? The specific question was whether Swedish economists could agree on suitable winners. Lindbeck said it could work. Nobel Prizes in science were awarded by the Royal Swedish Academy of Sciences, and Lindbeck suggested consulting with four of its economist members, Gunnar Myrdal, Bertil Ohlin, Erik Lundberg, and Ingvar Svennilson (he was not yet a member himself). Lindbeck contacted Myrdal directly, while the latter two

---

64. Lindbeck, *Ekonomi* (2013), 109.
65. Per Åsbrink to Bent Hansen, 15 February 1965, Swedish Central Bank Archive: P. Åsbrink Korrespondens 1965.

kept in touch.[66] There was resistance in the Academy, primarily from physicists, but the economists pushed hard, insisting that it should be a proper Nobel Prize.[67] The bank's Jubilee Research Fund already gave it considerable sway over Swedish academics.

The date of 15 May 1968 was chosen for the jubilee. The Nobel Foundation (which managed the prize) was dominated by businessmen. Lindbeck acted as the go-between.[68] He mentioned Wallenberg, one of the brothers Jacob or Marcus, heads of the foremost economic dynasty in Sweden. Both were on the Nobel Foundation board. Lindbeck had dealt with Marcus Wallenberg while writing studies for the business-funded IUI, of which the banker was the long-standing chair.[69]

Negotiations went down to the wire. The Nobel family had to consent, perhaps to using its name. Peter Nobel, a descendant of the benefactor's brother and a critic of the prize, says that five days before the jubilee, foundation executives visited the oldest living member of the family, who was eighty-seven at the time. She understood that refusal was impossible but insisted on setting the new prize apart by naming it 'The Prize in Economic Science in Memory of Alfred Nobel.'[70] This showed a remarkable presence of mind, since the awkward title has continued to tarnish the award ever since. Peter Nobel also believes that the foundation was given incentives to cooperate with the Riksbank, either with regard to its tax-free status, or over the range of permissible investments.[71]

Time was short. The Riksbank board was told of the prize only one day before the Jubilee event.[72] It would be administered by the Nobel Foundation on the same terms as other prizes. The prize money, paid by the bank, would also be the same, plus a 65 percent annual fee for the foundation. The bank would endow the prize with a bundle of specific securities. This fund

---

66. Lindbeck was unsure about the date, but 1967 was more likely, as we shall see, than the first half of 1968, which he also suggested as possible. Lindbeck, *Ekonomi* (2012), 111; 'The Prize in Economics' (1985), 37.

67. Lindbeck, 'The Prize in Economics' (1985), 38; *Ekonomi* (2012), 112.

68. Note from Assar Lindbeck to Per Åsbrink, 25 March 1968, Swedish Central Bank Archive, Stockholm: P. Åsbrink Korrespondens 1968.

69. Lindbeck, 'Assar Minns: Mina Tre Perioder på IUI' (2009), 248.

70. 'Gökungen i Nobelprisens Bo', debate published on the Swedish public service television network website, 11 October 2010, http://debatt.svt.se/2010/10/11/vi-i-nobelfamiljen-tar-av stand-fran-ekonomipriset/. Also interview with Peter Nobel, 22 November 2010.

71. Interview, 22 November 2010.

72. Minutes, Board of the Bank of Sweden Meeting, 14 May 1968, Swedish Central Bank Archive, Stockholm: Fullmäktiges Protokoll för År 1968.

would exist off the balance sheet, but could be drawn upon for the bank's operations. Scores of central bank governors came to Sweden on the day, 'all affirming what a great honor it was to receive invitations to the Jubilee, to which they brought expensive gifts from their home countries.'[73] The prize was only disclosed as a surprise at the end.[74]

Bancoposten, the bank's internal newsletter, explained that the purpose was to attract a little limelight: 'It has in other words been a PR matter for the Riksbank. Experience shows that it is necessary to be quite lavish to get any effect in this matter.'[75] After the celebrations it was time to work out the details. Was the prime minister consulted? According to a Social Democratic newspaper, Åsbrink had raised the idea several years before, and was given approval.[76] Maybe. The paper speculated wrongly that Gunnar Myrdal would receive the initial prize. The Riksbank had established the prize without permission from Parliament, its putative owner (another assertion of independence). Detailed provision was discussed retroactively at the next Riksbank board meeting in June 1968. The prize would be paid in perpetuity by the bank. A little more than half the earmarked assets were housing bonds and bonds of local authorities, and the rest were bond issues of industrial and power companies.[77]

Permission was not sought from Parliament: the banking committee was informed by letter one day before the festivities.[78] But the chairs of the political parties had been consulted, and they approved. The parliamentary auditor investigated whether the bank had exceeded its powers. A professor of administrative law was invited to judge.[79] He found that 'all activity that has not been specified in the central bank law, is to be a decision for Parliament as the principal of the Riksbank,' and that these activities were 'to run the banking service, to run printing service in its print shop, and to run paper production at its paper mill.'[80] The bank had overstepped its limits, and this

---

73. Anon., 'Riksbankens Jubileum' (1968), *Bancoposten*, 53,2, 3.
74. Anon., 'Sveriges Riksbank 300 År'(1968), *Bancoposten*, 53,2, 5.
75. Ibid., 9.
76. 'Gunnar Myrdal, Blir Han den Förste som Får Nobelpris i Ekonomi?', *Aftonbladet*, 6 August 1969.
77. Minutes, Board of the Bank of Sweden Meeting, 14 May 1968, Swedish Central Bank Archive, Stockholm: Fullmäktiges Protokoll för År 1968.
78. 'Bankoutskottets Utlåtande Nr 11 År 1969', 7, 15.
79. Ibid., 7.
80. Petrén, Gustav, 'PM', *Bihang till Riksdagens Protokoll År 1969* (1969), Bilaga B, 2 saml. 2 Bandet., Riksdagen, 5.

could only be put right by Parliament. The board loftily dismissed these criticisms, but Parliament now insisted on a vote.[81] Parliament's central bank committee advised Parliament to acquiesce and so it did, with no debate.[82]

For the third time running, Åsbrink had pulled off a coup. This time, on the face of it, a great deal less was at stake. The sums involved, although large for the recipients, were trivial for the bank: the capital was a mere 10 percent of the Jubilee Research Fund. By earmarking funds for the Nobel Prize, it merely protected them from the Treasury. An economics prize appeared innocuous. The post-war Social Democratic 'golden age' of economic growth, low unemployment, and expanding welfare states, then at its very height, was widely attributed to Keynesian demand management. It was easy to regard economists as technocratic facilitators. Economics education was on the brink of expanding in Sweden, but the discipline had not yet penetrated deeply into policy.[83] Gunnar Myrdal, the leading Social Democratic economist, had described economists just a year before as the 'cavalry of the social sciences.'[84] Tage Erlander, the prime minister, who had read some economics at university, believed that the Keynesian/Stockholm School synthesis was consistent with, and indeed supportive of Social Democracy, and could eliminate harmful slumps.[85] His favourite economist was now John Kenneth Galbraith, whose book *The Affluent Society* he quoted, a book which he regarded as a cornerstone of a renewed Social Democratic movement, one more sensitive to individual needs and their public provision.[86]

Åsbrink's strategy was to announce the prize as a fait accompli. The international loss of face would have been too much in case of reversal. The stakes appeared to be low, and if corners were cut, it was not worth a fight. The bank was no longer (if ever it was) an independent economic policy force. Although a Nobel Prize was of high symbolic value, once the jubilee was over little of this reflected off the central bank. It took several years for the weight of the prize to shift behind the resistance to Social Democracy, and by then Åsbrink was no longer in office. The cost to Swedish taxpayers was a

---

81. 'Bankoutskottets Utlåtande Nr 11' (1969), C23, 17.
82. Swedish Parliament, *Första Kammarens Protokoll 1969* Nr. 14–22 [First Chamber Debates] (1969), No. 16, 63; *Andra Kammarens Protokoll* Nr. 15–20 [Second Chamber Debates] (1969), No. 17, 124.
83. Wadensjö, 'Recruiting a New Generation' (1992); Hugemark, *Den Fängslande Marknaden* (1994), chs. 2–3.
84. Myrdal, *Asian Drama* (1968), I, 28.
85. Above, 78–79.
86. Östberg, *Olof Palme* (2010), 144.

mere drop in the social expenditure of the most interventionist government outside the Soviet Bloc.

FOR WHOSE BENEFIT?

The prize was a transaction in the economy of esteem, in which economic assets are exchanged for social position.[87] The question is whether it was called for at all. In justifying it to Parliament, Åsbrink (speaking through the chairman of the parliamentary bank committee, Kjell-Olof Feldt), listed Swedish achievements that needed to be celebrated: The Riksbank's successful three centuries, Sweden's economic and social success, its fine record in economics (Wicksell, Cassel, Heckscher, the Stockholm School), two Swedes (Rooth and Jacobsson) as successive directors of the IMF, the bank's advice to developing countries, and Sweden's recent access to the top-tier economic association of 'Group of Ten' countries. All of this could be crowned by the Nobel Prize.[88]

Let us try to chart the flows of prestige. The prize was instigated as a vanity project. The governor had lived up to his reputation for cleverness. The money he allocated, a mere 21 million kronor, unlocked the prestige of science, and focused its beam on the bank and its governor. Peter Nobel, Alfred's great-great nephew, later wrote that: 'The Economics prize has nestled itself in and is awarded as if it were a Nobel Prize. But it is a PR coup by economists to improve their reputation.'[89] For the Nobel Foundation, the payoff (apart from any relief from backroom arm-twisting) was to extend its domain, and a generous fee. The foundation had to balance this temptation against the risk of diluting the prize. But the Nobel scientific brand was already diluted by the prizes for peace and literature, so the downside was small. The other body was the Royal Swedish Academy of Sciences. The prize came as a windfall for its economist members and as a boost for the standing of the discipline, and its status within the academy. Two members soon received the award themselves. Their task was to persuade the academy. We are not privy to these discussions, but several natural scientists objected to granting what they regarded as unwarranted scientific standing to economics. If this was a reasonable position to take, it was not easy to sustain in a collegiate setting like the academy.

---

87. Brennan and Pettit, *Economy of Esteem* (2004).
88. 'Bankoutskottets Utlåtande Nr 11 År 1969', C23, 15.
89. Peter Nobel, 'The Local', 28 September 2005, http://www.thelocal.se/20120102/2173.

In German-style universities such as Uppsala and Lund, all full professors were equal members of the Senate up to the late 1960s. Within national academies as well, all fellows enjoy an equal status. Whatever their disciplines, they all had an equal vote. In the UK, the natural sciences had their own Royal Society. In Sweden, if the core sciences of physics, chemistry and medicine were indeed special, the pass had already been sold a long time before by admitting social scientists to the academy. To deny the economists their prize would be uncollegiate. And status, while being psychologically all-important, is also easy to shrug off as not being of the essence, and thus easy to concede. The core business of academies is not research, but the endorsement of status. Their main activities are to select their members, and to publish obituaries. The academy might also have been reluctant to antagonize the bank, with its massive Jubilee Research Fund. The permanent winner was the academic discipline of economics. Doubts about its validity would be mitigated by association with the Academy of Sciences and the Nobel Foundation.

'A CUCKOO IN THE NOBEL PRIZE NEST'

The happy windfall of the prize was seized eagerly by Sweden's anti-socialist economists, and was kept firmly in their grip.[90] The academy had less than a year to prepare for the new prize, but almost seventy years of experience, and it followed established procedures.[91] Assar Lindbeck joined the initial selection committee (perhaps to look after the bank's interest). Unlike the others, he was not a member of the academy. He eventually served the longest (twenty-five years), and was also the longest-serving chair (fourteen years, from 1980 to 1994). By all accounts, he came to dominate the committee.

Two of the members of the founding committee had once been associated with the conservative Mont Pèlerin Society. Bertil Ohlin, a future prize winner, currently led the Liberals in Parliament, an opposition party to the right of the Social Democrats. Ohlin was present at the inaugural Mont Pèlerin Society meeting in 1947, but did not join the society. Erik Lundberg was elected to it in 1958, but was a no longer there in 1966; he left no mark on

90. Quote in section title attributed to Peter Nobel. Henderson, 'The Cuckoo's Egg in the Nobel Prize Nest' (2006).
91. Lindbeck, 'The Prize in Economics' (1985); Ståhl, 'Maurice Allais and the Prize in Economics' (1990).

society conferences.[92] Ingemar Ståhl joined the Nobel Committee in succession to Lundberg in 1980 and also the Mont Pèlerin Society in the same
year.[93]

The links with business were tighter. Herman Wold, a professor of statistics, was engaged in an abortive industry-funded project to construct a
quantitative model of the whole economy.[94] Erik Lundberg, an original
Stockholm School economist, was the first director of the government *Konjunkturinstitutet* (the National Institute of Economic Research) in 1937. In
the late 1940s, he was signed up by the business-funded Centre for Business
and Policy Studies (SNS) to write a book about the effects of post-war regulation. The business fund that created the SNS had also underwritten the
Swedish translation of Hayek's *Road to Serfdom* in 1944. When published in
1953, Lundberg's book contained a harsh critique of the post-war policy. It
objected to Myrdal's enthusiasm for planning. As long as the economy was
in equilibrium no intervention was required.[95] The book gave rise to heated
debate, not least with the labour union economists who wrote that Lundberg's book ended in a 'lyrical homage to the invisible hand.'[96]

In 1939, Swedish businessmen had created the Industrial Institute for Economic and Social Research (IUI) to challenge the government institute. The
IUI earned a reputation for solid research, but there could be no mistake
about its sympathies. Of the members of the founding Nobel Committee,
Ingvar Svennilson directed the IUI between 1941 and 1949, and Ragnar Bent-
zel, secretary of the committee for its first fifteen years, did so between 1961
and 1966. Assar Lindbeck, although nominally still a Social Democrat, had
undertaken two critiques for IUI of rent control and agricultural protection,
co-written with Ingemar Ståhl, another future renegade from Social Democracy. These were core Social Democratic policies, the one placing a cap on
household dwelling costs while the party embarked on its 'million house'
project, while the other affected the Agrarian Party, the erstwhile coalition
partner, and was central to Social Democratic modernizing preoccupations.

---

92. Leeson, 'Introduction' (2013), 28; 'no mark' in Mont Pèlerin Papers, and Friedrich von
Hayek Papers, Hoover Institution.
93. More on Ståhl, below, 212–213, 223, 249.
94. 'Lättare Bedöma Konjunktur', *Dagens Nyheter*, 19 November 1961.
95. Lundberg, *Konjunkturer och Ekonomisk Politik* (1953); Nycander, 'Assar Lindbecks Succé
Skadar Nationalekonomin', *Dagens Nyheter*, 10 April 2005.
96. Nycander, 'Assar Lindbecks Succé Skadar Nationalekonomin', *Dagens Nyheter*, 10 April
2005.

Four out of six of the original Nobel Committee members were thus strong market advocates, and associated with IUI.

Sweden also had distinguished left-leaning economists. Gunnar Myrdal (NPW, 1974), by far the best known Swedish economist of the time, was not on the committee. Another was Rudolf Meidner, of the Trade Union Federation, LO. In terms of real-world achievements, Meidner may be regarded as the foremost economist in Sweden in the twentieth century. Together with Gösta Rehn, he worked some earlier suggestions of Erik Lindahl and Ingvar Svennilson into the Rehn-Meidner model of wage determination, which was adopted in 1951. It implemented wage compression, and trained and redeployed workers in order to shift the economy into more productive industries. This was the foundation of Swedish economic success in the 1950s and 1960s, and its effect lingered on into the 2000s, in the form of low inequality and high productivity. Robin Blackburn wrote in an obituary:

> If Meidner had not been a Swedish citizen, and still a controversial figure at the age of 91, he would very likely have been awarded the Nobel Prize for economics. Meidner was, after all, the co-architect—with Gösta Rehn—of the Swedish welfare state, an achievement which, by itself, would have merited such a nomination. Those responsible for this prize tend to prefer theory to policy but it should be clear to everyone that the Rehn/Meidner model was based on its own distinctive theoretical insights and that policy-oriented economics is anyway deserving of recognition.[97]

But the prize was defined as 'scientific', which in practice meant academic, and the committee was thus protected from left-wing interlopers. The national association of Swedish economists, with better discrimination, included an article by Rehn in its centennial anniversary volume in 1977. As we shall see, most economists (despite a reputation to the contrary) lean towards left-of-centre values. But no left-leaner would penetrate the circle of Nobel selection until the 1990s.

---

97. Blackburn, 'Rudolf Meidner' (2005).

CHAPTER 5

DOES ECONOMICS HAVE A POLITICAL BIAS?

Counting journal citations illuminates the main clusters of economic authority, the pulse of economic opinion and thought, the reputations of particular individuals, and Nobel selection strategy. The Nobel selectors sought a middle ground between the ideological left and right, but veered rightwards towards the end of Assar Lindbeck's long chairmanship (1980–1994), in line with his strident interventions in Swedish politics. They moved back to the centre shortly after his departure. In contrast, surveys of economists' opinions taken over the same years show a two-thirds majority among American and European economists in favour of Social Democratic norms, and a third strongly opposed.

CITATIONS

Among scholars, priority of discovery is acknowledged in footnotes and references, and the number of citations is a measure of the impact of innovation. Citation counts also provide an estimate of how large the discipline of economics figures in the broader world of scholarship. Within the discipline, they trace the rise and fall of schools, and the trajectories of individuals. They are frequently used to evaluate academic performance.

All citation counts have biases.[1] Foremost among them is the Thomson-Reuters ISI database, which is accessed using the online 'Web of Science' tool and includes the Social Science Citation Index (SSCI). It has several weaknesses. It is proprietary and, at least for some applications, not easy to use. At

---

1. Harzing, *Publish or Perish Book* (2011).

the time of this analysis (January 2012), its citations were uneven before 1980 and virtually non-existent before 1960. It cited only first authors (this later changed), and did not count books directly. Elsevier's more recent Scopus database included many journals (over 5,300 in the social sciences alone), but it had poor coverage before the 1990s. In contrast, Google Scholar was intuitive to use, and it counted both books and articles in languages other than English. More problematically, it reported citations from sources as diverse as Microsoft Word documents and PowerPoint presentations, resulting in inflated, undiscriminating, and constantly changing scores. With Google Scholar as with the other standard bibliometric databases, it was not easy at the time to extract annual citation counts for any length of time.

The data here come from a different source, the JSTOR project to digitize scholarly journals. This database was started in 1995 with a core of the most important US academic journals in most humanities and social science fields, and has since expanded to include the main English-language journals, and increasingly other disciplines and the peripheries of scholarship.[2] Unlike other databases, JSTOR reaches back to the initial year of its journals, sometimes into the nineteenth century. Its coverage ends behind a 'moving wall' a few years before the present. The journals can be taken to comprise the most highly regarded scholarship in the English language since the late nineteenth century. The most important finding in citation studies is that the bulk of cited articles are published by a minority of authors in a minority of journals.[3] On that basis, JSTOR's coverage of a substantial number of the most important journals is adequate; it does not provide a population count, but a large high-quality sample. Current total citations in Google Scholar are substantially higher, in some cases by an order of magnitude, so JSTOR (like Thomson-Reuters 'Web of Science' and Scopus) should be considered as a selective sample. JSTOR does not encompass everything, but is unlikely to misrepresent trends. The total number of journals in JSTOR in January 2012 was 1,984, with 409 of them in economics, business and finance.[4]

Our dataset was assembled using the JSTOR online Data for Research service.[5] Citations were derived from JSTOR articles, by year of publication, and provide a continuous record over time. The most tedious procedure is

---

2. Schonfeld, *JSTOR: A History* (2003).
3. De Bellis. *Bibliometrics* (2009), ch. 4.
4. Bjork et al., 'Time-Series Citation Data: The Nobel Prize in Economics' (2014), 186.
5. JSTOR, 'Data for Research' (2012).

the need to count all different forms of an author's name, and to exclude authors with similar names. JSTOR did not include books directly at the time, but like ISI it did count them in journal citations, so books were amply represented. Citations were taken only from the reference sections (including footnotes), and not from the body of the text. A name was counted only once, regardless of the number of times it was cited in an article (that was also the case with Thomson-ISI). The main disadvantage of JSTOR was the virtual exclusion at the time of publications not in English. In consequence, a few reputations here (for example, Ohlin) appear abruptly, after a previous history of publication in a different language. JSTOR makes it possible to start counting from a scholar's first publication in English. We began in 1930 and stopped in 2005, when JSTOR totals began to drop steeply. That also set the endpoint for the study as a whole.

The number of journals and their size have grown over this period, so it would be misleading to report raw citation figures. A low citation count in 1970 might be a greater achievement in relative terms than a high one in 2000. To control for the changing size of the literature, citations are reported as an index number, which represents a proportion of all publications. Some NPWs have made an impact beyond economics, and a few NPWs in economics were not even economists. Consequently, the index is calculated as the ratio of a person's JSTOR citations in all disciplines to the total of all JSTOR articles (the total number of citations was not available, and the number of articles is a suitable deflator).

Kenneth Arrow, one of the very top economists, had the highest individual NPW annual score up to the year 2000, and this provides a benchmark for comparison with the others. The index number is expressed as a percentage of Arrow's highest single year citation ratio (in 1976), which is given the score of 100. These percentages are termed 'Arrows'. In that year, Arrow was cited in 0.335 percent of all JSTOR articles. His absolute number of citations that year was 289. An 'Arrow' was therefore worth 2.89 JSTOR citations a year in 1976. This value changed from one year to another, depending on the number of JSTOR articles and the number of NPW citations. One hundred Arrows equals 0.335 percent of JSTOR articles in any year. In 2000, for example, an Arrow was worth 3.54 citations.

The number of prize winners built up gradually, from two in 1969, up to fifty-seven in 2005. One would expect the share of NPW citations in the total stock of economic citations to increase over time, as the number of winners increased. But the economics profession also expanded rapidly during this period, which worked to offset the increase of NPWs. Between the mid-1970s and 1997, the two trends offset each other more or less, with the NPW citations maintaining their share of economics citations. There was a spike in the early years of the prize, suggesting a backlog of exceptional candidates in the initial cohorts.

The Nobel Committee did not set much store by mechanical citation counts, and they said as much.[6] Table 5.1 shows the citation ranking: The top total count (Friedman, 3,382 Arrows) was twenty-five times as high as the lowest one (Kantorovich, 132); The most cited per year (a better measure) was Stiglitz (60 Arrows), with Kantorovich (who mostly published in Russian) again bringing up the rear with 2.

IDEOLOGICAL ORIENTATION

Economists can be classified according to ideological orientation. They have a good opinion of markets, but are divided on the role of government. Some think that government needs to regulate and complement market activity; others that governments handicap markets and get in the way. Labels are confusing, with North Americans and Europeans using the word 'liberal' in opposite senses. In North America 'liberal' is the opposite of conservative, while in Europe, 'liberal' is the opposite of Social Democrat. In line with common usage, we use the term 'liberal' in the North American left-leaning sense, and 'market-liberal' in the European right-leaning sense. Even conservative economists concede a limited role for government in protecting property and upholding contracts. In contrast, liberal economists see an active role for government in raising efficiency and output, in reducing inequity and insuring against life-cycle contingencies.[7]

Economic opinion varies on several dimensions, but in most cases it is not too difficult to allocate Nobel economists to the left or the right. A few are elusive, because their work has little bearing on policy orientation, like some econometric theoreticians and game theorists. Others, like Arrow (inclining left), and North (inclining right), have not been entirely consistent

---

6. Lindbeck, 'The Prize in Economic Science in Memory of Alfred Nobel' (1985), 51; Ståhl, 'The Prize in Economic Science and Maurice Allais' (1990), 7–8.
7. Buchanan and Musgrave, *Public Finance and Public Choice* (1999).

Table 5.1. Ranking by Cumulative and Per Year Arrow Counts, 1930–2005

Rank	Cumulative	Arrows	Per year	Arrows	Years
1	Friedman	3,382	Stiglitz	60	40
2	Arrow	3,287	Becker	57	46
3	Simon	3,222	Arrow	57	58
4	Samuelson	2,737	Simon	55	59
5	Becker	2,613	Heckman	49	34
6	Stiglitz	2,406	Friedman	47	72
7	Stigler	2,179	Merton	42	41
8	Buchanan	1,988	Samuelson	39	70
9	Miller	1,904	Buchanan	34	58
10	Lewis	1,840	Lucas	33	46
11	Merton	1,702	Stigler	33	66
12	Heckman	1,664	Miller	33	58
13	Hicks	1,609	Sen	31	46
14	Tobin	1,526	Kahneman	30	37
15	Lucas	1,522	Lewis	28	65
16	Klein	1,483	Solow	27	54
17	Solow	1,456	Tobin	25	60
18	Sen	1,425	Granger	25	43
19	Modigliani	1,413	Engle	24	36
20	Myrdal	1,291	Klein	24	63
21	Kuznets	1,184	Modigliani	23	61
22	Kahneman	1,109	Hicks	22	72
23	Schultz	1,087	Prescott	22	37
24	Granger	1,074	Spence	20	34
25	Koopmans	1,026	Scholes	19	39
26	Coase	930	Smith	18	48
27	Hayek	892	Myrdal	18	72
28	Smith	884	Akerlof	18	37
29	North	865	North	17	52
30	Engle	852	McFadden	16	41
31	Schelling	830	Kuznets	16	74

continued

Table 5.1. Continued

Rank	Cumulative	Arrows	Per year	Arrows	Years
32	Prescott	813	Schultz	16	68
33	Scholes	751	Sharpe	15	46
34	Sharpe	713	Schelling	15	55
35	Spence	685	Koopmans	15	68
36	Akerlof	659	Coase	15	64
37	McFadden	659	Hayek	12	75
38	Debreu	636	Debreu	12	55
39	Meade	571	Markowitz	10	53
40	Tinbergen	559	Mundell	10	46
41	Markowitz	551	Kydland	10	31
42	Leontief	548	Mirrlees	9	43
43	Stone	539	Nash	9	55
44	Nash	504	Fogel	9	44
45	Mundell	474	Aumann	9	49
46	Frisch	472	Tinbergen	9	64
47	Aumann	435	Harsanyi	9	50
48	Harsanyi	426	Stone	8	64
49	Fogel	399	Leontief	8	67
50	Mirrlees	396	Meade	8	70
51	Kydland	311	Selten	7	39
52	Vickrey	301	Frisch	6	76
53	Selten	277	Vickrey	5	61
54	Ohlin	252	Allais	4	56
55	Haavelmo	226	Haavelmo	3	65
56	Allais	203	Ohlin	3	76
57	Kantorovich	132	Kantorovich	2	53

in this respect, and yet others have changed their minds.[8] Some economists have expressed left-of-centre values and advocated right-of-centre policies (Mirrlees) while others could be interpreted as doing the opposite (Coase, North). In a recent study, Daniel Klein has classified NPWs along a nine-point scale from 'most Classical Liberal' to 'least', followed by an extensive

---

8. Klein, 'The Ideological Migration of the Economics Laureates' (2013).

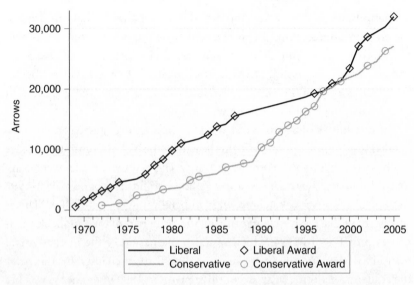

Figure 5.1. Cumulative citation scores for liberal and conservative NPWs, c. 1969–2005.
Note: Liberal (in chronological order of award): Frisch, Tinbergen, Samuelson, Kuznets, Arrow, Leontief, Myrdal, Ohlin, Meade, Simon, Lewis, Klein, Tobin, Stone, Modigliani, Solow, Vickrey, Sen, McFadden, Heckman, Akerlof, Spence, Stiglitz, Kahneman, Schelling. Conservative (in chronological order of award): Hicks, Hayek, Friedman, Schultz, Stigler, Debreu, Buchanan, Allais, Markowitz, Miller, Sharpe, Coase, Becker, Fogel, North, Nash, Lucas, Mirrlees, Merton, Scholes, Mundell, Smith, Kydland, Prescott. Some economists (Simon, Kahneman, Schelling) are allocated to the first group because their views are not consistent with market equilibrium. Nash is allocated to the second group for the opposite reason. The econometricians/game theorists Koopmans, Kantorovich, Haavelmo, Harsanyi, Selten, Engle, Granger, and Aumann are excluded.

discussion of each.[9] Opinions are not always easy to pin down.[10] For the purpose of classification, we do take account of economists' personal values, but give priority to whether or not their doctrinal position supports the Social Democratic preference for positive government intervention. Our classification was carried out before the publication of Klein's study. His allocations largely overlap with our own. His left-right range is arrayed in nine columns. We take the four columns on either side of his table as representing left and right, and the middle column as subject to discretion. Four of our NPWs (two on each side) are allocated differently by Klein so that the overall balance remains the same.

Figure 5.1 applies a rough and ready classification of liberal and conservative economists (in the American sense of the terms). It cumulates the stock

9. Ibid., fig. 2, 235.
10. Colander, 'On the Ideological Migration of the Economics Laureates' (2013).

of citations, while the markers indicate the year of award. Citations prior to the prize are allocated in the year of award, since they acquire the Nobel halo only in that year. The numbers on each side can be taken as equal (26:25 liberal). In terms of aggregate Arrow scores, the ratio is 1.18 to 1 for the liberals. So in terms of citation impact overall, those who supported government action had a small lead over those who did not.

The committee's balancing of left and right might suggest a certain even-handedness (or perhaps caution) on the part of the Nobel Committee. Figure 5.1, however, tells a more complicated story. The first two decades were dominated by liberals, with conservatives falling behind. The period 1990–1997 was one of conservative catch-up, with a liberal resurgence after 2000. This is consistent with a regime change during the latter part of the Lindbeck chairmanship of 1980 to 1994, which was also the period of the market-liberal turn in Sweden and the financial crisis described in chapter 10. Whatever the academic reasons, the award of three prizes in 1990 in finance gave a big boost of academic visibility/credibility to conservative doctrine.

Daniel Klein, who covers later years as well and does not exclude any NPWs comes up with thirty-five liberals and twenty-six conservatives, excluding the middle column (nine names). Counting the middle column as conservative (it includes three of our liberals) the sides are equally matched. The four cases where we allocate differently from Klein also suggest that on the boundary differences can be small. Schelling is taken by Klein to be moderately classic liberal. In contrast, he described himself as a political liberal (that is, Democrat) throughout, but has recently taken a non-liberal position as a climate-change sceptic, a supporter of market-oriented health-care, and an opponent of anti-sweatshop regulation.[11] What makes him a liberal (in our view) is that his work in all its phases has demonstrated that individual choice does not converge on equilibrium, let alone a benign one. This applied to the Cold War stand-off, to racial segregation, and to cognitive biases in individual choice. Bertil Ohlin (NPW, 1997), whom we classify as liberal, was a political opponent of Social Democracy in Sweden (as leader of the Liberal Party), but was also a life-long Keynesian and a supporter of social insurance. In most other countries, he would be placed left of centre. On the opposite side (in our view), James Mirrlees (NPW, 1996) is an avowed Social Democrat, but his two central contributions, on optimal taxation and project appraisal, have both affected Social Democracy adversely, as

---

11. Klein et al., 'Schelling' (2013).

we show in detail below, and as others have argued too.[12] The fourth disagreement is about Gerard Debreu (NPW, 1983), an apolitical mathematician whose general equilibrium result is the foundation of modern invisible hand claims (for example, those of Lucas). But Debreu also contributed to the Sonnenschein-Mantel-Debreu result that undermines this finding, by demonstrating that the aggregation of individual choices is indeterminate. This devastating result is less known than the earlier one.[13]

Other NPW classifications are ambiguous too: Douglass North (NPW, 1993) provided a neoclassical equilibrium account of long-run economic development in his early work, but is better known for his later work on institutional failure. Robert Fogel (NPW, 1993) was a communist youth organizer, but ended up as a Chicago economist. His work on railroads and slavery was not welcomed by liberals, but his later anthropometric studies are not controversial. What tips the balance for us is his recent support for privatizing social security, but it is a close call.[14] Franco Modigliani (NPW, 1985) is (like Mirrlees) another ambiguous case. He staked a strong personal position as a Social Democrat and life-long Keynesian, but of his main contributions, the life-cycle model of consumption assumes that dependency can be managed by individual market choices. With Merton Miller (NPW, 1990), he put forward a theorem that firms could be indifferent between finance from debt and from equity (that is, own capital), which is one of the foundations of the conservative efficient market hypothesis. He also supported a shift from pay-as-you go social insurance to pre-funding it with financial assets (not in itself completely inconsistent with Social Democracy), but he opposed the Bush proposals for part-privatization of social security.[15] John Hicks is a borderline case, positioned by Klein just right of centre (with which we concur), partly on the strength of two pamphlets he wrote (in 1966 and 1975) for the Institute of Economic Affairs, the English offshoot of the Mont Pèlerin Society.[16]

At the margin, then, allocations are not hard and fast; this is consistent with our argument that economic doctrines and norms sometimes suffer from internal contradiction, and that the equilibrium doctrines of economics are in conflict with Social Democracy, whatever the personal political inclinations

---

12. Klein et al., 'Mirrlees' (2013); below, chapter 7, 170–173, and chapter 11, 232.
13. Rizvi, 'The Sonnenschein-Mantel-Debreu Results after Thirty Years' (2006).
14. Klein et al., 'Fogel' (2013).
15. Barnett and Solow, 'Modigliani' (2007), 106; Klein and Daza, 'Modigliani' (2013), 483–484.
16. Klein and Daza, 'John R. Hicks' (2013), 366–377.

of the economists involved. The politics that these positions refer to have not been stable either: New Labour in Britain embraced market-liberal norms; the Democrats in the United States moved in the same direction; and as we shall see in chapters 9 to 11, so did Swedish Social Democracy.

THE BALANCE OF OPINION WITHIN ECONOMICS MORE BROADLY

Were the Nobel selectors biased? An external standard of comparison is required. A reasonable one would be the balance of opinion within the discipline as a whole, if such could be found.

George Stigler (NPW, 1982), a conservative Chicago economist, wrote that 'the professional study of economics makes one politically conservative', and more so than other social scientists.[17] Murray Rothbard, the American libertarian, expressed a similar view:

> the proportion of believers in laissez faire is much greater among economists than in other academic disciplines, and . . . the 'average' point on the ideological spectrum in economics is considerably 'to the right' of the average in other fields of study. It appears that the economic discipline, per se, imposes a rightward shift in ideological belief.[18]

If economists on average fall to the right of other academics, does that make them right-wing? The evidence points the other way.

Since the 1970s, a sequence of surveys has polled economists on their attitudes to a variety of issues. Several such surveys were taken about a decade apart in the United States, with a single wave of surveys in Europe in the early 1980s. The number of questions was large, typically between twenty and forty, and the samples were substantial, with one exception ranging from the low hundreds up to one thousand. The surveys shown in figure 5.2 are from the United States in 1976, 1990, and 2000; from four countries in Europe in the early 1980s (France, Germany, Switzerland, Austria); and from the UK in 1990.[19] The total number of individual responses was 8,037 (9,366 including Canada, the results for which are quite similar to the United States, but are left out for reasons of space).[20] The response rate was reasonable, between 30

---

17.   Stigler, 'The Politics of Political Economists' (1959), 522.
18.   Rothbard, 'The Politics of Political Economists: Comment' (1960), 665.
19.   The set of comparable surveys also includes Canada in 1986, and Europe by country. References follow figure 5.2, below.
20.   Block, 'Entropy in the Canadian Economics Profession' (1988).

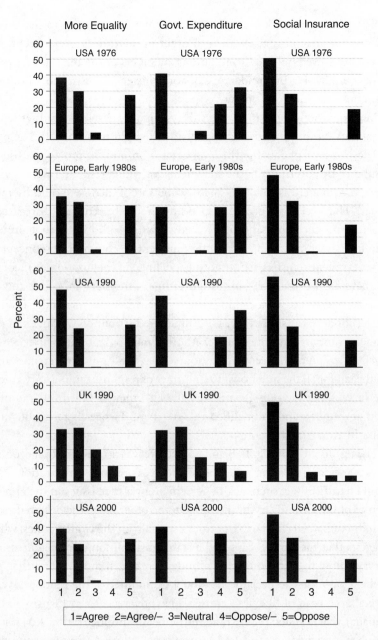

Figure 5.2. Distribution of economists' opinions, c. 1976–2000.

Source: Kearl et al., 'A Confusion of Economists' (1979); Frey et al., 'Consensus and Dissension among Economists' (1984); Alston et al., 'Is There a Consensus among Economists in the 1990s?' (1992); Ricketts and Shoesmith, *British Economic Opinion: A Survey* (1990); idem, 'British Economic Opinion: Positive Science or Normative Judgment?' (1992).

and 50 percent, and these surveys are roughly representative. In the United States, they are consistent with each other in the three survey sweeps. The respondents were selected from among members of the main professional association, with a preponderance of academic economists, and a minority from business and government.

Most questions recur in all the surveys. Figure 5.2 selects a subset which highlights the enduring issues that divide the right from the left. These are the desired level of equality, the level of taxation, and the provision of social insurance by government. The statements for which responses were invited are approximately as follows: 'The distribution of income should be more equal'; 'The level of government spending should be reduced (disregarding expenditures for stabilisation)'; 'The redistribution of income is a legitimate role for government.' The latter one represents a common misconception of government transfers as promoting a deliberate equalization of incomes. We have argued that the bulk of government transfers are across the life cycle in the context of social insurance.[21] We think this was understood by the responders: the support for government redistribution was much higher than the support for more equality. Another manipulation in figure 5.2 is to reverse the sign of the second question, so that left-leaning preferences align on the left for all the questions. The number of response options vary among the surveys, but typically (apart from the UK) they included full and qualified agreement, and unqualified disagreement. Hence there is not much point in averaging the scores.

The results are striking. To begin with, there was no unanimity. If economics was a science, there was no agreement on its core policy implications. One would hardly expect such lack of agreement over core issues in the application of physics, chemistry, or biology. On the other hand, the distribution of opinion remained constant over time, especially in the United States, which suggests that the surveys captured a stable distribution of preferences. The surveys show that economists as a body were much more liberal than the Nobel Committee, especially the Nobel Committee of the Lindbeck years. Overall, the ratio of liberal to conservative preferences was 1.81 (including Canada), that is, much higher than the Nobel Committee ratios (1.04 for the number of individuals, and 1.18 for citations). North American economists (1.9 for the United States, 1.5 for Canada) were more liberal than European ones (1.41), and the French were much more liberal than other Europeans

---

21. Offer, 'Economy of Obligation' (2011); introduction, above, 5–7.

(2.21 versus 1.21).[22] British economists (with a large sample of 981) were by far the most liberal (a ratio of 5.59), a finding consistent with an earlier survey from 1973.[23] The US responses remained consistent throughout, with a slight decline in support for equality. Other surveys, not precisely in the same format and mostly taken later, have returned similar results.[24]

Leaning left is typical, not only of economists, but even more of other social scientists.[25] A group of doctoral students in economics in the top six American university departments was surveyed in 1985, and again some fifteen years later, in the early 2000s. In graduate school, 50 percent were liberal and another 20 percent 'radical', that is, even more to the left. Fifteen years later as practising economists (two-thirds of them in universities), 55 percent were liberal and 7 percent still 'radical': in both cases, some two-thirds were left of centre, rather like our main sample.[26] Among American Economic Association (AEA) members who gave money to political parties (fewer than a tenth), five times as many gave to Democrats as to Republicans. The top of the profession leant even more towards the Democrats. AEA officers and authors in the *American Economic Review* were about nine times more likely to give to Democrats, and authors in flagship non-refereed (but prestigious) AEA journals (*Journal of Economic Perspectives* [*JEP*] and *Journal of Economic Literature* [*JEL*]) were 38 times more likely to contribute to Democrats. Among all the givers in the AEA elite, 182 gave money to the Democrats and only 10 to Republicans. Perhaps Republican supporters, as proponents of selfishness, were disinclined to give. Or were they less successful in a liberal-leaning profession, and so with less money to donate? Be that as it may, those who openly identified as Republicans gave much less each than comparably identified Democrats.[27] Finally, a poll by the *Economist* in 2008 found that 46 percent of senior American economists who responded identified as Democrats, 10 percent as Republicans, and 44 percent as independent. 80 percent supported Obama's policies.[28]

22. Weighted average—each survey given equal weight. Neutrals and don't knows (a small proportion) not counted.

23. Ricketts and Shoesmith, *British Economic Opinion: A Survey of a Thousand Economists* (1990).

24. Klein and Stern, 'Is There a Free-Market Economist in the House?' (2007); Whaples, 'The Policy Views of American Economic Association Members' (2009).

25. Davis and Figgins, 'Do Economists Believe American Democracy Is Working?' (2009); Cardiff and Klein, 'Faculty Partisan Affiliations in All Disciplines' (2005).

26. Colander, *The Making of an Economist, Redux* (2007), 84–87.

27. McEachern, 'AEA Ideology: Campaign Contributions of American Economic Association Members' (2006).

28. 'The Economist Poll of Economists', *Economist*, 2 October 2008.

These findings take us back to the validity of the rational expectations hypothesis, at the core of the New Classical Macroeconomics (NCM), which was discussed in chapter 1. It is obvious from figure 5.2 that economists are not of a single mind, and that only a minority hold strong market-liberal views. This calls into question a central conceit of rational expectations theory, namely that there is a single objectively correct economic model, which is applied in decision-making by experts and laypersons alike.[29] Two of the US surveys, ten years apart, asked economists whether they believed that rational expectations moderated swings in output. Only one-fifth agreed without reservations, and some 40 percent generally disagreed.[30] Rational expectations theory assumes that economic agents and economists share the same models. One survey put the identical questions to a sample of economists and to one made up of the general public. There was a large divergence between lay and professional viewpoints, with the general public inclining more to the right. For example, as a reason why the economy was not doing better, 61 percent of the public said that taxes were too high, but only 18 percent of economists.[31] Another survey, in 2010–2012, showed that when a panel of forty-one elite economists were given a set of policy questions, their average percentage of agreement with the statement was 35 percentage points to the left of the average response in a large panel of the general public.[32]

How effective a critique is this of rational expectations? The doctrine has the scholarly virtue of being counter-intuitive and therefore interesting as a hypothesis. Had it been able to predict economic outcomes successfully, it might have been possible to dismiss the unreality of its premises as being irrelevant (not a view that we would share). The premises are manifestly wrong, and the survey evidence shows how fanciful they are. It indicates that the premises bear no relation to reality, and that the theory relies entirely on the rigorous and elegant relation it develops between arbitrary premises and arbitrary results. Rational expectations theory may be suggestive of something, and may be worth pursuing as an intellectual exercise, but, however elegant, it can tell us little about reality. It is no more than a falsified hypothesis, and certainly does not have the normative authority to reject

29. Chapter 1, above, 25–26.
30. Fuller and Geide-Stevenson, 'Consensus among Economists: Revisited' (2003), 374, q. 11.
31. Blendon et al., 'Bridging the Gap' (1997), table 6, 113.
32. Sapienza and Zingales, 'Economic Experts versus Average Americans' (2013); Gordon and Dahl, 'Views among Economists: Professional Consensus or Point-Counterpoint?' (2013).

policy interventions which its advocates insist on. To be blunt, does rational expectations theory still deserve the benefit of the doubt?

Despite the influence of rational expectations doctrine, during the first twenty-five years of the Nobel Prize's existence, none of its creators was honoured by a Nobel Prize.[33] Perhaps Lindbeck, whose committee withheld the prize from the accomplished Social Democrat J. K. Galbraith, and from the highly cited liberals Stiglitz and Akerlof, may have taken rational expectations theories as being a step too far in the other direction. In an interview, Lindbeck said that he himself had never believed in rational expectations.[34] One year after Lindbeck's resignation from the committee, the prize did go to Lucas, who by then had moved on to other interests. Subsequent prizes were given to other rational expectations economists including, in 2011, to Thomas Sargent, 'for [his] empirical research on cause and effect in the macroeconomy'. Some commentators were puzzled.[35]

In awarding the prize to the rational expectations theorists Lucas (NPW, 1995), Kydland and Prescott (NPWs, 2004), and Sargent (NPW, 2011), the Nobel Committee endorsed the disciplinary norm that high theory could not be invalidated by mere empirical scrutiny. In order to maintain the credibility of the prize, the committee had to align itself with professional opinion. Although doubts were sometimes expressed about a particular selection, in general the committee succeeded in maintaining the reputation of the prize.

METHODOLOGY

Methodology is not the same as political orientation. One distinction is between theoretical and applied economists (elaborated further in chapter 7, between 'formalists' and 'empiricists'). All winners made a contribution, large or small, to theory.[36] These theorists fell into two main groups: On the one side, those equilibrium theorists whose work assumes that markets normally clear, and on the other, those more concerned with market failure. The first group contained Chicago School economists, who believed that actual market outcomes could be regarded for practical purposes as being

---

33. Nasar, *A Beautiful Mind* (1998), 371–373.
34. Lindbeck interview with AO, 3 December 2012.
35. For example, Kay, 'The Random Shock That Clinched a Brave Nobel Prize' (2011).
36. Lindbeck, 'The Prize in Economic Science in Memory of Alfred Nobel' (1984), 54.

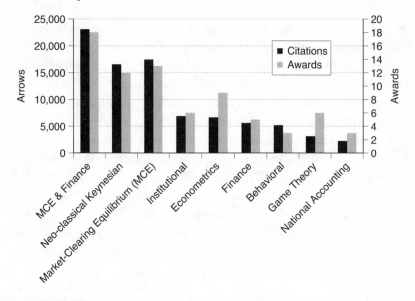

Figure 5.3. Citations and awards by method, 1969–2005.

close enough to the optimal.[37] An economic agent can obtain this optimal outcome for himself, and economists can calculate it. Similar models were provided by finance theorists in economics, who generally advocated versions of the 'efficient market hypothesis.'

The second group of theorists we call neoclassical Keynesians. These economists generally embrace the axioms of neoclassical economics which specify rational agents operating with complete knowledge. They also seek an efficient market equilibrium, but they identify circumstances in which markets can fail. Both the market efficiency advocates and the neoclassical Keynesians believe implicitly in the stability of human motivation, and in a stable set of causal relations in the economy, which extends from the past into the future so that the economic future is already predetermined.[38] Together, the market-clearing theorists and the neoclassical Keynesians have received about two-thirds of Nobel Prizes, and account for most citations (figure 5.3).

In figure 5.3, aggregate citation scores are compared to the number of awards in each of the sub-disciplines.[39] In the main fields of theory, the cor-

37. Reder, 'Chicago Economics' (1982).
38. Davidson, 'Reality and Economic Theory' (1996).
39. Other breakdowns, Shalev, *100 Years of Nobel Prizes* (2002); Ghosh, 'Beautiful Minds' (2015).

respondence is close, and appears to validate the committee selections. In the smaller fields, econometrics and game theory appear to be rated more highly by the committee than by the discipline as a whole, taking citations as a measure of esteem. The winners outside the two big theory fields together form an eclectic group. Some are in the top citation ranks, while others remain obscure. With the exception of game theorists, the eclectic 'others' have engaged more with reality than the two large groups of theorists. The strong performances of institutional economists and of behavioural economists in the flow of citations is striking (chapter 6, appendix). In the 1970s, three prizes were given to development economists: Myrdal, Schultz, and Lewis. Thereafter, the Nobel Committee lost its interest in economic development until Amartya Sen's award in 1998. Nevertheless (and unlike many of the other NPWs), the citation profile of these economists suggest contributions of enduring value.[40] Two other institutional awards were made to economic historians Fogel and North. Economic historians are inclined to rank Fogel higher, but North has a much stronger citation record, and is among the few NPWs whose citations are still on an accelerating growth trajectory. A bold award in 1978 to Herbert Simon, for his behavioural concept of bounded rationality, may nevertheless be seen as belated in view of his citation ranking (no. 3 cumulative, no. 4 per year). No other behavioural prizes were given until Kahneman and Smith's awards in 2002. Our own view is that (to use the terms of the Nobel benefaction) the greatest benefit conferred by economics on mankind has been the development and deployment of the system of national accounts, which has made it possible to monitor the performance of the economy and to try to control it. Three prizes were awarded in that category, to Kuznets, Leontief, and Stone. Their contribution has become an established technology. But on the evidence of citations, national accounting stagnated as a research programme, and its powerful breakthrough was already a thing of the past. Game theory was first recognized only in 1994, with another batch in 2004. In contrast, econometrics was recognized in the very first award, and periodically ever since.

To conclude: from an ideological point of view, the Nobel Committee was even-handed in its awards, but the balance it achieved was biased to the right in comparison with opinion within the discipline, especially during the 1990s. With regard to sub-disciplines, the committee made a virtue of its

---

40. All individual NPW citation trajectories are plotted below, either in the body of chapter 6, or in an appendix, where they are arranged in order of year of the prize.

pluralism, and this is borne out in the awards.[41] A committee made up of the editors of the top American journals during the same years is likely to have shown more sectarian bias. Nevertheless, the following chapter shows that the Nobel electors made deliberate omissions on the basis of ideological orientation, and possibly gender as well.

---

41. Lindbeck, 'The Prize in Economic Science in Memory of Alfred Nobel' (1985), 56.

CHAPTER 6
INDIVIDUAL REPUTATIONS
With Samuel Bjork

The citation trajectory of an individual can be understood as tracing the diffusion of an innovation. The Bass model of innovation is widely used in marketing research to investigate the diffusion of new products, and is applied here to intellectual innovation. Modelling academic reputations in this way makes it possible to determine how transient or durable they are, and to monitor the ebb and flow of intellectual innovation more generally.

THE BASS CURVE

The Bass equation was inspired by epidemiological models of the spread of contagious disease in closed populations. They describe the cumulative social adoption of a trait. Adoption is a learning (or 'contagion') process. At the start, a few early adopters embrace the innovation. Information and emulation spread the word, and take-up accelerates. Diffusion then slows down as the innovation approaches its maximum appeal. Following the shallow lead of early adoption, there is an exponential (convex) increase up to an inflection point, and then a concave section which flattens out at the peak of adoptions. In such models, the probability and timing of new adoptions (in our case, of new citations) is determined by the quantity and pace of previous ones. The trajectory of citations over time is approximately bell-shaped, peaking at the point of inflection of the cumulative curve. Figure 6.1 fits this model to the citation record of Paul Samuelson, one of the most celebrated NPWs. The flow of citations takes a typical bell shape, rising towards a maximum as diffusion accelerates, and declining when most new adoptions have taken place.

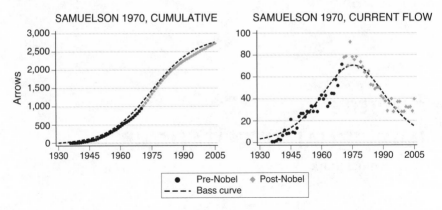

Figure 6.1. Bass innovation diffusion curves of citations: the example of Paul Samuelson (NPW, 1970).

The Bass model is a mathematical curve-fitting procedure.[1] It has three unknown variables that describe the pace of adoption and its maximum. For prediction, three initial values need to be guessed at, and the computation will then converge iteratively on a stable value. Advocates of the model claim some explanatory meaning to these variables. We think this can be ignored: The Bass model is just an inspired algorithm. The model is often used to forecast future diffusion patterns, but its use here is primarily descriptive: what is notable is that the influence of NPWs tends to wax and wane in accordance with a Bass diffusion model, rather than the prediction of future trajectories. Stable and robust parameter estimates require that data should be available at least up to the inflection point. We have data for the whole curve, and are interested in description rather than prediction. Nothing needs to be guessed, except for the initial seeding values. The Bass model provides a remarkably useful tool for characterizing NPW citation trajectories, and the exceptions, noted below, are also revealing.

Figure 6.2 shows an average of the Nobel Prize citation trajectories, with all fifty-seven winners from 1969–2005 normalized to centre on their prize year. The average citation trajectory fits well with an almost symmetrical Bass curve (the skew is largely imparted by the later winners, who have fewer years after the prize). There is a small and brief 'prize citation premium', and reputational decline sets in a few years after the award. At its most basic, the good fit indicates that old novelties are displaced by new ones over time, and

1.   Lilien and Rangaswamy, *Marketing Engineering* (1997), 195–203; Bjork et al., 'Time Series Citation Data' (2014), 187–188.

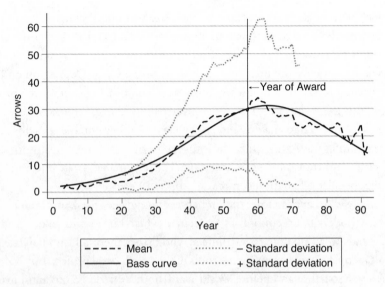

Figure 6.2. Average citation trajectory of fifty-seven Nobel Prize winners.
Note: Standard deviation where numbers ≥ 30.

that what goes up, eventually comes down, at least as far as direct citation is concerned. Another interpretation is that some innovations become so pervasive that they no longer need to be cited, but simply enter common usage. But if this is argued for Samuelson, one needs to explain why it does not apply to the same extent to Friedman, Arrow, and several others (see figure 6.5, below).

It is not clear whether the peak tends to attract the prize, or whether the prize provokes the decline. In general, the Nobel Committee tended to nominate NPWs near their citation peak, that is, at the very height of their reputations. On the average at least, it played safe, and awarded prizes to those already endorsed by the profession as being currently productive. This had the effect of enhancing the credibility of the prize.[2] Armed with this credibility, the committee was then able to diverge from its prudent course and to make a few choices that were more controversial.

HAYEK AND MONT PÈLERIN

This kind of discretion was first used to award the prize to Friedrich von Hayek, who won it in 1974. This may well have been the most significant

---

2. Ståhl, 'The Prize in Economic Science and Maurice Allais' (1990), 9.

Nobel Prize of all. Hayek's claim to the prize was not obvious. Early in his career, he developed an Austrian theory of capital and of self-correcting business cycles, which was published in 1929–1930. This was sidelined by Keynesian and Friedmanite interpretations of the Great Depression and is rarely cited today, although it was given as the nominal reason for the prize. From the 1930s onwards, Hayek was overshadowed as an economist by the success of Keynesian analysis and policy. Hayek's other notable contribution to economics was to highlight the importance of markets as a means for discovering and transmitting information. This originated as an intervention in the socialist calculation controversy in the 1930s.

Some six decades before, the French economic theorist Leon Walras devised a model of the economy as a system in which buyers and sellers submit price bids to an imaginary auctioneer, who brings them all into balance simultaneously. This was one of the roots of the neoclassical project. But Walras was also a socialist, and before World War I, both Vilfredo Pareto and Enrico Barone showed how his model could be applied in a socialist society, that is, one without private ownership of the means of production. In the 1920s and 1930s, several socialist economists (especially Oscar Lange) showed that if there were markets in labour and consumer goods, then Walrasian socialism would work. More recently, the socialist calculation problem (as formulated by the left-leaning Frank Ramsey in 1928) has reappeared as the problem of choice faced by a single-person economy (a representative agent) in Chicago right-leaning real business cycle models of the 1970s and 1980s.[3]

Hayek's riposte, developed over a decade, was acutely written. He built on a prior contribution by Ludwig by von Mises, who argued that socialist planning was impossible without the input of genuine market signals.[4] Hayek added that economic agents were circumscribed in their knowledge by local horizons and individual capacity. But the economic decisions of millions of uncoordinated individuals added up to the price signals that allowed a market economy to function efficiently. This spontaneous order could not be matched by the deliberate efforts of the socialist central planner.

Hayek's argument was also a challenge to the conventional premises of orthodox neoclassical economics, which assumed that rational agents op-

---

3. Ingrao and Israel, *Invisible Hand* (1990), 252–253; King, *Microfoundations Delusion* (2012), 106–107; Jael, 'Socialist Calculation and Market Socialism' (2015).
4. Mises, 'Economic Calculation in the Socialist Commonwealth' (1920/1935); Lane, 'The Genesis and Reception of *The Road to Serfdom*' (2013).

erated with complete knowledge of prices.[5] It was also inconsistent with the Walrasian general equilibrium. It had drastic implications for market-clearing economics: if the socialist calculation was impossible, so was the neoclassical assumption of omniscience. A perfectly informed central planner would be little different from a Walrasian auctioneer. The two theorems of welfare economics, proven in the 1950s by Arrow and Debreu (both of them NPWs), which dominated high theory in the 1960s and 1970s, also assumed that agents had complete information. This contrarian position set Hayek completely apart from other anti-socialists at the University of Chicago, and was, for him, a dead end. From the 1950s onwards, he no longer published any economics, but engaged in elaborating a classical liberal political philosophy. At the University of Chicago, he was not a member of the economics department.

Hayek received the prize jointly with the Social Democrat economist, politician, and development scholar Gunnar Myrdal. Even the citation was joint to both of them, 'for their pioneering work in the theory of money and economic fluctuations and for their penetrating analysis of the interdependence of economic, social and institutional phenomena.'[6] There was more than a touch of irony about this, since it would have been difficult to find two NPWs who were less in harmony with each other, and they barely acknowledged each other's existence during the festivities.

Hayek's supporters resented the joint award, and speculated that Myrdal was given the prize as a sop to the left and as a Scandinavian favourite son. But at the time, Myrdal had a much stronger citation record, and was only overtaken by Hayek in the 1990s (Myrdal was still placed seven citation ranks above Hayek in 2005). Like Hayek, Myrdal had made interesting and even important contributions to macroeconomics in the 1920s and 1930s, which were cited by the committee, but he had moved away from theory and acquired a much larger reputation as the author of two great studies in human development, *An American Dilemma* (about the condition of blacks in America in the 1930s) and *Asian Drama* (on South Asian development in the 1960s), in addition to ministerial office and service in international agencies. It is no wonder that Myrdal treated the prize as a snub. At a party

5. Overview, Levy and Peart, 'Socialist Calculation Debate' (2008); Jael, 'Socialist Calculation and Market Socialism' (2015).
6. Hoover Institution Papers, Nobel Citation 1974, Hayek Papers 47–10.

in honour of the two, 'Myrdal demonstratively turned his back to Hayek and said he had no desire to speak to what he called "such a person".'[7]

Despite their almost polar differences, the winners of 1974 had one thing in common. Among all recipients of the prize, these two were its only public critics. In his acceptance speech, Hayek questioned the 'scientistic' pretensions of the Nobel Prize, in accordance with his view that economic agents (and economists as well) had to act on incomplete understanding and information.[8] Two years later, Myrdal criticized what he saw as the politicization of the prize, when it was given to Milton Friedman. He regretted having accepted it himself.[9]

Hayek's biographers accept that his reputation had reached a low ebb in the early 1970s. He was depressed, financially insecure, and disposed to drink. One of his biographers wrote: 'If Hayek had not received the Nobel Prize in Economic Science, it is an open question what his reputation would be now.'[10] This is confirmed in a Bass model of Hayek's citations. Figure 6.3 shows Hayek's citation record over time (solid line, right-hand scale), and fits two Bass flow trajectories, the first up to the prize in 1974, and second beginning in 1975. The first trajectory shows Hayek as having exhausted his potential as an innovator by 1974. Receiving the prize shifted him onto a much higher trajectory, although he had reached a second peak by 2005. This was not entirely unique. Visual inspection suggests similar patterns for Stone (NPW, 1984) and Vickrey (NPW, 1996) (appendix, below).

The prize also had an invigorating effect on the Mont Pèlerin Society which Hayek had founded. Its official historian wrote in 1995, at the end of the Lindbeck era:

> A main reason for the heightened profile of the Society was the awarding of the Nobel prize in economics to seven of its members between 1974 and 1991: Hayek in 1974, Friedman in 1976, Stigler in 1982, Buchanan in 1986, Allais in 1988, Coase in 1991, and Gary Becker in 1992. Of these, Hayek, Friedman, Stigler, and Allais were at the 1947 meeting, and Buchanan and Coase were early members; Hayek, Friedman, Stigler, Buchanan, and Becker became presidents of the Society, and all but Allais and Coase have been actively engaged in the Society throughout its history. Although differ-

---

7. Lindbeck, *Ekonomi* (2012), 115.
8. Hayek, 'The Pretence of Knowledge' (1974).
9. Myrdal, 'The Nobel Prize in Economic Sciences' (1977).
10. Ebenstein, *Friedrich Hayek* (2001), 261.

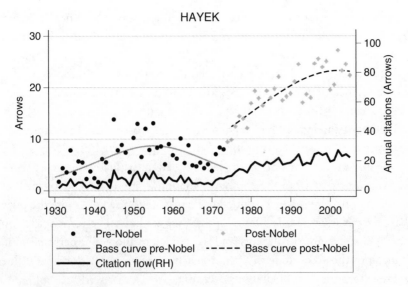

Figure 6.3. Bass diffusion trajectories for Hayek, before and after the Nobel Prize.

ing in their technical contributions to economic theory, the laureates had much in common, particularly their support of the free market and of the right of the individual to choose without coercive constraints. Thus they recognized the need to limit government, to curb socialist tendencies in the democracies, and to be suspicious of appeals to social aggregates like 'the public interest'. There is no doubt that the Nobel prizes, with their worldwide recognition, strengthened the intellectual status of the Society and thus, in the world at large, its influence in the formation of a more liberal conception of society and its workings.[11]

Up to 2005, thirteen out of fifty-seven NPWs were directly or indirectly attached to the University of Chicago, far more than any other institution.[12]

INDIVIDUAL TRAJECTORIES

For both economists and the general public, the most compelling aspect of the prizes is who gets them and who doesn't. Also of interest is the effect of the prize on winners' careers. A larger question is whether the prize has

11. Hartwell, *History of the Mont Pelèrin Society* (1995), 160.
12. Ghose, 'Beautiful Minds' (2015), 10.

amplified the authority of any particular winner, or of all winners together. Finally, the impact of the prize on individuals may tell us something about economics more generally.

The trajectories fall into patterns, and this section shows samples of each of them. An appendix contains Bass diagrams for all the NPWs whose trajectories are not in the body of the text.[13] These figures all have two vertical axes, on the right and left, both of them measuring Arrow scores. To recapitulate, Arrow scores measure the number of citations per year, adjusted for the size of the literature.[14] The one on the left is scaled individually for each person, to make use of the whole height for the citations scattergram, and for the Bass curve (a dotted line) which is fitted to them. Citation scores before the prize have dark markers, while after the prize they are light. The vertical scale on the right is the same in all plots, and is intended to allow interpersonal comparison of the absolute level of citations. It provides a scale for a solid line representing the flow of citations over time.

The Bass citation curve for two of the early winners, Jan Tinbergen (1969) and John Hicks (1972), is typical of symmetrical bell-shaped citation trajectories which peak around the time of the Nobel award (figure 6.4). It indicates that breakthroughs in economics have something in common with other innovations: a novelty value which peaks, and then declines. This does not depend on the absolute level of citations. Tinbergen peaked six years before his award with 16.5 Arrows in 1963, while Paul Samuelson, who received the prize in 1970, achieved his peak four years later with his highest annual score of 91 Arrows in 1974 (see figure 6.1 above). Thereafter, they both steadily declined. This symmetrical bell-curve was the most common pattern (22 out of 57).

A second group are innovators with staying power (figure 6.5). These also peaked around the time of the prize, but did not decline very much thereafter. The strongest performance here was by Arrow and Friedman, who were also the most cited NPWs overall. A close third, with equally strong staying power, was Simon, thus explaining what to many appeared to be an outlier award in 1978. Also impressive has been the staying power of the development economists, Myrdal, Lewis, and Schultz.

A third group are ten who were still well below the inflection point when they received the prize (figure 6.6, left). This group of the still-rising

13. Below, 143–148.
14. Above, 109.

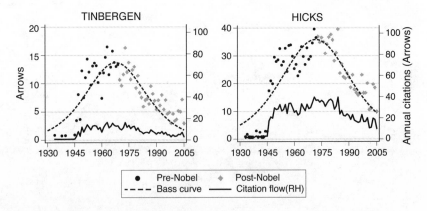

Figure 6.4. Personal trajectories: (1) symmetrical.

Note: Similar patterns (peak close to award with symmetric bell-shaped trajectory) for Kuznets, Samuelson, Leontief, Kantorovich, Koopmans, Meade, Klein, Tobin, Stigler (borderline), Debreu, Modigliani, Harsanyi, Nash, Selten, Fogel, Lucas, Mirrlees, Scholes, Spence, Schelling. Later awards have truncated futures, and in some cases are indeterminate.

includes (in addition to Hayek) Coase, Becker, North, Heckman (the single-year superstar, with a maximum score of 135), Akerlof, Stiglitz (borderline), Kahneman, Smith, Engle, Prescott, and Aumann. Apart from Hayek, they all received their prize from the 1990s onwards. These awards indicate, on the one hand, a drift towards earlier recognition, but these NPWs are also highly cited. In their case the 'Nobel premium' may simply be a case of earlier recognition. For another group, recognition came late. The most striking cases

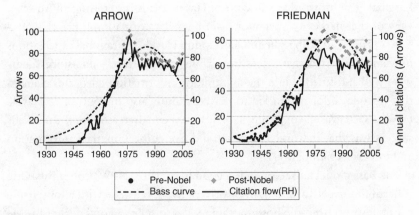

Figure 6.5. Personal trajectories: (2) staying power.

Note: Similar patterns (peak close to award, with persisting high scores) for Myrdal, Simon, Lewis, Schultz, Stigler, Buchanan, Solow, Miller, Merton. Later awards are not conclusive.

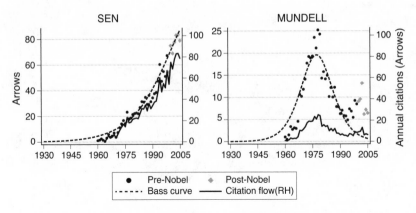

Figure 6.6. Personal trajectories: (3) rising (Sen); (4) over the hill (Mundell).

are Haavelmo, Markowitz, Sharpe, and Mundell, all of whom were recognized by the prize long after their citation peak, although they had a brief second wind after the prize, like Mundell, shown in figure 6.6 (right). More moderate belated recognition came to Klein, Modigliani, and Solow.

Another group had to wait a long time before their Arrow citation eminence was acknowledged by the prize. These were the information theorists, both the anti-government proponents of rational expectations (Lucas, Prescott, and Kydland), and the market-failure exponents of asymmetric information, especially the NPW 2001 trio of Akerlof, Spence, and Stiglitz. In Arrow citation score terms, they all became eligible during the 1980s or early 1990s. Their failure to win the prize may be explicable if we take Assar Lindbeck, the Nobel kingmaker, at his word as a disciple of Hayek, that is, as holding an Austrian view of the market as integrator of imperfect information.[15] Hayek's position was rejected both right and left. Contra Hayek, the rational expectations movement asserted that prices were close to their 'true' value since agents were well informed, while the asymmetric information advocates claimed that unequal information led to market failure, also in contrast to Hayek. Hayek's view was the opposite, namely that the main reason for the market's success was that it worked to offset and overcome imperfect information and imperfect rationality.

The Bass model fails to provide a good fit for three NPW economists. One is Bertil Ohlin (NPW, 1977), who was a native-son Swede with a low Arrow count, four up from the bottom (table 5.1). He spent a good deal of his life

---

15. Below, 188.

as a leader of the centrist Liberal Party, in that respect in opposition to his Social Democratic co-member of the so-called Stockholm School Myrdal, who received the prize before him.[16] Ohlin's prize, so soon after Myrdal's, looks like a balancing gesture in Swedish economics and politics. Ohlin is best known for his model of foreign trade (with Heckscher) which was first proposed in the 1920s, and his limited impact takes the unusual form of a flat and declining Bass line. Another poor fit is for Richard Stone, the main creator of the standard national accounting system, and William Vickrey. Like Hayek, both have a bi-modal citation distribution, with an initial peak more than twenty years before the prize, and a second, higher one after it. In the case of Vickrey, this peak was posthumous.

THE *REFUSÉS*

It is easy to compile a list of economists who would have been plausible NPWs. The American Economic Association elected up to four Distinguished Fellows a year, with automatic election for past presidents. Among them were Moses Abramovitz, Armen Alchian, Abram Bergson, Edward Denison, Victor Fuchs, Alexander Gerschenkron, Harold Hotelling, Hendrick Houthakker, Harry Johnson, Charles Kindleberger, Kelvin Lancaster, Abba Lerner, Jacob Marschak, Jacob Mincer, Ludwig von Mises, Oskar Morgenstern, Richard Musgrave, Herbert Scarf, Anna Schwartz, Tibor Scitovsky, and Gordon Tullock. Any of these would have been accepted as NPWs by the discipline. Presidents of the American Economic Association also included William Baumol, J. K. Galbraith, Arnold Harberger, Dale Jorgensen, and Marc Nerlove. Not in these lists but highly cited are Robert Barro, Zvi Griliches, and Paul Romer. Among British economists, Anthony Atkinson, Partha Dasgupta, Roy Harrod, Nicholas Kaldor, and Joan Robinson might also be mentioned. In the 1980s, about 150 candidates were nominated for the prize every year by competent authorities.[17] These lists highlight the preponderance of Americans at the pinnacle of economics during the Nobel Prize years. Bruno Frey explains the shortfall of Europeans by the different conception of merit in Europe, where economists' eminence arises from a high position in policy advice, and not from theoretical innovation.[18]

---

16. Above, 77–80.
17. Ingemar Ståhl, 'The Prize in Economic Science and Maurice Allais' (1990).
18. Frey, 'Economics and Economists: A European Perspective' (1992).

For most of the winners, the prize came close to the peak of citation impact. The prize manifestly did not have an incentive effect for those who already won it. Many of them were quite old, and were unlikely to go on producing with the vigour of youth. But among the many plausible aspirants (some of whom went on to get the prize), it is reasonable to assume that some were stimulated by the prospect of receiving it.

This might imply that there was an underlying true merit ranking to discover, and that the Nobel Committee's task was to uncover it. What the names of the *Refusés* suggest is the extent to which the selection of winners was a task of construction, which could have gone differently without affecting the prestige of the prize. It highlights the discretion available to the committee, especially during the later Lindbeck chairmanship years, the period of right-wing ascendancy in the 1990s.

It is consistent with our method so far to compare citation scores of winners and non-winners. In 1989, Marshall Medoff published a list of plausible non-winners, including many of those mentioned above.[19] It is instructive to compare their citation scores with those of the winners. His list did not contain any super-cited economist at the level of Arrow, Becker, Friedman, Sen, Simon, or Stiglitz, But a few non-winners came close, and many of them would have fitted comfortably in the centre of the Nobel field. We have used this list as a point of departure, have taken out a few and included a few others to make up an eclectic list of a dozen. The number is limited for reasons of space, but it is consistent with the status of the *Refusés* that, however good they may have been, we cannot treat them equally with the winners. Such is the power of anointment. Lindbeck and another former chairman of the committee have both suggested in interview that our list of near-misses was accurate, and that many of the scholars in question had been discussed by the committee.[20]

Joan Robinson and J. K. Galbraith were the most celebrated among those who failed to get the prize. Their claims were strong. Robinson was a highly cited co-originator of the influential theory of monopolistic competition, and a credible woman candidate. The first woman NPW Elinor Ostrom was not elected until 2010. Robinson also had citation staying power. In 2005, she would have ranked eleventh from the top in our citation list, just after Lewis, above Lucas, Solow, and Sen, and two places higher than Hicks, who

19. Medoff, 'The Ranking of Economists' (1989).
20. AO interview with Assar Lindbeck and Jörgen Weibull, 4 December 2012.

was her contemporary. In 1975, *Business Week*, after sounding out the American economics profession, featured her as a prospective winner. The magazine may not have appreciated how much further left than opinion on the committee American economists were at that time. Robinson would have been the left-wing counterpart of the previous year's selection of Hayek, and with a much stronger citation record. Against her chances, however, was the implication of her theory that the appearance of market competition was deceptive. By the time the prize came into being, she had become heterodox, had repudiated her best-known contribution, had sympathized publicly with student radicals, and was writing appreciatively of China and North Korea. In the Cold War atmosphere of the 1970s, a prize for Robinson was probably a step too far. Instead, the committee made a gesture to détente that year with its award to the Soviet economist Leonid Kantorovich. His contribution to linear programming posed no threat to the imaginary machine programme; indeed, it was an aspect of it.

In contrast, Galbraith was the foremost English-speaking exponent of Social Democracy, an articulate, visible, influential, acute, and prolific writer. He may be compared to some other 'literary economist' NPWs, Lewis, Hayek, Myrdal, Buchanan, Coase, and North, and arguably had a greater impact on economic thinking and policy than all but Hayek and Buchanan. He had been a favourite of the Social Democratic prime minister Tage Erlander, and in the labour movement more generally, whose publishing house had translated and brought out his book *The Affluent Society*.[21] Among the Nobel Prize winners, he would have ranked foureenth in total citations in 2005, and behind only Robinson, Baumol, and Griliches in our group of *Refusés*. It is consistent with our account of the origins and purpose of the Nobel Prize that Galbraith was blackballed for his advocacy of the welfare state and for his scepticism about market perfection. He was dismissed by Lindbeck in his autobiography (and in conversation as well) as a social essayist, with a pronounced economic historical focus, comparable to Myrdal but without the latter's depth and originality.[22] This indicates the conviction with which the committee held to their (not always consistent) vision of economics as the construction of abstract models.[23] From a less fundamentalist point of view, the prizes for Hayek and Buchanan on the right could have been

21. Chapter 4, above, 102; Andersson, *Between Growth and Security* (2006), 33, 40, n. 19, 44.
22. Lindbeck, *Ekonomi* (2012), 70.
23. Lindbeck, 'The Prize in Economic Science in Memory of Alfred Nobel' (1985), 54.

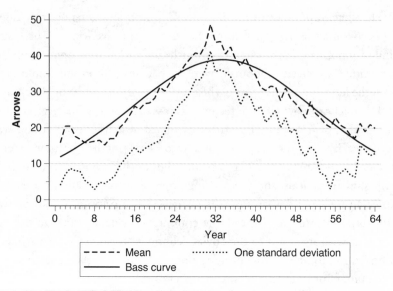

Figure 6.7. Twelve non-winners, normalized on year of maximum citations.
Note: Names: Anthony Atkinson, Robert Barro, Martin Feldstein, John Kenneth Galbraith, Zvi Griliches, Albert Hirschman, Mancur Olson, Joan Robinson, Walt Whitman Rostow, Henri Theil, Gordon Tullock.

matched by one for Galbraith, whose stature on the left was comparable. Rejected by the economics discipline, Galbraith became increasingly jaundiced about its pretensions, of which he made gentle fun in his novel *A Tenured Professor* (1990).

Figure 6.7 shows the average citation trajectory of our group of non-winners. It is normalized to centre on the peak citation year. The dispersion is actually smaller than that of the winners in figure 6.8, and the peak for this group is considerably higher, but in other respects the trajectory does not look very different from that of the winners.

Figure 6.8 permits a closer examination of this group. It confirms the strong citation performance of non-winners. This group cuts a swathe through the middle height, and the number of Nobel winners below them was larger than the number above. Both Galbraith and Robinson put in strong performances, but Baumol and Griliches, quite technical neoclassical economists, were always ahead of Galbraith. During the 1960s, probably his period of highest renown, Galbraith was completely overshadowed by Rostow (made famous by his *Stages of Economic Growth* [1960] and highly visible in the Kennedy administration—these years are not shown here). From the 1980s onwards, Galbraith was only in mild decline, at the bottom of a cluster

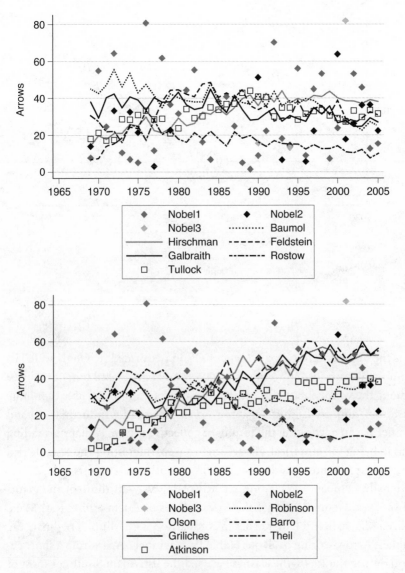

Figure 6.8. Citation flows of some leading *Refusés*.
Note: Nobel1, Nobel2, and Nobel3 refer to Arrow scores of NPWs in the particular year.

of non-winners, which includes such right-wing heroes as Feldstein, Tullock, and Barro, and the development economist and historian of thought Albert Hirschman. Joan Robinson emerged early, and peaked in the 1970s. Her stock never collapsed, and continued at a level similar to that of Galbraith, below the very top ranks of the non-winners although in the aggregate it

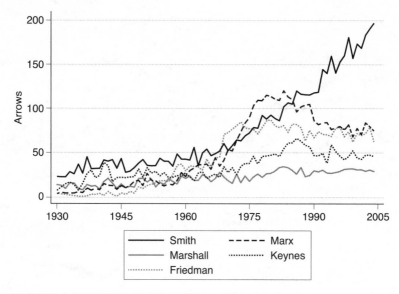

Figure 6.9. Citation flows of enduring reputations, 1930–2005.

was the highest in this group. Mancur Olson performed strikingly well. His cumulative score of 1407 Arrows in 2005 would have placed him number 19 among the winners, but well behind Robinson. Olson was an able economic historian, and his *Logic of Collective Action* was mostly influential beyond economics in advocating the futility of collective action. Perhaps his failing was in being too empirical. His arguments were interesting and testable and may have given hostages to reality, which few other economists did.

Finally, compare the citation records of NPWs with those of the giants of the past. Figure 6.9 shows the Arrow scores of Adam Smith, Karl Marx, Alfred Marshall, and J. M. Keynes in comparison with Milton Friedman, the highest Arrow-scoring of all our Nobel Prize winners. Apart from a short period during the 1970s, the classics have led the list, Adam Smith for most of the time, and Karl Marx from the mid-1970s to the late 1980s. In recent years, Smith has scored much higher than any Nobel Prize winner. His great surge from the 1990s onwards may be related to the false embrace of neoliberalism. But in recent years, his *Theory of Moral Sentiments*, which is premised on reciprocity rather than self-regard, has also received a great many citations. Friedman had an exceptional heyday during the late-1960s to mid-1970s, when he outscored everyone else (except for Arrow, who had a similar trajectory and scored even higher in the 1970s). But reaction came quickly: Smith was overtaken by Marx, who had an even greater visibility during the 1980s, and who has never since dipped lower than Friedman. If times turn bad, he may be due for a revival. In contrast, Keynes has been a steady but not spectacular performer, and Marshall has hung on. The classics would have earned a towering position in the Nobel cumulative citation ranking, with Smith and Marx placing first and third respectively. What distinguishes both of them from the advocates of the imaginary machine was their open-ended ethical understanding of economy and society. 'Value-free' they were not.

CONCLUSION

In Axel Leijonhufvud's satirical masterpiece,'Life among the Econ', he writes, 'There has been a great deal of debate in recent years over whether certain Econ [models] and the associated belief-systems are best to be regarded as religious, folklore and mythology, philosophical and "scientific," or as sports and games. Each category has its vocal proponents among Econologists of repute but very little headway has been made in the debate.'[24] The Bank of Sweden's Nobel Prize strove to endow economics with the authority of science, and invested tens of millions of dollars in this aspiration. The Nobel Committee's conception of science reflected the tribal rankings of the Econ as depicted by the satirist: 'The priestly caste (the Math-Econ) for example, is a higher 'field' than either Micro or Macro, while the Devlops just as definitely rank lower.'[25]

If the Nobel Committee's task was to make the prize credible, they have largely succeeded, at least up to 2005 (when our study ends). Credibility required them not to stray too far from the discipline's internal prestige rankings. Once achieved, this credibility fed back into the winners' reputations. It also gave the committee room to exercise discretion. In its political stance, the committee achieved a mechanical balance overall, with almost equal numbers of right- and left-leaning economists. On closer examination, left-leaning economists achieved about a fifth more citations. The most important instance of discretion was the prize awarded to Hayek in 1974. Between 1990 and 1997, all the winners inclined to the right. This was consistent with the latter-day policy agenda of the chairman, Assar Lindbeck.[26] It also

---

24. Leijonhufvud, 'Life among the Econ' (1973), 334.
25. Leijonhufvud, ibid., 329.
26. Chapter 9 below.

enhanced the prestige of the reactionary Mont Pèlerin Society. In comparison with the balance of opinion in the profession in both the United States and Europe during the 1980s and 1990s, the choices of the committee were distinctly biased to the right.

The credibility of the prizes allows us to treat them as a high-quality sample of the discipline. Axel Leijonhufvud wrote that: 'The dominant feature which makes status relations among the Econ of unique interests to the serious student, is the way that status is tied to the manufacture of certain types of implements, called "modls".[27] In terms of methodological orientation, his account is borne out: to get a prize, it was necessary to make models, even for those whose main line of work was empirical.

The prize was dominated by two groups of theorists, the market-clearing equilibrium advocates clustered around Chicago, and the Keynesian neoclassicals in the mould of Samuelson and Solow, roughly, freshwater versus saltwater. About two-thirds of the prizes went to these groups, with numbers of prize winners closely matching citation scores.

The best-known of those economists who did not win the prize cannot be distinguished from the winners merely by their citation records. In the list of those who were denied the prize, it is difficult not to conclude that Robinson and Galbraith were kept out for ideological reasons. Among neoclassical economists, the active American neoclassicals Baumol and Griliches achieved their peaks of reputation during the 1980s, a time when Nobel awards were given to the low-scoring Europeans Allais and Haavelmo, both of whom had peaked a long time earlier. Olson was a contender on the right who scored remarkably high but did not receive the prize. His theories of collective action may have helped to form the pessimism about co-operation that characterized the 1970s and the 1980s. A prize to Hirschman would have recognized a highly cited development economist and also a significant historian of economic thought.

The Nobel Prize in economics invested tens of millions of dollars of Swedish taxpayers' money in promoting economics as a science. It sent a costly signal, and succeeded. For the Swedish advocates of market liberalism, it was cheap at the price, it not being their money either. The Nobel imprimatur created an aura of authority around the winners. The aura extended to the marketizing policy agenda that was pursued by conservatives both in Sweden and internationally at the time.

---

27. Leijonhufvud, ibid., 328.

APPENDIX

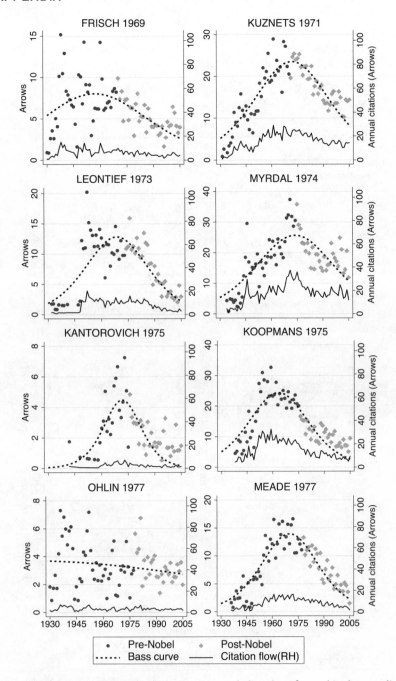

Appendix Figure 6.A. NPW individual trajectories, excluding those featured in the preceding figures. The construction of the figures is described on p. 132 above.

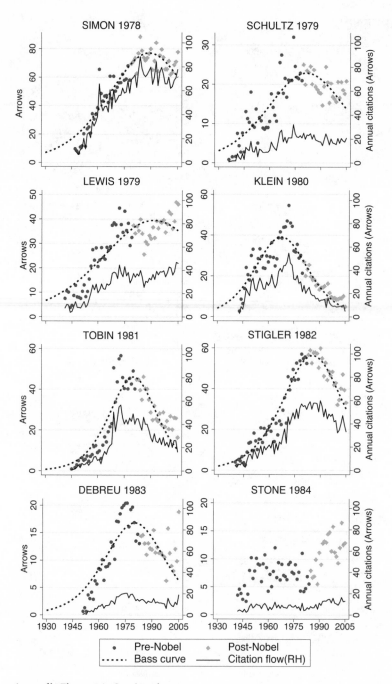

Appendix Figure 6.A. Continued

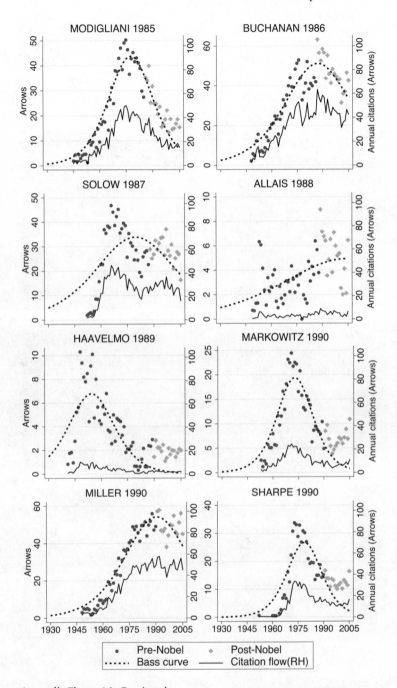

Appendix Figure 6.A. Continued

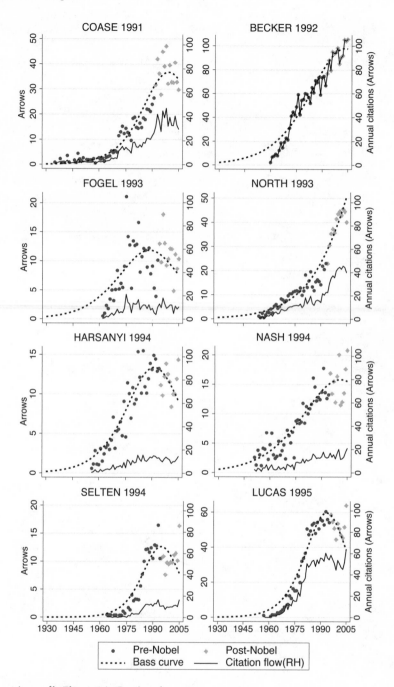

Appendix Figure 6.A. Continued

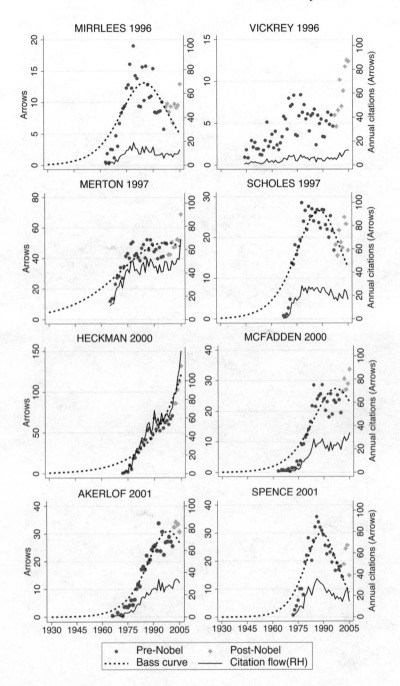

Appendix Figure 6.A. Continued

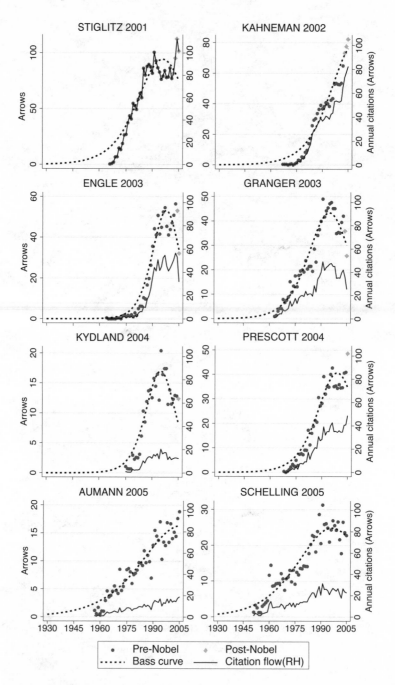

Appendix Figure 6.A. Continued

CHAPTER 7

NOBEL ECONOMICS AND SOCIAL DEMOCRACY

Achieving well-being involves a trade-off between satisfaction now and satisfaction later.[1] How to manage this trade-off is what largely divides neoclassical economics from Social Democracy. In both approaches, people are 'forward looking'. In economics, the future has a value in the present. The individual makes a choice that will maximize this present value. But in order to do this, the future needs to be known, and general equilibrium economics assumes that it is known: preferences, products, quantities, prices, everything. Uncertainty is dealt with by assuming that future outcomes have a known probability, and that even if particular individuals are in error, on average they are right. Uncertainty thus becomes 'certainty equivalence' and is simply defined away. People allocate their endowment and effort between present and future by trading in markets. If they are short of cash, they can always borrow, and if they have cash to spare, they can always save. For future contingencies, insurance can be purchased. Contracts are assumed to be costless and secure. Individuals provide for themselves.

In contrast, Social Democracy has worked to secure the future by means of collective action, initially through trade unions, and then by means of parliamentary democracy. Social Democracy acts for those whose prior endowments are modest, with no boost from inheritance, ability, or luck. Their future is uncertain and they are always at risk. Social Democracy has aimed to mitigate uncertainty and risk by two means. One was to build up personal resilience through education, healthcare, and housing. The other was to insure against life-cycle contingencies, primarily unemployment, poverty,

---

1. Offer, *Challenge of Affluence* (2006), chs. 3–4.

ill health, and old age, by pooling these risks for society as a whole. Both of these objectives are achieved by means of lateral transfers between the generations, out of progressive taxation on a pay-as-you-go basis. The tax paid monthly out of a moderate salary finds its way that very month into somebody else's pension or hospital treatment.[2]

The challenge of unemployment appears differently in the two approaches. For Social Democracy, it arises during the life cycle; for orthodox economics, in the course of the business cycle. Unemployment hurts: it inflicts economic loss, social isolation, and mental pain. The New Classical Macroeconomics (NCM) does not acknowledge pain. Just the opposite. It regards unemployment as a voluntary choice, a preference for agreeable idleness over working at the current market rate.[3] Economics before the 1930s, to the extent that it acknowledged the business cycle, regarded unemployment as largely self-correcting. In contrast, trade unions and friendly societies began to insure workers against unemployment in the nineteenth century, and governments extended the coverage between the wars. Keynes defined unemployment as a collective challenge, not an individual one: it arose from a market failure, and was caused by a shortfall of aggregate demand. The solution was to raise demand by means of government spending. For Social Democracy, unemployment was a recurring feature of the market economy, and the policy response was to pay the unemployed until they could find work again, and to enhance their mobility and skills. Keynesians and Social Democrats both regarded worklessness as intolerable.

FORMALISTS AND EMPIRICS

Nobel awards go to the most accomplished work in the discipline. But distinction takes time to emerge, so the awards lag behind the cutting edge. On the other hand, the work selected for the prize has stood the test of time. For its influence on policy, it is useful to divide NPWs into formalists and empiricists (or more concisely, 'empirics', thus avoiding any association with empiricism in philosophy). The prize is not given for purely descriptive work: theoretical or conceptual innovation is required. But there are degrees of theorizing. Empirics are innovators in 'empirical science theory.' They take the natural sciences as their model, and the observable world as their sub-

---

2. Offer, 'Economy of Obligation' (2012); Hills, *Good Times, Bad Times* (2015).
3. Lucas, *Models of Business Cycles* (1987), 54–69.

ject. They confront theory with measurement, and accept the discipline of evidence.[4] Formalists take their cue from mathematics and logic. They begin with premises which are taken as true. Results are then derived deductively and rigorously and (assuming there is no mistake) are always correct for this particular set of premises.[5] In the words of the visionary poet William Blake: 'Truth can never be told so as to be understood and not be believ'd.'[6]

It might be assumed that for policy guidance theory needs to have been validated empirically, but the opposite is the case. Economists are prone to overconfidence, that is, to more confidence in their views than the evidence merits. The main reason for this is a general human tendency to overconfidence. Most people regard themselves as being above average, for example, smarter, more attractive, and better drivers than they actually are. In controlled experiments, however, the tendency to overconfidence can be undermined by empirical feedback. In the absence of such feedback, economic formalists will be more confident in their positions than empirical economists, and this is borne out by the record.[7] Among Nobel economists as well, the most prescriptive, the boldest in laying down policy guidance have been the formalists, those whose authority is based on reason, with no validation from experience.

Figure 7.1 shows the respective numbers and citation paths of the two groups among NPWs. Most economists are easy to allocate to one group or the other, while some have done work in both modes. All econometricians are taken as empirics; all game theorists as formalists. In cases of doubt, we have made a judgment, based on the scholar's most important contributions, and taking account of the reasons given for their Nobel award. Article citations are taken from JSTOR, and expressed as an index proportional to the whole JSTOR literature, measured in 'Arrows', that is, relative to Kenneth Arrow's score in 1976, which is normalized to 100.[8] There was a rough numerical parity for the two approaches, with alternating awards. The first five years of advantage for the formalists were followed by a big empirical surge from the mid-1970s to the mid-1980s. A formalist surge around 1990 was

---

4. Ward, *What's Wrong with Economics?* (1972), 40; Mayer, *Truth and Precision in Economics* (1993); Hutchison, *On the Methodology of Economics and the Formalist Revolution* (2000).
5. Mayer, *Truth and Precision in Economics* (1993), 24–31.
6. Samuelson, 'Economists and the History of Ideas' (1962), 18, acknowledged to the philosopher and economist Frank Ramsey. The source is William Blake, *The Marriage of Heaven and Hell* (1790), no. 69.
7. Angner, 'Economists as Experts: Overconfidence in Theory and Practice' (2006); Milberg, 'The Rhetoric of Policy Relevance in International Economics' (1996), 243, 247, 250.
8. Chapter 5, above, 109.

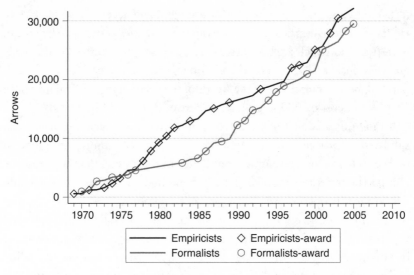

Figure 7.1. 'Empirical scientist' and 'formalist' cumulative citation counts for Nobel Prize winners, 1969–2005.
Note: Empirics (in order of award): Frisch and Tinbergen, Kuznets, Leontief, Myrdal, Kantorovich, Koopmans, Friedman, Simon, Lewis and Schultz, Klein, Tobin, Stigler, Stone, Solow, Haavelmo, North, Fogel, Merton and Scholes, Sen, McFadden and Heckman, Kahneman and Smith, Engle and Granger. Formalists (in order of award): Samuelson, Arrow and Hicks, Hayek, Meade and Ohlin, Debreu, Modigliani, Buchanan, Allais, Markowitz and Miller and Sharpe, Coase, Becker, Harsanyi and Nash and Selten, Lucas, Mirrlees and Vickrey, Mundell, Akerlof and Spence and Stiglitz, Kydland and Prescott, Aumann and Schelling.

aligned with the conservative one seen earlier in figure 5.1. It was followed with two empirical wavelets after 1997 and 2000. As in the case of political orientation, the numbers are evenly matched, with twenty-eight empirics and twenty-nine formalists over the period as a whole, and empirics slightly ahead in the citation count. Empirics and formalists were found on both sides of politics.

EMPIRICS

There is a view that the Nobel Prize is dominated by theory, and is quite remote from reality. According to Jon Elster,

> Many of the economists who have received the Alfred Nobel Memorial Prize for Economic Science work within the paradigms of rational choice theory and statistical modeling. Yet is a noteworthy fact that not a single one of them has been awarded the prize for confirmed empirical predictions.[9]

---

9. Elster, 'Excessive Ambitions' (2009), 20. He made an exception for Kahneman.

Phrased in this way, the statement may be correct. But in his article, Elster applies a different test, which is the discovery of 'novel facts'.[10] Empirical NPWs have provided these in abundance.

NATIONAL ACCOUNTS

The best empirical program in twentieth-century economics was national accounting. Estimates of the aggregate income, output, and wealth of nations go back to William Petty and Gregory King in the seventeenth century, and continued periodically with growing sophistication in many countries.[11] The first official estimates were prepared initially in the United States by Simon Kuznets (NPW, 1971) and published by the federal government from the mid-1930s onwards. In Britain, the first official estimates were published in 1941. John Maynard Keynes caused them to be prepared in the Treasury, by James Meade (NPW, 1977) and Richard Stone (NPW, 1984).

'National accounts' provide a comprehensive quantitative double-entry bookkeeping model of the economy as a whole, with total income on one side, expenditure on the other, and output as a check on both. The income on one side appears as expenditure on the other. Each aggregate table is constructed bottom-up from statistical data on segments and sectors of the economy. The ability to monitor the movement of the economy annually, quarterly, and even monthly is immensely useful to government, business, commentators, academics, and voters. It did not take long for the numbers to enter into everyday use.

National accounting was an empirical, pragmatic, and practical model of general equilibrium, based on a deep understanding and knowledge of the economy. The founders gave primacy to observation over theory. They did not reject mathematical logic or statistical rigour. What they questioned were deductive models of general equilibrium originating with Walras, Pareto, Hicks, Samuelson, and Arrow-Debreu, which implied that markets necessarily allocated resources efficiently, that market outcomes were always for the best. Simon Kuznets (NPW, 1971), their doyen, thought that the task of theory was to specify what needs to be measured. Theory was not immutable.

---

10.   Ibid., 6, 23–24.
11.   The next few pages derive from Offer, 'Charles Hilliard Feinstein' (2008); Studenski, *The Income of Nations* (1967); Kendrick, 'Historical Development of National-Income Accounts' (1970); Carson, 'History of the United States National Income and Product Accounts' (1975); Vanoli, *A History of National Accounting* (2005).

It identified a set of empirical regularities, which needed to be revised in the light of new knowledge and changing social values. It was unwise to accept data without understanding how they came into being. More than one model could be fitted to any set of data, and a good statistical fit could not in itself guarantee correctness. His method was essentially inductive: 'from measurement to estimation to classification to explanation to speculation.'[12]

Richard Stone (NPW, 1984) also questioned grand theory. For the epigraph of one of his national income volumes, he chose a dialogue from the satirical novel *Crochet Castle* (1831) by Thomas Love Peacock. Mr Mac Quedy praises the modern political economy as 'the science of sciences'. He is mocked by

THE REV. DR FOLLIOTT. 'A hyperbarbarous technology, that no Athenian ear could have borne. Premises assumed without evidence, or in spite of it; and conclusions drawn from them so logically, that they must necessarily be erroneous.'[13]

A second epigraph from Alfred Marshall spelled out the proper relation between theory and practice:

the work of the economist is 'to disentangle the interwoven effects of complex causes'; and that for this, general reasoning is essential, but a wide and thorough study of facts is equally essential, and that a combination of the two sides of the work is *alone* economics *proper*.[14]

Wassily Leontief (NPW, 1973), the inter-war developer of input-output analysis (another system of general equilibrium that partly overlaps with national accounting and is now integral to it) made similar points.[15] In an interview towards the end of his life he said, 'Essentially, theory organizes facts. . . . Practical advice could and should be more based on understanding how the system works.'[16] Unlike Arrow-Debreu general equilibrium, which is only known to 'exist', input-output analysis has numerical solutions and allows practical policy analysis.

Kuznets, Stone, and Leontief were not mindless empiricists. Kuznets originated cyclical theories of economic activity and inequality. Leontief was

---

12. Lundberg, 'Simon Kuznets' Contribution to Economics' (1971), 460; Fogel, 'Simon S. Kuznets' (2000).
13. Stone and Rowe, *The Measurement of Consumers' Expenditure and Behaviour* (1954), xxiv.
14. Italics in original.
15. Leontief, 'Implicit Theorizing' (1937); idem, 'Theoretical Assumptions and Nonobserved Facts' (1971).
16. Foley, 'Interview with Leontief' (1998), 121, 126.

a mathematician and theorist. In an interview he said: 'When I developed input-output analysis it was as a response to the weaknesses of classical-neoclassical supply-and-demand analysis. . . . I felt that general equilibrium theory does not see how to integrate the facts.'[17]

Like other innovations of the 1930s (in radar, electronic computing, jet propulsion, and nuclear physics), what began as an academic challenge, became a technology in service of government within less than a decade. It is enduring and pervasive. It works unobtrusively in business, scholarship, politics and the media. Government took up national accounting as a lever for action; to influence the aggregates of income, expenditure and output, they had to be measured. For national accountants, both observation and deduction have a role in science, and they discipline each other. Its rationalist, deductive rivals (especially the New Classical Macro) are less modest in their ambitions, but (with their assumption of rational behaviour) resemble belief systems more than failsafe techniques.

National accounting made it easier for governments to provide those services that only governments can provide, or those they provide more efficiently (education, health, social insurance, central banking, infrastructure), and thus to satisfy the aspirations of voters. It is the core tool of Social Democracy. Indeed, national accounting has gone beyond measuring the spending choices of voters and into shaping their aspirations, by setting up the gross domestic product (GDP) as a prosperity target, and by tracing it from quarter to quarter. This success in devising a working model of the economy is one reason why governments have become so large and indispensable, why in many countries even conservatives have acted like Social Democrats, in order to satisfy the popular expectations that Social Democracy created. Since the 1980s, the construction of national accounts has passed into the hands of government statistical offices, away from the scrutiny of academics, where they have become susceptible to administrative mismanagement and political manipulation.[18]

National accounting opened up a tremendous trove of new data, which is constantly expanding and unfolding. The components and aggregates were novel scientific facts, aspects of reality which could not be measured before. In his Nobel Lecture of 1984, Richard Stone sketched out the inductive approach to policy (figure 7.2), with a feedback relation between theory and

17. Ibid., 117–118.
18. Martin, 'Resurrecting the UK Historic Sector National Accounts' (2009); Williams, 'John Williams' Shadow Government Statistics'.

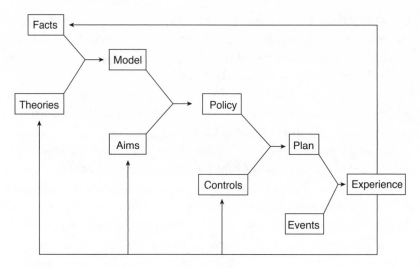

Figure 7.2. Richard Stone, 'Models, Policies and Plans'.
Source: Stone, 'The Accounts of Society', Nobel Lecture 1984, 116.

policy. The crucial link is the feedback loop from experience to theory, the assumption that theory and policy should both be responsive and flexible. This looks like the 'piecemeal social engineering' recommended by Karl Popper as the antidote to utopian thinking in *The Open Society and Its Enemies*.[19] National accounting was progressive, in the scientific sense that it originated innovation at Nobel Prize–level standard. Jan Tinbergen (NPW, 1969) was the first to construct a dynamic empirical national income model of the economy. Using a different approach, Lawrence Klein (NPW, 1980) constructed macroeconomic models of the US economy based on national accounting data, for use in forecasting.

Klein's approach was the target of a famous critique in 1976, by Robert Lucas (NPW, 1995), on the grounds that past regularities were no guide to the future: when a policy change was announced, people would anticipate its effect, and their action to avoid it would undo the policy. Hence policy intervention was futile. Instead, Lucas pursued the real business cycle approach, mentioned in chapter 1. For empirical support ('calibration', also described above), it still depended on comparisons with national accounting data. But the real business cycles approach had a poor empirical record, and was not conducive to effective policy-making. The adjustment predicted by

---

19. Popper, *The Open Society and Its Enemies* (1945/1957), II, 222.

the Lucas critique proved difficult to detect. In contrast, the large econometric models pioneered by Klein continue to be used by central banks and government, although, like national accounting, they are no longer constructed
in universities.[20]

James Tobin (NPW, 1981) worked to incorporate money and taxation
into Keynesian macroeconomic policy, to extend national accounting to encompass non-market variables such as household production, and to take
account of the negative aspects of economic growth. Robert Solow (NPW,
1987) developed an aggregate growth model using national accounting data
which showed, in particular, that conventional factors of production (capital and labour) leave approximately half of economic growth unaccounted
for. This 'residual' was identified with innovation and technical change. National accounting was a fecund source of good models and novel facts, and
a great success story.

MILTON FRIEDMAN AND CHICAGO EMPIRICS

Empirics were not exclusively on the left. If Social Democracy is the benchmark, then Milton Friedman (NPW, 1976) was its most influential adversary.
Early on, he criticized rent control, a social intervention intended to mitigate
monopoly pricing. His permanent income model of consumption implied
that Social Democracy was unnecessary (not its main purpose, which was to
query the consumption function, an aspect of Keynesian economics). The
future could be provided for by saving and borrowing. But he acknowledged
poverty as a problem, and its relief as an obligation. He proposed a negative
income tax to bring incomes up to a social minimum, and several trials
were conducted. Although designed as an alternative to Social Democracy
(perhaps as a way of making it unnecessary, or to make it easy to abolish),
it overlapped with the Social Democratic aspiration to place a floor under
incomes.

One of Friedman's preoccupations was financial and price stability. His
Monetary History of the United States attempted to demonstrate empirically
that a contraction of the money supply was the main cause of the Great Depression. The cure ('monetarism') was to replace central bank discretion with
a rule: for the central bank to increase the money supply at a steady and predictable rate consistent with the trend of economic growth. This turned out

---

20. Chapter 1, above, 28–33.

to be impractical because the money supply was not fully understood. This failure should be taken as a virtue of Friedman's empirical method, which exposed itself to falsification.[21] Monetarism was also a substitute for the Keynesian (and Social Democratic) objective of trying to keep down the level of unemployment. Friedman asserted the existence of a 'natural' non-inflationary level of unemployment (itself a version of the Keynesian Phillips Curve relation between unemployment and inflation). Like the money supply, it has proven difficult to pin down, which has not diminished its popularity in policy discourse.[22]

Friedman was hostile to trade unions (and indeed to all professional organizations), on the grounds that they restricted competition. Inconsistently, he and his followers did not regard business monopolies as anti-competitive in the same way. His innovations supported the business challenge to Social Democracy, and he eventually took over from Hayek as the leading figure in the Mont Pèlerin Society. In the early 1970s, at the height of his influence, he was among the most cited economists of all, overtaking Adam Smith and Karl Marx for a while. Like the national accountants, the empirical tradition he stood for was further acknowledged by the Nobel, in the persons of his Chicago colleagues Theodore Schultz (NPW, 1979) and George Stigler (NPW, 1982), who applied a similar empirical approach to economic development, and to regulation and information, respectively.

INSTITUTIONALISTS

Six NPW institutionalists each showed differently how social organization affected economic outcomes. This defied methodological individualism, but only two of them were on the left.

In the course of his career, Gunnar Myrdal (NPW, 1974), travelled all the way from conservative to Social Democrat, and from formalist to institutionalist. After a doctoral thesis in 1927 (which the Nobel Committee cited in its award), he published a compelling book showing how economic doctrines were saturated with value biases.[23] In particular, he rejected the harmony of interests implied by equilibrium theory. After a detour into monetary theory, he abandoned economic analysis for large social surveys and

---

21. Mayer, 'The Twilight of the Monetarism Debate' (1990).
22. Mayer, 'The Twilight of the Monetarism Debate' (1990); Pierce, 'Monetarism: The Good, the Bad and the Ugly' (1995).
23. Myrdal, *Political Element in the Development of Economic Theory* (1930/1990).

senior policy positions. His most notable subsequent achievements were two massive studies of the condition of black people in the United States and of development in Southeast Asia. Among Nobel economists, he was unique as a theorist and activist of Social Democracy and of the welfare state.[24]

Arthur Lewis and Theodore Schultz (NPWs, 1979) were both development economists and institutionalists. Lewis's 'dual economy' model insisted that rural overpopulation made incentives futile in agriculture, and that development called for 'big push' urbanization and industrial development. In contrast, Schultz demonstrated that third world peasants responded rationally to incentives, and made the best of their opportunities. The Norwegian Trygve Haavelmo (NPW, 1989) received the prize for econometric innovation made more than four decades before, but in his Nobel Lecture chose to focus on the failures of econometrics, which he attributed to its association with individualist economic theory. 'Consider this,' he said, 'In the world today there are more than five billion people. If they should try to live without being members of some society, I suppose most of them would be dead in a few weeks.'[25]

In his Nobel Lecture, Ronald Coase (NPW, 1991) condemned the 'blackboard economics' that treated the firm as an individual, without seeking to open its 'black box' or consider its internal mechanisms. Markets failed because transactions were costly. The counterfactual 'Coase theorem' (a term coined by Stigler, not Coase) stated that if transactions were costless, markets would deliver resources into hands best qualified to use them, regardless of their initial ownership. But this was a utopian doctrine, as unreal as other versions of the invisible hand. Firms existed because trading was costly. The economic historian Douglass North (NPW, 1993) estimated that 45 percent of US gross national product (GNP) consisted of transaction costs. His Nobel Lecture stated bluntly that neoclassical economics failed because it ignored institutions and historical time.[26] The other economic historian that year, Robert Fogel (NPW, 1993), wrote about the institution of slavery in the United States, arguing that it was economically as efficient as free farming. What he meant to say was that it was as profitable, which is not the same thing. This finding was hardly consistent with the economic conception of

24. Cherrier, 'Gunnar Myrdal and the Scientific Way to Social Democracy' (2009); Jackson, *Gunnar Myrdal and America's Conscience* (1990); Barber, *Gunnar Myrdal* (2008).
25. Haavelmo, 'Econometrics and the Welfare State', Nobel Lecture 1989.
26. North, 'Economic Performance through Time', Nobel Lecture 1993.

efficiency, which stressed free choice, or with its focus on individual welfare, such individuals presumably including slaves.

James Buchanan (NPW, 1986) was a formalist but also an institutionalist, an originator of public choice doctrine, whose central premise was that majority rule undermined the efficiency of free markets. Electoral majorities were inclined to tax wealthy minorities, while public servants were just as likely as anyone to look after themselves. The solution was to bind majorities with constitutional rules, ideally by supermajorities. This actually obtains in the United States, where constitutional changes, impeachment of senior officials, and overriding presidential vetoes require large majorities, and even routine legislation in Congress effectively requires the approval of 60 percent of the Senate. The consequences are policy gridlock working against the liberal majority, as envisaged by public choice theory. It is rarely noticed that the public choice requirement for unanimity is identical to the standard economic optimality target of 'Pareto efficiency', in which a single holdout is allowed to veto any change, and prior endowments are privileged.

AGAINST ORTHODOXY

The last three groups of empirics consist of experimentalists, econometricians, and behavioural economists, already reviewed in chapter 2. What they had in common was agnosticism or even outright rejection of equilibrium doctrines, and the combination of invisible hand and rational choice. Among the behaviourists, Herbert Simon (NPW, 1978) and Daniel Kahneman (NPW, 2002) reported empirical findings not compatible with the assumption of rationality, in its formal sense of consistency.

People strove to do the best for themselves, but were frustrated by cognitive limitations, their inability to acquire and process sufficient information. They suffered from innate biases, notably in experiencing losses more acutely than gains of the same magnitude. This asymmetry of gain and loss undermined the standard economic technique of defining value in terms of foregone alternatives ('opportunity cost'). That actual preferences fail the test of consistency had already been demonstrated experimentally in the 1950s by the formalist Allais (NPW, 1988) in the paradox named for him. A third behavioural economist, Vernon Smith (NPW, 2002), reported that a large proportion of participants in social experiments rejected selfish options. Most of them followed a norm of reciprocity, rather than of fairness or altruism.[27] In market simulations, however, results converged onto efficient outcomes, regardless of how poorly informed the players were. This was at odds with the perfect information assumptions of rational choice, game theory, and microeconomics more generally, but accorded with Hayek's view of the market as a price-discovery system working to compensate for the cognitive and informational limitations of individuals, and also with Friedman's claim that markets work as if firms maximized profits and markets were perfectly competitive.[28]

MARKET ALTERNATIVES TO SOCIAL DEMOCRACY

Empirics did not take up the challenge of Social Democracy. That challenge was how to provide access to resources over the life cycle in the face of uncertainty. Social Democracy's solution, as we have seen, was lateral transfers between the generations and investment in education, health, and infrastructure. Among the Nobel empirics, neither social insurance nor public finance received any recognition, and they did not loom large as academic fields. Among the empirical prize winners, Milton Friedman's basic income entitlement (in the form of a negative income tax) did not provide for contingencies like serious illness or acute dependency. Two empirical economists did however grapple directly with the issue, by applying the standard orthodox approach, namely the use of financial markets.

Robert Merton and Myron Scholes (NPWs, 1997) were among the originators of efficient markets theory in finance, and the latter in particular being an originator of the Black-Scholes model of option prices, which guided market financial strategies from the 1980s onwards. The two also consulted commercially, and Merton in particular, in his Nobel Lecture, made a virtue of this activity. They both became directors of Long-Term Capital Management, a hedge fund which applied their methods on a grand scale. Less than a year after their Nobel award, the fund collapsed, and was bailed out by the Federal Reserve and Wall Street firms to forestall the possibility of contagion. In October 2007, with the great crash unfolding, their scholarship and

---

27.   Smith, 'Constructivist and Ecological Rationality in the Economics', Nobel Lecture 2002; Offer, 'Between the Gift and the Market: The Economy of Regard' (1997).
28.   Smith, 'Constructivist and Ecological Rationality in the Economics', Nobel Lecture 2002.

the Nobel Prize were thrashed in the *Financial Times* by Nassim Nicholas Taleb, a contrarian author and market trader:

> in 1997, the Royal Swedish Academy of Sciences awarded the prize to Robert Merton and Myron Scholes for their option pricing formula. I (and many traders) find the prize offensive. . . . The environment in financial economics is reminiscent of medieval medicine, which refused to incorporate the observations and experiences of the plebeian barbers and surgeons. Medicine used to kill more patients than it saved—just as financial economics endangers the system by creating, not reducing, risk. But how did financial economics take on the appearance of a science? Not by experiments (perhaps the only true scientist who got the prize was Daniel Kahneman, who happens to be a psychologist, not an economist). It did so by drowning us in mathematics with abstract 'theorems'. Prof Merton's book *Continuous Time Finance* contains 339 mentions of the word 'theorem' (or equivalent). An average physics book of the same length has 25 such mentions. Yet while economic models, it has been shown, work hardly better than random guesses or the intuition of cab drivers, physics can predict a wide range of phenomena with a tenth decimal precision. Every time I have questioned these methods I have been abruptly countered with: 'they have the Nobel', which I have found impossible to argue with.[29]

JUST WORLD THEORY AGAIN

Just World Theories state that everyone gets what they deserve. Both Social Democracy and market liberalism were Just World Theories.[30] Market liberalism was firmly individualist, insisting that prior endowments of wealth and personal attributes, and the outcomes of market trading, were both efficient and just, and should not be interfered with. In contrast, the Social Democratic version was all-embracing and universalistic, assuming that everyone was entitled by virtue of membership in the community.

From the outset, market-clearing equilibrium economics was a harmony theory: It justified the existing distribution of property and income. Neoclassical formalists of a more liberal inclination might acknowledge that their efficiency criterion of 'Pareto optimality' (all resources fully used) was ethically unattractive: it did not exclude the possibility of one person having

---

29. Taleb, 'The Pseudoscience Hurting Markets' (2007).
30. Introduction, above, 3–4.

everything and everyone else nothing. Their concession took the form of acknowledging that equity might require a more equal distribution of incomes, but this should only happen by means of redistributive taxation after markets have delivered their outcomes. Markets were efficient and taxation was not. Effectively, this was a choice for a different distribution of assets, which would allow a different Pareto-optimal distribution. Those liberals who made this concession (for example, Mirrlees in his Nobel Lecture of 1996) were not entirely clear about whether the justification was compassion or a concession to politics. Whatever it was, redistribution was economically inefficient, and gave rise to the so-called equity/efficiency trade-off.[31]

Formalism is a kind of faith. At its heart is a set of unquestioned premises. Gary Becker (NPW, 1992) summarized his own version: 'The combined assumptions of maximizing behavior, market equilibrium, and stable preferences, used relentlessly and unflinchingly, form the heart of the economic approach as I see it.'[32] The neoclassical solution to the life-cycle welfare problem is to lock in financial claims, and to trade them in financial markets. Rational individuals allocated resources over their life cycle in order to smooth consumption, by borrowing when income was low, saving when it was high, and dis-saving when the need arose, especially in old age. The life-cycle consumption model, first developed by Richard Brumberg and Franco Modigliani (NPW, 1985), assumes (1) access to credit, and to credible savings contracts; (2) costless transactions; (3) perfect information (personal, or at least in the aggregate); (4) that any contingency (however large) can be managed with an individual household's resources, or insured in financial markets.

Credible contracts imply either perfect information for all time, costless enforcement, or pervasive good faith. Effectively, such models abolish the future. With no uncertainty, there is no future to worry about, and since preferences are innate and people are smart, the economic problem is merely the computational one of maximizing present value. Welfare should be provided by market institutions: private health, private education, private insurance and private pension markets.[33] For conservative economists, this implied that if everyone provided privately for themselves, then taxes could come down for the better off, ideally to their ultra-low levels before 1914.

---

31. Okun, *Equality and Efficiency: The Big Tradeoff* (1975).
32. Becker, *Economic Approach to Human Behavior* (1976), 5.
33. An extreme proponent is the otherwise sceptical NPW Shiller, *The New Financial Order* (2003).

In Sweden, for example, the two leading economists in the 1920s and 1930s (Cassel and Heckscher) railed against the progressive taxation of the nascent Social Democracy.[34] The stalwarts of the status quo responded to high-tax post-war regimes with a succession of landmark moves: Hayek's *The Road to Serfdom* (1944) and his creation of the Mont Pèlerin Society in 1947; Milton Friedman's *Capitalism and Freedom* (1962); and Buchanan and Tullock's *The Calculus of Consent* (1962). All of these received the Nobel Prize, with members of the Mont Pèlerin Society collecting a total of eight by 2005. Their resistance was not futile: top tax rates fell sharply in the 1980s, while the total tax take did not, thus helping to drive a sharp rise in inequality in English-speaking countries during the 1980s.[35]

FROM HARMONY TO BAD FAITH

After World War II, Social Democracy replaced laissez faire as the new status quo. One response in economics, especially on the formalist side, was a shift from extolling the harmony of interests to an assumption of bad faith. In an inversion of Just World Theory, people no longer received what they deserved, but reached out for what they did not deserve. A sequence of innovations developed this message in various forms, and most were eventually acknowledged by a Nobel Prize. They brought a fresh realism into the discipline. But realism came at a cost: no longer a single best outcome, which economists could recommend with confidence. Instead, a range of possible equilibria, none of them certain and many of them bad.

The most consequential innovation for economic method was game theory, which models the interaction of individuals each seeking an advantage. The two main implications (from our point of view) are the opportunities for strategic behaviour, namely the exploitation of uncertainty and dissimulation, and the consequent result of many possible outcomes, depending on who has prevailed. In contrast, the previous good-faith economics had converged on one equilibrium outcome, which was also the best one. Welfare economics was normative: economists could tell you what to do: eliminate market 'distortions', and you would be better off. Game theory was indeterminate: outcomes depended on cunning, not wisdom, that is, on how well the strategies worked out in adversarial settings. Market outcomes could no

---

34. Myrdal, *Political Element* (1930/1990), xli; Carlson, *The State as Monster* (1994), 198–203.
35. Alvaredo et al., 'The Top 1 Percent in Historical Perspective' (2013).

longer be taken as optimal. Anthony Downs and Mancur Olson developed economic theories of democracy, in which the common good was thwarted. Buchanan and Tullock's public choice theory conveyed the same message, and argued that democracy undermined both freedom and efficiency.[36]

The motivational doctrine of rational choice that swept through the social sciences and philosophy in the 1960s and 1970s placed self-regard at the heart of even the popular ethical theory of John Rawls.[37] The Coase theorem seemed to promote the cause of allocative market efficiency, only to gum it up with transaction costs in its descriptive version.[38] Arnold Harberger showed how taxation was always a 'deadweight cost.'[39] George Stigler demonstrated that market regulation was bound to be ineffective, while Anne Krueger depicted public officials as handing out favours to highest bidders.[40]

Innovations from the left had a similar effect of undermining confidence in the Social Democratic status quo. The novelty was to assume asymmetric information. For example, welfare claimants might fake a disability. On the other hand, asymmetric information reinforced Social Democracy by undermining belief in the invisible hand. Early work was done during the 1970s, by Kenneth Arrow, George Akerlof, James Mirrlees, Joseph Stiglitz, and Michael Spence, to mention only NPWs. Concepts such as principal/agent, the market for lemons, signalling, moral hazard, adverse selection, incomplete contracts, all indicated that market outcomes were neither wholesome nor trustworthy. The prevailing (and appropriate) attitude in markets was no longer good faith, but (in the words of Oliver Williamson, NPW, 2009) 'opportunism', defined as 'self-interest seeking with guile.'[41] In sum, markets were no longer guided by an invisible hand, but could equally inflict an 'invisible backhand.'[42]

NPWs included, among the formalists, a large group sympathetic to Social Democracy, who tried to bend the market frame to make room for their values. They suggested two modifications. The first was the assumption of

---

36. Downs, *An Economic Theory of Democracy* (1957); Olson, *The Logic of Collective Action* (1965); Kreps, *Game Theory and Economic Modelling* (1990); Buchanan and Tullock, *The Calculus of Consent* (1962). See above, 24, 160.

37. Rawls, *A Theory of Justice* (1971); Green and Shapiro, *Pathologies of Rational Choice Theory* (1994).

38. Coase, 'The Institutional Structure of Production', Nobel Lecture 1991.

39. Hines, 'Three Sides of Harberger Triangles' (1999); and see below, 199–203.

40. Stigler, 'Economic Theory of Regulation' (1971); Krueger, 'The Political Economy of the Rent-Seeking Society' (1974).

41. Williamson, 'Transaction-Cost Economics' (1979), 234n.

42. Brennan and Pettit, 'Hands Invisible and Intangible' (1993), 191.

finite lives. Paul Samuelson (NPW, 1970) showed the way with his model of two overlapping generations, one working and one retired. It was difficult for the two generations to strike a credible deal to make sure that workers supported pensioners. In a suggestive concluding statement, Samuelson said that the problem could be solved either by social insurance, or through the medium of money, by means of financial markets.[43] Quite separately, he also endorsed and formalized the concept of 'public goods', those which everyone wanted, but which it was in nobody's interest to pay for himself. He also dropped a hint that universal provision would dispense with the need for cheating.[44]

The second modification was asymmetric information. If some parties had better information than others, then a role emerged for society. Kenneth Arrow (NPW, 1972) gave the example of healthcare, where patients depended critically on professional expertise (opaque to them) of doctors and nurses. Government could help by regulating qualifications and services.[45] Perhaps Arrow was provoked by Milton Friedman's idea of deregulating medical practice, and placing the onus of quality control on the patients.[46] But for both Samuelson and Arrow, their endorsement of non-market solutions was lukewarm. Arrow went out of his way to criticize the British system of voluntary blood donations, insisting that markets for blood were better.[47] He had previously argued that it was impossible to scale up individual interests into a consistent, agreed, and ethically acceptable set of social priorities (his 'impossibility theorem' of 1951). This latter was later contested by Amartya Sen (NPW, 1998), who demonstrated that consistency was achievable with a slightly different set of priors.[48] Arrow did acknowledge a role for public (that is, non-market) goods by later participating in studies of climate change, and even in something close to heresy in neoclassical terms, a report on whether Western societies were consuming too much; approached from an environmental, 'public bads' point of view, not that of the sovereign individual.[49]

---

43. Samuelson, 'An Exact Consumption-Loan Model of Interest with or without the Social Contrivance of Money' (1958).
44. Samuelson, 'Aspects of Public-Expenditure Theories' (1958), 336.
45. Arrow, 'Uncertainty and the Welfare Economics of Medical Care' (1963).
46. Friedman, *Capitalism and Freedom* (1962), ch. 9; first explored in Friedman and Kuznets, *Income from Independent Professional Practice* (1945).
47. Arrow, 'Gifts and Exchanges' (1972); McLean and Poulton, 'Good Blood, Bad Blood' (1986); Mellstrom and Johannesson, 'Crowding Out in Blood Donation' (2008).
48. Sen, 'The Possibility of Social Choice', Nobel Lecture 1998.
49. Arrow et al., 'Are We Consuming Too Much?' (2004).

Of the formalists, the most orthodoxly Keynesian was James Meade (NPW, 1977), who perceived the economic problem as one of achieving a full-employment equilibrium. The latent inconsistency between Social Democratic values and the formalist orientation came out in the case of Franco Modigliani (NPW, 1985), a liberal associated with two innovations. In the Modigliani-Miller theorem, it made no difference if investment was funded by equity or debt. This appeared to justify the large overhang of debt built up by business and finance from the 1980s onwards, which contributed eventually to the financial crisis of 2008. The other innovation was his life-cycle theory of consumption (already mentioned), which assumed that it was possible to smooth consumption by borrowing early in the life cycle, and running down savings towards the end. During the 1980s and 1990s, economists, policy-makers, and financial corporations followed this lead, and promoted a 'personal responsibility agenda' to wean American workers from collective retirement systems, whether employers' defined-benefit pensions, or the Social Democratic ones of Social Security.[50] Corporate final salary pension schemes were mostly wound down (for workers, not for executives), and the risk transferred to savers through 401(k) funds, in which savings accumulated tax-free but with lower contributions from employers, and heavy charges paid to financial companies. This system generally works much worse than the one it replaced.[51]

In an interview in 1999, Modigliani said that 'we need to abandon the pay-as-you-go system, which is a wasteful and inefficient system and replace it with a fully funded system', that is, a system in which savings are invested in financial claims which pay out retirement income in due course.[52] But evidence points the other way. Pay-as-you-go, the Social Democratic alternative, is an order of magnitude cheaper to administer than a funded system, and its resource base, taxable income, is much larger and more stable than financial asset returns. It is true that it depends on social agreement about the level of transfers, but that level expresses the distributional preferences of society at a particular time, and can be re-negotiated as necessary. A 'funded' system also depends on social consensus (that financial claims will be kept in being for decades and will be honoured come what may).[53] In a later

50. Hacker, *The Great Risk Shift* (2006); Hacker and Pierson, *Winner-Takes-All Politics* (2013); Sabadish and Morrisey, 'Retirement Inequality Chartbook' (2013).
51. Offer, 'Economy of Obligation' (2012); Bogle, *Battle for the Soul of Capitalism* (2005), ch. 7.
52. Barnett and Solow, 'Interview with Franco Modigliani' (2007), 106.
53. Offer, 'Economy of Obligation' (2012).

publication, Modigliani conceded a role for pay-as-you-go, but made a great deal of the contribution of funding to productive savings. Like most economists of the time, he overlooked the fact that most financial assets (especially the largest—mortgages lent against existing real estate) were speculative and volatile, and were conducive to financial instability.[54] Martin Feldstein, an empiricist Harvard economist and a professed Republican, has devoted a good part of his career to criticizing the welfare state, and promoting the very transition to funding that Modigliani advocated.[55] But his own aims were more modest: 'I would move gradually to make a system that preserves some of the current pay-as-you-go structure but at a reduced level combine it with personal retirement accounts.'[56] Modigliani, with his prior commitment to Social Democratic values, subsequently affirmed that only government could guarantee a decent retirement income for everyone in old age. He sought to combine some pay-as-you go taxation with elements of capital market and government funding.[57] In 1959, Social Democratic Sweden set up a funding system for occupational pensions, albeit restricted to investment in public sector securities. Subsequent conservative governments returned to a pay-as-you-go system which preserves some pretence of funding, and has some similarities with Modigliani's proposals.[58]

Asymmetric information was an important modification. Without equal sharing of information, the benefits of perfect competition (such as they are) were not available, and the range of possible outcomes is less benign. The assumption of asymmetric information relaxes the rigid market model, and aligns it with the reality of unequally distributed knowledge and bargaining power. It is the work of the 1970s, in the opposite direction to the rational expectations movement of the same decade (described in chapter 1). George Akerlof, Michael Spence, and Joseph Stiglitz (all NPWs, 2001) demonstrated, each in a different way, that the outcome of market exchange depended on the partial information available to the different parties, and that asymmetries were likely to persist. This was subversive, showing that market outcomes could not be predicted, and that there was a potential role

---

54. Modigliani and Muralidhar, *Rethinking Pension Reform* (2004), ch. 2; Turner, *Between Debt and the Devil* (2015).
55. For example, Feldstein, 'Rethinking Social Insurance' (2005).
56. Poterba, 'Interview with Martin Feldstein' (2007), 202.
57. Modigliani and Muralidhar, *Rethinking Pension Reform* (2004).
58. Hagen, 'History of the Swedish Pension System' (2013).

for society to intervene, if only to equalize bargaining power. Their speculations were amply confirmed in subsequent experiments under laboratory conditions, in which, given the choice, some participants chose to take advantage of their trading partners, while others did not.[59] Two NPWs have recently shown that bad faith is pervasive in the American economy today.[60]

The remaining formalists made no concessions at all to Social Democracy. Most (not all) of them were inclined towards the right. To the extent that they even acknowledged the problems of uncertainty and economic insecurity, they thought that markets would provide. Some of their work has already been considered (for example, Hayek; Lucas and his NCM colleagues). Alone among the formalists, Gary Becker (NPW, 1992) extended his range to social institutions. For Becker, the family and criminality were markets under other names. To make allocation within the household tractable, however, he made a concession of a joint utility within the family, and demonstrated that mutual obligation within the household could be explained that way.

Buchanan, Stigler, and Krueger all stressed the problems of 'government failure', due to the opportunism of officials. But the theoretical efficiency properties of free markets also depended on assumption of good faith, on the absence of opportunism and fraud (or what comes to the same thing, on their costless suppression). But bad faith (behind the veil of asymmetric information) is just as likely in private transactions as in public ones. The formalists were comparing real-life institutions with the perfection of 'Nirvana economics'. And once the primacy of bad faith is accepted, it is not clear why economists themselves should be regarded as impartial sources of advice.

Chicago's response to the economics of bad faith was to develop new models of market-clearing equilibrium, which retained the preferred normative optimality results. From the 1970s onwards, these models took their subject as the whole economy, populated by 'representative agents', typically one consumer and one firm, driven over time by the microeconomic theory that explained individual actions. These theories dispensed with competition, money, finance, government, and public goods, and depended on complicated mathematics. Their empirical performance was poor, and we have covered them in detail in chapter 1.

59. Some described by Smith, 'Constructivist and Ecological Rationality in Economics', Nobel Lecture 2002.
60. Akerlof and Shiller, *Phishing for Phools* (2015).

OPTIMAL TAXATION: FORMALISM APPLIED

The most prescriptive of all Nobel Lectures up to 2005 was delivered in 1996 by James Mirrlees, a formalist who won the prize mostly for his development in 1971 of a theory of 'optimal taxation'.[61] The problem in taxation can be thought of as how to raise revenue at the lowest cost to the economy. It is not the question of how much government expenditure is best. Mirrlees, whose first degree was in mathematics, set out to model 'optimal taxation' using the standard assumptions of neoclassical economics, that is, individual self-seeking, market competition, and equilibrium, with the optimality properties of welfare economics and general equilibrium in mind. The assumption was the standard one that the unfettered exercise of individual choice maximizes aggregate welfare. In his model, people differed only in earning capacity, which was reflected in their wage rate; there was no inheritance or capital income; everyone had identical preferences between leisure and income, and could vary their working time smoothly in response to incentives. The government revenue requirement was given externally. It could be zero if the only purpose was redistribution. Marginal income was equal to marginal productivity, that is, in the labour market, everyone got what they put in.

The one departure from the standard assumptions of complete information was that individual ability could not be observed. Able taxpayers might reduce their effort in order to take advantage of lower tax rates on low incomes, undetected by government. The optimal tax schedule therefore had to be 'incentive-compatible', that is, designed to induce effort and to thwart the gaming of tax brackets. The intuition was that in view of the temptation to mimic low ability, steep marginal taxes were potentially self-defeating.

Even with such unrealistic premises, the exercise turned out to be analytically difficult, and only produced a few general results. Mirrlees highlighted some findings which were strongly counter-intuitive. The most striking one (which Mirrlees never tired of stressing) was that the marginal tax rate on the very top earner (the tax payable on her next increment of income) should be zero. Simulations pointed towards a low linear tax (that is, a fixed proportion of income) of around 20 to 30 percent with optimal marginal tax rates declining as income increased, to discourage withdrawal of effort.[62] This was massively lower than the steeply progressive tax rates imposed by Social Democracy.

---

61. Mirrlees, 'Information and Incentives: The Economics of Carrots and Sticks', Nobel Lecture 1996.
62. 'Optimal Progressivity', elsa.berkeley.edu/~burch/conf04/d2.pdf.

The mathematics were difficult to follow, but the results were a challenge to the high-tax regimes of Social Democracy, and they helped to justify the reduction in tax rates which began soon afterwards.[63] Mirrlees presented them again in his Nobel Lecture of 1996, and later led an official review of UK taxation, which recommended lower income taxes for top earners, and higher consumption taxes for everyone else, at a time of austerity.[64] But these results were only as robust as the assumptions. Indeed, as in the case of Ricardo, they were embodied in the assumptions. Some of them were strongly normative. It was clear to Mirrlees, for example, that 'in general, taxes reduce welfare'.[65] Despite repeatedly invoking a holistic conception of welfare, covering life-cycle and non-monetary satisfactions, in practice his model assumed that private market goods (including leisure) were the only source of well-being (or in economics parlance, 'welfare'). The purpose of tax design was to remove 'distortions', that is, incentives that were not consistent with market signals. The implicit assumptions included that market outcomes were 'efficient', if only in terms of allowing free rein to individual choices. All trade-offs between taxation and leisure were uniform and unchanging for all (that is, stable preferences). Individuals had perfect information (required for the market efficiency result), but government did not. But the assumption that the removal of 'distortions', that is, deviations from untrammelled preferences, is sufficient to ensure optimality (in the Pareto sense) is merely an article of faith. And the Pareto objective of maximizing the sum of individual utilities (subject to a rule of no individual loss) is far from compelling as a welfare objective for society. It says nothing about who gets the increments of welfare.

The model is open to many other criticisms: once asymmetric information is conceded, it is not clear why ignorance and cunning should be applied only to taxation and not to exchange, only to government not to trade. Nor is it clear that people are so sensitive to high levels of taxation, or that leisure is so much more attractive to them than highly taxed work, or that their preferences are uniform. The assumption that payouts are equal to contributions overlooks the role of bargaining power.[66] If corporate executives today earn ten times more (relative to their workers) than they did three decades ago, there is no evidence that their contribution to output (their marginal productivity)

63. Mankiw et al., 'Optimal Taxation in Theory and Practice' (2009).
64. Mirrlees et al., *Tax by Design* (2011).
65. Ibid., vol. 2, 32.
66. Piketty et al., 'Optimal Taxation of Top Labor Incomes' (2014), 238.

has increased so much. This was conceded by Mirrlees, suggesting that these pay grades should perhaps fall outside the model.[67] But how to tax these pay grades is precisely the purpose of the model. It also ignores personal preferences for collective and public goods, which have broad electoral support. A practical example shows how wrong such a model could be. The UK National Health Service (NHS), free at the point of service and paid for by taxation, is assumed in the terms of such models to reduce welfare by the amount of the tax. American healthcare, bought in the market, is about twice as expensive per head, and delivers worse outcomes.[68] Nor is it always obtainable at affordable cost. But in Mirrlees's model, the cost of American healthcare would be an addition to welfare, while the cost of the NHS would reduce welfare.

Criticism continues to mount. Under different plausible assumptions, Peter Diamond (NPW, 2012) and Emmanuel Saez have worked out that the top marginal tax rates should be 78 percent, and not zero. With asymmetric information assumed to be pervasive, there is no reason to think that marginal incomes equal marginal products, or that leisure/work/tax trade-offs are constant.[69] Myopia, addiction, and other cognitive biases suggest that consumer choices do not necessarily maximize their welfare.[70] Mirrlees was aware of these criticisms. He homed in on one form of asymmetric information, namely 'moral hazard'. The term comes from the analysis of insurance contracts, and the temptation to make false claims once insurance is taken out. He conceded that once asymmetric information was admitted, the problem of optimal taxation became insoluble. With donnish understatement he said, 'it is particularly hard to give any general rules ... when the relationship between principal and agent involves moral hazard'.[71] This is another way of making our own point, that bad faith undermines the normative authority of market models. The concessions by Mirrlees did not register, even with himself: the model of optimal taxation continued to hold its canonical authority, and the reservations were not repeated in his government report.[72]

---

67.   Mirrlees, 'Information and Incentives: The Economics of Carrots and Sticks', Nobel Lecture 1996, 33.
68.   Davis et al., *Mirror, Mirror on the Wall* (2010); Offer, 'Warrant for Pain' (2012); Pritchard, 'Comparing the USA, UK and 17 Western Countries' (2011).
69.   Diamond and Saez, 'The Case for a Progressive Tax' (2011); Atkinson, 'The Mirrlees Review' (2012); Piketty et al., 'Optimal Taxation of Top Labor Incomes' (2014); Boadway, *From Optimal Tax Theory to Tax Policy* (2012).
70.   Offer, *The Challenge of Affluence* (2006), chs. 3–4; Atkinson, 'The Mirrlees Review' (2012), 778–779.
71.   Mirrlees, Nobel Lecture, 32.
72.   Atkinson, 'The Mirrlees Review' (2012).

There are other reasons to question Mirrlees's example of normative prescription. Mirrlees assumed an equity/efficiency trade-off and took equity as a legitimate objective: 'There will always be some willingness to sacrifice a part of national income in order to achieve distributional objectives.' But there is no evidence that less equal societies are more successful economically (or happier). The empirical consensus is now the opposite, namely, that redistribution enhances efficiency.[73] And overall, economic performance in advanced societies during the high-tax period after World War II was superior to the more unequal tax-cutting period which followed. Mirrlees never considered a role for tax as social insurance, which we have argued is its main purpose.

Optimal taxation demonstrates how liberal formalists could end up endorsing conservative norms. They put together hybrid theories which combined the bad faith of asymmetric information with the good faith implicitly assumed in equilibrium analysis.[74] This cannot be justified. Optimality implies a single outcome, and bad faith outcomes are indeterminate. This failure of prescriptive economic theory is rarely acknowledged. Unlike members of the Mont Pèlerin Society, Mirrlees had no overt political agenda, and was not of the right. He accepted the legitimacy of equity and re-distribution. Critics show that the model, with its prescriptive thrust, depends on its assumptions. In his taxation report, Mirrlees looked for empirical support, but the evidence did not justify the confidence of the recommendations.[75] The French economist Thomas Piketty (himself an optimal taxation theorist) has written that

> Some economists have an unfortunate tendency to defend their private interest while implausibly claiming to champion the general interest. . . . For example, by using abstruse theoretical models designed to prove that the richest people should pay zero tax or even receive subsidies.[76]

There is no reason to assume that Mirrlees had any ulterior motives. What optimal taxation shows is the power of theory alone, with assumptions adopted by convention, to arrive at conclusions that serve the privileged.

---

73.   Osberg, 'The Equity/Efficiency Tradeoff in Retrospect' (1995); Ostry et al., 'Redistribution, Inequality, and Growth' (2014); Cingano, 'Trends in Income Inequality and Its Impact on Economic Growth' (2014); Dabla-Norris et al., 'Causes and Consequences of Income Inequality' (2015).
74.   On hybrid theories, Kohn, 'Value and Exchange' (2004).
75.   Atkinson, 'The Mirrlees Review' (2012), 774.
76.   Piketty, *Capital in the Twenty-First Century* (2014), 514, and n. 55, 640.

CHAPTER 8

MODELS INTO POLICY: ASSAR LINDBECK AND SWEDISH SOCIAL DEMOCRACY

THE CONCEPT OF SOCIAL DEMOCRACY

Economists first took their place among the Nobel Prize winners in 1969, at the height of the golden age of Social Democracy in Sweden. The prize was paid by the central bank out of public money. It eventually turned into something of a Trojan horse: Swedish Social Democracy was challenged in the name of doctrines honoured by the prize it had created.

Social Democracy arose in defiance of market-clearing equilibrium economics. To simplify, orthodox economics takes the allocation mechanism of market exchange as being inherently superior to any alternatives. It has no issue with the inequality of assets that people bring with them into the market, their different endowments of wealth, connections, ability, education and health; nor does it query the unequal rewards they receive. In Europe between the wars, this belief in market norms was shaken by the traumas of unemployment and poverty. In contrast, Social Democracy regarded the market for labour as predatory and wasteful. It refused to privilege prior endowments and market allocations, and when it came into power, it intervened to modify them. Up to the 1930s, Sweden had turbulent industrial relations, with demonstrations, lockouts, and strikes. The Swedish Social Democratic Party (SAP), already the largest in Parliament from 1914 onwards, attained stable power in 1932. In 1938, employers and trade unions agreed to negotiate wage levels centrally, and industrial unrest became a thing of the past. That was another rejection of raw market outcomes, and, on the face of it, also an efficient one.

For many economists, these interventions went against the grain of their beliefs. Social Democracy might achieve more equity, but in doing so, it was likely to hold back prosperity. In the absence of market incentives, why should anyone make an effort? Neoclassical economic theory asserted that market competition would maximize efficiency.[1] The theory was premised on 'perfect competition', an abstract construct in which people existed only as individual producers and consumers, buyers and sellers. This matchstick model was extrapolated by analogy: policy should strive to expose production, distribution, and exchange to the prices prevailing in functioning markets.

This doctrine of efficiency has never been proven analytically for any conditions approaching reality. It is not even easy to define what such efficiency would consist of. Efficiency for whom? We have discussed its shortcomings in previous chapters, and it is good to keep them in mind. Economic textbooks acknowledged that markets might fail, but market exchange was always the point of departure. In Sweden after World War I, economic teaching was driven by the 'very uncompromising laissez faire doctrine' of Gustav Cassel, Eli Heckscher, and Gösta Bagge.[2] Responding to this Victorian obstinacy as its point of departure, the method of Social Democracy was to seek to influence market outcomes. It offered a vision of reciprocal solidarity, in which immediate self-interest was subordinated to collective advantage. Already in the 1930s, Swedish Social Democrats took their objectives to be not only equitable, not only compassionate, but also productive and efficient.[3] To achieve these objectives, Social Democracy was willing to pull health, education, welfare, and housing out of the market, to de-commodify the provision of well-being.[4]

After World War II, Western Europe and the United States constructed their economies on foundations of manufacturing and exports. The people who worked in these industries tended to vote for Social Democracy. They often had excellent skills, but many had not been given the opportunity to complete a secondary school education.[5] Under Social Democratic governments, and with strong trade unions, workers did better than

---

1. Above, 3–4, 18–19.
2. Bergström, 'Nationalekonomerna'; Korpi, 'Eurosclerosis and the Sclerosis of Objectivity' (1977), 382; Carlson, *The State as Monster* (1994), ch. 11; quote from Myrdal, *The Political Element* (1930/1990), xli.
3. Myrdal, 'Ett Bra Land' (1977), 242–243; Andersson, *Between Growth and Security* (2006), ch. 2.
4. Esping-Andersen, *Three Worlds of Welfare Capitalism* (1990).
5. Korpi, *The Working-class in Welfare Capitalism* (1978).

had they bargained on their own. In Sweden, the Social Democratic Party (SAP) built up a sociable environment for its rank and file. It took supporters into its confidence with a large-circulation daily newspaper, a system of adult education, and a profusion of meetings and local events. Its slogan 'The People's Home' reached out to society more widely.[6] But the wealthy continued to provide for themselves, and the educated, managerial and professional middle classes might have preferred to earn enough to do so. Social Democracy was popular, but it rarely achieved a parliamentary majority in the Swedish lower house, even after governing for decades. Social Democracy was a considerable economic success. By 1969, the year of the first Nobel Prize, Sweden was among the four wealthiest countries in the world, along with the United States, Switzerland, and Canada.

In the immediate post-war years, the SAP's first priority in government was full employment, and this was pursued by keeping interest rates below their notional market-clearing levels. At the same time, farm prices were set above world market levels. The SAP remembered wartime shortages, and owed its parliamentary allies, the Agrarian Party. Rent control on urban dwellings, inherited from the war years, was not repealed. Housing is a challenge for market societies. If both labour and housing markets are competitive, low earners are likely to be priced out of dwellings. So rents were controlled, while (starting in the 1960s) Sweden carried out a 'million house' building programme, in a country of little more than eight million inhabitants.

In 1951, the trade union economists Gösta Rehn and Rudolf Meidner devised a wage-bargaining framework, the solidarity wage, with a norm of equal pay for equal work, intended to compress wage differentials. This bore heavily on weaker industries and firms, and prevented workers in stronger ones from making full use of their market power. It encouraged workers and businesspeople to move from low to high productivity activities, with assistance from an active labour market policy to retrain workers and subsidize the disabled, immobile, and old. It was also intended to contain inflationary wage pressures. Over time, income differentials between a cabinet minister and skilled manual worker fell from 8:1 in 1938 to 2:1 in 1980. Against the Rehn-Meidner model, it was argued that heavy taxes on income (which financed social insurance and public goods) discouraged initiative and effort.

---

6. Berman, 'The *Folkhem* Was a Success Story' (2004).

But taxes on business were kept low in order to encourage investment, and government subsidized some industries.[7]

For an economist nurtured on the smooth elegance of market allocation, Social Democracy was not easy to justify. For the policy to work, it required a commitment to solidarity, trust, and reciprocity among trade union members, and an ability to perceive larger goals beyond their immediate market interests which workers in English-speaking countries have largely failed to achieve. External observers were right to identify these nebulous norms as the heart of Swedish Social Democracy.[8] For proletarian voters (the main source of SAP support), the pursuit of a rough equality was reasonable: they were not in competition with each other. Social insurance and reciprocity reduced insecurity and dependency for manual workers.[9] Other classes might find equality less compelling, but the proletarians were numerous, and their norm of equality, as formed in the Social Democratic community, came to inspire society more widely, and in important respects continues to do so today. The alternative economic vision of market allocation was actually quite nebulous, and allowed, among pragmatic economists, a variety of exceptions which made it as amorphous as Social Democracy. Most economists in English-speaking and European countries were personally inclined towards Social Democracy and have continued to be so.[10]

Nevertheless, for the last four decades, policy has been dominated by market advocates, and the defenders of Social Democracy are subdued. Market advocates have captured historical Social Democratic parties in many countries, most notably the Democrats in the United States and the Labour Party in Britain, and to some extent in Scandinavia as well. In Sweden, the political breakthrough of market-liberal norms took place (as elsewhere) in the 1980s.[11] But despite this ideological retreat and the alternation of political parties in power, Social Democratic policies continued to prevail in Europe, and arguably even in North America. Economies have largely shifted from manufacturing to services, people are better educated and most (at least in Europe) are also better off. Inequality has risen, and trade unions have declined (less so in Scandinavia). But the priorities of Social Democracy

---

7. Drawing on Heclo and Madsen, *Policy and Politics in Sweden* (1987); Milner, *Sweden: Social Democracy* (1989), ch. 6, and Whyman, *Sweden and the 'Third Way'* (2003).

8. Milner, *Sweden: Social Democracy* (1989), 38–39, and chs. 2–3.

9. Korpi, *The Working-class in Welfare Capitalism* (1978).

10. Chapter 5, above, 116–119.

11. Blyth, 'The Transformation of the Swedish Model' (2001); Lindvall, *The Politics of Purpose* (2004).

continue to govern public expenditure, with extensive social insurance and public goods, supplied or mandated primarily by government. The reason is that Social Democracy is efficient and robust in practice, while the economic case against it, even when made in good faith, is based on models which cannot be made to work even in theory.[12] Arguably, a good deal of market advocacy is driven by the interests of social, business and money elites.[13] But the house that Social Democracy built has proved hard to pull down even as its social and ideological foundations were sinking.

ASSAR LINDBECK'S DILEMMA

A great deal has been written about Sweden in the 1970s and 1980s, even in English.[14] A chronic economic crisis in the 1970s drove voters away from Social Democracy and towards a market liberalism which finally prevailed (for a while) in the 1990s.[15] The focus here is on the role of economic theory. For this purpose, the travails of Social Democracy are followed as they affected the public trajectory of Assar Lindbeck (b. 1930), 'the key figure in Swedish economics.'[16] The discipline of economics in Sweden mostly spoke with one voice in this period,[17] so this method provides for a sharp focus and fewer words.

Emerging initially from the heart of Social Democracy, Lindbeck eventually became one of its most vocal opponents. In the early 1950s, he was a student activist and a confidant of Social Democratic ministers. Four decades later, in 1992, a 'bourgeois' (centre-right) coalition government appointed him to lead an important policy commission, which endorsed and extended the market-liberal agenda that he had advocated for more than two decades. Lindbeck's career shows how the authority of economic theory shifted the course of policy. It may be regarded as a natural experiment: the eventual failure of the policies he advocated reflects back on the validity of the theory that informed them.

---

12. Offer, 'Self-Interest, Sympathy, and the Invisible Hand' (2012); idem, 'A Warrant for Pain' (2012); idem, 'Economy of Obligation' (2012); Rizvi, 'The Sonnenschein-Mantel-Debreu Results' (2006).
13. Bergström, 'Nationalekonomerna' (1977); Lönnroth, *Schamanerna* (1993).
14. Much of it cited below. Most recently in Sejersted, *Age of Social Democracy* (2011), which cites profusely.
15. Blyth, 'The Transformation of the Swedish Model' (2001), 4–5.
16. Blyth, *Great Transformations* (2002), 215.
17. Ibid., 238.

Lindbeck also dominated the selection of Nobel Prize winners during the first twenty-five years of the prize. The prize may not have been his idea in the first place, but he was among the first to be consulted.[18] Despite being less than forty in 1969 and not yet a member of the Swedish Academy, he joined the initial Nobel economics selection committee, and remained a member for twenty-five years, far longer than anyone else. For fourteen years between 1980 and 1994, he chaired the committee, and was seen as its king-maker.[19]

Face to face, Lindbeck was energetic, charismatic, and likeable.[20] In writing, he is powerful and engaged. As director of the Stockholm University Institute of International Economics from 1971 (in succession at one remove to Gunnar Myrdal), he was at the top of the Swedish economics profession, in a position to make and break academic careers, and, according to a Nobel Committee colleague, 'a kind of a mafia leader, a fixer.'[21] Lindbeck's special field was public policy, on which he had strong views, not only as a technical expert, but as a public intellectual, always an advocate for economic reason, with an unremitting flow of books, articles, committee reports, public lectures, newspaper features and broadcasting, some 300 professional and popular publications in all, and another 180 press and media interviews.[22]

Lindbeck was initially a *wunderkind* of Swedish public policy. He came from a working-class and Social Democratic family background in the province of Norrland, remote from the capital. His parents were both SAP members, his father an industrial worker who became a local government administrator. Lindbeck excelled as a gymnasium student not only academically, but also in music, literature, and art. At university, he read economics and politics and formed a lasting friendship with Olof Palme, a student contemporary and future Social Democratic prime minister. As a conscript in 1953, he was assigned to work on statistics for the Army General Staff, while also moonlighting in the Treasury and Defence Departments.[23] Soon out of the army, for several years afterwards he advised ministers, wrote editorials and pamphlets for them, and rubbed shoulders with party and trade union

18. Lindbeck, *Ekonomi* (2012), 112.
19. Nasar, *Beautiful Mind* (1998), 359–360. The only published account of the Nobel election criteria is Lindbeck, 'The Prize in Economic Science' (1985).
20. AO interview and dinner, Stockholm, 3–4 December 2012.
21. Karl-Gustaf Löfgren, quoted by Nasar, *Beautiful Mind* (1998), 359.
22. Lindbeck, *Ekonomi* (2012), 'Bibliografi', 426–446.
23. Biographical details from Lindbeck, *Ekonomi* (2012), unless indicated otherwise.

leaders, while undertaking applied research at the Treasury and teaching courses at Stockholm universities.

In 1957–1958, he spent time at Yale and Michigan. The liberal wing of American economics was taming Keynesian doctrine into alignment with market optimality, and Lindbeck was impressed by its vigour and authority. He internalized its vision of markets as a template for society. A 1959 Swedish volume on the prospects for socialism included a chapter by Lindbeck on 'Anticipated Developments', which contains both his credo and a set of contradictions he never resolved. Call them 'Lindbeck's Dilemma', a conflict between economic principles and his personal values as a Social Democrat (a familiar dilemma in economics at the time). Efficiency required competitive pricing and market exchange. Regulations, restrictions, and tariffs should all be reduced. Private services like retailing should be rationalized, scale economies promoted, and needs satisfied by private choice in competitive markets. Lindbeck was harsh on the persistence of wartime regulations in a time of affluence, on agricultural protection and on rent control.

On the other hand, raw market outcomes were often unacceptable: that was the point of Social Democracy. The correct norm was to apply the price mechanism in allocation. The burden of proof should lie with those who would turn away from it. This ('obviously' he wrote) did not mean that the state in all fields needed passively to accept the results of unbridled competition. On equality, social insurance, and government expenditure, Lindbeck (like most economists of his day) was on the left. There were many cases, he wrote, where interference could be defended from an economic, social, cultural, medical or other factual standpoint. State policy should seek out such cases and take appropriate action.[24] Attractively (to the present authors), the young market advocate Lindbeck also singled out literature, culture, and art as deserving of support. He had been an amateur musician and in later years he took up painting, even exhibiting in a Stockholm gallery.

According to Lindbeck, the choice of market prices or other forms of allocation was a matter of discretion for government (voters are not mentioned). But no guidance is provided on how it should be exercised, except that there should be 'a factual standpoint.'[25] This is weak, because among the listed 'standpoints' are social and cultural ones, where judgment has to be

---

24. Lindbeck, 'Att Förutse Utvecklingen' (1959), 68–69.
25. Ibid., 68.

informed by values. Indeed, one can say the same for the other 'standpoints', the economic and medical ones.

A dozen years later, in 1971, Lindbeck published another book chapter, 'The Efficiency of Competition and Planning'. It was his best effort to engage with the dilemma theoretically, and was still his credo forty years later.[26] It opens with a simple microeconomic model of 'market efficiency'. This is achieved when two inputs are combined in the most effective proportion by a producer and a consumer jointly and simultaneously. When pressed at our interview in 2012 about his understanding of the concept of 'efficiency', Lindbeck stood up, went to the whiteboard, drew a graphic, and referred to this 1971 chapter, which he later fetched in hard copy.

The graphic represented the criteria of 'static allocative efficiency and optimality ... as traditionally defined in static price theory'.[27] In this model, there are two commodities. Each different combination of the two commodities can be thought of as a 'product'. A consumer chooses the most efficient combination of two commodities (that is, a particular product); a producer combines the two commodities optimally to make the same product. The cost-price equilibrium in question is one in which the price of two commodities relative to each other (their 'marginal rate of substitution') is equal both in production and in consumption. Efficiency is maximized when the two choices (of producer and consumer) coincide in a single 'product'. Such simple models (two commodities, two agents) exemplify microeconomic reasoning, as described in chapter 1. The convergence just described (shown graphically in the Edgeworth Box and its variants) is typically used to demonstrate how to maximize efficiency in exchange, or in production using two factors.[28] With only one product, this model of efficiency is simple, not to say simplistic. But Lindbeck implies that command of this theory unlocks the talismanic aims of 'efficiency' and 'optimality'. The problem with this ingenious toy model as a policy norm is fundamental and simple. It cannot be scaled up. It provides no guidance on the choices that individuals and policy-makers need to make among the innumerable options that face them in real life.

As if conceding these shortcomings, Lindbeck quickly moves on (in the article) to describe five other efficiency models, all but one incompatible

26. Interview, 3 December 2012.
27. Lindbeck, 'The Efficiency of Competition and Planning' (1971), 83.
28. Humphrey, 'The Early History of the Box Diagram' (1996).

with the first. After an inter-temporal variant of the first model comes Schumpeter's model of entrepreneurship. Here, efficiency is achieved not by the optimal combination of two inputs, but through 'creative destruction' by businessmen whose innovative products overthrow established ones. The next model is Herbert Simon's insight into the cognitive limitations of managers within the firm (NPW, 1978). Lindbeck then considers central planning as practised in Eastern Europe, which cannot possibly acquire and process the information required for the best combination of output and consumer satisfaction due to the socialist calculation problem. This difficulty is resolved in another model, Friedrich Hayek's account of the market as a source of information, in which every individual, as a consumer and producer, knows only that part of the economy that affects him or her directly, by means of the prices (or psychic costs) attached to the choices available to them. Market exchange co-ordinates this multitude of individual choices, and gives rise to 'spontaneous order.' This appealed to Lindbeck. In retrospect, he regarded it as the most abiding lesson he took from economics.[29] Hayek, soon to be a Nobel Prize winner, is invoked nine times. But planning was still required, to provide collective goods and undo collective bads, and to provide overall co-ordination and investment. In a society where government allocated half or more of GDP, that was no small matter: 'For in reality the issue is, of course, not competition *versus* planning, but rather the optimum combination of competition and planning.' His conclusion was that the 'the crucial thing would presumably not be whether perfect competition, in the context of a domestic markets, exists or not, but whether strong competitive pressure *of some sort* prevails, even rivalry between a limited number of firms, so that the incentives to reduce costs and develop new products are strong.'[30]

This eclectic pragmatism speaks in Lindbeck's favour. A true believer in markets might have looked, for example, to provide social insurance by private means, but for Lindbeck this was a step too far. Hence his commitment to the efficiency of market competition, always at the core of his advocacy, rested on weak foundations. As argued in chapter 1, the theoretical case for market efficiency depends on two conditions: on all markets clearing simultaneously, with no excess supply or demand, and on the resulting allocation being equitable. In 1971, this analytical objective of general equilibrium still

---

29. Lindbeck, 'Reflektioner om Nationalekonomins Styrka och Begränsningar' (2012).
30. Lindbeck, 'The Efficiency of Competition' (1971), 102, 103.

seemed to be within the reach of economics, but around that time it was also shown to be unattainable.[31] Lindbeck never invokes general equilibrium. Unlike Lucas, for example, he did not regard economics as an encompassing and interlocking system, but rather as a toolbox, or a 'flashlight', to illuminate some particular issue or aspect.[32] His advocacy was incomplete: he could never demonstrate its ramifications throughout the economy and society, and, wisely, he never tried. Apart from his powerful drive and from participation in public affairs, his claim to expertise was founded on a bundle of disparate notions, a set of inconsistent ideas held together by force of personality. Never mind. In our story, Lindbeck invokes questionable theory for partisan ends. But his pragmatic approach may still be intellectually better than the 'blackboard science' of competitive equilibrium. With his sense of the limitations of economics, Lindbeck was less of a market fundamentalist than some of his colleagues. His interventions were (arguably) more political than analytic. But he had a plausible case to make, either in fact or value, quite separately from the untenable economic models which he invoked in support.

SWEDISH SOCIAL DEMOCRACY IN THE 1970S

The political success of Social Democracy was founded on its association with economic prosperity, underpinned in Sweden by a diversified mode of production. There was a legacy of natural resources, of timber, iron, coal, water power, and metals; a powerful manufacturing sector, at the cutting edge of technology in electronics and avionics, but also mass producing consumer goods, household appliances, cars, furniture and fashion, all distinguished by quality designs. A capital goods industry assembled ships, trucks, office equipment, armaments, agricultural equipment, civil engineering plants, and electrical machinery. Government pitched in with massive housebuilding, with roads and urban infrastructure, and invested in education, sport, and the arts. Production and public sector workers were the core of Social Democratic support, and the main beneficiaries of its collective provision.

---

31. Arrow and Hahn, *General Competitive Analysis* (1971); Kirman, 'Whom or What Does the Representative Individual Represent?' (1992); Rizvi, 'The Sonnenschein-Mantel-Debreu Results' (2006). Above, 19–20, 26–27.
32. Lindbeck 'Förvanskningar om Ekonomerna och Arbetarrörelsen' (1978), 36; Lindbeck interview, 3 December 2012.

This mode of production came under pressure in the 1970s. Factories in East Asia, applying technology and design talent similar to Sweden's, but with much cheaper labour, began to undermine the Swedish ability to compete. Productivity growth began to fall, while worker expectations were still rising. First to go were the textile industries. The shipyards, which had overtaken Britain's as the most advanced, were overtaken in their turn by Japan and Korea, and finally died in the 1980s. Facit, a world leader in mechanical calculators and typewriters with 14,000 workers, folded almost overnight in the early 1970s.

Another challenge was instability from the outside: The end of the Bretton Woods regime of fixed-exchange rates, the floating of the dollar and sterling, the volatility of the business cycle, the oil shock of 1973, the world recession of 1973–1974 and the higher inflation that followed, were more than Keynesian demand surges could cope with for long. Repeated devaluations only stoked up inflation.

In response to this buffeting, Swedish firms performed remarkably well, rather better than in Britain or the United States.[33] Alfa Laval, Asea, Astra, Atlas Copco, Bofors, Electrolux, Ericsson, Hasselblad, IKEA, Saab, Scania, SKF, Tetrapak, and Volvo remained or even emerged newly as worldwide brands. Swedish creativity took other forms: Ingmar Bergman in cinema, Björn Borg in tennis, ABBA in popular music.[34]

De-industrialization only gradually reduced the numbers and bargaining power of manual workers. In Sweden as in other countries, both private and public services grew. Increasingly, they employed more women, and more of the educated who came out of expanding universities and secondary schools.[35] They enrolled in white-collar unions outside the LO federation of manual workers, and sometimes in opposition to it.

ACADEMIC ECONOMICS IN SWEDEN

The authority of Swedish Social Democracy was also undercut by intellectual forces from the outside, and mainly from North America. One of them was the short-lived but compelling New Left movement of the late 1960s

33. Leamer, 'Changes to the Global Market' (2010).
34. Bergman's self-exile from Sweden in 1976 was not a protest against the tax level, but a reaction to a particular charge of tax evasion, a charge which was shown to be groundless.
35. Leamer, 'Changes to Global Markets' (2010), 314–315; Edin and Topel, 'Wage Policy' (1997), figs. 4.6, 4.13, 164, 174.

and early 1970s, which can be detected in the surge of Karl Marx's citations during this period (see figure 6.9, above). Lindbeck, who was on leave at Columbia and Berkeley in 1969, responded to the unrest with his most popular book, *The Political Economy of the New Left* (1971). He dismissed New Left utopianism more in sorrow than in anger. The book carried a long endorsement by Paul Samuelson (NPW, 1970). The *Swedish Journal of Economics* (later the *Scandinavian Journal of Economics*) had already changed its language from Swedish to English in 1965. In 1973, Lindbeck co-founded a Swedish-language economics journal, *Ekonomisk Debatt*, partly as a platform against left-wing and environmental movements.[36]

Higher education also opened new doors for economics. Achieving a doctorate in economics had previously been a rocky road: an average of one per year was completed in the seventy-five years to 1969. Professors remained in post for decades, and blocked the way for newcomers.[37] Quality was high: many of the names are familiar; they influenced policy, but were too few to dominate it.[38] More people achieved the licentiate, an intermediary graduate degree, but hardly enough to leave a strong mark on the elite. In 1969, the system was reformed, and the output of doctorates increased tenfold: within twenty years, 220 new ones were qualified. These people were employed in business and government, and spread the notions of neoclassical rationality through economy, politics, and administration. An elite of young technocrats (many without doctorates), all conversant with the most recent jargon of neoclassical efficiency, diffused through the elites and took control of policy. They displaced an earlier generation of New-Leftish administrators initially trained as social workers. These had undermined Swedish Social Democracy from the left during the 1960s and 1970s, by drawing attention to the social exclusion of women, the old, the disabled, the worn-out, the misfits, the poor, and immigrants. Such outsiders had previously fallen beyond the ken of the productive workers whom Social Democratic policies strove to benefit.[39]

Another beachhead of foreign economics was the Nobel Prize established in 1969. which promoted 'scientific' economics, over the communitarian

---

36. Lundgren, 'Tidsandan Framfödde *Ekonomisk Debatt*' (2002), 505.
37. Wadensjö, 'Recruiting a New Generation' (1992), table 4.3, 74; Jonung and Gunnarsson, 'Economics the Swedish Way' (1992), table 2.5, 35.
38. Wadensjö, 'Appendix D. Doctoral Theses in Economics in Sweden 1895–1989' (1992).
39. Hugemark, *Den Fängslande Marknaden* (1994); Andersson, *Between Growth and Security* (2006), ch. 6.

solidarity of Social Democracy. Its winners were celebrated at the pinnacle of Swedish society, in the limelight of international publicity. Their faces featured in the national media. The *Scandinavian Journal of Economics* printed the Nobel citation and an expert appreciation. A leading critic wrote in retrospect that 'the setting up of the Nobel Prize in economics in the 1960s greatly enhanced the national as well as international prestige of Swedish economists', and Lindbeck, in our interview of 2012, did not disagree.[40] At first, the implications were not entirely clear. Economics in the late 1960s had a progressive, Keynesian inclination. Gunnar Myrdal, the Social Democratic economist, was prone in the 1960s to regard the discipline as politically neutral.[41] The very first awards went to Ragnar Frisch and Jan Tinbergen, a Norwegian and a Dutchman respectively, both of them Social Democratic advocates of planning.

Planning has since faded out of economics, but for Lindbeck in the 1960s it was key. There was something to be learned, he thought, even from the Soviet Union.[42] The economist was a technocrat of the mixed economy.[43] Viewing the Nobel Prizes from the retrospect of 2012, he still considered the crucial issue as having been planning versus markets.[44] From this point of view, seven of the first eight NPWs, although mostly committed to market principles, were also sympathetic to Social Democracy, and their views were not inconsistent at various points with a measure of planning. Frisch and Tinbergen, in the very first cohort, had advocated it directly. Samuelson and Arrow, the high theorists of general equilibrium, also wrote in support of social insurance ('overlapping generations' by Samuelson, asymmetric information in healthcare by Arrow). Only Hicks was neutral, or slightly hostile. Leontief (NPW, 1973) had devised input-output analysis, a paradigm of planning, and the work of the Soviet economist Kantorovich (NPW, 1975) in linear programming lent itself to the same use. Myrdal (NPW, 1974) had co-authored the Social Democratic planning manifesto of 1944.[45]

The prize to Hayek in 1974, however, was a clear break with planning.[46] He was known as its foremost critic, both the mild Keynesian version, and

40. Korpi, 'Eurosclerosis and the Sclerosis of Objectivity' (1996), 1728.
41. Myrdal, *Asian Drama* (1968), I, 28.
42. Lönnroth, *Schamanerna* (1993), 216.
43. Lönnroth, *Schamanerna* (1993), 220. Note the title of Lindbeck, 'The Efficiency of Competition and Planning' (1971).
44. Interview, 3 December 2012.
45. Landsorganisationen, *The Postwar Programme of Swedish Labour* (1944/1946).
46. Above, 8–9, 127–129.

the Soviet one. His greatest public impact was to depict the welfare state as *The Road to Serfdom* (1944). The book was also freighted with political significance in Sweden. In the late 1940s, Swedish Social Democracy encountered fierce ideological resistance from the right, culminating in an electoral setback in 1948 that forced it to moderate its ambitions.[47] The focal point for this controversy was a translation of Hayek's *Road to Serfdom*, financed by a business foundation. Erik Lundberg, head of the official National Institute for Economic Research, left it to write an influential book against planning, funded by the same foundation.[48] Lundberg was Lindbeck's dissertation supervisor, chair of the Nobel selection committee in its first ten years, and a member for another five. Among the five Nobel selection committee members, Lundberg, although quite open-minded, had been a member of the Mont Pèlerin Society in the late 1950s and early 1960s.[49] Another member of the Nobel Committee (and a future NPW) was Bertil Ohlin (who was present at Mont Pèlerin in 1947 but did not join the society due to a prior commitment to a competing organization). He was also a centrist politician and party leader. Of these two, Lindbeck testified in 2006,

> Ohlin's and Lundberg's main imprint on Swedish society, I believe, is that they helped to dampen the political enthusiasm for central planning and nationalization during the first decade after World War II. They were also important advocates of free trade. Lundberg, moreover, convinced many Swedish economists about the limits, indeed dangers, of attempts to "fine tune" macroeconomic policies. He also helped Swedish economists to appreciate the advantages of well-functioning markets, although the work that clarified this point most effectively for me was Hayek's little article "The Use of Knowledge in Society," in the *American Economic Review* in 1945—an article also highly appreciated by Lundberg.[50]

Awarding the Prize to Hayek was a gesture that moved Lindbeck personally: 'He'd been in a very deep depression he told me. It was terribly satisfying to indicate his greatness.'[51] The prize had a more positive effect on Hayek's visibility and reputation than on any other recipient.[52]

---

47. Olsen, *The Struggle for Economic Democracy* (1992), 57.
48. Lundberg, *Konjunkturer och Ekonomisk Politik* (1953).
49. Mont Pèlerin Society membership list 1961, Hoover Institution, Hayek Papers 71/3. Above, 104–105, n. 92.
50. Gylfason, 'An Interview with Assar Lindbeck' (2006), 108
51. Lindbeck in a 1997 interview, quoted in Nasar, *A Beautiful Mind* (1998), 367.
52. Chapter 6, above, 127–131.

Hayek's famous article of 1945 was at odds with the North American neo-classical market-clearing equilibrium approach of Samuelson and Arrow. For their mathematical models to work, the person making an economic choice had to know all the options available. This bland requirement implied the more far-fetched one of complete information about all commodities and services and their prices relative to each other, not only in the present but for all time. In contrast, Hayek assumed (more realistically) that every individual in the economy could know only a small part of the whole, conveyed to him by prices. Markets co-ordinated this multitude of individual choices and gave rise to the 'spontaneous order' of the liberal society. This order was assumed, not proven with any rigour.

Hayek's imaginary world may have been ordered, but was not necessarily benign. It was not an invisible hand utopia, and indeed had some authoritarian undertones.[53] But it was superior to central planning as practised in the Soviet Union, and if it fell short of the imaginary best, Hayek regarded it as the best available. The imaginary auctioneer of general equilibrium, who brought prices into agreement for all time, was suspiciously similar to the socialist central planner, an affinity exploited by some socialist equilibrium economists.[54] Walras (who originated modern general equilibrium in the 1870s) had been a socialist. Hayek expressed his disdain for such models in his Nobel speech, stating (correctly, in our view) that their certainty was not science, but 'scientism.'

Hayek provided a more usable theoretical underpinning for Lindbeck than static equilibrium efficiency analysis. Like his Austrian mentors, Hayek wrote in ordinary language. At this stage, so did Lindbeck. Hayek seemed to provide the decisive argument against any form of planning: no central planner could hope to acquire all the information required. In Lindbeck's hands, however, the two approaches, the Austrian and neoclassical, were used opportunistically. He did not acknowledge any disharmony and continued to invoke the authority of both.

1976: A PIVOTAL YEAR

It was an election year in 1976, and for Lindbeck, a fork in the road. The previous contest in 1973 had been the first triennial election for a single-house parliament, a constitutional reform which worked permanently against the

---

53. Mirowski, 'Postface: Defining Neoliberalism' (2009).
54. Lavoie, *Rivalry and Central Planning* (1985).

SAP. In 1976, the manual workers' trade union federation (LO) adopted a proposal to establish so-called 'wage funds', causing some electoral embarrassment to the SAP. And on 19 September, the party lost power in Sweden for the first time in more than forty years.

Some dilution of private ownership was already a Social Democratic objective in the 1920s.[55] Its core social insurance aspiration had been achieved by the 1960s, and, in a setting of enduring prosperity, the trade union movement returned to its quest for industrial democracy. This was also in keeping with the utopian spirit of New Left radicalism, and 'blue collar blues' motivated some successful strikes and reforms in Sweden at the beginning of the 1970s. At Volvo's new Kalmar automobile plant in 1971, the assembly line was replaced by small teams rotating tasks among themselves. This was Sweden's largest industrial firm, and the innovation spread throughout the company and beyond.[56] Industrial democracy was in the air: in Germany, workers sat on company boards, and profit-sharing schemes were being examined throughout Europe. Sweden had had consultative works councils since 1946, and, during the 1970s, worker delegates were also admitted to company boards, with little resistance from management.[57] A European Union draft directive recommended worker representation in 1975, and a British Royal Commission reported in favour of it in 1977. In the United States, management consultants questioned assembly-line Taylorism, and work discipline in the mighty automobile industry was purchased with generous pay, pensions, and medical care. A trade union official was even admitted to the Chrysler board in 1980.[58]

One way of aligning the workers with the enterprise was to give them an ownership stake. This idea had a lineage in industrial capitalism; a proposal of this kind was made in the early 1970s by Bertil Ohlin's 'bourgeois' Liberal Party, and another in 1976 by the employers' organization.[59] A complacent trade union movement had been one of the targets of the workers' unrest at the end of the 1960s, and the unions responded with a 'Workers' Funds' proposal, devised in the early 1970s by the trade union economist Rudolf Meidner.[60] He argued that the 'solidarity' wage compression gave successful

---

55. Berman, *The Social Democratic Moment* (1998), 162–163.
56. Milner, *Sweden: Social Democracy in Practice* (1989),146–147.
57. Olsen, *The Struggle for Industrial Democracy in Sweden* (1992), ch. 2.
58. Cumbers, *Reclaiming Public Ownership* (2012), 41.
59. Ryner, *Capitalist Restructuring* (2002), 125, 144, 168.
60. A detailed favourable account in Whyman, *Sweden and the 'Third Way'* (2003), ch. 5.

companies an undeserved profit. Workers were frustrated by wage restraint while profits surged.[61] A 10 to 20 percent tax on corporate profits could be used to buy corporate shares, to be vested in funds administered by the trade unions for the benefit of their members.[62] Despite scepticism among party leaders, the funds proposal attracted the union rank and file, although socialization or nationalization had never been central to labour movement agendas. In response, Swedish business mobilized against the funds and they became the flashpoint of politics.

In this stand-off, Lindbeck chose the side of business. When the proposals were published in 1975, he responded critically, first in the Social Democratic journal *Arbetet*, and then in the daily newspaper of opinion, the 'bourgeois' *Dagens Nyheter*. In the run-up to the 1976 elections, he published several more biting articles in that paper, which helped the opposition.[63] Lindbeck explicitly invoked Hayek's *Road to Serfdom*. Extending share ownership to trade unionism would create such a dominant force in society as to stifle pluralism. Looking back, he wrote,

> The proposed fund would be an economic power colossus without parallel in any democratic country. In a country where unions already had great power over the leading political party, including by placing money and staff at SAP's disposal, it was obvious—at least for me—that such a merger of ownership power, trade union power, employer power and political power would drastically reduce opportunities to preserve pluralism in a society. Who would dare use his right to speak to criticize such power blocs?[64]

The Meidner society, shouted one of his articles, would be a 'Silent Society.'[65]

Lindbeck's arguments are not entirely convincing. Private ownership was also concentrated, with the ten families and their foundations already exercising a voting power on corporate boards that was disproportionate to their actual share ownership. The Wallenbergs dominated finance and had controlling shareholdings in many companies.[66] The build-up of wage funds

61. Ibid., 66.
62. Meidner, *Employee Investment Funds* (1978); Meidner, 'Why Did the Swedish Model Fail?' (1993).
63. Lönnroth, *Schamanerna* (1993), ch. 4, 242.
64. Lindbeck, *Ekonomi* (2012), 255.
65. *Dagens Nyheter*, 25 March 1976, cited in Bergström, 'Nationalekonomerna' (1977), 151.
66. Magnusson, *Economic History of Sweden* (2000), 214–221. The Wallenberg Foundation helped to finance Lindbeck's Stockholm Institution; the Bonnier media empire owned *Dagens Nyheter*, and the publisher of Lindbeck's memoirs.

was going to be gradual, with the most profitable firms being socialized first. Small firms would be exempt. The proposal covered about two-thirds of private sector workers and excluded the public and co-operative sector. Hence, it was going to benefit only a minority even of SAP supporters, although one writer argues credibly that the wage funds were not initially vote losers.[67] Assuming capital value at ten times profits, and the wage fund tax at 20 percent of profits, it would take fifteen years for the wages fund to build up a thirty percent stake in successful companies.[68] During this time, the effects of the policy would be subject to scrutiny in four general elections. In fact, it took two more general elections for the funds to be implemented in a weakened form, and another two for them to be abolished.[69]

The principle was not new. The supplementary state pension system (ATP), established in 1959 (by a parliamentary majority of one) after intense controversy and a referendum, built up three large funds which financed Swedish housing and infrastructure (they only lent to public bodies). A fourth one, added in 1974, invested in equities, had up to 60 percent trade unionists on its board, and was not resisted by business.[70] In any case, institutional ownership of equities was already dominant in Sweden.[71]

The main effect of private shareholding has been to increase wealth and income inequality, which the funds would have mitigated. On the other side, it might be argued that the trade unions were not necessarily the best custodians for popular share ownership, although possibly no worse than mutual fund managers or insurance company executives.[72] Microeconomics in the 1970s was largely silent on the matter of ownership. In that theory, the whole firm behaves as an individual, but ownership had long been separated from control in Western capitalism. In that same year, 1976, a seminal article appeared which advocated ownership equity incentives for managers so as to align their interests with those of the shareholders.[73] The long-term consequence of this idea has been the systematic plundering of companies by managers at the expense of the shareholders. But that was still in the future.

---

67. Whyman, *Sweden and the 'Third Way'* (2003), 73; Also Ryner, *Capitalist Restructuring* (2002), 167–168.
68. Detailed examples in Whyman, *Sweden and the 'Third Way'* (2003), 69.
69. Olsen, *The Struggle for Economic Democracy in Sweden* (1992).
70. Milner, *Sweden* (1989), 128–30; Whyman, *Sweden and the 'Third Way'* (2003), 64.
71. Norrman and McLure, 'Tax Policy in Sweden' (1997), fig. 3.1, 112.
72. Bogle, *Battle for the Soul of Capitalism* (2005).
73. Jensen and Meckling, 'Theory of the Firm' (1976); Jensen and Murphy, 'CEO Incentives—It's Not How Much You Pay' (1990).

Lindbeck did not concern himself greatly about the quasi-royal position, for example, of the Wallenbergs in Swedish economic life, or with the heavy concentration of media ownership.[74] He did not even object to the principle of popular ownership, and endorsed the Liberal Party's proposal of civic funds as an alternative, with individual ownership of shares.[75]

What Lindbeck mainly objected to was that the funds would promote trade union values, which Lindbeck thought had too much influence in Swedish society already. In reality, manual workers were receding in numbers and influence even as the funds were being proposed, and this affected the fate of the scheme. Lindbeck was happy to align with Social Democracy when (in the 1950s and 1960s) it was a rising force, but now that conditions had changed, he turned his back on manual workers, their culture and values. Despite his origins, this was not a world in which he felt at ease.

A similar distancing of political and economic specialists from the trade unions occurred in the UK and the United States, and comes out in the contrast between the UK Labour Party's everyday leader Neil Kinnock in the 1980s, and his slick successor Tony Blair in the 1990s. A centrist group in the UK split off the Labour Party in 1981 to form the Social Democratic Party (note the name), which eventually merged with the more centrist Liberals. In the 1990s, the Labour Party was captured by another centrist neoliberal group (Tony Blair, Gordon Brown, Peter Mandelson), which renamed the party 'New Labour'. This party, which governed Britain between 1997 and 2010, turned its back on its trade union heritage, and embraced the market liberalism of Thatcher and its cultural trappings as well. Its leaders were more comfortable with bankers (with whom they surrounded themselves, and whose ranks some of them eventually came to join) than with the working-class people who continued to vote for them.[76] The centrist 'New Democrats' in the United States likewise had a period in power under Bill Clinton.

In Sweden in 1980 and 1981, a high-ranking 'Crisis Group' within the SAP developed the 'Future for Sweden', a programme of economic reform designed to improve incentives for business by holding down wages and government expenditure.[77] This so-called Third Way Social Democracy looked

74. Magnusson, *Economic History of Sweden* (2000), 217–218, 220.
75. Lindbeck, *Ekonomi* (2012), 256.
76. Offer, 'British Manual Workers' (2008), 545; Ramsay, *Rise of New Labour* (2002), esp. ch. 5.
77. Lindvall, *The Politics of Purpose* (2004), 75–78.

to an alliance with business without sacrificing the commitment to social insurance.[78]

THE NOBEL PRIZE IN 1976

The Nobel Committee was also busy in the summer of 1976, and in October the academy announced its choice for the economics prize as Milton Friedman of Chicago. This was the second break from its left-of-centre run of awards up to that point, after the prize to Hayek in 1974. A prize to Friedman was inevitable given his towering reputation and the orthodox composition of the selection committee. Chicago economics was somewhat marginalized in the United States during the two-decade golden age after World War II, but in the late 1960s Friedman led an insurgency within the discipline against Keynesian analysis.[79] His alternative inflation-focused monetarism had not yet been tried, and in the early 1970s he was among the most cited economists in the world.[80] He had also replaced Hayek as the leading figure of the Mont Pèlerin Society and had become an icon of market liberalism, for which he had written the canonical text, *Capitalism and Freedom*.[81] He had several outstanding scholarly achievements, all of them lending academic credibility to his political agenda.

The award to Friedman exposed the Swedish Academy of Sciences to some of the darker forces at work in the world. Particularly awkward in Sweden was Friedman's outspoken support for Pinochet's Chile, where he went several times to advise and endorse the dictatorship's economic policies. In the opening session of the 1973 Parliament, Prime Minister Olof Palme had memorably eulogized the murdered Chilean President Salvador Allende. In 1976, the Friedman award was criticized in the press, and four Nobel Prize winners wrote to the *New York Times* in protest.[82] At the award ceremony, immediately after Erik Lundberg's speech, a demonstrator shouted 'down with capitalism, freedom for Chile', while thousands marched outside in the winter cold.[83] On the day of the Nobel award, Gunnar Myrdal (the Social

---

78. Blyth, *Great Transformations* (2002), 219–221; Ryner, *Capitalist Restructuring* (2002), 148; Andersson, *Between Growth and Security* (2006), ch. 6.
79. Above, 10, 24–25.
80. See chapter 6, figure 6.9.
81. Friedman and Friedman, *Capitalism and Freedom* (1962).
82. 'Letters to the Editor: The Laureate', *New York Times*, 24 October 1976, 166.
83. Friedman and Friedman, *Two Lucky People* (1998), 451.

Democrat economist) wrote at length in *Dagens Nyheter*, criticizing the secretive procedure by which the economics committee presented the academy with a fait accompli. He thought the award to Friedman had fatally discredited the prize, and regretted accepting the prize himself two years before.[84]

In response, the academy commissioned an investigation into the press allegations of Friedman's involvement with Chile. A reviewer in *Ekonomisk Debatt* dismissed its book-length report as whitewash.[85] A group of students published a protest against the award. The academy flew Lindbeck home from Yale to meet them.[86] Was there a case to answer? We return to this question below.[87] In his memoirs, Friedman dwelt at length on this episode and was manifestly shaken by the vehement opposition that he (and his wife) attracted. But he was not contrite.[88] Of his critics, he wrote,

> What we were doing was, according to them, deliberately mean, nasty, inhuman—not stated explicitly but implied because we were said to support a fascist military junta that allegedly took delight in torturing people. It was taken for granted that theirs was an obvious preferable alternative that sensitive human beings could have recommended—but no writer ever spelled out what it was.[89]

Thousands died, suffered torture or disappeared in Chile. Recall our definition of a Just World Theory: everybody gets what they deserve.[90] That was Friedman's definition of the just entitlement to property and effort that we used above. A Just World Theory is a licence to inflict pain. Gunnar Myrdal and the five thousand demonstrators in Stockholm understood this. Friedman implies (in the lines above) that it was a matter of one Just World Theory against another, and that is correct, but he put his weight behind the one that inflicted the pain. It might be argued that the previous year's winner, Kantorovich, had worked for the equally obnoxious Soviet regime, but Kantorovich was a genuine technician, and advocated using market prices in Russia. Six years later in another Nobel Lecture, the writer Gabriel García

---

84. *Dagens Nyheter*, 14 December 1976. English translation, Myrdal, 'Nobel Prize in Economic Science' (1977).

85. Axell and Swedenborg, *Milton Friedman och Ekonomipriset* (1977); Englund and Heikensten, 'Böcker: Bo Axell-Birgitta Swedenborg, Milton Friedman och Ekonomipriset' (1977).

86. Lindbeck, *Ekonomi* (2012), 119.

87. See ch. 11, 234, below.

88. Friedman and Friedman, *Two Lucky People* (1998), 400–404, 448–452, and appendix A.

89. Ibid., 401.

90. Introduction, above, 3–4.

Márquez invoked the suffering of Latin America under its military dictatorships: 'One million people have fled Chile . . . that is, ten percent of its population. . . . I dare to think that it is this outsized reality, and not just its literary expression, that has deserved the attention of the Swedish Academy of Letters.'[91]

THE WAGE-EARNER FUNDS SHOWDOWN

By the end of 1976, Lindbeck had transferred his loyalty from labour to capital. It is understandable if Social Democrats regarded his actions as treachery. In 1976, Lindbeck had abandoned them in a sequence of public gestures. When he later came back from leave (partly spent at the Hoover Institution, a Conservative bastion), he found that the former prime minister Olof Palme, a long-time confidant, neighbour, and friend of the family, would no longer speak to him.[92] In a centenary volume for the Swedish Economic Association in 1977, the trade union economist Villy Bergström cast the history of economics in Sweden as one long legacy of hostility to Social Democracy, motivated by class animosity. The atomistic actors of market economics were at odds with the communitarian vision of Social Democracy. The elders of Swedish economics in the 1920s and 1930s, Heckscher and Cassel, had resisted Social Democracy. Their class was threatened. Subsequently, economists made a qualified peace with the Social Democratic project, but now class resistance had re-emerged and Lindbeck's arguments were no better than those of Cassel.[93] Lindbeck exploded. In an article in *Ekonomisk Debatt*, he insisted on the scientific nature of economic analysis, on a boundary line between politics and disinterested analysis, that many economists had actually supported Social Democracy, and that economics was a toolbox open to all. Such falsification in an official publication of the Economic Association was unforgivable, he wrote, and left him no option but to resign from the society.[94] Erik Lundberg, a more accomplished economist than Lindbeck and not a man of the left, conceded in the same volume that Bergström was correct overall.[95] For a figure of Lindbeck's centrality to storm out of the

91. Gabriel García Márquez, 'The Solitude of Latin America', Nobel Lecture 1982.
92. Lindbeck, *Ekonomi* (2012), 263.
93. Bergström, 'Nationalekonomerna och Arbetarrörelsen' (1977).
94. Lindbeck, 'Förvanskningar Om Ekonomerna och Arbetarrörelsen' (1978).
95. Lundberg, 'Ekonomernas Debatt Om Ekonomisk Politik' (1977), 159; also idem, 'The Rise and Fall of the Swedish Model' (1985), 12.

Economics Association was tantamount to stating that non-orthodox approaches to the discipline were not legitimate, and in particular, to discredit the trade union economists who had designed the Social Democratic model.

The funds debate reached a strident pitch in the early 1980s. At the Mont Pèlerin Society meeting in Stanford in 1980, a Swedish contribution cited Hayek on its title page as saying,

> What is threatened by our present political trends is not just economic prosperity, not just our comfort, or the rate of economic growth. It is very much more. It is what I mean by the phrase 'our civilization'.[96]

The Mont Pèlerin Society annual conference came to Stockholm in 1981, perhaps to fish in troubled waters. The list of those attending included many Swedish businesspeople, but most of Sweden's top economists stayed away. In our interview, Lindbeck said that he was never attracted to the society, though he did address it when it came again in 2009.

As the labour movement wound down its wage-fund proposals, business cranked up its resistance. Industry became more concentrated in Sweden during the 1970s, and the different factions of capital made up some of their differences and learned (following the example of other countries in the west) to focus their political efforts. Two neoliberal think tanks, Timbro and SNS, energized by newly aggressive leaders, provided well-funded intellectual support. They were part of an informal international array of think-tanks looking for inspiration to the Mont Pèlerin Society. In the election campaign of 1982, the employer's federation (SAF) spent about five times as much as all five political parties together campaigning against the funds, and mobilized about ten times as much money as the trade unions.[97] But if this looked to be Sweden's Thatcher moment, it was not to be. The left won an overall majority in 1982, and after a bitter debate in parliament, the Social Democratic government passed a watered-down wage fund. Property and money had won the intellectual argument, which was increasingly accepted by the Social Democratic Party, but the bourgeois parties did not win political power for another nine years, and then in the context of a deep crisis caused by market-liberal policies. By then their historical opportunity had passed.[98]

---

96. Sven Rydenfelt, 'The Limits of Taxation: Lessons from the Swedish Welfare State' (1980), Hoover Institution, Mont Pèlerin Society Papers Box 24/1, September 1980, 1.
97. Olsen, *The Struggle for Economic Democracy* (1992), 75–84; Blyth, *Great Transformations* (2002), 209–219.
98. Steinmo, *Evolution of Modern States* (2010), ch. 2.

This business agitation agreed with the spirit of the times. There was a disjuncture between the ambitions still embodied in the wage funds, and the waning power of manual workers. Class conflict continued. On 4 October 1983, about 100,000 anti-socialists came from all over Sweden to march in Stockholm, and 115,000 marched the next year at fifteen different locations.[99] No wonder: by the early 1980s, the after-tax income share of the top one percent had fallen to its lowest level ever, a mere 4 percent, about half of its level in 1950 and again in 2010, and income inequalities had also fallen to a record low.[100]

It is customary to regard the wage-fund controversy as a wrong turn in labour strategy in Sweden, but if it was electorally unpopular, this was not enough to lose it the 1982 election.[101] There may have been a positive consequence for Social Democracy. It is possible that its most important legacy was to deflect the market-liberal attack from the welfare state itself, which consequently remained shielded from the impact of the 'market turn' in Sweden for another ten years. Prime Minister Olof Palme thought so.[102]

---

99. Whyman, *Sweden and the 'Third Way'* (2003), 78; Blyth, 'Transformation of the Swedish Model' (2001), 16; Copetas, 'The Revolt of the Capitalists' (1985).

100. Edin and Topel, 'Wage Policy and Restructuring' (1997), fig. 4.2, 160; Roine, 'Varför har Balansen Mellan Kapital och Löner Förändrats?' (2013).

101. Ryner, *Capitalist Restructuring* (2002), 167–168.

102. Viktorov, 'Swedish Employers and the Wage-Earners Funds Debate' (2009), 14.

CHAPTER 9

SWEDOSCLEROSIS OR PSEUDOSCLEROSIS? SWEDEN IN THE 1980S

Between 1976 and 1982, Sweden suffered a sequence of economic buffetings. The turmoil of the times is captured in figure 9.1. Government expenditure rose to more than 60 percent of GDP, and public employment embraced one-third of the workforce. In response, business flung itself into massive protest, setting up think tanks which published massively, agitating in parliament, the press and even in the streets. The discipline of economics mobilized too. Assar Lindbeck cranked up criticism of his old party, and finally resigned from it in 1982 over the wage-fund issue, a few weeks before the election. But in defiance of his forebodings, the eight years of Social Democratic government after 1982 were economically more successful than the previous six under centre-right ('bourgeois') governments: inflation fell most of the time, output increased, and unemployment stayed low (figure 9.1).

AN ECONOMICS OF INEFFICIENCY

Lindbeck used theory to promote policy. His argument was simple: the tax-heavy Swedish welfare state destroyed incentives and reduced efficiency. High taxes and high welfare benefits discouraged work for wages. This criticism deployed an innovation in economic theory (with roots in previous work), the 'Harberger Triangle'.[1] Its purpose was to demonstrate the economic cost

---

1. Lindbeck, *Political Economy of the New Left* (1977), 78–79; idem, *The Welfare State* (1993), 117 [first published 1981], 165 [first published 1982]. Hines, 'Three Sides of Harberger Triangles' (1999); Banzhaf, 'The Chicago School of Welfare Economics'(2010).

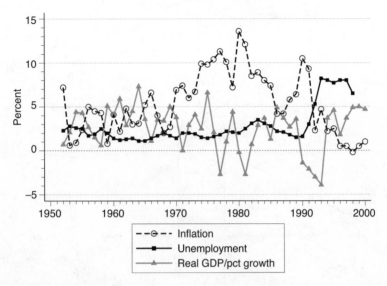

Figure 9.1. The Swedish economy: main performance indicators, c. 1952–2000.
Source: Inflation: Swedish Bureau of Statistics, http://www.scb.se/Pages/TableAndChart____33831.aspx.
GDP per capita: Swedish Bureau of Statistics, http://www.scb.se/Pages/ProductTables____38450.aspx; http://
www.scb.se/Pages/TableAndChart____35666.aspx. Unemployment: Mitchell, *International Historical Statistics*
(2003), 168–169.

of taxation. The idea is simple. It begins with an imaginary 'invisible hand'
economy, which has no government, only workers and capitalists trading
with each other. In conditions of perfect competition (nobody can impose
a price), both capitalists and workers receive the equivalent value of the last
unit of their effort or capital. In such an economy, workers and capitalists ration out what they give, depending on what they receive. Reward is matched
to effort, and this ensures efficiency. That is the ideal. If workers have to
pay taxes, that distorts their incentives: wages paid diverge from wages received. 'Distortions' can be plotted, and have a triangular shape, hence they
are called 'wedges' (figure 9.2). Their geometry shows that the magnitude of
harm (the 'distortion') is approximately the square of the linear size of the
distortion (see note to figure 9.2 for an explanation).

The concept of 'distortion' makes use of a common move in economic
policy argument, of using a commonplace word in a different technical
sense, while still implying its common-sense meaning.[2] In this case, it implies that the expert economist (whom the layperson cannot follow) has
found that the whole of Social Democracy was a 'distortion'. The rhetorical

---

2. A variant of the 'Ricardian Vice' (above, 22–23).

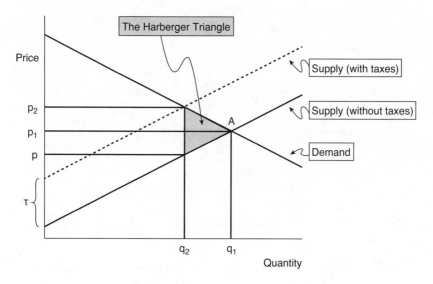

Figure 9.2. The Harberger Triangle.

Source: Hines, 'Three Sides of Harberger Triangles' (1999), fig. 1, 169, with permission from the author and the American Economic Association.

Note: The distortion is a tax that increases the price of labour from p_1 to p_2. The quantity produced (in this case, labour effort) is reduced from q_1 to q_2. The harm is $(p_2-p_1)*(q_1-q_2)$ (the shaded area in the diagram), or roughly $(p_2-p_1)^2$.

effect is powerful. For example, extensions of this model 'demonstrated' during the 1980s that social insurance was 'welfare-reducing', in comparison with a perfectly competitive economy with costless private insurance.[3]

On the face of it, this model seems to allow for precise measurement of the harmful effects of 'distortions' such as tariffs, monopolies, and taxes. The procedure is to compare a real magnitude (the size of a tax) with an imaginary state of no taxes at all (what has been called a 'Nirvana economy').[4] This imaginary state might be regarded by sceptics as a distortion in its own right (Harberger himself conceded the irrelevance of 'full optima').[5] As Harberger also points out, it might be possible to be more practical and compare for example, two different tax regimes, but Lindbeck and his acolytes did not do that. Moreover, the model is shot through with assumptions and value judgments. For one thing, it is a 'representative agent' model, that is, the economy

3. Survey and counter-argument in Peterman, 'A Historical Welfare Analysis of Social Security' (2014).
4. Above, 22.
5. Harberger, 'Three Basic Postulates' (1971), 795.

viewed as two people, a consumer and producer. By implication, everyone is assumed to have a uniform set of preferences (or 'utility function'; that is what the downward-sloping demand curve means in this context), violating the standard assumption that utilities of different people cannot be compared. Utility is assumed to be constant throughout (the first and last dollar of income are worth the same), violating the standard assumption of diminishing returns (the final dollar is worth less). Harberger offered a dubious defence, that similar assumptions of uniform valuation pervade national income accounting.[6] But national income accounting makes no assumptions about unobservable utilities: it only measures prices and quantities. If politicians and other policy-makers treat GDP as a measure of welfare or well-being, they do so as practical people who take all dollars as equal, and not as economists. National accounting is not a normative activity. Growth theory uses national accounting merely as a data source, and much of it is open to the same criticism as Harberger Triangles. In brief, adopting constraints or rejecting them seems to be motivated in these welfare models by the ideological agendas of avoiding the issue of distribution in one context, or denouncing government in another.

In Sweden, the outcome of interest was the workers' effort, expressed in hours of labour. The model assumes that wages represent the value of the worker's output at some level of effort. But the 'pure' undistorted state is imaginary, hence there is no wage level to compare with. And the worker's effort depends also on alternative satisfactions available outside the market (family, domestic work, and leisure), on the prices of all the other goods, services, and opportunities; and on knowing what these prices are (perfect information and general equilibrium).

This model is similar to the Mirrlees model of optimal taxation presented in chapter 7, and similar criticisms apply.[7] The problem that Mirrlees set out to solve was that a progressive income tax (its rate rising with income) might induce workers to reduce their effort. His model assumed that effort responded directly to pay, and to pay alone, and vice versa, that pay responds directly to effort. Neither of these is necessarily the case. In response to lower pay, the worker might actually increase her effort (the income effect) rather than reduce it (the substitution effect). It is not clear that in the absence of

---

6. Ibid., 786–787.
7. Above, 170–173. For example, Atkinson, 'The Mirrlees Review' (2012); idem, *Public Economics in an Age of Austerity* (2014), ch. 2.

distortions (whatever that might mean), the individual worker's observed effort would be the one that is good either for that worker, or for society as a whole, however that good is defined. From the point of view of equity overall (the Pareto criterion in equilibrium economics), there is no advantage for one worker to get extra pay, if another one loses more than that sum, or indeed, if he loses anything at all. Finally, what are taxes for? Sophisticated Harberger-type analysis gets around this question by assuming that the tax is returned to the worker in cash to spend as they wish. But the tax might be spent on a public or collective good (such as defence or social insurance) which is not for sale to individuals. Harberger's response to that is to model a distortion that leaves out what workers would relinquish to keep the service in question. But this would require an omniscient rationality on the part of workers, whose subordinate position in the division of labour is assumed to arise precisely from the limitations of their cognitive ability. In brief, the Harberger diagram is a clear, tractable, and spurious piece of class rhetoric. Admittedly so—Harberger insisted that distributional equity considerations should be left out of policy analysis, and of economics more generally.[8] It defines an imaginary market exchange of atomistic individuals as the ideal norm, and the ordinary arrangements of society as 'distortions.'

Harberger himself was a member of the Mont Pèlerin Society, whose objective was to resist and roll back the welfare state.[9] He led the Chicago programme to train Latin America's 'Chicago boy' economists, and was a frequent visitor and advisor to the Pinochet regime in Chile. In line with Chicago priors, it is not surprising that his own efforts at estimation showed the 'distortions' caused by monopoly to be negligible, and those of taxation to be large. Harberger's model was first published in 1954,[10] and was in vogue during the 1980s. It declined in popularity in the 1990s, one would like to think due to its inherent implausibility, but more likely because economists found that 'Harberger Triangles are small.' The harmful effects were hard to identify empirically.[11]

---

8. Harberger, 'Three Basic Postulates' (1971), 785–786.
9. See Introduction, above, 9–10.
10. Harberger, 'Monopoly and Resource Allocation' (1954).
11. Citations to Harberger Triangles in JSTOR start rising sharply in 1980 (after a few earlier scattered ones), peaked in 1991, and settled at less than half this level subsequently. Numbers are small. Citations to 'welfare triangles' (which can also have other meanings) started to rise in the 1970s, also peaked in 1991, and then declined to about a third of the former level. Hines found a similar pattern, 'Three Sides of Harberger Triangles' (1999), 181–182. Quote from McCloskey, 'A Neo-Institutionalism of Measurement' (2013), 368. On empirical failings, Atkinson and Mogensen, *Welfare and Work Incentives* (1993), chs. 2–3.

The economic harm of tax 'wedges' was the main theme of Lindbeck's attack on Swedish Social Democracy in the 1980s. It appeared in many publications of various kinds, but is most accessible as a series of essays and journal articles published in English and subsequently collected in his book *The Welfare State* (1993).[12] They all follow the same pattern and repeat the same arguments, in much the same style. The argument was that the Swedish welfare model had come to undermine economic incentives. Marginal tax rates were too high and discouraged effort. The consequence was a general reduction in the flexibility and mobility of labour. Increasing absenteeism was especially difficult for small firms. Jobs were chosen with a view to their utility in tax-free leisure-time, rather than money income. Students preferred easy and enjoyable subjects rather than demanding ones that might subsequently yield higher earnings. There was less striving for promotion and higher skills, and a trend to employ, promote, and dismiss in line with seniority rather than competence. Readily available welfare benefits encouraged dishonesty and fiddling.[13]

FROM THEORY TO POLICY

'Personally,' Lindbeck declared in 1983, 'I find it hard to believe that a modern economy can function in the long run with even moderate demands on efficiency if the connection between effort and reward is cut off as drastically as in Sweden.'[14] Sclerosis was creeping over Northwestern Europe.[15] 'Eurosclerosis' wrote one Mont Pèlerin economist; 'Suedosclerosis' (that is, Swedishsclerosis) wrote another.[16] The remedy was to wind down the welfare state, reduce worker protections, lower social benefits and levy fees for government services, in order to force the share of labour in national income down, and the share of profits up: 'deregulate the markets and modify the remaining regulations in order to restore flexibility in labour, goods and services, and capital markets and business.'[17]

---

12. Lindbeck, *The Welfare State* (1993).
13. Attempt to measure the distortions, Lindbeck, 'Interpreting Income Distribution in a Welfare State' (1983).
14. Lindbeck, 'Mekanismer för en Bättre Samhällsekonomi' (1983), 157.
15. Lindbeck claimed first use of the term, *Ekonomi* (2012), 214; idem, 'Emerging Arteriosclerosis' (1982).
16. Giersch, 'Eurosclerosis' (1985); Ståhl and Wickman, *Suedosclerosis* (1993). The latter published by Timbro, the Swedish neoliberal think tank. The Mont Pèlerin Society members were the German Herbert Giersch and the Swedish Ingemar Ståhl, respectively. See also Lindbeck, *Ekonomi* (2012), 215–216.
17. Lindbeck, 'Overshooting, Retreat and Reform of the Welfare State' (1993), 10–21. Quote from Lindbeck, 'Problem i Industriländernas Strukturanpassning' (1981), 87.

The Social Democratic leadership bought in. The market fundamentalism of the late-1970s instigated a 'gestalt switch' among the SAP's economic intelligentsia.[18] Compared to the golden age of the 1960s, the economy appeared to be lurching from one crisis to another. During their six years in power, the centre-right parties had been no more successful. In such circumstances, wizards with nostrums found it easy to get a hearing. The finance minister Kjell-Olof Feldt (1982–1990) and his officials were exposed to market-liberal views during their frequent visits to the OECD, the Bank of International Settlements, and the IMF.[19] The message they brought back was to stop attempting to control the economy, and to expose Social Democracy to international competition. More than ten years after the university reform, the ministries were replete with civil servants trained in economics, for whom this way of thinking was literally axiomatic.

For example, Klas Eklund entered the Stockholm School of Economics in 1972, and spent a decade as a student and then a teacher of economics. He converted from the Marxist 'New Left', but found mathematical economics too difficult and never finished his doctorate. He transferred the intensity of his New Left convictions to neoclassical theory. In 1979, he helped to form a society of Social Democratic economists which soon numbered about a hundred. With enthusiasm and energy, they set out to re-educate the party and the public in 'modern economic theory'. The society sponsored scores of lectures, seminars and articles. This ideological campaign against historical Social Democracy and especially the trade unions became known as the 'war of the roses' (the red rose was adopted as the Social Democratic icon in 1979; the late-medieval dynastic wars of the roses in England pitted red against white roses). Members of the group wrote party economic tracts for the 1982 election. Eklund then went to work with the 'Third Way' finance minister Feldt, and remained in government until the late 1980s, attempting to turn theory into policy.[20] Trade union economists accused the finance ministry of abdicating to the neoliberal spirit of the age.[21]

James Buchanan (NPW, 1986), the leading advocate of public choice theory and a political scientist, was like Friedman, Hayek and Harberger another keen advisor to Pinochet's Chile. His co-author, Gordon Tullock

18. Blyth, 'The Transformation of the Swedish Model' (2001).
19. Ryner, *Capitalist Restructuring* (2002), 174–187.
20. Eklund, 'En Intellektuell Biografi' (1995).
21. Ryner, *Capitalist Restructuring* (2002), 175–176; Andersson, *Between Growth and Security* (2006), ch. 6.

(also involved in Chile), wrote a report for the Swedish Employers Association (SAF) in 1978 (which made him perhaps too partisan a figure in Sweden to share in his co-author Buchanan's Nobel Prize).[22] Lindbeck was inspired by these two to develop a theory of 'the captive politician', who subordinated principle and the common good in the service of vested interests: 'We are increasingly approaching a Vote Purchasing Democracy where politicians by generous promises to different groups perpetually overload our resources. Sooner or later a major crash is bound to come.'[23] Following Buchanan, he suggested reducing the power of politicians to intervene in markets. Lindbeck reports being asked why he did not go a step further and treat the economist himself as an intrinsic part of the model 'both when focusing on economic analysis and when you act as economic political adviser?' In his memoirs he wrote, 'I still do not have a good answer to that question.'[24]

Lindbeck's arguments proceeded from 'first principles'. No evidence, no facts. The principles are speculative. They were logical, coherent and made sense to their advocates, but like the theories for which his committee was handing out Nobel Prizes, they did not engage much with empirical reality. In the last six years of Lindbeck's chairmanship (up to 1994), the Nobel Committee veered to the right in its awards, and away from empiricism towards formalism (figures 5.1 and 7.1, above). The argument depended entirely on the presumed power of incentives (the assumption of 'greed', which was an article of faith).[25] But economists cannot determine the power of incentives a priori. That has to be observed empirically. Responding to incentives implies rising supply curves (as in figure 9.2), but as Paul Krugman (a sceptical NPW), writes, 'We do know that demand curves generally slope down; it's a lot harder to give good examples of supply curves that slope up (as a textbook author, believe me, I've looked).'[26] And this also applies to the supply of labour in response to pay.

Lindbeck's papers contain hardly any evidence. Take the argument that taxes and benefits distorted incentives, and thus suppressed production and output. That is a commonplace of microeconomic models, but how valid is it as argument, and how good was the evidence? At the very least, it depends on

22. Tullock, *Svenskarna och Deras Fonder* (1978).
23. Lindbeck quoted in Rydenfelt, 'The Limits of Taxation' (1980), n.p. [5].
24. Lindbeck, *Ekonomi* (2012), 223.
25. Hausman, *The Inexact and Separate Science of Economics* (1992), 31, 32.
26. Krugman, 'Irregular Economics' *New York Times*, 25 August 2011.

several assumptions, each one of which is open to question. It assumes that the purposes for which tax is collected are less valuable than if the money had been spent directly by the consumer. Even if we accept that there is no measure of value other than consumer choice, the level of taxes may still be regarded as a democratic choice to acquire collective and public goods by means of taxation rather than to buy them over the counter, just as consumers chose their spouses and produced their children without recourse to the price mechanism. If the product in question is social insurance, the market alternatives are inferior or non-existent.[27] Swedish voters (and voters in most other Western countries) have persisted in this choice despite the pleadings of Lindbeck and his followers.[28]

Lindbeck's theory had little predictive power. As pointed out above, in response to high taxes, workers could actually choose to *increase* their effort.[29] His argument depended entirely on the assumption that they would choose to reduce their effort (the substitution effect), mostly in favour of leisure and household production (for example, gardening or do-it-yourself). He was honest in admitting that there was no evidence in support:

> Admittedly, these judgements about the importance of various kinds of effects in the labour market are heuristic, based on scattered empirical information, rather than conclusions that can be supported by systematic and noncontroversial scholarly evidence.[30]

This absence of empirical research had already been noted as an oddity by Gunnar Myrdal, in view of the large issues at stake.[31]

When empirical research was finally undertaken in the 1980s and the 1990s, it found that tax levels had little effect on working hours. The response to tax levels was low for men. Women, who responded more to incentives, increased their labour force participation steeply, from about 55 percent in 1965, to more than 80 percent in 1990.[32] One competent empirical review 'does not suggest strong general conclusions about incentive effects on labour supply at the microlevel, and there is even less to say about gen-

---

27. Offer, 'Economy of Obligation' (2012).
28. Wittman, *The Myth of Democratic Failure* (1995).
29. Above, 201–202.
30. Lindbeck, 'Disincentive Problems' (1981/1993), 84.
31. Myrdal, 'Ett Bra Land' (1977), 243.
32. Edin and Topel, 'Wage Policy and Restructuring' (1997), fig. 4.6, 164.

eral equilibrium effects.'[33] Another competent survey found 'little response in labor force participation and hours of work.'[34]

Very low unemployment levels in Sweden in the Social Democratic years (figure 9.1) do not suggest a reluctance to work. The 'Beveridge Curve' measures the relation between vacancies and unemployment, that is, the inertia in filling jobs. If Swedes had been work-shy, this inertia would be high. In fact, Sweden ranked best on this measure within the OECD, and no lower than average if those in training (itself a market participation incentive) are regarded as unemployed.[35] At the level of the economy as a whole, it is difficult to see how any 'distortions' in labour supply incentives could have had much effect on the full-employment Swedish economy. Men were already working forty hours or more per week. With better incentives, they might work a little more, but the forgone increase would only make the tiniest of differences to Swedish output or growth rates. That is why Harberger effects are small, as Harberger found for himself. Lindbeck acknowledged that Harberger distortions were minimal, but insisted in the same breath, and with no reasons given, that they could potentially be very large.[36]

Sweden had some of the shortest working hours per person employed in Europe during the 1980s (though not its production workers).[37] But societies work less as they become wealthier. Normal manual working hours in Sweden decreased from 72 in 1860 to 40 in 1973. In a selection of twenty-two European countries, the poorest countries worked the longest hours between 1980 and 1990.[38] Sweden was in a tight cluster with other prosperous short-working-hour countries: Norway, Netherlands, Denmark, France, West Germany, and Belgium. A high proportion of women in the workforce was another reason for shorter working hours, since many women prefer to work part-time. This effect can be offset by measuring hours worked per capita, and in these terms Sweden was the seventh most hard-working out of nineteen (other factors, not considered here, were an older population in Sweden, and on the other side, lower unemployment).[39]

33. Gustafsson and Klevmarken, 'Taxes and Transfers in Sweden' (1993), 131.
34. Aronsson and Walker, 'The Effects of Sweden's Welfare State' (1997), 253.
35. Ryner, *Capitalist Restructuring* (2002), 50–52.
36. Lindbeck, *Political Economy of the New Left* (1977), 78–79.
37. Huberman and Minns, 'The Times They Are Not Changin'' (2007), table 1, 542; other data source in note 39, below.
38. Correlation coefficient $(r) = 0.69$.
39. Calculated from Conference Board, 'Total Economy Database' (2012) on decadal averages.

In the 1990s, and again in the following decade, two substantial studies were carried out by teams of Swedish and American economists. They set out to compare the Swedish labour market under the welfare state with the flexible and free American labour market, and they used Harberger-type analysis to discuss the Swedish case.[40] In the United States, labour productivity more than doubled between 1975 and 2010, with hardly any increase in hourly wages. An enormous 'wedge' opened up between labour productivity and labour wages, almost entirely for the benefit of a thin sliver of wealthy capitalists.[41] American capitalists discovered on their own that 'distortions' and incentives did not really matter, and the gap between productivity and pay did not trouble them. Stick was as good as carrot: workers worked as hard. In the Swedish-American comparisons, no Harberger diagrams were wheeled out to examine this anomaly. At the risk of overstating the case, this indicates the class bias of Harberger analysis, and its use in the market liberal campaign to undermine the welfare state. The welfare state and its 'wedges' protected Swedish workers from the fate of American ones (figure 9.3).[42]

One of Lindbeck's complaints was that compressed income differentials would turn students away from demanding subjects, and reduce the human capital formation required for an advanced economy. The calculated rate of return on education in Sweden was indeed found to be much lower than in the United States,[43] presumably due to lower inequality. Despite this supposed handicap Sweden ranked near the very top on various indices of R&D and higher education, and was producing twice as many doctorates as the United States (pro rata) in science and engineering subjects, even setting aside the high proportion of foreigners doing American Ph.Ds.[44] The distortion argument was clearly capable of empirical testing, and was found wanting, but not by Lindbeck.

The assumption that market incentives produce greater efficiency depends for its validity on comparison with an imaginary benchmark (invisible hand perfect-competition general equilibrium). Even with such unrealistic assumptions, as we have seen, invisible hand arguments cannot be made to work.[45] The best of such models, that of Arrow and Debreu, was honoured with two Nobel Prizes, although its originators came to deny its relevance to

---

40. Aronsson and Walker, 'The Effects of Sweden's Welfare State' (1997), 204–214.
41. Mishel, 'The Wedges between Productivity and Median Compensation' (2012).
42. OECD, *Growing Unequal?* (2008), fig. 3.3, 82.
43. Fredriksson and Topel, 'Wage Determination and Employment' (2010), 108–109.
44. Björklund and Freeman, 'Searching for Optimal Inequality/Incentives' (2010), 51.
45. See above, 19–20.

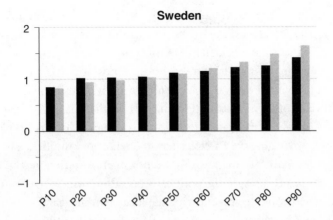

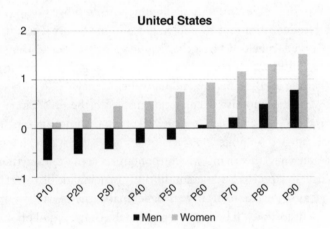

Figure 9.3. Real earnings growth for men and women working full time by income decile, 1980–2005, Sweden and the United States.

Source: OECD, *Growing Unequal?* (2008), fig. 3.3, 82.

Note: Average growth rate per year, in percentage. Decile: tenth of the income distribution, moving from lowest to highest. Women: lighter bars.

policy. When Debreu addressed the issue of distortions, he insisted that they should be demonstrated at the level of GDP, not of individuals.[46] It should be said that maximized GDP does not maximize welfare, merely aggregates output, not all of it good, and not always better than the unmeasured satisfactions of leisure and production at home.[47]

---

46. Hines, 'Three Sides of Harberger Triangles' (1999), 178, n. 11.
47. Jackson and Marks, *Measuring Sustainable Economic Welfare* (1994); Offer, *Challenge of Affluence* (2006), ch. 2; Philipsen, *The Little Big Number* (2015).

The wedge approach was pursued by other Swedish economists, who compared the actual working of Swedish labour markets and welfare institutions with the notional efficiency of imagined perfect market allocation.[48] Some also criticized social insurance on grounds of fairness or neutrality. Their notion of fairness was that payoffs to individuals should reflect the actuarial value of their contribution, that is, rejecting the Social Democratic principles of solidarity, reciprocity, and redistribution. This is simply to assume what privileging the Pareto criterion of efficiency implies, namely that prior endowments and inequalities are not open to question, and should be protected, in contrast to the political aims of Swedish Social Democracy.

The Harberger mode of comparing the ideal with the real was institutionalized in Sweden by means of a public agency founded in 1981, the ESO (Expert Group for Studies in Public Economics), to improve the operation of Swedish public institutions by applying economic theory. This intellectual gambit worked. It helped break the 'cognitive lock' of Social Democracy, a paradigm shift in which progressive redistribution gave way to the market-liberal rhetoric of consumerism and market efficiency.[49]

In the 1980s, economists increasingly displaced the professional knowledge of the doctors, architects, social workers, and administrators who had previously advised on policy.[50] Professional knowledge was replaced by the abstract 'efficiency' theorizing which economists apply to everything. ESO reports usually applied a static equilibrium benchmark of the Harberger kind, and took deviations from this benchmark (the so-called wedges) as evidence of distortion.[51] It bears repeating that the general equilibrium benchmark cannot be shown to be optimal even in the limited 'Pareto efficiency' sense. The procedure is quite arbitrary, and is merely designed to show public provision in a bad light. It does not compare with real, existing market delivery, where employers are often grasping, workers underpaid, traders opportunistic, prices opaque, and service uneven, but rather depends on the assumption that in perfect markets quality control is costless and automatic, and that payoffs to workers and owners represent their respective contribution. This not tested, just assumed. These procedures, already invalidated by

48. This paragraph and the following one are based largely on Hugemark, *Den Fängslande Marknaden* (1994), for example, 112, 115–119, chs. 6–7.
49. Blyth, 'Transformation of the Swedish Model' (2001), esp. 16–17; Lindvall, *Politics of Purpose* (2004), esp. 145–152.
50. Andersson, *Between Growth and Security* (2006), ch. 4.
51. For example, Expertgruppen [ESO], 'Är Subventioner Effektiva?' (1984), 41–47.

theory (but still common in practice), were designed to favour marketization of public services, quite frequently (as we have shown in other work) to the detriment of the public.[52]

It is axiomatic in neoclassical analysis that consumers are fully informed, that their choices are motivated by innate and well-ordered preferences, and that they maximize the well-being of those who make them. Lindbeck was inclined to fall into this argument from time to time, but only anecdotally, based on his own atypical experiences. Rent control was bad, because he himself had to queue for an apartment. Choice was good, because he was able to choose the best nursing home for his wife.[53] What he failed to ask was if the service was free at the point of delivery, why should anyone choose anything but the best? And if it had to be paid for, did choice not depend on the ability to pay? Implicit in his support for the 'choice' agenda is the silent message that choice would allow the middle class to separate itself (with government subsidy) from less privileged citizens. This was a displacement of Social Democracy's original objective of helping to overcome the insecurities and injuries of manual working life, and it may have eased the welfare state transition away from the proletarian mode of production in which it was created.[54]

Behavioural economics has shown that people cannot always trust themselves to make the best choice. Mirrlees conceded this in his Nobel Lecture although it went against his advocacy of 'optimal taxation'.[55] An instance of this is obesity. Nobody wants to be obese, but it is an outcome of prior choices. Obesity is much higher in market-friendly countries than in strong welfare states.[56] Another instance is smoking, which even advocates of consumer choice are now willing to discourage. Market liberals on the right often support the 'war on drugs' on the grounds that consumers cannot all make an informed choice (more libertarian ones prefer de-regulation). If consumers are innately focused on the short term and find it difficult to make long-term commitments (for which there is a good deal of evidence), then the most difficult choices involve making a sacrifice now for the sake of something better later.[57] The welfare state may be considered as a 'commitment agent'

52. Offer, 'A Warrant for Pain' (2012); Offer, 'Economy of Obligation' (2012).
53. Lindbeck, *Ekonomi* (2012), 125, 335.
54. Offer, 'British Manual Workers: From Producers to Consumers' (2008).
55. Chapter 7, above, 171–172.
56. Offer et al., 'Obesity under Affluence varies by Welfare Regimes' (2010).
57. Offer, *Challenge of Affluence* (2006), chs. 3–4.

for myopic individuals.[58] An aspect of consumer choice that Lindbeck never considers, is that market expansion into services like health and education disadvantages the worst off, since the poor need them more, and find it more difficult to pay for them. The efficiency argument for the pricing of welfare services, as pursued by Lindbeck, was class conflict by other means.

But not all the way. General equilibrium, despite the 'wedges' rhetoric, may have been a step too far for Lindbeck, since he continued to support the principle of social insurance (though not perhaps the extent and method of its application) and never embraced an encompassing invisible hand market model. He was not a stickler for consistency. Given the flimsy validity of invisible hand doctrine, that speaks in his favour. His arguments about incentives had little analytical validity, although there may have been other reasons (perhaps even good ones) to support them. If theory is invoked, it requires evidence as well. The socialist economist Gunnar Myrdal wrote persuasively that the norms of public finance had no scientific grounding but represented special pleading, whether conscious or not. When (in 1978) he made a case quite similar to Lindbeck's, he relied on nothing but his intuitions.[59] Ultimately, the trade-off between economic incentives and welfare objectives is a matter of judgment which has to be resolved politically, and not by economists. The normative argument (in our view) was the only valid form of argument. Theoretical mumbo-jumbo was essentially deceptive.

Lindbeck increasingly insisted that free provision of welfare services caused them to be over-consumed. Three decades of experience with market liberalism has not left much of this argument standing. The marketized American health system is about twice as expensive as not-for-profit European ones, encourages harmful overtreatment, leaves tens of millions unprotected, and is associated with inferior services and health.[60] Nor is there much convincing evidence that privatization has benefited either consumers or workers; the evidence is mixed. The winners are investors and managers.[61]

The loudest exponent of Swedish sclerosis (who also coined the term 'Suedosclerosis') was Ingemar Ståhl, a professor of Lindbeck's generation, who also began as a Social Democrat. In 1963, with Lindbeck (and with

---

58. Offer, 'Economy of Obligation' (2012), 15–16.
59. Myrdal, *Political Element* (1953), ch. 7; Myrdal, 'Dags för ett Bättre Skattesystem!' (1978), 493.
60. Offer, 'A Warrant for Pain' (2012).
61. Florio, *The Great Divestiture* (2004), ch. 10; Cumbers, *Reclaiming Public Ownership* (2012), 50–55.

Ragnar Benzel, later the first Secretary of the Nobel selection committee), he published a study of housing that attacked rent control and advocated a market solution. It was commissioned by the Research Institute of Industrial Economics (IUI), a business-funded research institute. Ståhl veered to the right earlier and more sharply than Lindbeck, and kept up a flow of writings in support of de-regulation. He also became a member of the Mont Pèlerin Society, almost alone among Swedish academic economists at the time. In 1980, he joined the Nobel selection committee, where his tenure (1980–1994) was longer than anyone other than Lindbeck.[62] On one account, he acted to oust Lindbeck from the committee in 1994, when his own candidate, Robert Lucas (NPW, 1995), was not taken forward.[63]

In methodological terms, the evidence for 'Suedosclerosis' is a joke. Swedosclerosis was a pseudo-malady.[64] It was criticized by Walter Korpi, a prominent sociologist who was Lindeck's most persistent critic. The 'Suedosclerosis' argument was that Swedish GDP and productivity growth lagged behind its OECD competitors. Korpi showed that any small difference arose because Lindbeck measured the Swedish economy from its peak in 1970 to a trough in 1992 (the latter a consequence of market-liberal deregulation). In fact, Swedish performance was no worse than that of competitors and comparators.[65] Korpi still played the game by Lindbeck's rules. But a proper statistical comparison would need to take account of confounding effects, that is, the many differences of prior endowment among the different countries. For example, poor countries have technological opportunities to catch up with wealthier ones (and often a younger workforce as well), and have the potential to grow faster. Taking growth per head over twenty-three OECD countries, the raw figures show that it declined very slightly when taxes rose as a share of GDP; that there was no statistical association between taxation and growth rates when controlling for differences in initial output levels; and that growth actually increased mildly with taxation, when controlling for the latter and for the age distribution.[66]

Growth statistics are biased against countries with large public services. The GDP value of public sector output, by statistical convention, is measured at

62. On Ståhl and Lindbeck, Söderberg, *Constructing Invisible Hands* (2013), ch. 4, 161–188.
63. Nasar, *A Beautiful Mind* (1998), 370–373.
64. Bogardi et al., 'Swedosclerosis or Pseudosclerosis' (2001).
65. Korpi, 'Eurosclerosis and the Sclerosis of Objectivity' (1996); Korpi, *Halkar Sverige Efter?* (1992).
66. Agell, 'Why Sweden's Welfare State Needed Reform' (1996), 1763.

cost, so any improvements for example, better teaching or healthcare, would not be captured as a productivity increase. The same services provided privately would show an increase in welfare if they became more expensive (or profitable) at the same level of use. This bias discriminated against a large public sector country like Sweden, and is sufficient in itself to invalidate Lindbeck's productivity comparisons. In reality, public sector social insurance is between one and two orders of magnitude cheaper and more efficient than market insurance for sickness, disability, and unemployment.[67] Using standard national accounting conventions, the American health system, which costs about twice as much in relative terms as the UK National Health Service (and more than that absolutely), and is associated with inferior health outcomes, contributes twice as much 'output' to GDP as the UK health service.[68] Likewise, due to good public health and a low birth rate, Sweden had a larger proportion of aged people. Controlling for such differences (and many others) is elementary statistical practice, which both Lindbeck and Korpi failed to apply. And if Swedish performance lagged behind (no sure thing), Lindbeck never demonstrates that the cause lay in inadequate incentives for labour or capital. A more careful Swedish economist, otherwise sympathetic to Lindbeck, called his sclerosis argument 'silly.'[69]

It is widely understood (by Lindbeck too) that GDP per head is not a good measure of welfare.[70] It did not capture the main achievements of Swedish Social Democracy, of high employment (sustained throughout this period), more equality, more security, and more dignity for ordinary people than in most OECD countries at the time. The United States had higher levels of GDP (though not growth per head in the relevant period) than Sweden, but lagged far behind on most measures of welfare, such as life expectancy, infant mortality, inequality, education, paid holidays, and even median income, that is, the income of the middle person in the distribution.[71] Measured properly, Gunnar Myrdal insisted, Swedish well-being was 'vastly superior' to the United States.[72] Lindbeck would have to show that under his implied counterfactual, any miniscule economic advantage Sweden might

67. Offer, 'Economy of Obligation' (2012), 17–23.
68. Offer, 'A Warrant for Pain' (2012), figs. 1–2, 92.
69. Agell, 'Why Sweden's Welfare State Needed Reform' (1996), 1769.
70. Lindbeck, *Ekonomi* (2012), 356.
71. Fullbrook, *Decline of the USA* (2012).
72. Myrdal, 'Ett Bra Land' (1977), 243.

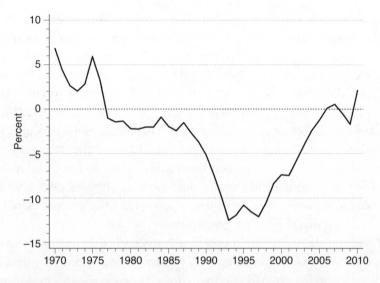

Figure 9.4. GDP per head (PPP, 2011 prices), Swedish difference from 'Europe 10.'
Source: Conference Board, 'Total Economy Database', September 2012, GDP Per Capita, in 2011 EKS$.
Note: 'Europe 10': Austria, Belgium, Denmark, Finland, France, Italy, Netherlands, Norway, Switzerland, United Kingdom. No data for Germany.

have obtained by the removal of 'distortions' would not have been bought with higher unemployment, lower incomes, inferior social services, and less security.

Lindbeck did not come out well from this debate, so in his autobiography of 2012, he returned with some new graphs, still comparing only GDP per head and no other data, showing alleged Swedish inferiority in growth rates in the period in question and using an inappropriate method to present its purported (small) magnitude.[73] That exercise is still open to all the criticisms made here. But to play the same game of GDP comparisons, levels of income are more secure comparators over time, since they do not depend on initial levels as much as annual growth measures. Our own figures compare the level of Swedish economic output per head with a comparable group of ten rich European countries, chosen for convenience (figure 9.4).[74]

If Sweden had been suffering from a special case of sclerosis, the gap would have widened gradually, but in fact it was discontinuous, with breaks around 1975, 1990, and 1997. These discontinuities were the consequence of

73. Lindbeck, *Ekonomi* (2012), 346–352.
74. A credible comparative study of raw output measures, is Lindert, *Growing Public* (2004), I, ch. 11.

macroeconomic shocks, not gradual stagnation. In 1975, Sweden caught up with the international crisis of 1973–1974, which it had delayed by means of Keynesian 'bridging' policies. The crisis of the 1990s was also the result of macroeconomic policy decisions, this time of a market-liberal kind. During the period of alleged 'Suedosclerosis' (c. 1975–1990) Sweden was level with the average, and about 2 percent below it, a difference that falls within measurement error. A study from the main Swedish business think tank indicates that GDP per head in Sweden was substantially above 'the [average of the] first 15 European Union member countries' from 1970 to 1990.[75] As we shall see (chapter 10, below), the subsequent economic collapse of 1990–1997 had nothing to do with Sweden's domestic labour rigidities, but was caused by the opposite, that is, excessive deregulation.[76]

Lindbeck was wise to avoid empirical analysis, since (as we have seen) the evidence told against him. Women, for example, responded to market incentives by preferring market work to domestic work, and this made Swedish labour participation rates among the highest in the world.[77] Lindbeck's response (consistent with his preference for a smaller welfare state) was to complain that instead of caring for their own children, women cared for those of others, by taking work in schools and nurseries. As an economist, he might have considered that unpaid domestic work entailed higher risks and more inequalities for women, depending on their individual family circumstances, number of children, level of income and other personal attributes. Collective provision in nurseries and schools could be more equitable and efficient: it empowered women both as mothers and as workers, without being clearly harmful in other respects. Apart from inconsistency, there is also a whiff of paternalism. Lindbeck generally insisted that work for wages was more productive than work at home; he applied this to men, but prescribed the opposite for women. Furthermore, his alarmist argument was clearly not borne out. Nordic high tax societies remain more productive and wealthy than most societies on earth. The *Economist*, a right-wing magazine which had gloated about the Swedish crisis in 1991–1993, has recently conceded Sweden's enduring success.[78] Moreover, Sweden and other Scandina-

---

75. Heyman et al., 'The Turnaround of Swedish Industry' (2015), fig. 1, 4.
76. Below, ch.10.
77. Meidner, 'Why Did the Swedish Model Fail?' (1993), 219; Forslund and Kreuger, 'Did Active Labor Market Policies Help Sweden Rebound?' (2010).
78. Lindert, *Growing Public* (2004), I, 265; Wooldridge, 'Special Report: The Nordic Countries: Northern Lights', *Economist*, 2 February 2013.

vian countries have not followed the English-speaking countries' example of suppressing their unions. Their affluence remains compatible with high union membership and labour market regulation.[79] Even Lindbeck's *bêtes noires* of the 1960s, rent control and agricultural subsidies, have never been wound down completely.

One of the consistent tropes in Lindbeck's criticism of the welfare state was that it promoted dishonesty. He made great play of the abuses of sick pay. Now tighter work disciplines for workers might be good for consumers, and arguably (given the temptations of shirking the job) even for the moral welfare of the workers themselves. Anthony Giddens made this purported 'moral hazard' the justification for a 'Third Way' between capitalism and socialism, which also influenced New Labour in Britain; the notions of shirking and scrounging have since become commonplaces of social discourse in Britain.[80] Even Gunnar Myrdal had famously written (in 1978) that the Swedes were becoming a nation of 'fiddlers' (he was referring mostly to tax deductions exploited by the middle class). Lindbeck followed this up by arguing that opportunities for tax evasion made honesty expensive.[81] In 1981 he wrote,

> Most well informed economists in Sweden, for instance, are by now quite convinced that the country entered the 1980s with very severe disincentive problems concerning work, saving, asset choice and entrepreneurship and with the considerable risk of a drastic deterioration in the honesty of individual citizens, particularly in their relations with the public authorities.[82]

But his evidence was merely anecdotal. Subsequent research showed that sick leave increased when demand for labour was high (that is, was used to cope with long working hours), and that absenteeism due to illness fell by about 20 percent when eligibility was tightened.[83] That this is a good thing relies on the assumption that for a person who is unwell, presence at work is more useful than staying at home, a judgment that professional workers (like Professor Lindbeck and the present authors) are allowed to make

---

79. Schmitt and Mitukiewicz, 'Politics Matter' (2012), fig. 2, p. 5.
80. Ryner, *Capitalist Restructuring* (2002), 13, 48–50; Taylor-Gooby, *Double Crisis of the Welfare State* (2013), chs. 2–3.
81. Myrdal, 'Dags för ett Bättre Skattesystem!' (1978), 500; Lindbeck, 'Disincentive Problems' (1981/1993), 90–91.
82. Lindbeck, 'Disincentive Problems' (1981/1993), 93.
83. Aronsson and Walker, 'Effects of Sweden's Welfare State on Labor Supply Incentives' (1997), 244–246; idem, 'Labor Supply, Tax Base, and Public Policy in Sweden' (2010), 140–141.

for themselves. Is the economic cost of absence from work greater than the harm of coercing the unwell to turn up? Either way, the effect on productivity was not likely to be large.

According to this view, high tax rates were also conducive to dishonesty. SAP Finance Minister Kjell-Olof Feldt followed Reagan and Thatcher in pursuit of lower taxes. In 1976, before the general election, the world-famous children's author Astrid Lindgren had published a fable in a newspaper as a way of inquiring why she was paying a marginal tax of 102 percent. She then got the better of the finance minister in a public exchange. This Pomperipossa affair (named after her alter-ego witch in the fable) did a good deal of harm to the Social Democrats in the election that year (she remained a loyal Social Democrat, however, for the rest of her life).[84] Feldt wrote in retrospect:

> The negative inheritance I received from my predecessor Gunnar Sträng (Minister of Finance 1955–1976) was a strongly progressive tax system with high marginal taxes. This was supposed to bring about a just and equal society. But I eventually came to the opinion that it simply didn't work out the way he concluded. Progressive taxes created instead a society of wranglers, cheaters, peculiar manipulations, false ambitions and new injustices. It took me at least a decade to get a part of the party to see this.[85]

But if the high marginal tax rates made honesty expensive, Swedes did not systematically choose to cheat. A reputable study reports that: 'The little evidence that exists does not suggest rampant tax evasion or other fraudulent behaviour.'[86] Sweden regularly scores very high in indices of integrity.[87] Is it possible that the outrage expressed by Myrdal, Lindbeck, and Feldt simply expressed a prevailing *aversion* to cheating in Sweden?

In the absence of concrete evidence, Lindbeck constructed a fable of his own: Sweden had industrialized rapidly, and most of its population migrated into the towns equipped with a work ethic and virtues of integrity appropriate to the reciprocal nature (or sometimes to the rugged individualism) of their backwoods existence. These virtues persisted among the first generation, but were likely to die out, and the welfare state would then be-

---

84. Östberg, *När Vinden Vände: Olof Palme 1969–1986* (2009), 182–183; Barkman, 'Brev från Astrid Lindgren Visar Hennes Stöd för S' (2010).
85. Sjöberg, 'Intervjun: Kjell-Olof Feldt' (1999).
86. Aronsson and Walker, 'Effects of Sweden's Welfare State on Labor Supply Incentives' (1997), 249–250.
87. Below, 256.

come unsustainable. Lindbeck devoted some ten academic articles to this fairy tale.[88] The argument is almost Marxist in the sense that 'being determines consciousness'. But again, Lindbeck provides no evidence, only mathematical models, typically co-authored with competent model builders. His most highly cited contribution to academic economics, the insider-outsider theory of labour markets, was compiled in collaboration with Dennis Snower. In these mathematical models, 'insiders' with higher skills and experience colluded to exclude and disadvantage 'outsiders'.[89] Ironically, it was 'New Left' sociologists and social workers in Sweden in the 1960s who identified a group of outsiders, made up of the disabled, migrants, and misfits, relatively few, though often in dire straits, and Lindbeck's concept was taken from this 1971 report.[90]

Lindbeck's model was not intended to integrate social 'outsiders'. The intention was to push the insiders out rather than pull the outsiders in. However compelling his model might be in other places and times, its relevance to Sweden was far-fetched. Some 85 percent of workers belonged to trade unions, and union work agreements covered most of the rest, while unemployment was almost non-existent.[91] The 'outsider' problem in Sweden in the 1980s was marginal at best, and more social than economic.

Another factor in the decline of Swedish Social Democracy was inwards migration, which peaked briefly in the mid-1960s, and then picked up again from the mid-1980s onwards. Swedish Social Democracy drew a good deal of its cohesion from a culturally homogenous working class. One of the lasting legacies of the New Left, however, was a respect for identity differences and minorities. Migration was accepted, even welcomed, on ethical grounds, especially refugee migration from outside the OECD. But in other countries, employers and right-wing parties have traditionally welcomed such migration as weakening the bargaining power of organized labour. A similar policy was adopted by New Labour in Britain after it came into power in 1997. Hence, a political consensus in support of migration acted to further weaken the cohesion of manual workers, and by 2011, about 15 percent of the population in Sweden were foreign-born.[92]

---

88. For example, Lindbeck et al., 'Social Norms and Economic Incentives in the Welfare State' (1999).
89. Lindbeck and Snower, *The Insider-Outsider Theory of Employment and Unemployment* (1988).
90. Andersson, *Between Growth and Security* (2006), ch. 3, esp. 50–51.
91. Rydenfelt, 'Trade Unions and Socialist Governments in Sweden' (1985).
92. Swedish Bureau of Statistics, 'Utrikes Födda 2012. Fortsatt Ökning av Utrikes Födda i Sverige' (2013), http://www.scb.se/sv_/hitta-statistik/artiklar/fortsatt-okning-av-utrikes-fodda-i -sverige/.

CHAPTER 10

THE REAL CRISIS: NOT WORK INCENTIVES BUT RUNAWAY CREDIT

While economists were fretting over incentives, the real action was taking place unremarked under their noses. When the major crash that Lindbeck predicted finally occurred, it had nothing to do with work incentives or the welfare state. Like the global financial crisis of 2007–2008, of which it might be considered a precursor, the Swedish (and indeed, the wider Nordic) crash originated in finance.[1] Lindbeck rarely wrote about finance, except for an occasional aside in favour of a more flexible capital market.[2]

CREDIT SET FREE

Towards the end of World War II, the leading Allied powers agreed to fix the exchange rates of their currencies in the Bretton Woods system. The repudiation of this system in the early 1970s by the United States caused macroeconomic disorder. There was little understanding, either in Sweden or elsewhere, of how much of the turbulence of the 1970s was caused by opening the floodgates of credit in the United States and Britain.[3] The conventional wisdom was that markets would be self-regulated by the prudence of lenders and borrowers. Despite the floating of currencies in English-speaking countries, Sweden continued to control credit centrally and persisted with a fixed

---

1. For analogies, Offer, 'Narrow Banking, Real Estate, and Financial Stability in the UK' (2014).
2. Above, chapter 9, note 17; Lönnroth, *Schamanerna* (1993), 267.
3. Wallander, 'En Effektivare Kreditpolitik' (1982). Wallander was a senior banker; Lindvall, *The Politics of Purpose* (2004), 116–119, 141.

exchange rate policy, which was seen as a discipline (working through the balance of trade) on wage pressures from labour. This could be maintained only by a succession of devaluations.

Credit became difficult to control as Swedish corporations expanded overseas and lending took place outside domestic banks. And government was already borrowing overseas. This made market opening more difficult to resist. Credit controls were loosened gradually, and the central bank unleashed the 'November revolution' of 1985, when mortgage lending caps were suddenly removed, as if in a fit of absence of mind.[4] Almost thirty years after Åsbrink's unilateral rate increase of 1957, liberal-minded financial technocrats once again threw Social Democracy off its balance.[5]

Failure is an orphan: the finance minister Feldt was market-minded, a liberal socialist (in the European sense).[6] He had been the Swedish representative to the IMF, the World Bank, the OECD, and the Group of Ten leading economies. In his memoirs, he claims to have acted under pressure from the central bank, without receiving any guidance from a distracted and exhausted prime minister.[7] In the central bank, the view was that financial markets had become so pervasive that regulations no longer worked, and therefore might as well be removed. It was assumed that all demand for credit was already taken up, and the drastic increase in lending was completely unexpected.[8] It was not understood at the time that commercial banks do not face a serious exogenous constraint on lending, apart from the access to credible borrowers with good collateral. Interest payments in Sweden were tax-deductible; given high tax rates and credit loosening, it was tempting for people to borrow in order to invest in financial assets and real estate. With hindsight, the consequences could have been predicted, and they followed soon enough. A surge of lending inflated the value of houses and shares. House prices rose by some sixty percent in five years, unemployment shrank almost to nothing, the economy boomed and then overheated. As if to endorse the new wisdom, the Nobel Prize in economics in 1990 was given to exponents of rational expectations and efficient markets

---

4. Lindvall, *The Politics of Purpose* (2004), 116–119, 141; Svensson, *Novemberrevolutionen* (1996); Blyth, *Great Transformations* (2002), 223–224.
5. Chapter 4, above.
6. Lundberg, 'The Rise and Fall of the Swedish Model' (1985), 32–33.
7. Feldt, *Alla Dessa Dagar* (1991), I, 254–255.
8. Lars Hansson, 'Mot en Marknadskonform Kreditpolitik', 28 August 1985, Stockholm, Swedish Central Bank Archive, Riksbankschefers Arkiv, Box: B. Dennis, Översyn av Kredit- och Valutapolitiken 1985, F1A:236.

finance, Markowitz, Miller, and Sharpe. It might be construed as a signal from members of the Swedish Nobel Committee that their silence on credit liberalization at home was in line with the best current theory. By the time the prize was awarded in December 1990, the boom had been reversed and the economy was falling rapidly (see figures 9.1 and 9.4, above).

In retrospect, those who supported the lifting of credit controls said that it did not go far enough: investors were still restricted to domestic assets; and interest on loans remained deductible from taxes, making investment in assets very cheap in high-tax Sweden.[9] Maybe. International capital controls were lifted in 1989 and interest deductibility, later abolished, has since been restored. In his memoir, Klas Eklund (the finance minister's 'Third Way' advisor) writes,

> The reality was much more difficult than the textbook. When I came to the Ministry of Trade I experienced an unexpected culture shock. It turned out that what blocked a rational economic strategy was not the lack of economic or theoretical expertise of those who were responsible for economic policy, but the difficulties in making policies of the theoretical insights. The problem was not that the finance minister had too few good economists at his disposal (which was what the self-conscious but naïve young commerce student believed) but rather that the Minister and his undeniably talented economists were unable to get the rest of the government, the party and the labor movement to see things the same way as them.[10]

This is revealing. The naïve economist had forgotten the premises underpinning his model, namely that the only condition under which it was valid was atomistic competition in an Arrow-Debreu general equilibrium model that did not resemble any reality. It surprised him that policy had to take account of real-life frictions. The Third Way tenure at the Ministry of Finance was a disaster: since the theory was poor, it was no wonder the policy failed. Finance Minister Feldt and his protégé Eklund were frustrated by the struggle, and both bailed out before their terms were up.

By 1990, the credit boom had run its course, and the onset of the global recession made it difficult for borrowers to service their loans. The boom turned into the worst slump in Sweden since the Great Depression, an economic setback that lasted for much of the next decade (see figures 9.1 and

---

9. Lindbeck interview, 3 December 2012. On the crisis, see Jonung et al., *The Great Financial Crisis* (2009), and Honkaphoja, 'The 1990's Financial Crisis in Nordic Countries' (2009).
10. Eklund, 'En Intellektuell Biografi' (1995).

9.4, above). The financial sector was devastated, and was salvaged by the government (in a pattern that has since become familiar), a subsidy for capitalism that was no part of the design of the welfare state, but was massive and unstinting nonetheless. Lindbeck and his Mont Pèlerin ally Ståhl never tired of advocating free markets in housing.[11] But the regulated Social Democratic housing system provided sustained high volumes of good quality affordable housing, while overcrowding ('Norm 2'—more than two per room) fell from 33 percent (1965) to 4 percent in 1985. Financial liberalization began with harmful house-price surges, while housebuilding fell by more than half from the Social Democratic to the market liberal period. Marketization led to a rise in vacancies, an increase in crowding, a decline of public housing, sharp housing inequalities, and a doubling of homelessness. Housing markets worked well for those who could afford them, and priced out the rest.[12] Looking at Britain, the liberalized housing market has left the country worse housed than most European countries, with a huge overhang of debt and default, and with more housing stress at the bottom of society than when Thatcher came to power in 1979.[13]

Its Keynesian response to the 1973 crisis protected Sweden from the worst. In the late 1980s, however, the Social Democratic government reacted to the new crisis with fiscal austerity, and shifted its priorities from full employment to low inflation. Inflation fell, but unemployment shot up from almost nothing to more than 8 percent (see figure 9.1, above), before settling down to quite high 'normal' European levels thereafter.[14] In 1991, the Social Democrats were replaced in government by a centre-right coalition. In the election campaign, Lindbeck beat the drums of economics in support of the non-socialist parties, as standing for 'market economy, decentralization and private ownership' in opposition to the 'extensive and interventionist regulations, centralism and collective ownership' of Social Democracy.[15]

In 1992, the new centre-right government appointed Lindbeck to lead a commission of inquiry into the crisis. He was given complete discretion, and staffed it with like-minded colleagues.[16] His old collaborator Ingemar Ståhl received the labour brief. Ståhl had long been a member of the Nobel

11. Meyerson et al., *Makten över Bostaden* (1990).
12. Clark and Johnson, 'The "System Switch" in Swedish Housing' (2009); Stenfors, 'The Swedish Financial System' (2014), 113–125.
13. Roberts-Hughes, *The Case for Space* (2011); Hills, *Ends and Means* (2007).
14. Ljungqvist and Sargent, 'How Sweden's Unemployment Became More Like Europe's' (2010).
15. Lönnroth, *Schamanerna* (1993), 269.
16. Lindbeck, *Ekonomi* (2012), 295.

Committee, and also of the Mont Pèlerin Society. The Lindbeck Commission took a mere three months to issue a report, with twenty-seven supporting papers.[17] In an instance of disaster capitalism,[18] it took the opportunity of the crisis to push through the incentives agenda that Lindbeck had been advocating for almost two decades. But 'severe disincentive problems' had little to do with the crisis,[19] which occurred only in the Scandinavian countries (Norway, Finland, and to some extent Denmark), all of which had liberalized credit at about the same time. Other countries were not affected (see figure 9.4, above). In its 113 recommendations, the Lindbeck Commission focused on work incentives, reducing welfare benefits and removing labour protections. In our interview, Lindbeck confirmed that this reflected his own personal priorities, and that no compromises or concessions were required of him. For all their apparent severity, on a larger view (which Lindbeck is inclined to take), the commission did not propose to privatize the welfare state (as suggested at the time by the employers' federation),[20] but merely to make it less compassionate, perhaps less of a soft touch, while making the market tougher for workers, and more benign for employers. Ironically, market failure was used as an excuse for market expansion. Then as now, economic science was invoked in support of reforms, with no regard for its failure to foresee the crisis: 'Mere empirical failure is not enough to discredit a mode of thought.'[21] In his memoirs, Lindbeck conceded that empirical support was often lacking.[22]

What happened next? A recent study from the leading Swedish business think tank reviewed the effectiveness of the reforms.[23] The Lindbeck Commission report, it is argued there, was followed by a productivity surge caused by market reforms. But this does not hold up well under scrutiny. There is the common subterfuge of measuring trends from the trough upwards, that is, from the deepest point in the recession.[24] This is particularly misleading when claiming superiority over other OECD countries which (apart from the Nordic ones), did not have recessions in the mid-1990s. The comparison

17. Soon published in English (without the supporting papers) as Lindbeck et al., *Turning Sweden Around* (1994).
18. Klein, *Shock Doctrine: The Rise of Disaster Capitalism* (2007).
19. Lindbeck in 1981: chapter 9, note 82, above.
20. Blyth, *Great Transformations* (2002), 228.
21. Ibid., 235.
22. Lindbeck, *Ekonomi*, 297–298.
23. Heyman et al., 'The Turnaround of Swedish Industry' (2015). Our discussion refers to this article. Also argued in Bergh and Henrekson, *Varför Går det Bra för Sverige?* (2012).
24. Heyman et al., 'The Turnaround of Swedish Industry' (2015), 4–6.

shows at least four other disparate countries (out of the fifteen compared) with similar productivity growth records (and one much better), suggesting that the reforms in themselves are not a sufficient or even a necessary explanation.[25] The recession was long and harmful. Recovery took ten years to catch up with the 1970–1989 growth trend, and sixteen years to make up for the lost output.[26] Another three years, and the economy experienced two successive years of recession again. During this long recession, unemployment rose about fourfold and the labour participation rate fell by about 10 percentage points, from a very high 85 percent to below 75 percent.[27] If the least productive workers are eliminated, productivity is bound to increase. The continued cost to (and of) unemployed workers is unmeasured by the productivity of people at work, and it reduces overall welfare.

Very little of the productivity surge is attributed by the authors to labour market reforms. Nor was there a great deal of it. The Social Democrats returned to power in 1994 and remained in government until 2006. Wage setting remained centralized, and the workforce remained highly unionized. The main practical reform was less regulation of temporary short-term contracts. Any resulting productivity increase has again to be offset by the unmeasured cost of employment insecurity. If bringing wages into alignment with productivity gains is a good incentive, then it did not occur in manufacturing. The correlation was higher in the services, but it is not disclosed how much this was affected by rising pay in finance, where the link to productivity is dubious.[28] Most of the productivity effect, such as it was, is attributed to institutional policies, most of which were maintained and developed further under Social Democracy. In particular, the high level of education and the generalized culture of trust, which are an important part of the argument, were priorities of Social Democracy, not the product of market competition. That Sweden performed better than most other countries during this period is hardly an argument for market liberalism: Sweden remained more highly regulated than the countries it outperformed.[29] The authors admit that 'it is difficult to obtain causal evidence for our general theoretical and institutional predictions in a single-country study such as ours.'[30]

---

25. Ibid., fig. 2, 5.
26. Calculated from GDP per capita at constant 2005 prices and PPPs, US dollars, OECD, *OECD.Stat* (2015).
27. See figure 9.1, above, and Heyman et al., 'The Turnaround of Swedish Industry', fig. 3, 5.
28. Ibid., fig. 15, 24.
29. Magnusson, 'Globalisering och den Svenska Modellen' (2014).
30. Heyman et al., 'The Turnaround of Swedish Industry' (2015), 3.

EVALUATION

Sweden (with the rest of Scandinavia) resisted the lure of financial liberalization until the mid-1980s, and when it succumbed, punishment came quickly. A severe financial crisis in the early 1990s was almost entirely the result of this liberalization, which also became the opportunity for a modest application of the 'incentives' agenda, leaving, however, much of the Social Democratic welfare state intact.

Up to the 1930s, economics in Sweden as elsewhere offered a vision of self-regulating social harmony created by market exchange.[31] This was in contrast to the turbulent course of industrial relations in Sweden. After achieving the universal franchise, Social Democracy came to power and intervened decisively in labour, welfare, and housebuilding in support of its electoral base, manual workers and small farmers. The Keynesian hegemony in macroeconomics from the 1940s to the 1960s (some of it anticipated by Stockholm School theorists), lent support to these policies, which coincided with and helped to drive rising Swedish economic performance and well-being. Manufacturing as a proportion of paid work peaked in Sweden in the 1960s, and thereafter the electoral base of Social Democracy began to contract.

Swedish economic opinion, led by Assar Lindbeck, pushed to restore market incentives, invoking Hayek in the 1970s and Harberger's disincentive 'wedges' in the 1980s. Economically, Sweden slipped down the performance rankings, and the period 1970 to 1994 was one of considerable volatility, much of it imported from outside. In these circumstances, the push for industrial democracy by the trade unions in the 1970s was mistimed, just as it was in Britain. Another view of the debate about 'incentives' is to regard it as a quest by the expanding middle classes to tighten the discipline of manual workers, to push them back into their 'proper' place and to take advantage of their declining market power. By 1989, the two unions of the salaried and academically qualified represented 42 percent of the workforce.[32]

What probably kept the welfare state in being was the large unionized public sector workforce, who were both its providers and its beneficiaries, and who made up about a third of the workforce. High levels of public employment took up the slack from declining factories. This large public sector was one reason why Swedish unemployment, while never down to the levels

---

31. Myrdal, *Political Element* (1953), ch. 1; Lönnroth, *Schamanerna* (1993), ch. 2; Carlson, *The State as Monster* (1994).

32. Steinmo, *Evolution of Modern States* (2010), 62.

seen before 1990, remained reasonable in comparison with Europe. Except for the crisis decade of the 1990s and some years after 2000, unemployment was lower than in the United States, with much lower levels of poverty and disadvantage, even without taking account of the millions of Americans in military service and in prison.[33]

In four out of the first five years of the 1990s, the Nobel Committee nominated economists from the University of Chicago (see figure 5.1, above). The Nobel Prize swelled the prestige of market liberalism just as its policies were starting to fail worldwide. And in 1994, after twenty-five years on the Nobel Committee, Lindbeck finally had to step off. Interviews with academy insiders suggest that his management style and some of his choices had finally alienated the Swedish Academy of Sciences, which convened two secret investigations and decided that it was time for change.[34]

Walter Korpi wrote that Lindbeck used his position at the pinnacle of Swedish economics and his easy access to the media to browbeat his colleagues into compliance or silence. It could hardly be a lack of professional competence, he wrote, that:

> in the Swedish case, the Sclerosis diagnosis has had its strongest supporters within the Nobel Prize Committee on Economics of the Royal Academy of Science as well as at the Institute for International Economics at Stockholm University [both led by Lindbeck], widely held to be the very best Swedish research institute in economics. . . . There remains the problem of the ethical responsibility of the professional community for important policy recommendations made in the name of the economics discipline. . . . Within the relatively small Swedish professional community, the existence of extremely prestigious bodies such as the Royal Academy of Science and its Nobel Prize Committee is likely to provide the base for a wide variety of influences, which need not necessarily be conducive to theoretical pluralism.[35]

A Swedish economist otherwise supportive of Lindbeck conceded that: 'In their capacity as policy advisors, academic economists far from always live up to the standards of the seminar room.'[36] 'In Sweden,' wrote two economists about this episode, 'there is only one choice on the menu.'[37]

33. ILO, 'ILO Comparable Estimates.'
34. Brittan, 'The Not So Noble Nobel Prize' (2003); Nasar, *A Beautiful Mind* (1998), 368–372.
35. Korpi, 'Eurosclerosis and the Sclerosis of Objectivity' (1996), 1744, nn. 43–44.
36. Agell, 'Why Sweden's Welfare State Needed Reform' (1996), 1760.
37. In 1993. Cited in Blyth, *Great Transformations* (2002), 238.

Economics is sometimes dismissed as an ideology for the better-off. Our account of the Nobel Prize does not support such a generalization, but an unkind observer might think that it accords with Lindbeck's advocacy during these years. From 1976 onwards, he plunged into the conflict over the wage-earners' funds. It is unusual to have an instance of class conflict so narrowly focused (in the Marxist sense) over control of the means of production. Lindbeck used economic theory to support the employers' case. In the 1990s in his role as chair of both the Lindbeck and the Nobel Prize committees, he drew down the prestige of expert impartiality for use as the currency of political debate.

That does not mean that Lindbeck or indeed the majority of Swedish economists were entirely wrong. Lindbeck never grounded his international growth comparisons in appropriate econometric methods, and there are doubts about the validity of such procedures even when carried out correctly. He provided no evidence for his incentives agenda, and the theories themselves remain unvalidated. Most of the market-liberal argument in *Ekonomisk Debatt* was from theory, not measurement.

But even if theory is invalid, arguments still have to be made. Indeed, if one disbelieves the theory, then normative arguments are the only guides. That is the abiding theme of Lindbeck's predecessor Gunnar Myrdal in his acute study, *The Political Element in Economic Theory* (1930). The incompleteness and theoretical weakness of Lindbeck's arguments may be held against him, but we regard his resistance to market fundamentalism as a virtue. It could well be that the public sector in Sweden had grown too large (although the raw figures were exaggerated—cash benefits were taxed, so net expenditure was lower, and taxes paid were well below the marginal rates, and were offset by a variety of deductions). Maybe work had become too onerous and leisure too easy. There is no objective standard by which to judge, independently of ideology and self-interest. Lindbeck claimed the authority of science, as burnished in the reflected glow of the Nobel Prize. But if there was a case to make, it could only be made with reference to values. Public sector too large for what? In whose interest? How much more was work and money better than leisure? How much better was mothering at home compared with wage independence for women? How far should the decline in manual workers' bargaining power be used to roll back their security? That was what the debate was really about, not spurious arguments about 'efficiency'. Efficiency for whom? And at whose expense? Those are the questions that Gunnar Myrdal would have asked.

Values need to be argued for, and Lindbeck argued for his values in his essays and lectures on the welfare state. Since there is no definitive economic knowledge, we have to decide in other ways. Lindbeck's positions are defensible, and not manifestly vicious (unlike a good deal of neoliberalism). He took pride in that. The 'science', however, could not carry the weight that Lindbeck claimed for it. He advocated a more market-liberal society, in which manual and low-paid service workers worked harder, earned less, and were less secure, while middle-class professionals and property owners had more and better choices. As a leading social scientist, the impartial arbiter of the Nobel Prize, his arguments and tactics do not always pass muster. But this preference of Lindbeck's was increasingly shared by voters in Nordic and other well off societies as their members became more affluent and moved out of the factories and into white-collar work.

Lindbeck was no more than partly successful. Swedish society resisted the enticements of market-liberal logic, perhaps because the evidence did not support it. It re-elected the Social Democrats in 1994 for another twelve years. Market forces failed when unleashed, and disaster did not follow when they were thwarted. Financial liberalization led to collapse; trade union rights did not destroy the economy. Sweden's taxes and benefits both remain high, inequality and poverty are low, though both are rising. Lindbeck himself never repudiated the welfare state, and did not propose its wholesale replacement by anything resembling the ideal market of perfect competition. The welfare state, he said, was a major contribution to Western civilization, but it was overshooting its natural limits. The purpose of the Lindbeck Commission, he wrote, was 'to save the welfare state rather than dismantle it'.[38] In defiance of invisible hand thinking, Scandinavian Social Democracy managed to transcend the decline of its working-class constituencies, and its policies and priorities are grudgingly upheld today, even by its political opponents.[39]

---

38. Lindbeck, 'Overshooting, Reform and Retreat of the Welfare State' (1993), 28.
39. Wooldridge, 'Special Report: The Nordic Countries', *Economist*, 2 February 2013.

CHAPTER 11

BEYOND SCANDINAVIA: WASHINGTON CONSENSUS TO MARKET CORRUPTION

Scandinavia was but a sideshow in a larger plot in which market-liberal advocates strove to capture the command of policy worldwide with the 'Washington Consensus'. Their doctrines are viewed here from three aspects: internal validity, empirical performance, and unintended consequences. In brief, these doctrines were inconsistent, failed repeatedly, and engulfed the public domain in a miasma of corruption, in developed countries as well as 'emerging' ones. The reason, we argue, is that these doctrines were founded on deficient models of reality, which is the central thread of this book. The Nobel Prize played a part in all of this, if only a minor one.

THE THEORY OF THE SECOND BEST

Joseph Stiglitz (NPW, 2001) mentions a pervasive folk theorem (which he does not subscribe to): 'Anything that the government can do, the private sector can do as well or better.'[1] This was loosely associated with the 'two theorems of welfare economics' proven by Arrow, Debreu and McKenzie in the 1950s, the post-war model which appeared to place the discipline on a rigorous scientific basis.[2] These theorems stated that any Arrow-Debreu competitive general equilibrium implies a Pareto efficient allocation of re-

---

1. Stiglitz, 'Keynesian Economics and the Critique of First Fundamental Theorem' (2002), 46.
2. Düppe and Weintraub, *Finding Equilibrium* (2014), xi; above, chapter 1.

sources (that is, no slack), and conversely, that such a Pareto efficient allocation can be attained in general equilibrium from any initial distribution, without imposing loss on any individual.[3] There are, however, two views on what the theorems implied. The common one was to take them as the modern incarnation of Adam Smith's 'invisible hand', which did not depend on a particular initial allocation. But the model required the existence of markets for all goods and for all risks, with all prices known into the future, that is, perfect information for all time, unaffected by individual action or choice. Pareto efficient redistribution required in addition that transfers had to be by lump sums, and that government had perfect information about tastes and technologies, and convexity, that is, (very approximately) diminishing returns to tastes and technologies. Such preconditions do not exist in any real world, so another interpretation was to regard the theorems as an effective *refutation* of the invisible hand, a position sometimes taken even by their originators.[4]

No sooner had the Arrow-Debreu result been published in 1954 than another spanner fell into the works: even if only one of the Arrow-Debreu conditions was not fulfilled, there was no presumption that satisfying the others could improve efficiency or welfare. Optimality was a matter of all or nothing, and 'all' was not a real-world possibility. It was called a theory of the 'second best', but this was misleading: no second best was available either. Real-world deviations from Arrow-Debreu (commonly depicted as 'distortions') were numerous and inescapable: uncompetitive markets, entry barriers, locational inequalities, inflexible wages and jobs, government regulation and taxation, incomplete and asymmetric information, externalities and spillovers, missing markets, and concern for other people. Technological change, assumed to be the driver of growth, was inescapably uncertain (otherwise no research would be required), but the model required foreknowledge. So (contrary to the Harberger Triangle assumptions) there was no halfway house to optimality.[5] It is notable (but not surprising) that Assar

---

3. On Pareto efficiency, see above, 3, 17.
4. Arrow and Hahn, *General Competitive Analysis* (1971), vii; Stiglitz, 'The Invisible Hand' (1991); Blaug, 'The Fundamental Theorems of Modern Welfare Economics' (2007); above, 19.
5. Lipsey and Lancaster, 'The General Theory of the Second Best' (1956); Lipsey, 'Reflections on the General Theory of Second Best' (1950), 350–351; Stiglitz, 'Keynesian Economics and the Critique of First Fundamental Theorem' (2002); anticipated by Little, *Critique of Welfare Economics* (1950/2002), preface to 2002 ed., vii–viii.

Lindbeck, in his campaign to remove distortions in Sweden, did not allude to the problem of second best, which would have invalidated his argument.

Economists were mesmerized by the Arrow-Debreu result, and were not going to give it up so easily.[6] Harberger showed how to do it in practice: removing distortions one by one (mostly the fault of government and labour), in order to let supply and demand intersect unhindered without worrying too much whether any of the other multitude of restrictive assumptions about equilibrium were satisfied.[7] This was justified as according with economic intuition, though (as we have seen in the case of Sweden) it worked primarily as a wedge for policies inimical to Social Democracy.[8]

In the 1960s and early 1970s, several efforts were made to implement this method in economic development. Of these efforts, the most prominent was by Ian Little and James Mirrlees (NPW, 1996), but all of them aspired 'to get the prices right.'[9] Earlier development priorities like forced industrialization had shifted prices away from their equilibrium levels. 'Project appraisal' made it possible to compare development projects with alternative ones. The key was to assign prices to capital, labour, money, and time, even when such prices were not readily available. The idea was that world market prices reflected the opportunity cost of any input, that is, what had to be sacrificed in order to use them in a particular project, even if no inputs were imported. Such 'real-world' prices (and market-simulating 'shadow prices' for wages and interest rates) were assumed to converge on those obtained by market equilibrium. For Harberger, this meant pretending that the real world approximated to the model. That was standard Chicago procedure.[10] But although presented as 'second-best' theory, this was wrong: competitive prices that satisfied the models did not exist, and the optimal attributes of partial equilibrium analysis were also dubious.[11] The prices used for reference (world prices, market wages, and so on) were just another set of those 'distorted' prices which it was desired to correct.

Project appraisal was a form of what we have called hybrid theory, in which the application was not consistent with the premises, not unlike Mirr-

6. Stiglitz, 'The Invisible Hand' (1991), 35; Düppe and Weintraub, *Finding Equilibrium* (2014); Blaug, 'The Fundamental Theorems of Modern Welfare Economics' (2007), 198–199.

7. Harberger, 'Three Basic Postulates for Applied Welfare Economics' (1971).

8. Chapter 9, above, 200–203.

9. Little and Mirrlees, *Project Appraisal and Planning* (1974).

10. Harberger, *Project Evaluation* (1972), 127; Reder, 'Chicago Economics—Permanence and Change' (1982), 10–13; also chapter 1, above, 24.

11. Above, 19; below, 261–262.

lees's other theory, that of optimal taxation.[12] It was 'schizophrenic',[13] on the one hand assuming the miracle of the market, on the other acknowledging that its prerequisites did not exist.[14] Project appraisal textbooks acknowledged the second-best problem, but only as afterthoughts. They argued that it was possible to identify a good optimum, but despite the confidence with which they were stated, there was no getting around the 'second-best' problem.[15] This was borne out in practice: general equilibrium theory applies to the economy as a whole, but the appraisers dealt only with single projects. Rigorous analysis had to be set aside and the experienced analyst could strive only for piecemeal improvement.[16]

For a few years in the 1970s, the World Bank, development agencies and governments tried to apply project appraisal methods, but they soon gave up; other agencies and governments did not even try. Little and Mirrlees complained that passing over their method was a false economy, but requisite data were difficult to collect, and the analysis left out too much. It was really a delusion: project appraisal was not consistent with general equilibrium, and there was no theoretical second best, only pragmatic judgment. This is not to dismiss these efforts: the discipline of evaluating a project by its notional opportunity cost (which is what the technique effectively required) was likely (in good hands) to provide much benefit.[17]

WASHINGTON CONSENSUS

In the 1950s and 1960s, developing countries attempted a big push to self-sufficiency partly inspired by what seemed to be working in the USSR: replacing imports with local factories and skills.[18] Foreign corporations and banks were held at arm's length, and some *dirigiste* regimes, for example, Cuba, Indonesia, India, Egypt, Syria, and Iraq, aligned politically with the Soviet Union.[19]

---

12. Above, 173.
13. Not in a pejorative sense, but used by several economists to indicate inconsistent positions.
14. The term is used in this sense by Blaug, 'Fundamental Theorems of Welfare Economics' (2007), 198; Stiglitz, 'Invisible Hand' (1991), 7; Samuelson, 'Succumbing to Keynesianism' (1985), 5.
15. For example, Little and Mirrlees, *Project Appraisal and Planning* (1974), 372–373; Lal, *Poverty of 'Development Economics'* (1983), 111–112.
16. Harberger, *Project Evaluation* (1972), 128–129.
17. Little and Mirrlees, 'Project Appraisal and Planning Twenty Years On' (1990), 372–373.
18. Hirschman 'Rise and Fall of Development Economics' (1981).
19. The term used, pejoratively, by Lal, *Poverty of 'Development Economics'* (1983).

In the United States, the Cold War and the quest for free markets were easily conflated, and pursued with equal zeal.[20] Dictatorial coups in Iran and Guatemala in the 1950s were instigated by American and British agents. America dispatched its own troops, allies and mercenaries to Cuba and Vietnam in the 1960s. Suharto's takeover in Indonesia (1965) set off the mass killing of about half a million people identified with the left, and more than a million were locked up. Colonels and Generals took power in Brazil, Argentina, and Chile, where they tortured, murdered, 'disappeared' their opponents, and expelled them. In Latin America alone, it is estimated that tens of thousands were killed, hundreds of thousands exiled. These coups took their playbook from the CIA and their economics from Berkeley and Chicago.[21] They were reversals for communism, loosely conceived, but no victories for democracy. The military tore down worker protections and slashed wages, cut back social programs, removed subsidies for food and fuel, and drove much of their populations into poverty. But they opened up to foreign companies and banks, and privatized government services and enterprises.[22] A reader of *Economist*, *Financial Times*, or *Wall Street Journal* editorials might well ask what is there not to like?[23]

By the end of the 1980s, most of the first-wave dictators had been deposed, or were soon to go. Their economic policies, however, remained in place, as well as many of their technocrats. And a new wave was about to begin, this time in the former Soviet empire and in Southeast Asia. It was at this point, at the end of the 1980s, that John Williamson published 'What Washington Means by Policy Reform'.[24] This celebrated text coined the term 'Washington Consensus'. Naming is knowing: the 'Washington Consensus' (henceforth WashCon) has become the term for globalization driven by external debt. Williamson's essay had the virtue of putting the best face on such policies, and provides a starting-point for assessing their validity. The 'Washington' of the 'Consensus' consisted of the World Bank, the International Monetary Fund, and the US Treasury, that between them made financial policy for a globalizing world. Wall Street banks were low-profile partners, together with their regulator the Federal Reserve.

20. Berger et al., 'Commercial Imperialism?' (2013).
21. Blum, *Killing Hope* (1993); Klein, *Shock Doctrine* (2007), 57–128.
22. Green, *Silent Revolution* (2003); Chossudovsky, *Globalization of Poverty* (2003).
23. *Economist*, 'Memory Is Not History' (2014), 50.
24. Williamson, 'What Washington Means by Policy Reform' (1990).

Williamson set out ten commandments for recipients of Washington largesse

- 'Fiscal deficits'—that is, no recourse to budget deficits. In practice, sharp cuts in expenditure and taxes.
- 'Public expenditure priorities'—military expenditures protected, otherwise switching from price subsidies for basic commodities towards education, health and infrastructure.
- 'Tax reform'—'tax base should be broad and marginal tax rates should be moderate', that is, a shift of taxation from the upper and middle class to the middle class and poor, in line with Mirrlees's (NPW, 1996) optimal tax principles.
- 'Interest rates'—determined in financial markets, and positive in real terms, that is, financial market liberalization.
- 'Exchange rate'—determined by market forces, and consistent with macroeconomic objectives.
- 'Trade policy'—that is, import liberalization. Protection of domestic industry created costly distortions. Tariffs better than import quotas, and some temporary protection was acceptable.
- 'Foreign direct investment'—liberalization of financial flows not a high priority, but foreign direct investment welcome, including swaps of debt for ownership.
- 'Privatization'—both for the sake of government revenue windfalls, and on the view that ownership is a better incentive than public service.
- 'Deregulation'—to promote competition and reduce capriciousness and corruption.
- 'Property rights'—not sufficiently secure in Latin America (the book is about that continent).

In conclusion, he wrote: 'A striking fact about the list of policies on which Washington does have a collective view is that they all stem from classical mainstream economic theory.'[25]

This may be a clue as to why the agencies were enamoured of theory: it coincided with the interests of finance and business. But the pretence of rigour had gone. In the same year, Ravi Kanbur, a senior World Bank and academic

---

25. Ibid., 19.

economist, suggested extending project appraisal methods to WashCon programmes. His paper indicated that no such analysis was being applied, and
that WashCon policies did not come out of rigorous analysis. Response to
the presentation was tepid and it was not followed up.[26]

Williamson himself in 1990 was a think tank agent of high finance. More
than any other individual, he worked to impart intellectual coherence to the
WashCon project; in a stream of conference papers, articles and books, his
name comes up repeatedly. He had been an academic economist and had
worked for the IMF and World Bank. His employer was the Institute for
International Economics, founded in 1981 by Peter G. Peterson, a big figure
in American finance and right-wing politics. A self-made Republican businessman, Peterson was a Nixon Cabinet member; head of Lehman Brothers
bank from 1973 to 1984; founder (in 1985) of the Blackstone Group, a large
private equity firm; and (in 2000–2004) chair of the Federal Reserve Bank of
New York and also of the influential Council on Foreign Relations (1985–
2007), where his successor was Robert Rubin, the Goldman Sachs Chairman, Clinton Treasury Secretary, and Citibank executive. In 2006, Peterson
gave a billion dollars to the institute that employed Williamson, and added
his name to the masthead. For Peterson, an avowed enemy of Social Democracy, rolling back the welfare state was a personal cause, in support of which
he wrote eight books and co-founded a 'Concord Coalition'.[27]

A LOST DECADE

The WashCon project descended indirectly from American military setbacks in
the 1960s and the early 1970s. Paying for Vietnam with an excess of dollars un-
moored the currency from its gold anchor in 1971. When Soviet-armed Egypt
and Syria attacked America's ally Israel two years later, Arab oil producers raised
prices fourfold in sympathy. Inflation followed. Without the discipline of dollar
redemption in gold, bank loans became easier to make and to take. Currencies
were allowed to fluctuate, and the IMF lost its role of defending fixed exchange
rates. Developing countries turned to British and American banks, which were
flush with funds recycled by the oil producers. With inflation persisting, interest
rates fell and borrower countries built up large debts.

---

26.   Kanbur, 'Projects versus Policy Reform' (1990).
27.   Bergsten, *The Peter G. Peterson Institution for International Economics* (2006); Peterson, *The
Education of an American Dreamer* (2009).

In 1979, another American setback, the Iranian revolution, pushed up oil prices fourfold again. The Federal Reserve set out to tame US inflation in November of that year and began to tighten credit. Rates approaching 20 percent knocked debtor countries off their feet. Some borrowers could no longer roll over their commercial loans, and went back to the IMF. In August 1982, Mexico ran out of dollars.[28] The top nine American banks' exposure to Latin America was reported as 1.76 times their capital, and for all less developed countries (LDCs), 2.88 times.[29] These debts appeared to threaten the solvency of the American financial system, and indeed, the stability of the world economy. But there are reasons for doubt. Capital levels in American and British banking were low, typically no more than 3 to 5 percent of lending.[30] Bank exposure overall (their 'leverage') was normally twenty to thirty times their capital. In the 1990s and 2000s, it rose as high as 40 to 50 times their capital. American regulators (the Federal Reserve and the Treasury) were relaxed about such levels of exposure. There was no suggestion that all LDC borrowers would default at once, and even if they did, the banks could be recapitalized by the Fed and not allowed to fail, as happened domestically when Continental Illinois (seventh-largest bank in the United States) collapsed in 1984. But for loans to the developing world, there was no forbearance. Borrowers had to pay, whatever it took: *Pacta sunt servanda* ('agreements must be kept'); the same principle applied so brutally to Greece in 2015.

Old-style development economists were purged from WashCon agencies in the early 1980s.[31] At the World Bank, the liberal Robert McNamara gave way to A. W. Clausen, a Wall Street banker. His approach to the debt crisis was

> to emphasize the role of free markets and private sector institutions. He saw a clear link between efficiency and ownership, and believed that preference should be given to the private sector. Developing countries should improve market signals and price incentives while substituting imports for expensive domestic production and increasing the efficiency of their export sectors.[32]

28. Green, *Silent Revolution* (2003), 60.
29. Sachs, 'International Policy Coordination: The Case of the Developing Country Debt Crisis' (1987), table 1, after 3.
30. Haldane, 'Banking on the State' (2009), chart 2, 14.
31. Stiglitz, *Globalization and Its Discontents* (2002), 13.
32. World Bank Archives, 'Alden Winship ("Tom") Clausen' (n.d.).

Clausen appointed Anne Krueger as his chief economist: she had developed the concept of 'rent seeking', in which it pays more to invest in political control of revenue streams than in productive enterprise. This was aimed at government ineffectiveness, but also turned out to be a foretaste of the effects of deregulation and privatization, of which she remains a leading advocate.[33] The agencies' template was adapted only minimally to individual country circumstances and was deployed at short notice by economic technicians with little local knowledge. If market equilibrium theory was universal and timeless, then detailed local understanding was not vital.

The IMF did not have the funds to replace commercial lenders to its client countries. Instead, it provided commercial banks with an implicit guarantee. Its conditionality requirements made borrowers more capable of debt service.[34] Thus, WashCon agency credit made it more likely that debtors would service their commercial loans.[35] The IMF 'gave the banks a virtual veto over the approval and financing of adjustment programs . . . they were able to use this power to force significant modifications.'[36] When defaults threatened, the IMF imposed settlements that rescued the bankers: the loans, however ill judged, would be serviced. The World Bank economist Deepak Lal, otherwise a WashCon advocate (and Mont Pèlerin Society member), wrote: 'The IMF has increasingly become the international debt collector for foreign money-centre banks, as well as an important tool of US foreign policy. It should be shut down.'[37] This norm of 'too big to fail' has held sway ever since and pointed the way to the financial crash of 2008, and to the Greek crisis of 2015.[38] The agencies (endowed by taxpayers) acted as lenders of last resort, but not to the banks at risk (as stipulated by the historical 'lender of last resort' doctrine). Instead, it was the borrowers who would be rescued with public money, which they would have to use to pay back the lenders, under pain of economic, diplomatic and political excommunication.

The consequence for many borrowers was a collapse of income, investment, and quality of life, as well as capital flight and soaring inflation, as governments printed money to defer cuts. But debts were serviced. In 1986,

33. Krueger, 'Political Economy of the Rent-Seeking Society' (1974).
34. Gould, *Money Talks* (2006).
35. Sachs and Williamson, 'Managing the LDC Debt Crisis' (1986), table 5, 407.
36. Boughton, *Silent Revolution* (2001), 406–407.
37. Lal, *The Poverty of 'Development Economics'* (1983/2002), 25–26.
38. Barth et al., 'Just How Big Is Too Big to Fail' (2014), 10–11.

For Latin America, the negative net resource transfer since 1982 has totalled more than $95 billion. Yet the years under the debt crisis and IMF-style austerity programs have been ones of extreme economic hardship and declining living standards in most of the debtor countries. In some of the worst cases, the declines are shocking, with 1985 real wage levels down to 50 or 75 percent of 1975 values. Social and political dislocations have been profound.[39]

'The single most consistent effect the IMF seems to have is the redistribution of income away from workers.'[40] A good deal of the loans were sidelined by corrupt elites into military spending and into their own pockets. By 2003, the tribute (the positive gap between debt service and capital imports) had risen to nearly $280bn.[41]

The conventional view of money is that lenders are constrained by their equity capital and the scale of deposits, some multiple of which they can lend safely. For such a key issue in economics, there is a surprisingly wide range of divergent views. Endogenous money theory, which appears to be gaining ground, regards lending as not constrained by capital and deposits, only by the prospects of the debts being serviced.[42] With a sovereign safety net (what WashCon essentially provided), the constraints of prudence could be relaxed, and commercial banks could lend ever-higher multiples of their capital. Much of the lending was channelled into existing real estate, that is, did not increase productive capacity. That is also what essentially happened in the UK economy from the 1980s to 2008.[43] For borrowers, however, loans in dollars were like a liability in gold in the olden days: a foreign currency, which had to be sweated for by exporting. For two decades, the poor countries of the world delivered a flow of tribute to the United States (and other metropolitan lenders) in the form of export goods.

The systemic threat to US banks (mentioned previously as a pretext for these actions) was largely contrived. Figure 11.1 shows the cycle of LDC indebtedness in Latin America and South-East Asia, the main areas of Wash-Con lending. Many of the countries involved had long episodes of high and

---

39. Sachs, 'Managing the LDC Debt Crisis' (1986), 399.
40. Pastor, *International Monetary Fund and Latin America* (1987), 89.
41. Kregel, 'Negative Net Resource Transfers' (2006), 15.
42. Mishkin, *The Economics of Money, Banking and Financial Markets* (1998), chs. 13–14; Wray, *Modern Money Theory* (2012); Palley, 'Horizontalists, Verticalists, and Structuralists' (2013); McLeay et al., 'Money Creation in the Modern Economy' (2014).
43. Offer, 'Narrow Banking' (2014).

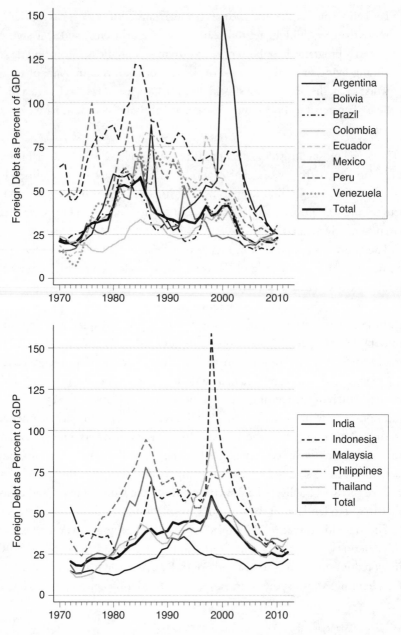

Figure 11.1. Foreign debt as percent of GDP, Latin America and South Asia, c. 1970–2012, current prices.

Source: Debt: World Bank, 'External Debt Stocks' (2014); GDP in current prices: Conference Board, 'Total Economy Database' (2014), Total GDP in Millions of Current USD.

hyper-inflation, so the figures cannot be entirely accurate. There was a good deal of variance among the different countries, and in their level over time. The weighted average ('Total') is dominated by the largest countries. Nevertheless some patterns emerge. In both regions, foreign debt rose up to the mid-1980s, and the WashCon export-oriented austerity policies managed to reverse this trend (in Latin America) or slow it (in Asia). Debt began to build up again in the 1990s, and peaked in the late 1990s. Several countries (Bolivia, Argentina, Thailand, Indonesia) crashed, while others (India, Malaysia, Colombia) avoided the pitfalls almost entirely. Foreign debts fell in both regions after 2000. Southeast Asian countries reinforced their export success, and built up large dollar reserves to prevent a recurrence of their humiliations in 1997. In South America, the fall of debt was due to a commodities boom, and also to a political swing which installed eleven left-of-centre governments.[44] After two WashCon decades, Social Democracy was making a comeback in the periphery, just as it was increasingly embattled in its heartlands.[45]

STRUCTURAL ADJUSTMENT

In the 1980s, there were doubts whether all borrowers could survive this onslaught, and several proposals for debt rescheduling and forgiveness. The principal economists involved showed only lukewarm support.[46] Instead, the Baker Plan (1985) formalized a co-partnership, with commercial banks providing credit, and WashCon agencies the persuasion. The IMF and World Bank had always imposed conditions on their loans. After the mid-1980s, these strove to reconstruct debtor economies on market-liberal lines. Conditionality hardened into 'structural adjustment programmes', tailor-made for each debtor country by the IMF or World Bank, often in consultation with each other.[47] The ingredients could be a currency devaluation, convertibility or pegging to the dollar; cuts in public spending; privatization, deregulation, and opening up: 'Stabilize, privatize, and liberalize' became the order

44. Cameron and Hershberg, *Latin America's Left Turns* (2010); Weyland et al., *Leftist Governments in Latin America* (2010).
45. Sandbrook et al., *Social Democracy in the Global Periphery* (2007), ch. 6; Weyland et al., *Leftist Governments in Latin America* (2010), ch. 1.
46. Sachs, 'Managing the LDC Debt Crisis' (1986), 432–440.
47. Polak, 'Changing Nature of IMF Conditionality' (1991); Boughton, *Silent Revolution* (2001), ch. 13.

of the day.[48] Aspirations also escalated: no longer just debt service and deficit reduction, but economic development and growth. In practice, as noted in one consultation, debt service and military expenditures were protected, and most of the cost of adjustment fell on labour.[49]

These norms stemmed from the University of Chicago, which together with Berkeley, Harvard, MIT, and Yale, had trained hundreds of Ph.D. economists from developing countries in the invisible hand/free trade models of general equilibrium microeconomics. These economists, in partnership with their North American mentors, implemented the market-liberal economic policies of Indonesia, Brazil, Argentina, and Chile in the 1960s and the 1970s. They focused on static efficiency, that is, reducing 'distortions' to squeeze the most out of domestic factors of production, in the manner advocated by Harberger. But the development challenge was not how to simulate a frictionless market—not how to abolish rents, but how to acquire them. Success when it came in Southeast Asia was achieved by means of imperfect competition, by combining poor, literate labour with production engineering to export well-made, well-priced manufactures, and earning the rents of market power.[50]

Nobel Prize winners were not prominent in WashCon conclaves, but some were there in spirit. For the first generation of post-war development economists, the problem of development had been one of dormant resources, especially 'unlimited supplies of labour' in the countryside.[51] This concern with idle hands was Keynesian, and the solutions were inherently *dirigiste*, a big push for industrial investment, foreign aid, industrialization, and a priority for basic needs (sanitation, education, income).[52] The eclipse of Keynes in the 1970s also diminished the old development economics. It was squeezed out by the neoclassical monoculture, which denied that LDCs required a different political economy: the road to development led into the global division of labour, making use of comparative advantage in domestic endowments, leaving the rest to be imported (in the manner of Ricardo). This changing of the economic guard was also played out in Stockholm, where the Nobel Prize for 1979 was given to the Caribbean economist Arthur Lewis of the 'old' school, and to Theodore Schultz, who applied a Chicago market approach to development.

48. Rodrik, 'Goodbye Washington Consensus' (2006), 973.
49. Meller, 'Comment' (1990), 33, 35.
50. World Bank, *East Asian Miracle* (1993).
51. Lewis, 'Economic Development with Unlimited Supply of Labour' (1954).
52. Hirschman, 'The Rise and Decline of Development Economics' (1981).

Schultz had initiated the training programme for Latin American economists financed by the US government in the 1950s, and by the Ford Foundation in the 1960s.[53] Milton Friedman (NPW, 1976) advised Pinochet in Chile. James Buchanan (NPW, 1986) visited Chile several times, and Hayek (NPW, 1974) went there twice, and spoke in support of the Pinochet regime.[54] Otherwise, the absence of top-flight Nobel-level economists in WashCon policy-making may be due to the lack of Nobel-quality rigour in its theoretical underpinning. The outstanding exception was Joseph Stiglitz (NPW, 2001), a one-time chief economist of the World Bank who was also WashCon's most persistent critic. The top-cited NPW of our whole period, he hammered at one point for three decades: 'The invisible hand must be taken as an article of faith, not a scientifically established proposition.'[55] His own contribution, for which he received the prize, was to show that 'whenever information is imperfect and markets incomplete, which is to say always, *and especially in developing countries*, then the invisible hand works most imperfectly.'[56] WashCon policies were 'market fundamentalism',

> made on the basis of what seemed a curious blend of ideology and bad economics, dogma that sometimes seemed to be thinly veiled special interests. ... Rarely did I see forecasts about what the policies would do to poverty. Rarely did I see thoughtful discussions and analysis of the consequences of alternative policies. There was a single prescription. Alternative opinions were not sought. Open, frank discussion was discouraged—there was no room for it.[57]

John Williamson himself, who coined the term 'Washington Consensus', later conceded that its prescriptions had no foundation in theory:

> One does not have to be some sort of market fundamentalist who believes that less government is better government and that externalities can safely be disregarded in order to recognize the benefits of using market forces to coordinate activity and motivate effort. This is a proposition that is such a basic part of economic thinking *that it is actually rather difficult to think of a*

---

53. Klein, *Shock Doctrine* (2007), 59–61.
54. Caldwell and Montes, 'Friedrich Hayek and His Visits to Chile' (2014).
55. Stiglitz, 'The Invisible Hand and Modern Welfare Economics' (1991), 35.
56. Stiglitz, *Globalization and Its Discontents* (2002), 73; idem,'Keynesian Economics and Critique of First Fundamental Theorem' (2002), quote n. 10, 60; idem, 'Round Table Discussion' (1990), 430; idem, 'Invisible Hand' (1991).
57. Stiglitz, *Globalization and Its Discontents* (2002), xii–xiv.

work that conclusively establishes its truth. But there are a variety of indirect confirmations.[58]

In other words, if WashCon was validated, it was by experience rather than theory. On this test, however, the record is just as poor. The first decade of WashCon policies has come to be known as the 'lost decade', in which Latin American incomes at the end were one-tenth lower than at the beginning.[59] A link between WashCon policies and economic growth could not be demonstrated.[60] The official historian of the IMF writes: 'There was no generally accepted model or paradigm linking specific structural policies either to macroeconomic performance or to external viability.'[61] Countries subject to IMF and World Bank 'conditionality' actually suffered inferior economic growth. Conditionality may have been a way for local elites to justify reforms that would work in their favour, against the interest of the rest.[62]

The decade that followed was another sequence of disasters. The transition out of communism in Eastern Europe plunged whole populations into indigence. The Mexican financial crisis of 1994 was followed by the East Asian and Russian crises of 1997–1998, and the collapse of Argentina in 2001. WashCon policies instigated these crises, and WashCon agencies mismanaged them. By the beginning of the 2000s, the 'Washington Consensus' had become 'a damaged brand'.[63]

By the 1990s, another commandment had silently joined the Washington Consensus, namely free capital movement.[64] This allowed Wall Street and other Western banks not only to make lucrative and secure adjustment loans, but also to acquire debtor country assets cheaply. The WashCon programmes imposed high interest rates (to retain and attract capital) and low exchange rates (to encourage exports), while tariff reductions were meant to invigorate local producers. Imports of Western consumer goods built up expensive tastes, and had to be funded by foreign loans.[65] Speculative money

58. Williamson, 'A Short History of the Washington Consensus' (2008), 26. Italics added.
59. Hayes, 'The U.S. and Latin America: A Lost Decade?' (1989).
60. Polak, *Changing Nature* (1991), 41–50.
61. Boughton, *Silent Revolution* (2001), 590; also ibid., 609, 612, 614.
62. Vreeland, *The IMF and Economic Development* (2003).
63. Naím, 'Washington Consensus: A Damaged Brand' (2002); Williamson, 'Our Agenda and the Washington Consensus' (2003), 325–329; Rodrik, 'Goodbye Washington Consensus' (2006); Stiglitz, *Globalization and Its Discontents* (2002).
64. Fischer, 'Comment' (1990), 26; Stiglitz, *Globalization and Its Discontents* (2002), ch. 4.
65. Baker, *Market and the Masses in Latin America* (2009).

flowed quickly into one country after another, instigated bubbles in finance and real estate, and then headed for the door.

Panics were contagious. The first happened in Mexico in 1994, where foreign capital arrived in response to high interest rates in a convertible currency. A well-managed economy collapsed when foreign investors panicked. President Carlos Salinas de Gortari, a Harvard economics Ph.D., left for exile under several different clouds. The IMF required Mexico to honour all the dollar debts. The same film ran even more vividly in 1997–1998, in a sequence of Southeast Asia 'dominoes', starting with Thailand, and followed by IMF clients Indonesia, the Philippines, and South Korea. In each of them, the IMF imposed punitive concessions, forcing governments to put local firms up for sale. The IMF implemented its standard package of austerity and privatization in countries whose fiscal condition was sound, who only required emergency aid due to the WashCon insistence on free capital movements. Incomes collapsed, riots followed, governments fell. Businesses closed, savings disappeared, hundreds of thousands lost their jobs, and the cost of living soared. The IMF later conceded that this had been an error, but the damage had been done.[66] Countries that had kept the IMF out (China, India, Taiwan, Singapore, Malaysia) weathered the crisis better.

In Eastern Europe, newly released from Soviet control, WashCon agencies (backed by the US and European governments) imposed their drastic agenda to devalue the currency, cut government services, social insurance, and price subsidies, and privatize government enterprises. These assets were picked up by former officials and their cronies, while foreign investors moved in to capture natural resources. Standards of living collapsed, Russian men lost about four years of life expectancy, while criminal gangs terrorized and captured a good deal of Russian business.[67] Overall, even WashCon agencies conceded that their policies had been a human disaster there.[68]

The faithful responded by saying that reforms had not gone far enough. Anne Krueger's title for a speech in 2004 was 'Meant Well, Tried Little, Failed Much.'[69] By then she was acting managing director of the IMF. She blamed, among other things, 'reform fatigue'. Her greatest regret was to have

---

66. Stiglitz, *Globalization and Its Discontents* (2002), chs. 4–5.
67. Wedel, *Collusion and Corruption* (1998); Reddaway and Glinski, *The Tragedy of Russia's Market Reforms* (2001); Cohen, *Failed Crusade* (2002); Cornia and Paniccià, *The Mortality Crisis in Transitional Economies* (2000); Stiglitz, *Globalization and Its Discontents* (2002), ch. 5.
68. Zagha and Nankani, *Economic Growth in the 1990s* (2005); Rodrik, 'Goodbye Washington Consensus' (2006).
69. Krueger, 'Meant Well' (2004).

neglected 'labour market reforms', that is, not having gone far enough to eviscerate worker protections. Market critics were inclined to condemn emergent welfare systems as favouring 'insiders' in government and in formal sector employment (a theory propounded by Lindbeck), but that is how welfare states began in the developed world as well: they began as clubs for favoured insiders, which eventually grew to encompass everybody.[70] To target these clubs in emerging countries was another retrograde step.

CORRUPTION ERUPTION

WashCon was a lenders' club, staking Western money in developing economies. As the flow of money increased, so did opportunities for embezzlement. By the 1990s, WashCon policies were inundated with corruption.[71] 'Petty corruption' is when individuals break the rules. 'Grand corruption' is when they are able to write them.[72] The development regimes of the 1950s and 1960s had a good deal of petty corruption by lower-level officials. In the Soviet Union, for example, 'fixing' (*blat*) was pervasive.[73] In contrast, WashCon reforms attracted 'grand corruption', that is, massive malfeasance at the top.[74] Whatever their other abuses, old-style development leaders did not become mega-rich unless and until they opened doors to international finance. Attatürk, Stalin, Mao, Nehru, Sukarno, Nyerere, Ho Chi Minh, Ben-Gurion, all had their dachas and banquets, but did not bequeath great wealth to their families, unlike Suharto and Mobuto, Marcos and Pinochet. Business-friendly coups in Indonesia, Argentina, Chile, Brazil, and elsewhere in the 1960s and 1970s made rulers and their cronies rich. The businesses sold off were typically natural monopolies, either public services or natural resources, and it was enough to sell them cheaply to insiders, and to keep their prices unregulated, to make enrichment possible.[75]

Corruption is not easy to measure or even to define, but indicators were soon compiled by several agencies, conferences convened, hundreds of books and articles published. In the space of a decade to the mid-1990s, refer-

---

70. Offer, *Why Has the Public Sector Grown So Large in Market Societies?* (2003), 3, 7–9, 12, 14–16.

71. Naím, 'Corruption Eruption'(1995).

72. For example, Bosman, 'Wisconsin Governor Signs Bill Limiting Political Corruption Inquiries' (2015).

73. Grossman, 'The "Second Economy" of the USSR' (1977).

74. Cockroft, *Global Corruption* (2012), ch. 2.

75. For example, Smith, 'Privatisation in Latin America' (2002); Cockroft, *Global Corruption* (2012), 26–32.

ences to corruption in the *Economist* increased fivefold, and almost doubled in JSTOR. In 1993, a former World Bank official set up Transparency International, an organization to monitor and fight corruption, which acquired local chapters in some ninety countries within ten years.

Corruption undermined the WashCon promise. Contracts could not be trusted and deals became uncertain. Competition was no longer on price and quality alone. If one imagines market outcomes to be ethical, then corruption rewarded insiders and criminals, and eroded public consent. The promise of reform itself was a con: 'Not one of the democratic governments that launched market-oriented reforms ran on a platform of free trade, price liberalization, and privatization. The drastic reforms of elected governments almost uniformly surprised Latin American voters.'[76] Privatization, whatever its purported benefits, alienated large majorities in Latin America, the more educated the more hostile.[77]

The experts were baffled: At WashCon conferences, economists and political scientists presented taxonomies of corruption, but no effective remedies.[78] The United States had already forbidden bribery overseas in 1978, and now complained of business lost to European and Japanese competitors. It promoted anti-corruption treaties in the UN and the OECD. WashCon agencies embarked on a costly anti-corruption effort, but to no avail: the indicators show no abatement, and corruption spread from developing countries back to the developed ones.[79]

Neither of the two tributaries of post-war economics provided much guidance. Of the two, bad faith economics regards corruption as the normal state of affairs. In contrast, invisible hand economics does not allow for corruption. Exchange is voluntary and informed, and everyone gets what they deserve. Traders act in good faith or enforcement is costless, the two assumptions being interchangeable. Adam Smith showed that competition on its own could offset bad faith: in domestic grain markets it was futile to cheat even if the traders were unscrupulous, because prices raised above

76. Naím, 'Latin America: Post-Adjustment Blues' (1993), 135.

77. For example, Martimort and Straub, 'Privatization and Changes in Corruption Patterns' (2006), 24–29; Nellis, 'Privatization—A Summary Assessment' (2006).

78. For example, Elliott, *Corruption and the Global Economy* (1997); Abed, *Governance, Corruption, and Economic Performance* (2003).

79. Transparency International, 'Corruptions Perception Index, 1995–2013, 27 Countries' (2013). The English-speaking countries in the index, Australia, Canada, Ireland, United Kingdom, United States, all declined a little. Also Hough, *Corruption, Anti-Corruption and Governance* (2013), ch. 1.

their natural level would soon be undercut.[80] This elegant model is correct on its own terms, but only with a single uniform commodity and many traders. Despite its brilliance, it is only a model. Reality was often different: eighteenth-century workers rioted for bread, and twentieth-century farmers in North America set up co-operatives.

With such notions at the back of their minds, WashCon exponents argued that expunging corruption required more of the same: 'Any reform that increases the competitiveness of the economy will reduce incentives for corrupt behaviour.'[81] That remained the WashCon view.[82] If corruption, according to the World Bank, was 'the abuse of public power for private benefit', then the solution was to diminish the public domain.[83] Never mind that countries with the largest public sectors were also (in general) those that were best governed, with the Nordic countries leading both in levels of taxation and in levels of integrity.[84] WashCon cheerleaders had an inkling that their policies were not antidotes to corruption, but possibly its drivers: 'It is a paradox that corruption is perceived to be erupting just as new global, political, and economic circumstances are creating unprecedented conditions for the decline of corruption.'[85] Critics saw things more clearly.[86]

Invisible hand economics was already in retreat. During the post-war decades, economics had turned away from harmony and embraced bad faith as the prime motivation.[87] The theory of rational choice stipulated that only self-interest counted. Neither of the two strands of economics, harmony or opportunism, had a conception of public good over and above the welfare of individuals. Despite a massive research and policy effort, economics was flying blind. For invisible hand harmony economists, corruption could not exist; in the economics of cheating, integrity was meaningless.

WashCon policies also proceeded from the assumption of bad faith. The 'distortions' they meant to correct arose from special interests acquiring

80.   Smith, *Wealth of Nations* (1976), IV.5.8–9, 528; Offer, 'Sympathy, Self-interest, and the Invisible Hand' (2012), 5–6.

81.   Naím, 'Corruption Eruption' (1995); World Bank, *World Development Report 1997: The State in a Changing World* (1997), 105.

82.   Abed and Gupta, 'The Economics of Corruption' (2003), 15; Hough, *Corruption, Anti-Corruption and Governance* (2013).

83.   Tanzi, 'Corruption around the World' (2003), 24–38, p. 25.

84.   La Porta et al., 'Quality of Government' (1999), 266; Rothstein, *Quality of Government* (2011), 10.

85.   Naím, 'Corruption Eruption' (1995).

86.   Hawley, 'Exporting Corruption' (2000).

87.   Chapter 7, above, 164–169.

what they did not deserve, through regulation, state intervention, tariffs, trades unions, and so on. Anne Krueger, chief economist of the World Bank (1982–1986) who identified the problem of 'rent-seeking', was herself part of the larger movement of 'public choice', associated (among NPWs) with George Stigler (NPW, 1982) and James Buchanan (NPW, 1986). These two prizes were awarded during the WashCon build-up of the 1980s, by a Nobel Committee chaired by Assar Lindbeck, who was pushing the same doctrines in Sweden together with his committee colleague Ingemar Ståhl, a keen member of the Mont Pèlerin Society.[88] What these doctrines had in common was the assumption that policy-making allowed opportunistic officials to misuse their authority for private gain. They did not worry about any 'rents' that might come out of private ownership.

George Stigler's (NPW, 1982) concept of 'capture' implied that regulators placed the interests of the industries they controlled ahead of those of the public. Buchanan's view was that for public servants to serve the public was actually wrong, because, in a democracy, a majority of the poor could coerce the wealthy minority.[89] Earlier development economists had invoked market failure to justify government intervention. Public choice turned this on its head, arguing that the problem was government failure.[90] A World Bank report explained that: 'Experience has ... shown nonmarket approaches to be less effective than had earlier been hoped and market failures to be more tractable than alleged.'[91]

Vito Tanzi, a senior IMF economist, wrote that the problem was not only bad policies, but often bad motivation:

> In this year [1987] when the Nobel Prize in economics has been given to James Buchanan for his contributions to public choice theory, it may be appropriate to conclude this paper with a few highly personal thoughts ... structural problems do not necessarily exist because policymakers have made technical mistakes in their policymaking. ... Rather, public choice theorists would argue that through these policies, policymakers have tried to promote their own political objectives.[92]

Tanzi did not ask whether a similar accusation might not be directed at his own agency as well.

---

88. Above, 204–205, 213.
89. Mueller, *Public Choice III* (2003).
90. Wolf, *Markets or Governments* (1993).
91. Shirley and Nellis, *Public Enterprise Reform* (1991), 1–2.
92. Tanzi, 'Fiscal Policy, Growth, and the Design of Stabilization Programs' (1987/1989), 30.

The WashCon agenda had been anticipated in an IMF policy board paper in 1981.[93] It contained the full menu apart from privatization, which was incorporated a little later after the audacious Thatcher sell-offs. Privatization was justified in terms of the effectiveness of market incentives. Public choice and principal-agent theories established a link between private ownership and efficiency.[94] This was another hybrid theory, in which private ownership had the efficiency attributes of the invisible hand, while the public sector was compromised by opportunism and corruption. But such models violated the invisible hand assumptions of perfect information, costless enforcement, and perfect competition. As the WashCon agencies lunged into Eastern Europe, Ronald Coase (NPW, 1991) warned in his Nobel Lecture that their privatization policy was not going to work. Stigler's invisible hand interpretation of his theory was wrong, and economic equilibrium theories were misguided in their disregard of economic frictions, institutions, and transaction costs.[95] In hybrid theories, corruption affects only the public sector. But large opportunities for corruption arise when assets are transferred from public to private hands, in the form of direct bribes, kickbacks, and lax regulation. In the absence of perfect competition (an ideal concept), or even of competitive markets, privatized services can easily exploit monopoly positions.[96]

Both the theory and the experience of privatization are ambiguous about the effect of ownership on efficiency.[97] In Britain and Northwestern Europe, the technical productivity of public utilities had long matched those in private ownership.[98] This suggests that efficiency was not driven by ownership incentives, but by technical competence at a lower level. Even supporters of privatization (for example, from the Peterson stable) acknowledged its uneven social effects, association with corruption, and unpopularity. Market tests in favour are not conclusive, since the purpose of public ownership was not to maximize profit.[99]

---

93. IMF, 'Supply-Oriented Adjustment Policies' (1981); Boughton, *Silent Revolution* (2001), 588–589.

94. Nellis, 'Is Privatisation Necessary?' (1994); Tanzi and Schuknecht, 'Reconsidering the Fiscal Role of Government' (1997), 168.

95. Coase, 'The Institutional Structure of Production', Nobel Lecture 1991.

96. For example, Manzetti, *Privatization South American Style* (1999).

97. Vickers and Yarrow, *Privatization* (1988).

98. Foreman-Peck and Millward, *Public and Private Ownership* (1994), 218–219; Millward, 'Political Economy' (2000), 170–173; Florio, *Great Divestiture* (2004), 119–126; Florio, *Network Industries* (2013), 331.

99. For example, Nellis, 'Privatization—A Summary Assessment' (2006).

Private ownership did not cauterize corruption, just the opposite. Recall Bernard de Mandeville's motivational assumption of 1714, 'private vices public benefits'.[100] If self-interest is the only motivation, who is going to guard the guardians? How was public benefit to be constructed and protected? Public choice had a response to that, of minimal government and strong rules, but it was not clear who would devise these rules and why they should be complied with. Moisés Naím, a prominent WashCon advocate, looked to 'strong moral values'.[101] But strong moral values were not part of economics. Why should contracts be honoured? This was a dilemma for an economics of greed. The conservative legal theorist Charles Fried (US solicitor general under Reagan and a Harvard law professor) argued that there was a moral obligation to fulfil promises that goes beyond individual self-interest.[102] Kenneth Arrow (NPW, 1970) pointed out that for markets to work, somebody needs to suspend self-interest. If judges and police (and others, like physicians, who owe a duty of care) act entirely in their own self-interest, markets cannot function.[103] The virtues required could not come out of the market itself.[104] And so from the outset, market-friendly reforms driven by unfettered self-interest became mired in corruption. Without internal validity, the model was not likely to work, except by accident.

Corruption in itself (it has been argued) is not always bad for development.[105] It has not prevented growth in China for more than three decades.[106] Students of Chinese corruption regard it as arising from the market turn in China—similar in that respect to corruption eruptions elsewhere. But China did not let the market rip. It kept a tight centralized control and a common-good developmental ideology, and, critically, did not expose itself to external predation.[107] Large anti-corruption efforts kept the problem from getting completely out of hand, and the windfalls of corruption accrued to the Chinese, and not to foreign finance.[108] At the other extreme, Nigeria,

---

100. Mandeville, *Fable of the Bees* (1714).
101. Naím, 'Corruption Eruption' (1995).
102. Fried, *Contract as Promise* (1981); Offer, 'Economy of Obligation' (2012), 7–12.
103. Arrow, 'Uncertainty and Medical Care' (1963), 948–951; Arrow, 'Gifts and Exchanges' (1972), 357.
104. Rothstein, *Quality of Government* (2011), ch. 10.
105. Rose-Ackerman, *Corruption* (1978), ch. 5; Naím, 'Bad Medicine' (2005); Tanzi, 'Corruption around the World' (2003), 42–44.
106. Wedeman, *Double Paradox* (2012).
107. Lin, *Demystifying the Chinese Economy* (2012).
108. Wedeman, *Double Paradox* (2012), 5–13; Ko and Weng, 'Structural Changes in Chinese Corruption' (2012).

despite large oil revenues, failed to deliver any improvements in the standard of living. Its WashCon financial reforms were easily captured by corrupt interests, both private and public.[109]

WashCon intellectuals identified the corruption fall-out with the code-words 'institutions' and 'governance'. The World Bank and the IMF began to attribute the failure to deficits of integrity, to the absence of impartial and competent administration. WashCon had overlooked that requirement.[110] When the laws enable corruption, the 'rule of law' is no solution. It is easier to abuse privilege when the privileged write the rules.[111] It is futile to expose corruption when the judges are corrupt. If the invisible hand did not work, then all that was left was self-interest, and it was not clear how anybody should be motivated by self-interest to stand up to corruption.

WashCon agencies were not above cooking the books themselves. A Caribbean economist, Davison Budhoo, a twelve-year veteran of conditionality, resigned from the IMF in 1988 in protest against deliberate under-reporting of economic performance in oil-rich Trinidad and Tobago, in order to justify reforms.[112] His allegations were never rebutted, and were subsequently confirmed by government investigations. Joseph Stiglitz (NPW, 2001) reported loose practice and unconscionable demands by the IMF's mission to Ethiopia.[113] Jeffrey Sachs reported similar IMF malpractice in Russia.[114] This suggests an excess of zeal on the part of IMF technicians. The WashCon agencies were not academic institutions, but bureaucracies with a chain of command, and fieldworkers are not expected to question policy. Important local interests in business, finance, and politics also stood to gain.

Agency economists were paid well, which provided a shield from temptation. But their salaries were tax-free: these staff made use of collective and public goods like everybody else, but avoided paying for them. It did not set a good example. Christine Lagarde, managing director of the IMF, exhorted Greeks to pay their taxes while paying no tax herself.[115] Timothy Geithner (US Treasury official, president of New York Fed) avoided some American

---

109.   Lewis and Stein, 'Shifting Fortunes' (1997); Cockroft, *Global Corruption* (2012), 14–19.
110.   Graham and Naím, 'The Political Economy of Institutional Reform' (1998); Hough, *Corruption and Anti-Corruption* (2013), ch. 2; Rodrik, 'Goodbye Washington Consensus' (2006), 977–978.
111.   Kaufmann and Vincente, 'Legal Corruption' (2011).
112.   Budhoo, *Enough Is Enough* (1990).
113.   Stiglitz, *Globalization and Its Discontents* (2002), 25–33.
114.   Sachs, 'Life in the Economic Emergency Room' (1994), 516–520, esp. 218.
115.   Willsher, 'Christine Lagarde, Scourge of Tax Evaders' (2012).

taxes during a stint at the IMF, which delayed his appointment as secretary of the Treasury only briefly in 2009. Two agency heads had to resign due to ethical irregularities, Paul Wolfowitz from the World Bank (favouritism), and Dominique Strauss-Kahn from the IMF (a murky sexual episode), while Christine Lagarde was under investigation in 2014 for irregularities in a previous post. Among prominent WashCon economists, it was publicly alleged in 2006 that Andrew Shleifer, a Harvard economist and protégé of Larry Summers (himself chief economist at the World Bank, and later secretary of the Treasury), used his position on a government-funded Harvard advisory mission in Russia to facilitate insider trading by his wife, making use of mission premises. Harvard paid the US government more than twenty million dollars in exculpation. Summers, by then president of Harvard, resigned shortly after the exposé. Harvard faculty voted no confidence in their president, and although attention was diverted by his derogatory comments on women scholars, the Russian affair appears to have contributed (he remained a 'University Professor', Harvard's highest professorial rank).[116] Shleifer published a much-cited analysis of 'corruption' in a top economics journal around the same time.[117]

WASHINGTON CONSENSUS VERSUS SOCIAL DEMOCRACY

WashCon policies came into direct conflict with Social Democracy over social insurance. The Social Democratic approach is pay-as-you-go: the taxes paid by workers cover the cost of pensions (sometimes with buffer funds). This is not consistent with the WashCon preference for private profit.[118] But pay-as-you-go is actually more efficient: it provides universal coverage, it draws on a large and stable revenue stream (the tax base), it has the largest risk pool, and it is an order of magnitude cheaper to administer. In contrast, privatized pension companies cream off typically between a quarter and forty percent of contributions as fees and profits; final payouts depend on financial market performance.[119] Chile in 1980 introduced a mandatory system of competing private pension funds. This was hailed by privatizers but ended

---

116. Wedel, *Collision and Collusion* (1998), 124–129; McClintick, 'How Harvard Lost Russia' (2006); Ivry, 'Did an Exposé Help Sink Harvard's President?' (2006).
117. Shleifer and Vishny, 'Corruption' (1993).
118. World Bank, *Averting the Old Age Crisis* (1994), chs. 4, 7.
119. Barr, 'The Truth about Pension Reform' (2001); Offer, 'Economy of Obligation' (2012); Orszag and Stiglitz, 'Rethinking Pension Reform: Ten Myths' (2001).

in failure. Charges were high, the funds were too profitable, pensions were low, and about half the population was not covered. Any redistribution was towards the better off.[120] In 2006, both left- and right-wing presidential candidates agreed that the system was not working, and promised to reform it.[121] At the other end, Sweden had right-of-centre governments from 1991 to 1994 and from 2006 to 2014. It genuflected towards market doctrine, allowing contributors to choose among private pension funds, but the choice applied only to about a seventh of the pension contribution, and has recently been curtailed. For the rest, Sweden has kept a pay-as-you-go system in which benefits are not pre-defined, but linked to contribution records and financial market performance.[122] Even the World Bank accepted that private pensions on their own do not work, and recommended a public system in conjunction with a mandatory one that is privately managed but tightly regulated.[123]

According to Gary Becker (NPW, 1992) in a *Newsweek* column, if we abolish the state, we abolish corruption.[124] But corruption arises wherever economic power can be abused, in the private sector as well. For the United States, suffice it to mention Enron, Tyco, and Global Crossing in the early 2000s, three American companies providing networked utility services (energy and communications), in which the managers and owners made large political contributions and plundered their companies. Pensions are also opportunities for private corruption. In 1986, the Thatcher government reneged on an element of UK state pension obligations by shifting them to an inferior cost-of-living index, and induced members to move into private schemes. Eventually, private pensions became such a bad deal that the government required the industry to compensate savers for 'misselling'.[125] Further episodes of misselling and compensation affected other corporate financial products, including mortgages and employment protection insurance (both of them traditional activities of Social Democracy).[126]

Beginning early in the nineteenth century, the whole of Northwestern Europe achieved a transition from official corruption to official integrity in the

120. Queisser, 'Pension Reform: Lessons from Latin America' (1999).
121. Rohter, 'Chile's Candidates Agree to Agree on Pension Woes' (2006).
122. Holzmann et al., *Nonfinancial Defined Contribution Pension Schemes* (2012).
123. World Bank, *Averting the Old-Age Crisis* (1994), ch. 7.
124. Tanzi, 'Corruption around the World' (2003), 26.
125. Ginn and Arber, 'Personal Pension Take-up in the 1990s' (2000).
126. Ferran, 'Regulatory Lessons from the Payment Protection Insurance Mis-selling Scandal' (2012).

course of a few decades.[127] The UK ended 'Old Corruption' and instituted a disinterested civil service, recruited and promoted on merit. The judiciary also improved.[128] But, during the 1980s market-liberal turn, corruption in high places returned.[129] Thatcher, Major, and Blair revoked a century of consensus and held out financial incentives for officials, out of faith in the motivation of greed, in the system of so-called new public management.[130] An historian of corruption wrote: 'I cannot think of another instance where a modern democracy has systematically undone the system by which uncorrupt public services were brought into being.'[131] In our own unpublished analysis of the satirical magazine *Private Eye*, reports of corruption increased tenfold from the 1970s to the 1990s, with the largest sub-category consisting of private-public interaction.

For the period after 2000, there is still no definitive overview, but red lights are flashing.[132] What they all signal, in one way or another, is the combination of privatization and corruption. In the UK during the 2000s, several ministers who implemented market-friendly policies found work in the industries they had regulated, while the head of the Audit Commission, in charge of policing government integrity, was forced out for personal corruption.[133] The prime minister, Tony Blair, blossomed after his resignation into a multi-millionaire many times over (on a comparable scale to Pinochet), on a million-dollar-plus annual retainer from J. P. Morgan. Nothing illegal here, on the face of it. In Germany, Premier Helmut Kohl was implicated in a financial scandal; two German presidents had to resign under a cloud; while ministerial and prime-ministerial scandals occurred in all the big EU countries, including Italy, France and Spain.[134] Israel, a country that is well known to one of us, implemented a strong market-liberal programme from

127. Neild, *Public Corruption* (2002); Rothstein, *Quality of Government* (2011), 111–119; Rubinstein, 'The End of "Old Corruption"' (1983); Harling, *The Waning of "Old Corruption"* (1996).
128. Neild, *Public Corruption* (2002), 107–116.
129. Business Week, 'Europe's New Morality' (1995); Bull and Newell, *Corruption in Contemporary Politics* (2003).
130. Ferlie et al., *Oxford Handbook of Public Management* (2005); Christensen and Laegreid, *New Public Management* (2011).
131. Neild, *Public Corruption* (2002), 198. Also Doig, 'Politics and Public Sector Ethics' (1996).
132. For example, Monbiot, *Captive State* (2000); Pollock, *NHS Plc.* (2004); Craig and Brooks, *Plundering the Public Sector* (2006); Oborne, *Triumph of the Political Class* (2007); Craig, *Squandered* (2008); Craig and Elliott, *Great European Rip-off* (2009); Leys and Player, *The Plot against the NHS* (2011); Shaxson, *Treasure Islands* (2013); Brooks, *The Great Tax Robbery* (2013); Meek, *Private Island* (2014); Jones, *The Establishment* (2014); Whyte, *How Corrupt Is Britain?* (2015).
133. Brooks, 'The Bourn Complicity' (2008); Transparency International, *Cabs for Hire* (2011).
134. Anderson, 'The Italian Disaster' (2014), 3.

the 1980s onwards. Ministers have been repeatedly implicated in corruption; some have gone to prison or committed suicide, a former prime minister is serving in prison, one president resigned, and another has served time. An Armed Forces chief of staff came under prolonged investigation, and the appointment of another was thwarted by exposure of corruption. And that is only at the very top, in those cases that were pursued. It remains a wonder that so many investigations are launched, and that some end in conviction. Closer to home, the great financial crisis of 2008 is still unfolding; investigations continue into the price-rigging LIBOR and FOREX scandals—so much for the virtues of 'getting the prices right'. The use of the HSBC bank in Switzerland for tax evasion was known to tax authorities in several countries for years, but no action followed.[135] Volkswagen blatantly cheated American emission tests.

Nordic Social Democratic countries, among the most heavily taxed and regulated, are also the least corrupt, with Denmark, Sweden, and Finland (not Norway) always in the very top ranks of integrity in the Corruption Perception Index. Social Democracy aimed to provide everybody with equal access to a good life, by means of a reciprocal exchange among the generations. The stress is on everybody and equal. Not complete equality of outcomes, but an equality of entitlement which makes sure that even if some get ahead, nobody is left behind. Workers support the young and the old, and are supported in their turn. This requires an enduring trust in officials and institutions.[136] Reciprocity accords better with Adam Smith's teaching than invocations of the 'invisible hand'. Smith argued that the prime motivation was to be worthy of other people's approbation, which was achieved by the exercise of civic virtue, by cultivating the public good.[137]

That is a clue to the success of Social Democracy, and also to its weakness. If trusting in others is a virtue, then Social Democracy appears to require it. And the experience of corruption can undermine that virtue. In Britain, a widespread belief in solidarity has given way to mutual suspicion and even a hatred of the poor.[138] Are the Nordics virtuous because of Social Democracy, or are they Social Democratic because they are virtuous? Be that as it may, Social Democracy in the Nordic countries, and in Sweden in particular, has

---

135. Leigh et al., 'HSBC Files: Swiss Bank Aggressively Pushed Way for Clients to Avoid New Tax' (2015).
136. Rothstein, *Quality of Government* (2011).
137. Offer, 'Self-Interest, Sympathy and the Invisible Hand' (2012).
138. Taylor-Gooby and Martin, 'Trends in Sympathy for the Poor' (2008).

achieved low-corruption institutions and high quality of life in defiance of market-liberal doctrines.

The discipline of economics is implicated in WashCon policies and doctrines, but how? Most of the policy-makers in the WashCon agencies were Ph.D. economists. They are what Thomas Kuhn called 'normal scientists', working within the paradigm, not probing foundations. The agencies themselves were driven by political and corporate imperatives. Thatcher, Reagan, Blair, and Bush had little grounding in economics themselves, and did not take their objectives from economics. It was important for the leaders (none of them deep thinkers), in their quest to extend the elbow room for business and finance, to believe that their doctrines and policies were underpinned by valid theory. Trusted advisors like Assar Lindbeck and John Williamson assured them that the project was well-founded. The reward was a place at the High Table of policy, professional prestige, and financial security.

On 11 October 2015, on the eve of the economics Nobel Prize announcement of that year, a member of the Swedish Academy of Sciences, the political scientist Bo Rothstein, published an article in the leading newspaper *Dagens Nyheter* to draw a link between corruption and the Nobel Prize.[139] Corruption, he wrote, adversely affected

> almost every measure of human welfare such as infant mortality, economic prosperity, life expectancy, the number of children living in poverty, access to clean water, the number of women who die in childbirth, willingness to handle environmental problems and more. Corruption has also recently been shown to be an important explanation for both the outbreak of civil wars and wars between states.

It also depressed private experience of life satisfaction, quality of life, and generalized trust. One reason for the rise of corruption was the ethics of elite managers in business and government, who increasingly had studied economics. Research showed that those who study economics were more prone to corruption than graduates in other subjects. This had been demonstrated in experimental settings, while members of the US Congress were twice as likely to have engaged in corrupt practices if they had a degree in economics.[140]

---

139. Rothstein, 'Ekonomipriset i Strid med Andan i Nobels Testamente' (2015).
140. For example, Frank et al., 'Do Economists Make Bad Citizens?' (1996); Zingales, *Capitalism for the People* (2012), ch. 10; Ruske, 'Does Economics Make Politicians Corrupt?' (2015).

Drawing on these findings, and on his own research into corruption over two decades, Rothstein wrote to the president of the Swedish Academy of Sciences: 'If it is true that studying economics increases tolerance for corruption and fraud, this is a very serious problem in the light of the above research findings.'[141] He proposed an inquiry (to be undertaken by non-social-science members of the academy) on whether a prize for economics was consistent with Alfred Nobel's intention of recognizing achievements that conferred a benefit on mankind. Until the inquiry was completed, he wrote, the economics prize should not be awarded.

---

141. Rothstein, 'Proposal for an Investigation by the Royal Swedish Academy' (2015). Includes a list of references.

CONCLUSION: LIKE PHYSICS
OR LIKE LITERATURE?

In 1968, the natural scientists of the Swedish Academy suppressed their doubts and allowed the prize in economics to go forth, but some members of the academy continued to resent it.[1] Dissent has flared up repeatedly in Sweden and elsewhere. Peter Nobel, a scion of the Nobel family, likened economics to a cuckoo's egg in the Nobel nest. On the Nobel Prize day in December 2004, Sweden's leading newspaper featured an argument that the prize in economics diminished the others. Naseem Taleb, a best-selling critic of efficient markets theory (an invisible hand financial doctrine) fulminated in the *Financial Times* in 2007: 'Academic economists are no more self-serving than other professions. You should blame those in the real world who give them the means to be taken seriously: those awarding that "Nobel" prize.'[2] Indifference is another form of criticism. In 2013, the outgoing Nobel Prize selection committee chairman Per Krussel complained that Swedish newspapers no longer took much notice of Nobel Prize announcements. We have already mentioned how in October 2015 a member of the Swedish Academy called for the prize to be suspended.[3] But all to no avail. Critics might snipe, but (as they complain) the prestige of the prize is undimmed.

The existence of a Nobel Prize in economics implied that the 'market turn' since the 1970s was scientifically grounded, and that it was objectively

---

1. Nasar, *A Beautiful Mind* (1998), 368; above, 100.
2. Taleb, 'The Pseudo-Science Hurting Markets' (2007).
3. Lönnroth et al., 'Ekononomipriset Förminskar Värdet på Alla Nobelpris' (2004); *Local*, 'Nobel Descendant Slams Economics Prize' (2005); Henderson, 'The Cuckoo's Egg in the Nobel Prize Nest' (2006); Fullbrook, *Real World Economics* (2007), pt. 2; Syll, 'Self-Righteous Drivel from Chairman of the Nobel Prize Committee' (2013); Nobel, 'Gökungen i Nobelprisen bo' (2010); Gabriel Söderberg Interview with Peter Nobel, 22 November 2010; Rothstein, 'Ekonomipriset i Strid med Andan i Nobels Testamente' (2015).

necessary. When Nobel Prize winners are mentioned in print, their prize is invariably cited: we do it ourselves. But what warrant does Nobel economics provide for the market turn? As science, not much. The Nobel Prize can be seen as a natural experiment, a discovery procedure for the nature of economics. As a body of knowledge, economics, even Nobel economics, does not hang together very well. It is rife with doctrines which are short on internal validity and at odds with each other. To show this is an achievement of the Nobel Prize. On three occasions (1974, 1979, and 2013), it was given to scholars whose doctrines were incompatible with each other. Prize winners have dismissed the work of other prize winners, most notably in the harsh words that Solow (NPW, 1987) and Krugman (NPW, 2008) had for the New Classical Macroeconomics of Robert Lucas (NPW, 1995). Eight NPWs have argued that the core doctrines of economics are wrong, and three others have expressed reservations.[4] Such dissension is unthinkable in other Nobel disciplines. But these inconsistent awards are neither arbitrary nor obtuse. For the Nobel selection committee, any overt bias would compromise its credibility. So for most of the time, it kept a mechanical balance between left and right, between empiricists and formalists, between Chicago and Keynes. The Nobel Committee delivered a scientific result: The need to be seen as impartial and credible drove it into a refutation of scientific economics.

The market turn pushback against Social Democracy was justified by the creed of market efficiency. The vision came from economics, the method was to remove 'distortions' such as tariffs, taxation and trade unions. The pushback had two important consequences. The first was lower taxes for the better-off. More of the cost was borne by the less affluent through regressive taxes on consumption, and through less progressivity elsewhere.[5] Inequality soared. The second main consequence was the outsourcing and privatization of welfare-state functions, of universal public services, and increasingly of social protection as well.

In consequence, money prevailed over work. One diagnostic is the fall in the share of work income in the total of all incomes, which has taken place in all advanced societies. The share of total output received by labour of all types (which includes even top executives) has typically fallen a great deal, for example, from about 60 percent of US national income in 1995,

---

4. Solow and Krugman, above, chapter 1, 40; eight NPWs, above, chapter 2, 65–66.
5. Alvaredo et al., 'The Top 1 Percent in International and Historical Perspective' (2013), 7–9; OECD, *Divided We Stand* (2011), 36–40; Brooks, *The Great Tax Robbery* (2013).

to about 50 percent in 2011.[6] Work gave much more than it took: labour productivity rose faster than pay in the top twenty economies (the G20); in the United States, productivity per worker has more than doubled since 1975, while hourly wages have risen hardly at all, after previously rising in step with productivity for almost thirty years.[7] For households in the broad middle class, annual earnings rose only 14 percent between 1979 and 2007, and two-thirds of that is accounted for by longer hours.[8] If only a small minority benefits from economic growth, it is not clear why it needs to be such a central objective for society.

The market-liberal breakthrough was political and intellectual, not scientific, and was achieved democratically in the West. One of its objectives has been to take the question of inequality out of economics.[9] Economics is invoked as a Just World Theory: when distortions are removed, everyone gets what they deserve. Self-seeking objectives are repackaged as technocratic ones, and the technocrats are economists. The purpose is destructive: to dismantle constraints on the wealthy, and to dismantle protections for everybody else. This process is resisted by the countervailing power of democracy. In less democratic places, it has been pushed through by the power of finance, backed up by coercion and violence. Writing in 2015, the coercion of Greece by the European Union, the European Central Bank, and the IMF is but the latest episode.

The scientific standing of economics is premised on the existence of a set of regularities which are supposed to underlie the confusing variety of experienced reality. Every economist is indoctrinated in this notion from the outset. It is 'thinking like an economist.'[10] But it is not easy to make it work. Being regularities, they ought to be captured (like the regularities of physics) in mathematics; ideally, in the smoothly incremental mathematics of the calculus, and, second-best, in the probabilistic ones of statistics. The core vision is simple: self-interest is harmonized by the invisible hand. The economy is driven by individuals, each seeking to maximize their private preferences. People bring their goods and endowments to market, and, when exchange

6. OECD, 'Unit Labour Costs—Annual Indicators: Labour Income Share Ratios' (2012); ILO, 'G20 Labour Markets' (2014), fig. 13, 13.
7. ILO, 'G20 Labour Markets' (2014), fig. 6, 6; Mishel, 'The Wedges between Productivity and Median Compensation' (2012).
8. Bivens et al., 'Raising America's Pay', 31.
9. Harberger, 'Three Basic Postulates for Applied Welfare Economics' (1971).
10. Mankiw, *Principles of Economics* (2008), chs. 1–2; Colander, *The Making of an Economist, Redux* (2009).

is over, the payouts scale up to an optimal state for society as a whole, in the sense that no better one can be had. This vision has been in the works for centuries now, and especially since the end of the nineteenth century: there are two-person versions, *n*-person versions, welfare-maximizing versions, general equilibrium versions. Beyond the simple two-person versions (and sometimes even then), they cannot be made to work in theory, let alone in practice.[11] A typical Chicago response to this failure (both the Harberger welfare analysis of the 1960s and the Lucas new classical 'representative agent' model of the 1980s) has been to reduce the whole economy to a two-person interaction.

One informed comment on the welfare-economics equilibrium version can stand for all the others: 'No one formula can be established which will be valid as a general principle.'[12] That suggests that something may be wrong with the assumption of innate regularity. That the vision not only fails to match reality, but may be inappropriate as a scientific strategy. Such heresy might be expected among heterodox economists, but is also arrived at by orthodox ones.[13] In the words of the philosopher Thomas Nagel, 'we have no grounds for confidence that questions about what there is reason to do always have determinate answers. By contrast, we are confident that questions of arithmetic always have determinate answers.'[14] Perhaps that is why economics seeks the supposed finality of mathematics. In the trade-off between rigour and relevance, rigour wins out.[15] But when theory is confronted by evidence, there is no secure foundation to be found, and everyone, to some extent, is whistling in the dark.[16]

But that is surely too harsh. Even the natural sciences never achieve finality, and are bedevilled by anomalies. What is wrong may be the pretence that finality is within reach, wrong even if the quest for finality (like the 'theory of everything' in physics) may help to drive the inquiry. And if no finality has been reached, it would be good to have less of the hectoring about efficiency, the purported theoretical justifications for labour market reforms meant to

---

11. Chapter 1, above, 19–20.
12. Ruggles, 'Recent Developments in the Theory of Marginal Cost Pricing' (1949–1950), 126.
13. Heterodox, McCloskey, *Rhetoric of Economics* (1985); Lawson, *Economics and Reality* (1997); more orthodox, Hey, 'Rationality Is as Rationality Does' (1993); Rubinstein, *Economic Fables* (2012), 34–36.
14. Nagel, 'Listening to Reason' (2014); a review of Scanlon, *Being Realistic about Reasons* (2014).
15. Blaug, *Methodology of Economics* (1992), 167.
16. Varoufakis et al., *Modern Political Economics* (2011), 260–279.

squeeze the lower-paid even more, and harking back to the cruel and uncertain world before Social Democracy. There is no warrant for confidence in real-world applications that do not always achieve internal consistency, let alone external validity.[17]

Another theoretical response to the failure of equilibrium economics is the economics of bad faith, still founded on self-interest, but without the invisible hand harmony legacy. This economics is not deterministic, and hence is more realistic, but (despite claims to the contrary) it is in no position to prescribe positive policies: it has had some localized successes (such as in auction theory), but it also endorses a metastasizing process of corruption and repression.[18] Hybrid combinations of harmony and bad faith attempt to save normative authority, but do not hang together consistently. In order to harness bad faith for good causes, it is necessary to reach beyond economics. If this were the whole of economics, it would be a cause for despair. It is not. But it does leave the political market turn without a scientific warrant.

The elite of economics is inclined to ignore and even silence those who disagree, but it cannot silence them entirely. Sometimes such critics (like the monetary economist Hyman Minsky) come back in from the cold. Central figures, like Veblen, Keynes, Schumpeter, and Hayek (NPW, 1974), have experienced long periods of disdain and neglect. Most of our own criticism was initially made within economics, sometimes by NPWs themselves. At the outset, we placed ourselves against the methodologists, and insisted on judging economics by empirical observation and results. At the end of the enquiry, economics does not appear to perform well on these criteria. Maybe the methodologists were right after all: empirical performance is too harsh a test for economics. For validity, it must fall back on other resources.

ANOTHER TEST: COMPUTABILITY

If the economy is driven by one individual choice after another in response to prices, this should be capable of being modelled on a computer. In the words of an eminent economist, consumer choice can be likened to a computer 'into whom we "feed" a sequence of market prices and from whom we

17. Myrdal, *Political Element* (1930/1990); Ruggles, 'Recent Developments in the Theory of Marginal Cost Pricing' (1949–1950); Little, *A Critique of Welfare Economics* (1950/1957); Lipsey and Lancaster, 'The General Theory of the Second Best' (1956).
18. Chapter 11, above, 246–258.

obtain a corresponding sequence of "solutions" in the form of specified opti-mum positions.'[19] The ranking of preferences determines the market choices of economic man. Arriving at this ranking can be modelled as a sequence of pairwise comparisons, for example, making a choice between strawberry and vanilla flavours (taking price into account), and comparing likewise all other options in sequence until the budget is exhausted. Such choices can be embodied in an algorithm (a calculation procedure) to run sequentially on a computer and provide a numerical result.[20]

But there is a snag: some algorithmic problems cannot be solved by a dig-ital computer. They either take too long to compute, are impossible to com-pute (that is, are 'non-computable'), or it is unknown whether they can be computed.[21] For example, the variable of interest may increase exponentially as the algorithm moves sequentially through time. A generic computer (known after its originator as a 'Turing machine', which can mimic any com-puter) fails to complete the algorithm and never comes to a halt. Such prob-lems can arise in deceptively simple tasks, for example, the 'travelling sales-man problem', which involves calculating the shortest route through several given locations, or designing efficient networks more generally. For every incremental move, the time required by the computer rises by a power: there may be a solution, but it requires an impossible length of time to compute.[22] In a more familiar example, encryption relying on the multiplication of two unknown prime numbers can be broken, but relies on solutions taking too long to complete.

The clockwork consumer maximizes her innate preferences in response to market prices. But there is a flaw in the design: the clockwork may not de-liver a result. It may have to run forever before making a single choice. This has been demonstrated formally several times. The ordering of individual preferences has been claimed to be 'non-computable', and Walrasian gen-eral equilibrium may be non-computable as well.[23] Non-computability in economics is little cited by mainstream scholars. On the face of it, it makes a mockery of the neoclassical notions of rationality and rigour, both of which imply finality. Economics however averts its gaze. In practice, since stand-

---

19.   Patinkin, *Money, Interest, and Prices* (1965), 7, cited in Velupillai, *Computable Economics* (2000), 33.

20.   Velupillai, *Computable Economics* (2000).

21.   Harel, *Computers Ltd.* (2000).

22.   Ibid., 98–100.

23.   Velupillai, *Computable Economics* (2000), chs. 2–3, 9; Mirowski, *Machine Dreams* (2002), 415–436.

ard microeconomics has never aspired to realism, it may be a reasonable response to say that it has formalisms that work, and that they constitute 'horses for courses'. But what cannot be claimed for such formalisms is a unique and binding authority in a theoretical, empirical, policy-normative sense, in the way that scientific consensus is binding.

Computation rears its head several times in Nobel economics. In the second Nobel Lecture, Ragnar Frisch described the task of the economist as validating and executing policy preferences by feeding them into computer models of the economy, and Milton Friedman expressed a similar idea in his Nobel Lecture of 1976.[24] Hayek (NPW, 1974) made his mark in the 'socialist calculation debate'.[25] Defenders of socialist planning (and of neoclassical economics) in the 1920s and 1930s argued that private ownership was not crucial: socialism could make use of markets, and that the requirements for socialist calculation were no more onerous than the ones assumed for neoclassical general equilibrium.[26] From then onwards, the debate should really be called 'the neoclassical calculation debate'. Joseph Stiglitz (NPW, 2001) perversely framed a devastating demolition of general equilibrium economics as a criticism of market socialism.[27] Kenneth Arrow (NPW, 1972), an architect of general equilibrium, pointed out (against general equilibrium) that in terms of computability, every person is her own 'socialist planner'—the task of rationally ordering even private preferences and choices (which Hayek and economics more generally takes for granted) looks too demanding. Under general equilibrium, if even a single person is in a position to set a price (as opposed to taking it as given), 'the superiority of the market over centralized planning disappears. Each individual agent is in effect using as much information as would be required by a central planner'.[28]

In response to the socialist neoclassical defence, Hayek and his supporters questioned the very possibility of rational calculation. Hayek acknowledged the interdependence of all prices. But the consumer and entrepreneur did not need to be omniscient, just to make use of local price signals and local knowledge to price their goods and choices. The problem was not the static once-and-for-all efficiency of general equilibrium, but coping with change. The

---

24. Above, chapter 2, 58, 61.
25. Levy and Peart, 'Socialist Calculation Debate' (2008); Jael, 'Socialist Calculation and Market Socialism' (2015); chapter 6, above, 128.
26. Jael, 'Socialist Calculation and Market Socialism' (2015), 11–15.
27. Stiglitz, *Whither Socialism?* (1994), chs. 2–3.
28. Arrow, 'Rationality of Self and Others' (1986), S392.

prices obtained fell well short of optimality (in the Pareto general equilibrium sense).[29] Hayek implied that this was the best that could be achieved. But how would we know? Joseph Stiglitz (NPW, 2001) does not think it is. Regulation can improve it.[30] Hayek's position fails as an argument against socialism: if capitalism can do without omniscience, why not a Hayekian market socialism without omniscience? A key part of Mises's original argument against socialism in 1920 was that that entrepreneurs require the motivation of profit, and that private ownership of the means of production was indispensable. But advanced economies are mixed economies: they have large public sectors, in which central banking, social insurance, and infrastructure, typically more than a third of the economy, are managed by governments or not-for-profit. They would be much less efficient to manage any other way.[31] In Britain, for example, with its privatized railways, the biggest investment decisions are still reserved for government: the rails are publicly owned, the trains are commissioned and purchased by government, and a major high speed line project (HS2) can only be undertaken by government. Despite Hayek, smaller public sectors are not associated with more affluent economies: The expensive Nordic Social Democratic societies demonstrate this.[32]

Herbert Simon (NPW, 1978) pointed out that individuals could not cope with the computational challenges they faced. They did the best they could with what they had, which he called 'bounded rationality.' The problem also appears in behavioural economics, where NPWs Allais, Selten, Kahneman, Smith, and Roth have all shown that real people diverge from the norms of rational choice, and that outcomes are therefore unlikely to scale up to 'efficient' equilibria. In a letter to the non-computability advocate Vela Velupillai, Simon spelled out the different degrees of cognitive capacity:[33]

There are many levels of complexity in problems, and corresponding boundaries between them. Turing computability is an outer boundary, and as you show, any theory that requires more power than that surely is irrele-

29. Lavoie, *Rivalry and Central Planning* (1985), 23, 108–111; Hayek, 'The Diffusion of Knowledge in Society' (1945), 527.
30. Stiglitz, *Whither Socialism* (1994), 24–25.
31. Offer, 'Why Is the Public Sector So Large in Market Societies?' (2003); idem, 'Economy of Obligation' (2012).
32. Lindert, *Growing Public* (2004), II.
33. Simon to Leijonhufvud and Velupillai, 25 May 2000, in Velupillai, *Computable Foundations for Economics* (2010), 409.

vant to any useful definition of human rationality. A slightly stricter boundary is posed by computational complexity, especially in its common 'worst case' form. We cannot expect people (and/or computers) to find exact solutions for large problems in computationally complex domains. This still leaves us far beyond what people and computers actually CAN do. The next boundary, but one for which we have few results ... is computational complexity for the 'average case', sometimes with an 'almost everywhere' loophole [that is, procedures that do not apply in all cases]. That begins to bring us closer to the realities of real-world and real-time computation. Finally, we get to the empirical boundary, measured by laboratory experiments on humans and by observation, of the level of complexity that humans actually can handle, with and without their computers, and—perhaps more important—what they actually do to solve problems that lie beyond this strict boundary even though they are within some of the broader limits.

The latter is an important point for economics, because we humans spend most of our lives making decisions that are far beyond any of the levels of complexity we can handle exactly; and this is where ... good-enough decisions take over.

This problem was also acknowledged by Milton Friedman (NPW, 1976). Surprisingly for a Chicago economist, he conceded that optimizing was difficult. His solution was to proceed 'as if' the choice had been optimized, without specifying how (the example he gives is of the billiards player, who implicitly solves complicated problems in physics every time he makes a successful shot).[34] Asymmetric information, at the core of bad faith economics, is partly a matter of inability to monitor even the moves of a collaborator or a counter-party. The new classical NPW economists (Lucas, Prescott, and Sargent) avoid the problem of computational complexity (and the difficulty of scaling up from heterogeneous individuals) by using a 'representative agent' to stand for the whole of the demand or supply side of the economy. Going back to where we started, 'imaginary machines', the reliance on models (that is, radically simplified mechanisms) arises from the difficulty of dealing with anything more complicated.

All this is just another way of saying that on plausible assumptions, the market-clearing procedures at the heart of normative economics (that is, its quest for 'efficiency') cannot work like computers. Having failed in the test

---

34. Friedman, 'Positive Economics' (1953).

of classic analysis, theory fails the test of computability as well. This suggests that actual human choices are not modelled correctly by economic theory, but are made some other way, with as much calculation as can be mustered, but also with short-cuts, intuitions, and other strategies. This is not far-fetched. Humans do things beyond the reach of computers, like carry out an everyday conversation. Policy is not made by computers, not by economists, but by imperfect politicians. Perhaps it is wrong to start with the individual—maybe equilibrium (such as it is) comes from the outside, from the relative stability of social conventions and institutions. This indeterminacy provides an analytical reason why understanding the economy needs to be pragmatic, pluralistic, and open to argument and evidence; an economic historian would say that we should embrace empirical complexity. Policy problems may be intractable to calculation, but most of them get resolved one way or another by the passage of time. History shows how. This may be taken as endorsing the pragmatism of Social Democracy, and of institutional and historical approaches which resemble the actual decision processes.

If economics is not science, what should we make of it? Economics has to be regarded as being one voice among many, not superior to other sources of authority, but not inferior to them either. In that respect, it is like Social Democracy. It commands an array of techniques, the proverbial 'toolkit' which economists use to perform concrete evaluations, including many varieties of cost-benefit analysis. It has other large assets as well: a belief system that commands allegiance, passion, commitment, groupthink, and rhetoric. Its amorality attracts the powerful in business, finance, and politics. It indoctrinates millions every year in universities, and its graduates find ready work in think tanks, in government, and in business. The press is full of its advocates. As an ideology, economics may be resistant to argument and evidence, but it is not entirely immune to them. Its nominal allegiance to scientific procedure ensures that the discipline responds to empirical anomalies, albeit slowly, embracing new approaches and discarding some of those that don't seem to work.

IS ECONOMICS ETHICALLY GOOD?

Economics is normative: it knows what we ought to do and it tells us how. It derives its authority from values it takes as self-evident. What is self-evident is aversive to evidence (by definition). Those self-evident values need to be examined. How attractive are they, and who do they attract? When we venture beyond science (and sometimes within science itself), there is an inclination to dismiss opposing views, and to wonder how other people can hold them seriously.[35]

In making the case against the vision of economics, we expect to come up against the intensity of conviction with which it is held. Moreover, since it is not science, the question of falsehood or truth is a subtle one: The vision of economics is immensely attractive to many people, and dominates policy-making today. It is held sincerely, and is a legitimate vision for society. Supporters of the right and left in politics may differ in temperament and even biology, and such preferences are also mediated by family, local, and class legacies.[36] In post-war elections, right and left have alternated in power, increasingly so in Scandinavia, while the erstwhile left has embraced and even led the market turn. There is thus a foundation of social support for the market-liberal vision.

But since market liberalism remains a matter of preference rather than of truth, it is appropriate to lay out the case against it. Consider first the objectives that economics holds out.[37] This is to maximize the fulfilment of individual preferences. In economic models, this is true by assumption. But is it attractive as an ideal, and is it empirically adequate? The premise is the liberal one of respecting personal choices. But in earlier years, in classical economics from Adam Smith to John Stuart Mill, the object of policy was not merely to gratify individuals, but the welfare of society as a whole. Adam Smith insisted on the primacy of the common good over self-interest:

> The wise and virtuous man is at all times willing that his own private interest should be sacrificed to the public interest of his own particular order or society. He is at all times willing, too, that the interests of this order or society should be sacrificed to the greater interest of the state sovereignty, in which it is only a subordinate part.[38]

Note the role for virtue and wisdom: man is not the slave of desire. He is capable of self-command, and of acknowledging a greater good beyond himself.

This was also the norm of nineteenth-century utilitarianism, an other-directed ethical doctrine whose precept was Jeremy Bentham's 'greatest good

---

35. Ross and Ward, 'Naïve Realism in Everyday Life' (1996); Pronin et al., 'Objectivity in the Eye of the Beholder' (2004).
36. Hibbing et al., *Predisposed: Liberals, Conservatives and the Biology of Political Differences* (2014).
37. What follows derives from Offer, 'Sympathy, Self-Interest and the Invisible Hand' (2012).
38. Adam Smith, *Theory of Moral Sentiments* (1759/1792/1976), VI.ii.3.3.

of the greatest number' (still endorsed by John Harsanyi, NPW, 1994). Following their eighteenth-century predecessors Smith, Hume, and Bentham, the Victorian economists J. S. Mill, Jevons, Sidgwick, Marshall, Edgeworth, and Pigou also held a view not unlike the Stoic doctrine that, in the words of Adam Smith: 'We should view ourselves, not in the light in which our own selfish passions are to place us, but in the light in which any other citizen of the world would view us.'[39] This is subtly different from the twentieth-century objective of Pareto efficiency, which seeks to maximize without any concern about who should benefit, so long as nobody loses.

More recent economics makes a virtue of selfishness: it prides itself on being counter-intuitive. Regard for others is soft-minded 'cheap talk' which may be an ethical injunction, but morality is just one idiosyncratic preference among others. Those who want to understand the world are told to separate 'ought' from 'is.' Modern social science prides itself on 'value freedom.'[40] Scientists describe things as they are, not as they ought to be. But the tough-minded economist who is indifferent to ethics is also taking an ethical stand. The Pareto efficiency criterion has nothing to say about prior endowment, which it takes as given. It is silent about equity. Disdain for ethics is an ethical position, which relies on the counter-intuitive assumption that well-being is entirely subjective and cannot be compared from one person to another. For Lionel Robbins, an influential exponent of neoclassical doctrine in the 1930s, 'me-first' was founded on the 'Indisputable Facts of Experience.'[41] Following from Robbins, 'me-first' is taken as a premise which needs no justification in standard microeconomic theory, for example, in the theory of household consumption.

But the facts of experience are no such thing. Counter-intuition is not compelling if it is wrong. As an empirical postulate, self-interest is tautological: any choice observed can be attributed to self-interest. If, however, it means that everyone is always maximizing their personal material or financial or market advantage, then it is manifestly false. The psychological model of unconstrained self-regard is wrong.[42] Individuals crave acceptance and are bound in a web of obligations. Friendship, love, loyalty, charity, patriotism, civility, solidarity, integrity, impartiality are ubiquitous and compelling, and

---

39. Ibid., III.3.11.
40. Bromley, 'The Ideology of Efficiency' (1990), 89–91.
41. Sugden, 'Can Economics Be Founded on "Indisputable Facts of Experience?"' (2009).
42. Karacuka and Zaman, 'The Empirical Evidence against Neoclassical Utility Theory' (2012).

falsify the premise of unbounded self-regard. Family, religion, profession, employment, the judiciary, the state, the nation, military service—some of the most powerful and enduring institutions would fail if everyone always put themselves first. Obligation is often more compelling than egotism, and preferences are not inscrutably subjective.

Economists ignore the ban on inter-personal comparisons when it suits them. Market liberals realized that for microeconomics to have any predictive power, it is necessary that preferences are 'assumed not to change substantially over time, not to be very different between wealthy and poor persons, or even between persons in different societies and cultures.'[43] They have worked this into macroeconomics with the device of the 'representative agent', a model of the economy as a whole in which multitudes of people are assumed to act as one. In advocating business-friendly deregulation, market liberals are happy to use cost-benefit analysis based on 'willingness to pay', and have no difficulty aggregating dollars which have different subjective value for different people. The focal points of market prices and their elasticities indicate a broad social consensus on what is valuable. Harberger (in his triangles) assumes constant and uniform utilities for everyone; he rejects diminishing returns, perhaps because that would justify redistribution.[44] Premises, it seems, are a matter of choice, when the purpose is to privilege markets and property.

The self-regarding actor also featured in 1950s game theory and in the Savage axioms of rationality, set out in the same decade. In the 1940s, Duncan Black defined the self-seeking rational voter and laid the foundation for Anthony Downs's *Economic Theory of Democracy* (1957). In the 1960s, Mancur Olson argued the futility of collective action.[45] By the 1970s, rational choice and methodological individualism had become standard assumptions in economics and political science.[46] These doctrines are so pervasive that it is easy to overlook how radical they were. This 'selfish turn' may be described neutrally as sociopathic, that is, inimical to social co-operation. In social science discourse, the criterion of common good was simply set aside. Rational choice theory does not even need to be blessed by the invisible hand.[47] The 'hand' is merely bolted on.

---

43. Becker, *The Economic Approach to Human Behaviour* (1976), 5.
44. Harberger, 'Three Basic Postulates for Applied Welfare Economics' (1971).
45. McLean, *Public Choice* (1987).
46. Green and Shapiro, *Pathologies of Rational Choice Theory* (1994).
47. Elster, 'The Nature and Scope of Rational-Choice Explanations' (2001).

There is a puzzle as to why, from the 1950s onwards, such an extreme form of selfishness should have beguiled academics in economics, political science, and philosophy, as being so manifestly self-evident. In evolutionary biology as well, the tide flowed from group to individual selection. Even John Rawls's *Theory of Justice* (1971), which dominated work in moral and political philosophy in the years of the market turn, took individual self-interest, 'behind the veil of ignorance', as its point of departure. It is not generally known that Rawls was, for a time, a member of the Mont Pèlerin Society. He was put forward for membership by Milton Friedman in 1968, and withdrew from the society three years later, just before the *Theory* was published.[48] In keeping with the society's orientation, Rawls privileged 'freedom' as the highest good. Many other philosophers and political scientists have followed his lead. Other social sciences, notably sociology, anthropology, and psychology, maintained a sceptical distance, and earned the disdain of 'tough-minded' rational choice colleagues.

Maybe this posture of 'toughness' provides a clue. Decisiveness can be attractive, and it is only a short step to extol the rough virtues of manliness. In American culture in particular, toughness is seen as good. A robust Social Darwinism coexisted in nineteenth-century America with an intense religiosity—indeed the two were regarded as complementary. Success was godly, failure deserved.[49] The style of argument in Chicago seminars (and in North American economics more generally) is notoriously abrasive and combative, and Friedman extolled the natural selection among business firms that made sure that only the fittest survived.[50]

Toughness is to be admired when it signifies the ability to endure pain. But in social and political rhetoric since the 1970s, toughness has mutated into a willingness to inflict pain: the rhetoric is 'hard choices' (hard for me to hurt you), 'cruel to be kind', or, more directly, 'if it ain't hurting, it ain't working.' When combined with a licence for self-seeking, such toughness might well inspire wariness rather than admiration. Just World Theories, like economics, warrant the infliction of pain.

---

48.   Mont Pèlerin Society, Proposals for Membership, September 1968, Mont Pèlerin Society Papers 44/1, Hoover Institution Archives; Mont Pèlerin Society, 'List of Members' [1970], Friedman Papers 87/5, Hoover Institution Archives; Mont Pèlerin Society, list of lapsed members, 1972, Friedman Papers 87/2.

49.   Hofstadter, *Social Darwinism in American Thought* (1955), especially ch. 3 on William Graham Sumner.

50.   Friedman, 'The Methodology of Positive Economics' (1953), 13–14.

The ideal of 'freedom' is also associated with toughness, to the extent that it means a defiant independence. Freedom has an exalted lineage in the historical struggle against religious oppression and political tyranny. The quest for freedom is replete with martyrdom. In the European tradition of Rousseau and Kant, 'freedom' is also about the scope for moral or personal autonomy. In the English-speaking tradition, however, it stands primarily for the security of property, although both other meanings are implied as well.[51] In the American and British traditions, 'freedom' was compatible with the ownership of slaves: indeed, it dignified the ownership of slaves.[52] In economics, efficiency means 'Pareto efficiency', a state in which any gain can be vetoed by the losers.[53] But slaves had no veto; no more than the victims of the Pinochet dictatorship, lauded for its market liberalism and advised by three Mont Pèlerin NPWs.

Property is commonly conflated with freedom, although property rights for some restrict the freedom of others.[54] In the market discourse of the twentieth century, 'freedom' has become another word for self-interest, and is ubiquitous on right-wing mastheads. 'Freedom' has a transcendental appeal in American culture and politics. But for a self-regarding rational individualist, it is only a matter of calculation: how much self-seeking is it useful to allow, if the same licence is available to others. The choice depends on socioeconomic standing: freedom from obligation is more valuable to the rich and powerful than to others, because they think there is more for them to lose. As in the case of toughness, personal virtue has mutated into social licence: freedom from tyranny has mutated into freedom from obligation. Among the followers of Ayn Rand, it is a kind of juvenile revulsion from parental tutelage. For the advocates of freedom, 'paternalism' is an abomination.

For all its rhetoric of freedom, neoclassical economics, at both micro and macro level, is not comfortable with actual choice. In microeconomic consumer theory, the agent has a set of immutable and innate preferences, in some versions not even personal to themselves. He or she is presented by reality with a complete set of opportunities, prices, and their probabilities. Given innate preferences and the information available, consumers can make only one choice, the one that maximizes their preferences. They have no more

51. MacPherson, *Possessive Individualism* (1962); MacGilvray, *Invention of Market Freedom* (2011).
52. Brown, 'Free Enterprise and Economics of Slavery' (2010); idem, 'Adam Smith's View of Slaves as Property' (2010) .
53. Introduction, 3–4 above.
54. Bentham, 'Principles of the Civil Code' (1838), 309.

discretion than a piece of clockwork. This rigid determinism leaves no room for ethical choice, and justifies any outcome as being inevitable. The 'public choice' doctrine of James Buchanan (NPW, 1986) was hostile to democracy, which he feared could vote away the rights of property. In that spirit, macroeconomic policy was taken away from elected governments and handed over to the technocrats of so-called independent central banks, whose discretion was restricted to achieving a given rate of inflation. Even that narrow discretion was a concession, designed to hold down the pressure of wage demands. When it came to asset price inflation, to the price of shares and houses, no intervention was allowed: one law for wages, another for capital.

Real choice can be difficult. In contrast with the premises of deterministic economic modelling, the future is unknown, and choice often intractable, with no optimizing algorithm available.[55] This indeterminacy opens up room for genuine discretion, including an ethical choice, for 'doing the right thing'. In the absence of failsafe clockwork procedures, people fall back on familiar social commitment devices, which allow them to place a larger conception of welfare above immediate impulse. These commitment devices are established conventions and strategies which embody ethical norms, and make it possible to overcome myopic preferences. Examples at a personal level are marriage, education, insurance, prudence, and patriotism; at the social level, constitutions, law, religion, money, calendars and clocks, government, and taxes. Some of these harness private virtues, others social ones. Before the amoral relativism of Robbins and his successors, the utilitarian values of Victorian economists were also commitment devices of this kind.

Many of these commitment devices can be thought of as 'ethical capital', for individuals as well as society. They form a stock of reliable expectations about how people are likely to act. They underpin trust and facilitate exchange. They economize on monitoring and enforcement. Ethical capital takes us back to Adam Smith, and his assumptions of a social good and of innate virtue. The 'selfish turn' of the 1960s and 1970s, the rise and acceptance of rational choice doctrines, can be seen as an episode of normative demolition, the plundering of ethical capital. No wonder it was followed by 'corruption eruption'.

Where do such self-regarding doctrines come from? They are not objective truth. Although they are captive to worldly interests and subservient to their needs, they are not entirely special pleading, no more than the doctrines of

---

55. Offer, *Challenge of Affluence* (2006), ch. 3.

the established religions. That comparison is often made, and may provide a clue.[56] Economics is not like a religion or a church, despite some similarities. It does not invoke transcendence and it despises spirituality. Rather, religious movements, institutions, and theologies are visions of social order which (like economics) can capture the imagination. The world religions used to be like that, but also conviction movements like the Reformation, the Counter-Reformation, the Enlightenment, Nationalism, Socialism, and Fascism. Market liberalism is a conviction movement too. We have no understanding of these great waves of certitude apart from historical contemplation. 'There are seasons in history, but they seem to have a mysterious, implacable dynamism that mere humans can only hope to ride like great waves, hoping to not get crushed.'[57] Whatever they were really about, all these movements had Just World Theories at their core, visions of inclusion and exclusion, of salvation and punishment. In retrospect, and from the outside, it is sometimes difficult to understand what the issues were about. Take the Reformation: whatever the theological issues, five hundred years later we are still none the wiser. But the burning of witches and heretics on both sides was real enough. Likewise, the metaphysics of economics can drive individuals like Friedman, Stigler, and Hayek with a conviction and passion which is quite baffling for those outside the faith.

Most economists did not actively enlist in the market-liberal crusade. The Nobel Prize winners between 1969 and 2005 were a group of gifted individuals; most (not all of them) subscribed to market analytics, but a great many (like members of the discipline more widely), were sceptical about harsh Chicago policy norms. Indeed, this lively variety of opinion, often expressed in the Nobel Lectures themselves, helped to maintain the credibility of the Nobel Prize, and by extension, of economics as an academic discipline, protecting it from backing into corners.

WHAT DO YOU KNOW ABOUT ECONOMICS, IF ALL YOU KNOW IS ECONOMICS?

If economics were abolished by decree, something would soon take its place. So the question is where to look for a more constructive form of inquiry. The first step is to accept the limitations of knowledge. This is not to forbid

---

56. Nelson, *Reaching for Heaven on Earth* (1991); idem, *Economics as Religion* (2001).
57. Kunstler, 'The Clash of Civilizations' (2015).

flights of fancy, but to accept them for the fancies that they are. In other words, to underpin desirable policies with secure knowledge, and if not, to state what values are driving policy. The justification then has to come out of politics, ethics, conviction, advantage, even temperament and biology. This is legitimate. There is not enough that we know for sure, action is necessary, and we differ in our interests and objectives. Value-transparency was advocated early on by Gunnar Myrdal.[58] If economics is to live up to its aspirations as a science, it needs to acknowledge the limitations of its grasp. If it is something other than science, then the scientistic pretence only muddies the water.[59]

Gunnar Myrdal wrote that scientific certitude was beyond reach, and urged candour about purpose. His alternative was Social Democracy. His daughter Sissela Bok showed how the Myrdals could be here carried away by the scientistic temptation. Of their joint book of 1934, she wrote,

> the most astounding points of view, sometimes emanating entirely from their own hopes or fears, are presented as facts. All writers are prone to such overstating, but Alva and Gunnar were so especially certain that what they said was 'scientific' and therefore incontestable. They could present hypotheses regarding the future in the same tone of self-evidence in which they put forth population statistics and offer personal interpretations of abstruse matters as obvious to all who have their eyes open. . . . At the same time one feels . . . how sharp their aim could be, how much they understood the problems that most people would never be able to sort out, how often they were in fact right, and how forcefully they conveyed the large outlines of a problem while capturing the links between so many circumstances.[60]

This could be written about a great deal of economics. What is absent, the daughter points out, is scientific grounding.

Let theorists do theory. But policy requires more humility, both in its understanding and in pushing for change. Economics has many powerful traditions to draw upon, many of them developed by Nobel Prize winners. A tradition of empirical investigation goes back to Adam Smith and political arithmetic before him. This almost amounts to another canon.[61] It is more

---

58. Myrdal, *Political Element* (1953).
59. Hayek, 'The Pretence of Knowledge', Nobel Lecture 1974.
60. Bok, *Alva Myrdal* (1991), 151.
61. Reinert and Daastel, 'The Other Canon' (2004).

modest in its claims from theory, but its findings and understanding are more secure. One stream goes back to the nineteenth-century tradition of statistical investigation, which has come back in the last two decades as the empirical revolution.[62] The German Historical School had a North American emulator in Thorstein Veblen and successors in Joseph Schumpeter and the National Bureau of Economic Research. It blossomed into national accounting, and is currently being enlarged by the study of happiness and well-being. The old development economics of Arthur Lewis and Gunnar Myrdal also belongs in this tradition. Another unbroken strand is that of economic history, modestly recognized by two Nobel awards in 1993, and indirectly in others.

Behavioural and experimental economics, with nineteenth-century roots in the psychology of Wilhelm Wundt and Frédéric Leplay, has been crowned by the award of Nobel Prizes to Simon (NPW, 1978) and Kahneman and Smith (NPWs, 2002). Most importantly, the massive empirical turn in economics during the last two decades, the work of field experiments and historical 'natural experiments', is a silent repudiation of equilibrium economics, a return to 'measurement without theory' (that is, only statistical inference). However challenging to carry out, it is a methodologically simple world in which the facts are allowed to speak for themselves, perhaps too much. The appeal of this type of factually grounded work is shown in Thomas Piketty's best-seller on inequality, *Capital in the Twenty-First Century* (2014). Its theory is disputable, and its power derives from rich historical data covering two centuries.

Textbook economics, like textbook science more generally, implies a finality which is belied by the value placed on research. If you don't know that theory in the past was different, it is hard to imagine that future theory will be different as well. A modest implication of the present study, and of the history of economic thought, is to show how much variety there continues to be. The discipline might take more guidance from earth sciences and biology, both of which deal with irreversible movement through time.[63] In the discipline of historical narrative, a system of causes rarely persists for long, changes follow a unique and unrepeatable course, and the future is unlike the past. To mine history for samples of regularity may have its uses, but to exclude the intellectual discipline of history is to exclude a vast amount of

---

62. Chapter 2, above, 56.
63. Rosenberg, 'If Economics Is a Science, What Kind of Science Is It?' (2009).

knowledge. A compelling alternative vision is presented by the economist Brian Arthur:

> the economy is not necessarily in equilibrium: economic agents (firms, consumers, investors) constantly change their actions and strategies in response to the outcome they mutually create. This further changes the outcome, which requires them to adjust afresh. Agents thus live in a world where their beliefs and strategies are constantly being 'tested' for survival within an outcome or 'ecology' these beliefs and strategies together create. Economics has largely avoided this nonequilibrium view in the past, but if we allow it, we see patterns or phenomena not visible to equilibrium analysis. These emerge probabilistically, last for some time and dissipate, and they correspond to complex structures in other fields. We also see the economy not as something given and existing but forming from a constantly developing set of technological innovations, institutions, and arrangements that draw forth further innovations, institutions and arrangements.[64]

To recapture validity, economics has to come down to the ground of argument, evidence, and counterargument, supported by reason and an open mind. In the quest for valid knowledge, for those of Enlightenment disposition, it is well to ignore black boxes, the magic of prizes, and the lure of immutable laws. Gunnar Myrdal and Friedrich von Hayek, two NPWs who detested each other but criticized their own prizes, would both have agreed.

---

64. Arthur, 'Complexity Economics: A Different Framework for Economic Thought' (2013); idem, *Complexity and the Economy* (2014).

BIBLIOGRAPHY

PRIMARY SOURCES

BELGIUM
Mont Pèlerin Society Papers, Liberaal Archief, Ghent.

SWEDEN

Erik Lindahl Papers, Lund University Archive, Lund.
Swedish Central Bank Archive, Stockholm.
Swedish National Archives, Marieberg, Stockholm.

UNITED STATES

Hoover Institution Archives, Stanford, CA.
   Friedrich von Hayek Papers.
   Milton Friedman Papers.
   Mont Pèlerin Society Papers.

SWEDISH OFFICIAL PUBLICATIONS

'Bankoutskottets Utlåtande Nr 13 År 1962' (1962). *Bihang till Riksdagens Protokoll År 1962*, C27 (Stockholm: Riksdagen). This is a published series of annexes to the parliamentary minutes. The particular source is from the permanent committee of parliament responsible for the central bank (Bankoutskottet). The series is hence *Bihang till Riksdagens Protokoll År 19xx*. (Stockholm: Riksdagen).
'Bankoutskottets Utlåtande Nr 11 År 1969' (1969). *Bihang till Riksdagens Protokoll År 1969*, C23 (Stockholm: Riksdagen).
Petrén, Gustaf (1969). 'PM', Riksdagens Revisorers Berättelse angående Riksbanken för År 1968, Bilaga B, *Bihang till Riksdagens Protokoll År 1969*, C13 (Stockholm: Riksdagen).
Swedish Parliament. *Första Kammarens Protokoll* [First Chamber Debates] (Stockholm: Riksdagen).
Swedish Parliament. *Andra Kammarens Protokoll* [Second Chamber Debates] (Stockholm: Riksdagen).

REFERENCES

Abed, George T., and Sanjeev Gupta (2003). 'The Economics of Corruption: An Overview', *Governance, Corruption & Economic Performance*, eds. George T. Abed and Sanjeev Gupta (Washington, DC: International Monetary Fund), 1–16.

Agell, Jonas (1996). 'Why Sweden's Welfare State Needed Reform', *Economic Journal*, 106,439, 1760–1771.

Ahamed, Liaquat (2009). *Lords of Finance: The Bankers Who Broke the World* (London: William Heinemann).

Ahlqvist, Anders, Johan Ahlqvist, John Hylton and Peter Nobel (2001). 'Falskt Pris i Nobels Namn', *Svenska Dagbladet*, 21 November 2001.

Akerlof, George A. (1970). 'The Market for Lemons—Quality Uncertainty and Market Mechanism', *Quarterly Journal of Economics*, 84,3, 488–500.

Akerlof, George A., and Robert J. Shiller (2015). *Phishing for Phools: The Economics of Manipulation and Deception* (Princeton, NJ: Princeton University Press).

Alpert, Daniel (2013). *The Age of Oversupply: Overcoming the Greatest Challenge to the Global Economy* (New York: Portfolio Penguin).

Alston, Richard M., J. R. Kearl and Michael B. Vaughan (1992). 'Is There a Consensus among Economists in the 1990's?' *American Economic Review*, 82,2, 203–209.

Alvaredo, Facundo, Anthony B. Atkinson, Thomas Piketty and Emmanuel Saez (2013). 'The Top 1 Percent in International and Historical Perspective', *Journal of Economic Perspectives*, 27,3, 3–20.

Alves, André Azevedo, and John Meadowcroft (2014). 'Hayek's Slippery Slope, the Stability of the Mixed Economy and the Dynamics of Rent Seeking', *Political Studies*, 62,4, 843–861.

Anderson, Perry (2014). 'The Italian Disaster', *New York Review of Books*, 22 May 2014, 3–16.

Andersson, Jenny (2006). *Between Growth and Security: Swedish Social Democracy from a Strong Society to a Third Way* (Manchester, UK: Manchester University Press).

Andersson, Staffan (2003). 'Political Corruption in Sweden', *Corruption in Contemporary Politics*, eds. Martin J. Bull and James Newell (Basingstoke, UK: Palgrave), 135–148.

Angner, Erik (2006). 'Economists as Experts: Overconfidence in Theory and Practice', *Journal of Economic Methodology*, 13,1, 1–24.

Anon. (n.d.). 'Optimal Progressivity', elsa.berkeley.edu/~burch/conf04/d2.pdf.

——— (1968). 'Riksbankens Jubileum', *Bancoposten*, 53,2, 3.

——— (1968). 'Sveriges Riksbank 300 År', *Bancoposten*, 53,2, 5.

——— (after 2012). 'Imre Lakatos', *World Heritage Encyclopaedia*, Project Gutenberg Self-Publishing Press, netlibrary.net/articles/Imre_Lakatos/articles/Imre_Lakatos.

Angrist, Joshua D., and Jorn-Steffen Pischke (2010). 'The Credibility Revolution in Empirical Economics: How Better Research Design Is Taking the Con Out of Econometrics', *Journal of Economic Perspectives*, 24,2, 3–30.

Archibald, G. C., Herbert A. Simon and Paul A. Samuelson (1963). 'Problems of Methodology: Discussion', *American Economic Review*, 53, 227–236.

Aronsson, Thomas, and James R. Walker (1997). 'The Effects of Sweden's Welfare State on Labor Supply Incentives', *The Welfare State in Transition: Reforming the Swedish Model*, eds. Richard B. Freeman, Robert Topel and Birgitta Swedenborg (Chicago: University of Chicago Press), 203–265.

——— (2010). 'Labor Supply, Tax Base, and Public Policy in Sweden', *Reforming the Welfare State: Recovery and Beyond in Sweden*, eds. Richard B. Freeman, Robert Topel and Birgitta Swedenborg (Chicago: University of Chicago Press), 127–158.

Arrow, K. J. (1963). 'Uncertainty and the Welfare Economics of Medical-Care', *American Economic Review*, 53, 5, 941–973.

——— (1972). 'Gifts and Exchanges', *Philosophy & Public Affairs*, 1,4, 343–362.

——— (1986). 'Rationality of Self and Others in an Economic-System', *Journal of Business*, 59,4, S385–S399.

——— (1987). 'Economic Theory and the Hypothesis of Rationality', *The New Palgrave Dictionary of Economics*, eds. John Eatwell and Murray Milgate (London: Macmillan), 70–74.

Arrow, K. J., P. Dasgupta, L. Goulder, G. Daily, P. Ehrlich, G. Heal, S. Levin, K. G. Maler, S. Schneider and D. Starrett (2004). 'Are We Consuming Too Much?' *Journal of Economic Perspectives*, 18,3, 147–172.

Arrow, K. J., and F. Hahn (1971). *General Competitive Analysis* (Amsterdam/Oxford: North-Holland).

Arthur, W. Brian (2013). 'Complexity Economics: A Different Framework for Economic Thought' (New York: Institute for New Economic Thinking). INET Research Note no. 033.

——— (2014). *Complexity and the Economy* (Oxford: Oxford University Press).

Athreya, Kartik B. (2015). *Big Ideas in Macroeconomics: A Nontechnical View* (Cambridge, MA: MIT Press).

Atkinson, Anthony B. (2012). 'The Mirrlees Review and the State of Public Economics', *Journal of Economic Literature*, 50,3, 770–780.

——— (2014). *Public Economics in an Age of Austerity* (Abingdon, UK: Routledge).

Atkinson, Anthony B., and Gunnar Viby Mogensen, eds. (1993). *Welfare and Work Incentives: A North European Perspective* (Oxford: Clarendon Press).

Auerbach, Paul, and Dimitris Sotiropoulos (2012). 'Revisiting the Socialist Calculation Debate: The Role of Markets and Finance in Hayek's Response to Lange's Challenge', Economics Discussion Paper 2012-6 (London: Kingston University Department of Economics).

Axell, Bo, and Birgitta Swedenborg (1977). *Milton Friedman och Ekonomipriset: En Sammanställning och Analys av Pressrapporteringen och Debatten om 1976 Års Ekonomipristagare* (Stockholm: Akademilitteratur).

Bachman, Daniel (1996). 'What Economic Forecasters Really Do' (Bala Cynwyd, PA: WEFA Group).

Backhouse, Roger (2012). 'The Rise and Fall of Popper and Lakatos in Economics', *Philosophy of Economics*, ed. Uskali Mäki (Oxford: North Holland Elsevier), 25–48.

Backhouse, Roger, ed. (1994). *New Directions in Economic Methodology* (London: Routledge).

Backhouse, Roger, and Béatrice Cherrier (2014). 'Becoming Applied: The Transformation of Economics after 1970', Department of Economics Discussion Paper 14-11 (Birmingham, UK: University of Birmingham).

Baker, Andy (2009). *The Market and the Masses in Latin America: Policy Reform and Consumption in Liberalizing Economies* (Cambridge: Cambridge University Press).

Ball, Laurence (1990). 'Intertemporal Substitution and Constraints on Labor Supply: Evidence from Panel Data', *Economic Inquiry*, 28,4, 706–724.

Baltensperger, Ernst (1999). *Fifty Years of the Deutsche Mark: Central Bank and the Currency in Germany since 1948* (Oxford: Oxford University Press).

Banzhaf, H. Spencer (2010). 'The Chicago School of Welfare Economics', *The Elgar Companion to the Chicago School of Economics*, ed. Ross B. Emmett (Cheltenham, UK: Edward Elgar), 59–69.

Barber, William J. (2008). *Gunnar Myrdal: An Intellectual Biography* (Basingstoke, UK: Palgrave Macmillan).

Barkman, Klas (2010). 'Brev från Astrid Lindgren Visar Hennes Stöd för S', *Dagens Nyheter*, 16 May 2010.

Barnett, William A., and Robert Solow (2007). 'An Interview with Franco Modigliani', *Inside the Economist's Mind: Conversations with Eminent Economists*, eds. Paul A. Samuelson and William A. Barnett (Malden, MA: Blackwell Publishing), 85–109.

Barr, N. A. (2001). *The Welfare State as Piggy Bank: Information, Risk, Uncertainty, and the Role of the State* (Oxford: Oxford University Press).

Barr, Nicholas (2001). 'The Truth about Pension Reform', *Finance & Development*, 38,3, 6–9.

——— (2012). *The Economics of the Welfare State*, 5th ed. (Oxford: Oxford University Press).

Barth, James R., Apanard Prabha and Phillip Swagel (2014). 'Just How Big Is the Too Big to Fail Problem?' (Santa Monica, CA: Milken Institute).

Becker, Gary S. (1976). *The Economic Approach to Human Behavior* (Chicago: University of Chicago Press).

Bentham, Jeremy (1838). 'Principles of the Civil Code', *The Works of Jeremy Bentham*, ed. John Bowring (Edinburgh: William Tait), 1, 297–365.

Berg, Claes, and Lars Jonung (1999). 'Pioneering Price Level Targeting: The Swedish Experience 1931–1937', *Journal of Monetary Economics*, 43,3, 525–551.

Berger, D., W. Easterly, N. Nunn and S. Satyanath (2013). 'Commercial Imperialism? Political Influence and Trade during the Cold War', *American Economic Review*, 103,2, 863–896.

Bergh, Andreas, and Magnus Henrekson (2012). *Varför Går det Bra för Sverige?: Om Sambanden Mellan Offentlig Sektor, Ekonomisk Frihet och Ekonomisk Utveckling* (Stockholm/Malmö: Fores Ivrig).

Bergsten, C. Fred (2006). *The Peter G. Peterson Institute for International Economics at Twenty Five* (Washington, DC: Peter G. Peterson Institute for International Economics).

Bergström, Villy (1977). 'Nationalekonomerna och Arbetarrörelsen', *Nationalekonomiska Föreningen 100 År: Ekonomisk Debatt och Ekonomisk Politik*, eds. Bertil Ohlin, Jan Herin and Lars Werin (Stockholm: Norstedts Förlag), 115–157.

Berman, Sheri (1998). *The Social Democratic Moment: Ideas and Politics in the Making of Interwar Europe* (Cambridge, MA: Harvard University Press).

—— (2004). 'The *Folkhem* Was a Success Story', *The Swedish Success Story?*, eds. Kurt Almqvist, Kay Glans and Paul Fischer (Stockholm: Axel and Margaret Ax:son Johnson Foundation), 61–65.

Bivens, Josh, Elise Gould, Lawrence Mishel and Heidi Shierholz (2014). 'Raising America's Pay: Why It's Our Central Economic Policy Challenge', Briefing Paper, 378, 4 June (Washington, DC: Economic Policy Institute).

Bjork, S., A. Offer and G. Söderberg (2014). 'Time Series Citation Data: The Nobel Prize in Economics', *Scientometrics*, 98,1, 185–196.

Björklund, Anders, and Richard B. Freeman (2010). 'Searching for Optimal Inequality/ Incentives', *Reforming the Welfare State: Recovery and Beyond in Sweden*, eds. Richard B. Freeman, Robert Topel and Birgitta Swedenborg (Chicago: University of Chicago Press), 25–56.

Blaazer, David (2005). 'Finance and the End of Appeasement: The Bank of England, the National Government and the Czech Gold', *Journal of Contemporary History*, 40,1, 25–39.

Blackburn, Robin (2005). 'Rudolf Meidner, 1914–2005: A Visionary Pragmatist', *Counterpunch*, 22 December 2005, http://www.counterpunch.org/2005/12/22/a-visonary-pragmatist/.

Blake, William (1790). *The Marriage of Heaven and Hell* (London: William Blake).

Blaug, Mark (1992). *The Methodology of Economics: Or, How Economists Explain*, 2nd ed. (Cambridge: Cambridge University Press).

—— (1994). 'Why I Am Not a Constructivist: Confessions of an Unrepentant Popperian', *New Directions in Economic Methodology*, ed. Roger E. Backhouse (London: Routledge), 109–136.

—— (1997). *Economic Theory in Retrospect*, 5th ed. (Cambridge: Cambridge University Press).

Blaug, Mark (2007). 'The Fundamental Theorems of Modern Welfare Economics, Historically Contemplated', *History of Political Economy*, 39,2, 185–207.

Blendon, Robert J., John M. Benson, Mollyann Brodie, Richard Morin, Drew E. Altman, Daniel Gitterman, Mario Brossard and Matt James (1997). 'Bridging the Gap between the Public's and Economists' Views of the Economy', *Journal of Economic Perspectives*, 11,3, 105–118.

Block, Walter, and Michael Walker (1988). 'Entropy in the Canadian Economics Profession: Sampling Consensus on the Major Issues', *Canadian Public Policy*, 14,2, 137–150.

Blum, William (2003). *Killing Hope: U.S. Military and CIA Interventions since World War II* (London: Zed Books).

Blyth, Mark (2001). 'The Transformation of the Swedish Model: Economic Ideas, Distributional Conflict, and Institutional Change', *World Politics*, 54, 1, 1–26.

—— (2002). *Great Transformations: The Rise and Decline of Embedded Liberalism* (New York: Cambridge University Press).

—— (2013). *Austerity: The History of a Dangerous Idea* (New York: Oxford University Press).

Boadway, Robin W. (2012). *From Optimal Tax Theory to Tax Policy: Retrospective and Prospective Views* (Cambridge, MA/London: MIT Press).

Bogardi, Peter, Andrew Knudsen and Carey Schildt (2001). 'Swedosclerosis or Pseudosclerosis', *Issues in Political Economy*, 10, org.elon.edu/ipe/sweden.pdf.

Bogle, John C. (2005). *The Battle for the Soul of Capitalism* (New Haven, CT: Yale University Press).

Bok, Sissela (1991). *Alva Myrdal: A Daughter's Memoir* (Reading, MA: Addison-Wesley).

Bosman, Julie (2015). 'Wisconsin Governor Signs Bill Limiting Political Corruption Inquiries', *New York Times*, 23 October 2015.

Boughton, James M. (2001). *Silent Revolution: The International Monetary Fund, 1979–1989* (Washington, DC: International Monetary Fund).

Boumans, Marcel (1999). 'Built-in Justification', *Models as Mediators: Perspectives on Natural and Social Science,* eds. Mary Morgan and Margaret Morrison (Cambridge: Cambridge University Press), 66–96.

Boyle, Andrew (1967). *Montagu Norman: A Biography* (London: Cassell).

Breit, William, and Barry T. Hirsch (2009). *Lives of the Laureates: Twenty-Three Nobel Economists*, 5th ed. (Cambridge, MA: MIT Press).

Brennan, Geoffrey, and Philip Pettit (1993). 'Hands Invisible and Intangible', *Synthese*, 94,2, 191–225.

—— (2004). *The Economy of Esteem: An Essay on Civil and Political Society* (Oxford: Oxford University Press).

Brittan, Samuel (2003). 'The Not So Noble Nobel Prize', *Financial Times*, 19 December 2003.

Bromley, Daniel W. (1990). 'The Ideology of Efficiency: Searching for a Theory of Policy Analysis', *Journal of Environmental Economics and Management*, 19,1, 86–107.

Brooks, Richard (2008). 'The Bourn Complicity', *Private Eye*, 5 September 2008, 17–25.

—— (2013). *The Great Tax Robbery: How Britain Became a Tax Haven for Fat Cats and Big Business* (London: Oneworld).

Brown, Marvin (2010). 'Free Enterprise and Economics of Slavery', *Real-world Economics Review*, 52, 28–39.

—— (2010). 'Adam Smith's View of Slaves as Property: A Response to Thomas Wells and Bruce Elmslie', *Real-World Economics Review*, 54, 124–125.

Buchanan, James M., and Richard A. Musgrave (1999). *Public Finance and Public Choice: Two Contrasting Visions of the State* (Cambridge, MA: MIT Press).

Buchanan, James M., and Gordon Tullock (1962). *The Calculus of Consent: Logical Foundations of Constitutional Democracy* (Ann Arbor: University of Michigan Press).

Budhoo, Davison L. (1990). *Enough Is Enough: Dear Mr. Camdessus—Open Letter of Resignation to the Managing Director of the International Monetary Fund* (New York: New Horizons Press).

Business Week International (1995). 'Dirty Money', 17 December 1995, http://www.bloomberg .com/bw/stories/1995-12-17/dirty-money-intl-edition.

—— (1995). 'Europe's New Morality', 17 December 1995, http://www.bloomberg.com/ news/articles/1995-12-17/europes-new-morality-intl-edition.

Buiter, Willem H. (1980). 'The Macroeconomics of Dr. Pangloss: A Critical Survey of the New Classical Macroeconomics', *Economic Journal*, 90,357, 34–50.

Bull, Martin J., and James Newell (2003). *Corruption in Contemporary Politics* (Houndmills/ Basingstoke, UK: Palgrave Macmillan).

Burgin, Angus (2012). *The Great Persuasion: Reinventing Free Markets since the Depression* (Cambridge, MA: Harvard University Press).

Caballero, R. J. (2010). 'Macroeconomics after the Crisis: Time to Deal with the Pretense-of-Knowledge Syndrome', *Journal of Economic Perspectives*, 24,4, 85–102.

Caldwell, Bruce (1982). *Beyond Positivism: Economic Methodology in the Twentieth Century* (London: Allen & Unwin).

Caldwell, Bruce, and Leonidas Montes (2014). 'Friedrich Hayek and His Visits to Chile', CHOPE Discussion Paper, 2014-12 (Durham, NC: Duke University).

Cameron, Maxwell A., and Eric Hershberg, ed. (2010). *Latin America's Left Turns: Politics, Policies, and Trajectories of Change* (Boulder, CO: Lynne Rienner).

Canterbery, E. Ray, and Robert J. Burkhardt (1983). 'What Do We Mean by Asking Whether Economics Is a Science?', *Why Economics Is Not a Science*, ed. Alfred S. Eichner (London: Macmillan), 15–40.

Card, David, Stefano DellaVigna and Ulrike Malmendier (2011). 'The Role of Theory in Field Experiments', *Journal of Economic Perspectives*, 25,3, 39–62.

Cardiff, C. F., and D. B. Klein (2005). 'Faculty Partisan Affiliations in All Disciplines: A Voter-Registration Study', *Critical Review*, 17,3, 237–256.

Carlaw, Kenneth I., and Richard G. Lipsey (2012). 'Does History Matter?: Empirical Analysis of Evolutionary versus Stationary Equilibrium Views of the Economy', *Journal of Evolutionary Economics*, 22, 735–736.

Carlson, Benny (1993). 'Den Enprocentiga Revolutionen: Debatten om Riksbankens Ställning i Samband Med Räntekuppen 1957', Lund Papers in Economic History 26 (Lund, Sweden: Lund University, Department of Economic History).

——— (1994). *The State as a Monster: Gustav Cassel and Eli Heckscher on the Role and Growth of the State* (Lanham, MD: University Press of America).

Carlson, Benny, and Lars Jonung (2006). 'Knut Wicksell, Gustav Cassel, Eli Heckscher, Bertil Ohlin and Gunnar Myrdal on the Role of the Economist in Public Debate', *Econ Journal Watch*, 3,3, 511–550.

Carson, Carol S. (1975). 'The History of the United States National Income and Product Accounts: The Development of an Analytical Tool', *Review of Income and Wealth*, 21,2, 153–181.

Carter, Michael, and Rodney Maddock (1984). *Rational Expectations: Macroeconomics for the 1980s?* (Basingstoke, UK: Macmillan Education).

Cassel, Gustav (1928). *Socialism Eller Framåtskridande* (Stockholm: Norstedt).

Chari, V. V. (2010). 'Statement of V. V. Chari', *US Congress Subcommittee on Investigations and Oversight, Committee on Science and Technology* (Washington, DC: US Government Printing Office), 32–34.

Cherrier, B. (2009). 'Gunnar Myrdal and the Scientific Way to Social Democracy, 1914–1968', *Journal of the History of Economic Thought*, 31,1, 33–55.

Childs, Marquis W. (1936). *Sweden: The Middle Way* (London: Faber).

Chossudovsky, Michel (2003). *The Globalization of Poverty and the New World Order*, 2nd ed. (Pincourt, Quebec: Global Research).

Christensen, Tom, and Per Lægreid, eds. (2011). *The Ashgate Research Companion to New Public Management* (Farnham, UK: Ashgate).

Cingano, Federico (2014). 'Trends in Income Inequality and Its Impact on Economic Growth', OECD Social, Employment and Migration Working Papers 163 (Paris: OECD), http://dx.doi.org/10.1787/5jxrjncwxv6j-en.

Clark, E., and K. Johnson (2009). 'Circumventing Circumscribed Neoliberalism: The "System Switch" in Swedish Housing', *Where the Other Half Lives: Lower Income Housing in a Neoliberal World*, ed. Sarah Glynn (London: Pluto), 173–194.

Clay, Henry (1957). *Lord Norman* (London: St. Martin's Press).

Cockroft, Laurence (2012). *Global Corruption: Money, Power and Ethics in the Modern World* (London: I. B. Tauris).

Cohen, Stephen F. (2000). *Failed Crusade: America and the Tragedy of Post-Communist Russia* (New York: Norton).

Colander, David C. (2013). 'On the Ideological Migration of the Economics Laureates', *Econ Journal Watch*, 10,3, 240–254.

Colander, David C., ed. (2009). *The Making of an Economist, Redux* (Princeton, NJ: Princeton University Press).

Conference Board (2012). 'Total Economy Database: Output, Labor and Labor Productivity Country Details, 1950–2011', http://www.conference-board.org/data/economydatabase/.

——— (2014). 'Total Economy Database: Output, Labor and Labor Productivity Country Details, 1950–2013', http://www.conference-board.org/data/economydatabase/.

Copeland, B. Jack, Carl J. Posy and Oron Shagrir, eds. (2013). *Computability: Turing, Gödel, Church, and Beyond* (Cambridge, MA: MIT Press).

Copetas, A. Craig (1985). 'The Revolt of the Capitalists', http://www.inc.com/magazine/1985 0901/4941.html.

Córdoba, Juan Carlos, and Geneviève Verdier (2007). 'Lucas vs. Lucas: On Inequality and Growth' IMF Working Paper WP/07/17 (Washington, DC: International Monetary Fund).

Cornia, Giovanni Andrea, and Renato Paniccià (2000). *The Mortality Crisis in Transitional Economies* (Oxford: Oxford University Press).

Craig, David (2008). *Squandered: How Gordon Brown Is Wasting over One Trillion Pounds of Our Money* (London: Constable).

Craig, David, and Richard Brooks (2006). *Plundering the Public Sector: How New Labour Are Letting Consultants Run Off with £70 Billion of Our Money* (London: Constable).

Craig, David, and Matthew Elliott (2009). *The Great European Rip-Off: How the Corrupt, Wasteful EU Is Taking Control of Our Lives* (London: Random House).

Creedy, J. (1980). 'Some Recent Interpretations of Mathematical Psychics', *History of Political Economy*, 12,2, 267–276.

Crosland, Anthony (1963). *The Future of Socialism*, rev. ed. (London: J. Cape).

Cullenberg, Stephen, Jack Amariglio and David F. Ruccio, eds. (2001). *Postmodernism, Economics and Knowledge* (London; New York: Routledge).

Cumbers, Andrew (2012). *Reclaiming Public Ownership: Making Space for Economic Democracy* (London: Zed Books).

Dabla-Norris, Era, Kalpana Kochhar, Nujin Suphaphiphat, Frantisek Ricka and Evridiki Tsounta (2015). 'Causes and Consequences of Income Inequality: A Global Perspective' (Washington, DC: International Monetary Fund).

Davidson, Paul (1996). 'Reality and Economic Theory', *Journal of Post Keynesian Economics*, 18,4, 479–508.

Davis, Karen, Cathy Schoen and Kristof Stremikis (2010). *Mirror, Mirror on the Wall: How the Performance of the U.S. Health Care System Compares Internationally* (New York: Commonwealth Fund).

Davis, William L., and Bob Figgins (2009). 'Do Economists Believe American Democracy Is Working?' *Econ Journal Watch*, 6,2, 195–202.

Dawid, Richard (2013). *String Theory and the Scientific Method* (Cambridge: Cambridge University Press).

Deane, Marjorie, Robert Pringle and Paul A. Volcker (1994). *The Central Banks* (London: Hamish Hamilton).

Deane, Phyllis (1983). 'The Scope and Method of Economic Science', *Economic Journal*, 93,369, 1–12.

De Bellis, Nicola (2009). *Bibliometrics and Citation Analysis: From the Science Citation Index to Cybermetrics* (Lanham, MD/Plymouth, UK: Scarecrow Press).

De Champs, Lena (2000). 'Organizing the Nobel Festival Day—Some Recollections', http://www.nobelprize.org/nobel_organizations/nobelfoundation/history/dechamps/index.html.

De Marchi, Neil (1988). *The Popperian Legacy in Economics: Papers Presented at a Symposium in Amsterdam, December 1985* (Cambridge: Cambridge University Press).

Demsetz, H. (1969). 'Information and Efficiency—Another Viewpoint', *Journal of Law & Economics*, 12,1, 1–22.

Diamond, P., and E. Saez (2011). 'The Case for a Progressive Tax: From Basic Research to Policy Recommendations', *Journal of Economic Perspectives*, 25,4, 165–190.

Dimsdale, N. H. (2013). 'The Bank of England and the British Economy, 1890–1913' Discussion Papers in Economic and Social History 123 (Oxford: University of Oxford)

Doig, Alan (1996). 'Politics and Public Sector Ethics: The Impact of Change in the United Kingdom', *Political Corruption in Europe and Latin America*, eds. Walter Little and Eduardo Posada-Carbó (Basingstoke, UK: Macmillan Press), 173–192.

Dou, Winston W., Andrew W. Lo and Ameya Muley (2015). 'Macroeconomic Models for Monetary Policies: A Critical Review from a Finance Perspective' (unpublished paper, Cambridge, MA).

Downs, Anthony (1957). *An Economic Theory of Democracy* (New York: Harper & Row).

Duarte, Pedro Garcia, and Gilberto Tadeu Lima, eds. (2012). *Microfoundations Reconsidered: The Relationship of Micro and Macroeconomics in Historical Perspective* (Cheltenham, UK: Edward Elgar).

Düppe, Till, and E. Roy Weintraub (2014). *Finding Equilibrium: Arrow, Debreu, McKenzie and the Problem of Scientific Credit* (Princeton, NJ: Princeton University Press).

Duvendack, Maren, Richard W. Palmer-Jones and W. Robert Reed (2014). 'Replications in Economics: A Progress Report', Working Paper 26/2014 (Canterbury, New Zealand: University of Canterbury).

Ebenstein, Alan O. (2001). *Friedrich Hayek: A Biography* (New York: Palgrave for St. Martin's Press).

Echenique, Federico (2014). 'Testing for Separability Is Hard', Discussion Paper arXiv:1401.4499 [cs.GT] (Pasadena: California Institute of Technology).

Economist (2008). 'The Economist Poll of Economists', 2 October 2008.

——— (2014). 'Memory Is Not History: "Dirty War" Memorials Should Not Be Used to Rewrite the Past', 13 September 2014, 50.

Edin, Per-Anders, and Robert Topel (1997). 'Wage Policy and Restructuring: The Swedish Labor Market since 1960', *The Welfare State in Transition: Reforming the Swedish Model*, eds. Richard B. Freeman, Robert Topel and Birgitta Swedenborg (Chicago: University of Chicago Press), 155–201.

Égert, Balazs (2013). 'The 90% Public Debt Threshold: The Rise and Fall of a Stylised Fact', OECD Economics Department Working Papers 1055 (Paris: OECD), http://search.proquest.com/docview/1416035616/abstract/embedded/D3DQFEVJGXTNKR3P?source=fedsrch.

Eklund, Klas (1995), 'En Intellektuell Biografi och Programförklaring', http://www.klaseklund.se/?page_id=82.

Elliott, Kimberly Ann (1997). *Corruption and the Global Economy* (Washington, DC: Institute for International Economics).

Elster, Jon (2001). 'The Nature and Scope of Rational Choice Explanation', *Readings in the Philosophy of Social Science*, eds. Michael Martin and Lee C. McIntyre (Cambridge, MA: MIT Press), 311–322.

——— (2009). 'Excessive Ambitions', *Capitalism and Society*, 4,2, article 1, 1–30.

Endres, A. M., and Grant A. Fleming (2002). *International Organizations and the Analysis of Economic Policy, 1919–1950: Analysis of Selected Institutions* (Cambridge: Cambridge University Press).

English, James F. (2005). *The Economy of Prestige: Prizes, Awards, and the Circulation of Cultural Value* (Cambridge, MA: Harvard University Press).

Englund, Peter, and Lars Heikensten (1977). 'Böcker: Bo Axell-Birgitta Swedenborg, Milton Friedman och Ekonomipriset', *Ekonomisk Debatt*, 5,77, 318–320.

Ericsson, Neil R., and John S. Irons (1995). 'The Lucas Critique in Practice: Theory without Measurement', International Finance Discussion Papers 506 (Washington, DC: Board of Governors of the Federal Reserve System).

Erlander, Tage (1976). *Tage Erlander. 1901–1939* (Stockholm: Tiden).

Erlander, Tage, and Sven Erlander (2001–2013). *Dagböcker*, 14 vols. (Hedemora: Gidlund).

Esping-Andersen, Gosta (1990). *The Three Worlds of Welfare Capitalism* (Cambridge: Polity).

Estrella, A., and J. C. Fuhrer (2002). 'Dynamic Inconsistencies: Counterfactual Implications of a Class of Rational-Expectations Models', *American Economic Review*, 92,4, 1013–1028.

Evans, G. W., S. Honkapohja and T. J. Sargent (2005). 'An Interview with Thomas J. Sargent', *Macroeconomic Dynamics*, 9,4, 561–583.

Expertgruppen för Studier i Offentlig Ekonomi (1984). 'Är Subventioner Effektiva? Rapport till Expertgruppen för Studier i Offentlig Ekonomi' (Stockholm: Liber/Allmänna förlaget).

Favero, Carlo, and David Hendry (1992). 'Testing the Lucas Critique: A Review', *Econometric Reviews*, 11, 3, 265–306.

Feldman, Burton (2000). *The Nobel Prize: A History of Genius, Controversy, and Prestige* (New York: Arcade).

Feldstein, M. (2005). 'Rethinking Social Insurance', *American Economic Review*, 95,1, 1–24.

Feldt, Kjell-Olof (1991). *Alla Dessa Dagar: I Regeringen 1982–1990* (Stockholm: Norstedt).

Ferlie, Ewan, Laurence E. Lynn and Christopher Pollitt (2005). *The Oxford Handbook of Public Management* (Oxford: Oxford University Press).

Ferran, E. (2012). 'Regulatory Lessons from the Payment Protection Insurance Mis-Selling Scandal in the UK', *European Business Organization Law Review*, 13,2, 247–270.

Feyerabend, Paul (1975). *Against Method: Outline of an Anarchistic Theory of Knowledge* (London: NLB Humanities Press).

Fischer, Stanley (1990). 'Comment', *Latin American Adjustment: How Much Has Happened?*, ed. John E. Williamson (Washington, DC: Institute for International Economics), 25–28.

Fisher, Franklin M. (2011). 'The Stability of General Equilibrium—What Do We Know and Why Is It Important?' *General Equilibrium Analysis: A Century after Walras*, ed. Pascal Bridel (London: Routledge), 34–45.

Florio, Massimo (2004). *The Great Divestiture: Evaluating the Welfare Impact of the British Privatizations, 1979–1997* (Cambridge, MA: MIT Press).

Florio, Massimo, ed. (2013). *Network Industries and Social Welfare: The Experiment That Reshuffled European Utilities* (Cambridge: Cambridge University Press).

Fogel, R. W. (2000). 'Simon S. Kuznets April 30, 1901–July 9, 1985', NBER Working Paper Series 0898–2937 (Cambridge, MA: NBER).

Foley, Duncan K. (1998). 'An Interview with Wassily Leontief', *Macroeconomic Dynamics*, 2,1, 116–140.

Forder, James (2014). *Macroeconomics and the Phillips Curve Myth* (Oxford: Oxford University Press).

Foreman-Peck, James, and Robert Millward (1994). *Public and Private Ownership of British Industry, 1820–1990* (Oxford: Clarendon Press).

Forslund, Anders, and Alan Krueger (2010). 'Did Active Labor Market Policies Help Sweden Rebound from the Depression of the Early 1990s?', *Reforming the Welfare State: Recovery and Beyond in Sweden*, eds. Richard B. Freeman, Birgitta Swedenborg and Robert Topel (Chicago: Chicago University Press), 159–187.

Fourcade, M., E. Ollion and Y. Algan (2015). 'The Superiority of Economists', *Journal of Economic Perspectives*, 29,1, 89–114.

Fox, Justin (2009). *The Myth of the Rational Market: A History of Risk, Reward, and Delusion on Wall Street* (New York: Harper Business).

Francis, Joe (2014), 'The Rise and Fall of Debate in Economics', http://www.joefrancis.info/economics-debate/.

Frank, R. H., T. D. Gilovich and D. T. Regan (1996). 'Do Economists Make Bad Citizens?' *Journal of Economic Perspectives*, 10,1, 187–192.

Fredriksson, Peter, and Robert Topel (2010). 'Wage Determination and Employment in Sweden since the Early 1990s: Wage Formation in a New Setting', *Reforming the Welfare State: Recovery and Beyond in Sweden*, eds. Richard B. Freeman, Birgitta Swedenborg and Robert Topel (Chicago: University of Chicago Press), 83–126.

Freeman, Richard B., Birgitta Swedenborg and Robert H. Topel (2010). *Reforming the Welfare State: Recovery and Beyond in Sweden* (Chicago: University of Chicago Press).

Freeth, Tony (2008). *The Antikythera Mechanism: Decoding an Ancient Greek Mystery: A Brief Research History* (Cambridge: Whipple Museum of the History of Science).

—— (2009). 'Decoding an Ancient Computer', *Scientific American*, 301,6, 76–83.

Freeth, Tony, Alexander Jones, John M. Steele and Yanis Bitsakis (2008). 'Calendars with Olympiad Display and Eclipse Prediction on the Antikythera Mechanism', *Nature*, 454, 7204, 614–617.

Frey, Bruno S., and Reiner Eichenberger (1992). 'Economics and Economists: A European Perspective', *American Economic Review*, 82,2, 216–220.

Frey, Bruno S., Werner W. Pommerehne, Friedrich Schneider and Guy Gilbert (1984). 'Consensus and Dissension among Economists: An Empirical Inquiry', *American Economic Review*, 74,5, 986–994.

Fried, Charles (1981). *Contract as Promise: A Theory of Contractual Obligation* (Cambridge, MA: Harvard University Press).

Friedman, Michael (1991). 'The Re-Evaluation of Logical Positivism', *Journal of Philosophy*, 88,10, 505–519.

—— (1999). *Reconsidering Logical Positivism* (Cambridge: Cambridge University Press).

Friedman, Milton (1953). 'The Methodology of Positive Economics', *Essays in Positive Economics*, ed. Milton Friedman (Chicago: Chicago University Press), 3–43.

—— (1968). 'The Role of Monetary Policy', *American Economic Review*, 58,1, 1–17.

Friedman, Milton, and Rose D. Friedman (1962). *Capitalism and Freedom* (Chicago: University of Chicago Press).

—— (1998). *Two Lucky People: Memoirs* (Chicago: University of Chicago Press).

Friedman, Milton, and Simon Smith Kuznets (1945). *Income from Independent Professional Practice* (New York: National Bureau of Economic Research).

Friedman, Robert Marc (2001). *The Politics of Excellence: Behind the Nobel Prize in Science* (New York: Times Books).

Frydman, Roman, and Michael D. Goldberg (2011). *Beyond Mechanical Markets: Asset Price Swings, Risk, and the Role of the State* (Princeton, NJ: Princeton University Press).

Frydman, Roman, and Edmund S. Phelps (1983). 'Introduction', *Individual Forecasting and Aggregate Outcomes: "Rational Expectations" Examined*, eds. Roman Frydman and Edmund S. Phelps (Cambridge: Cambridge University Press), 1–30.

Fullbrook, Edward (2007). *Real World Economics: A Post-Autistic Economics Reader* (London: Anthem).

—— (2012). *Decline of the USA* (Bristol, UK: Real-World Economics Books).

Fuller, Dan, and Doris Geide-Stevenson (2003). 'Consensus among Economists: Revisited', *Journal of Economic Education*, 34,4, 369–387.

Gaffney, Mason, and Harrison, Fred (1994). *Corruption of Economics* (London: Shepheard-Walwyn).

Ghosh, Saibal (2015). 'Beautiful Minds: The Nobel Memorial Prize in Economics', MPRA Paper 66216 (Munich: Munich Personal RePEc Archive), https://mpra.ub.uni-muenchen.de/66216/.

Giersch, Herbert (1985). 'Eurosclerosis', Kiel Discussion Papers 112 (Kiel: Institut für Weltwirtschaft Kiel).

Ginn, J., and S. Arber (2000). 'Personal Pension Take-up in the 1990s in Relation to Position in the Labour Market', *Journal of Social Policy*, 29, 205–228.

Gordon, R., and G. B. Dahl (2013). 'Views among Economists: Professional Consensus or Point-Counterpoint?' *American Economic Review*, 103, 3, 629–635.

Gould, Erica R. (2006). *Money Talks: The International Monetary Fund, Conditionality, and Supplementary Financiers* (Stanford, CA: Stanford University Press).

Graham, Carol, and Moisés Naím (1998). 'The Political Economy of Institutional Reform in Latin America', *Beyond Tradeoffs: Market Reforms and Equitable Growth in Latin America*, eds. Nancy Birdsall, Carol Graham and R. H. Sabot (Washington, DC: Inter-American Development Bank: Brookings Institution Press), 322–362.

Green, Donald P., and Ian Shapiro (1994). *Pathologies of Rational Choice Theory: A Critique of Applications in Political Science* (New Haven, CT: Yale University Press).

Green, Duncan (2003). *Silent Revolution: The Rise and Crisis of Market Economics in Latin America*, 2nd ed. (New York: Monthly Review Press).

Grimes, Arthur (2014). 'Four Lectures on Central Banking', MOTU Working Paper 14–02 (Auckland, New Zealand: MOTU Economic and Policy Research and the University of Auckland), motu-www.motu.org.nz/wpapers/14–02.pdf.

Grossman, G. (1977). 'The "Second Economy" of the USSR', *Problems of Communism*, 26, 25–40.

Grüske, Karl-Dieter, and Horst Claus Recktenwald (1994). *Die Nobelpreisträger Der Ökonomischen Wissenschaft: Kritisches Zum Werden Neuer Tradition: Selbstportrait, Lesung, Auswahl, Kritik* (Düsseldorf: Verlag Wirtschaft und Finanzen).

Gürkaynak, R. S., B. Kisacikoglu and B. Rossi (2013). 'Do DSGE Models Forecast More Accurately Out-of-Sample than VAR Models?' *Advances in Econometrics: VAR Models in Macroeconomics— New Developments and Applications: Essays in Honor of Christopher A Sims*, 32, 27–80.

Gustafsson, Björn, and N. Anders Klevmarken (1993). 'Taxes and Transfers in Sweden: Incentive Effects on Labour Supply', *Welfare and Work Incentives: A North European Perspective*, eds. Anthony B. Atkinson and Gunnar Viby Mogensen (Oxford: Oxford University Press), 135–160.

Gylfason, T. (2006). 'An Interview with A. Lindbeck', *Macroeconomic Dynamics*, 10,1, 101–130.

Haavisto, Tarmo, and Lars Jonung (1999). 'Central Banking in Sweden and Finland in the Twentieth Century', *The Emergence of Modern Central Banking from 1918 to the Present*, eds. Carl-L. Holtfrerich, Jaime Reis and Gianni Toniolo (Aldershot, UK: Ashgate), 111–143.

Hacker, Jacob S. (2006). *The Great Risk Shift: The Assault on American Jobs, Families, Health Care and Retirement and How You Can Fight Back* (New York: Oxford University Press).

Hacker, Jacob S., and Paul Pierson (2013). *Winner-Take-All Politics: How Washington Made the Rich Richer and Turned Its Back on the Middle Class* (New York: Simon & Schuster).

Hagen, Johannes (2013). 'A History of the Swedish Pension System', Working Paper 2013:7 (Uppsala: Uppsala Center for Fiscal Studies).

Hahn, Frank H. (1973). *On the Notion of Equilibrium in Economics: An Inaugural Lecture* (London: Cambridge University Press).

——— (1981). 'A Neoclassical Analysis of Macroeconomic Policy, by Michael Beenstock, (Book Review)', *Economic Journal*, 91,364, 1036.

——— (1981/1984). 'General Equilibrium Theory', *Equilibrium and Macroeconomics*, ed. Frank H. Hahn (Oxford: Blackwell), 72–87.

——— (1982/1984). 'Reflections on the Invisible Hand', *Equilibrium and Macroeconomics*, ed. Frank H. Hahn (Oxford: Blackwell), 111–132.

Hahn, Frank H., and Robert M. Solow (1995). *A Critical Essay on Modern Macroeconomic Theory* (Oxford: Blackwell).

Haldane, Andrew G., and Piergiorgio Alessandri (2009). 'Banking on the State', Presentation at the Federal Reserve Bank of Chicago, 25 September (London: Bank of England), http://www.bis.org/review/r091111e.pdf.

Hamermesh, Daniel S. (2013). 'Six Decades of Top Economics Publishing: Who and How?' *Journal of Economic Literature*, 51,1, 162–172.

Hammarskjöld, Dag (1935). 'Centralbankerna i Nutidens Ekonomiska Liv: Föredrag Vid 1935 Års Ordinarie Bankmöte' *Skrifter Utgivna av Svenska Bankföreningen* 61 (Stockholm: Svenska Bankföreningen).

Hansen, L. P., and J. J. Heckman (1996). 'The Empirical Foundations of Calibration', *Journal of Economic Perspectives*, 10, 1, 87–104.

Harberger, Arnold C. (1954). 'Monopoly and Resource Allocation', *American Economic Review*, 44,3, 77–87.

——— (1971). 'Three Basic Postulates for Applied Welfare Economics: An Interpretive Essay', *Journal of Economic Literature*, 9,3, 785–797.

——— (1972). *Project Evaluation: Collected Papers* (London: Macmillan).

Harel, David (2004). *Computers Ltd: What They Really Can't Do* (Oxford: Oxford University Press).

Harling, Philip (1996). *The Waning of "Old Corruption": The Politics of Economical Reform in Britain, 1779–1846* (Oxford: Clarendon Press).

Hartley, James E. (1997). *The Representative Agent in Macroeconomics* (London: Routledge).

Hartwell, R. M. (1995). *A History of the Mont Pelerin Society* (Indianapolis: Liberty Fund).

Harzing, Anne-Wil (2011). *The Publish or Perish Book: Your Guide to Effective and Responsible Citation Analysis* (Melbourne: Tarma Software Research Pty Ltd).

Hausman, Daniel M. (1992). *The Inexact and Separate Science of Economics* (Cambridge: Cambridge University Press).

Hawley, Susan (2000). 'Exporting Corruption: Privatisation, Multinationals and Bribery' (London: Corner House), 21 August 2000, http://www.thecornerhouse.org.uk/sites/thecorner house.org.UK/files/19bribe_0.pdf.

Hayek, F. A. (1942). 'Scientism and the Study of Society. Pt. I', *Economica, NS*, 9, 267–291.

——— (1943). 'Scientism and the Study of Society Part II', *Economica*, 10, 34–63.

——— (1944). *The Road to Serfdom*, popular edition (London: G. Routledge & Sons)

——— (1944). 'Scientism and the Study of Society. Part III', *Economica*, 11, 27–39.

Hayes, M. D. (1989). 'The United-States and Latin-America—A Lost Decade', *Foreign Affairs*, 68,1, 180–198.

Headey, Bruce W. (1978). *Housing Policy in the Developed Economy: The United Kingdom, Sweden and the United States* (London: Croom Helm).

Heap, Shaun Hargreaves (1993). 'Post-Modernity and New Conceptions of Rationality in Economics', *The Economics of Rationality*, ed. Bill Gerrard (London: Routledge), 68–90.

Heclo, Hugh, and Henrik Madsen (1987). *Policy and Politics in Sweden: Principled Pragmatism* (Philadelphia: Temple University Press).

Henderson, Hazel (2006), 'The Cuckoo's Egg in the Nobel Prize Nest', www.hazelhenderson.com/2006/10/30/the-cuckoos-egg-in-the-nobel-prize-nest-october-2006/.

Hendry, David F. (1980). 'Econometrics—Alchemy or Science?' *Economica*, 47, 387–406.

——— (2002). 'Forecast Failure, Expectations Formation and the Lucas Critique', *Annales d'Economie et de Statistique*, 67–68, July, 21–40.

——— (2004). 'The Nobel Memorial Prize for Clive W. J. Granger', *Scandinavian Journal of Economics*, 106,2, 187–213.

Hey, John D. (1993). 'Rationality Is as Rationality Does', *The Economics of Rationality*, ed. Bill Gerrard (London: Routledge), 6–21.

Heyman, Fredrik, Pehr-Johan Norbäck and Lars Persson (2015), 'The Turnaround of Swedish Industry: Reforms, Firm Diversity and Job and Productivity Dynamics', IFN Working Paper 1079 (Stockholm: Research Institute for Industrial Economics).

Hibbing, John R., Kevin B. Smith and John R. Alford (2014). *Predisposed Liberals, Conservatives, and the Biology of Political Differences* (Hoboken, NJ: Taylor and Francis).

Hicks, John (1979). *Causality in Economics* (Oxford: Blackwell).

Hills, John (2007). 'Ends and Means: The Future Roles of Social Housing in England', CASE Report 1334, 1465-3001 (London: ESRC Research Centre for Analysis of Social Exclusion).

——— (2015). *Good Times, Bad Times: The Welfare Myth of Them and Us* (Bristol, UK: Policy Press).

Hines, J. R. (1999). 'Three Sides of Harberger Triangles', *Journal of Economic Perspectives*, 13,2, 167–188.

Hirschman, Albert O. (1981). 'The Rise and Decline of Development Economics', *Essays in Trespassing: Economics to Politics and Beyond*, ed. Albert O. Hirschman (Cambridge: Cambridge University Press), 1–24.

—— (1991). *The Rhetoric of Reaction: Perversity, Futility, Jeopardy* (Cambridge, MA/London: Belknap Press of Harvard University Press).

Hofstadter, Richard (1955). *Social Darwinism in American Thought*, rev. ed. (Boston: Beacon Press).

Hogarth, Robin M., and Melvin Warren Reder, eds. (1987). *Rational Choice: The Contrast between Economics and Psychology* (Chicago: University of Chicago Press).

Holzmann, Robert, Edward E. Palmer and David A. Robalino (2012). *Nonfinancial Defined Contribution Pension Schemes in a Changing Pension World* (Washington, DC: World Bank).

Honkaphoja, S. (2009). 'The 1990's Financial Crises in Nordic Countries' (Helsinki: Bank of Finland).

Hoover, Kevin D. (1988). *The New Classical Macroeconomics: A Sceptical Inquiry* (Oxford: Basil Blackwell).

—— (1995). 'Facts and Artifacts: Calibration and the Empirical Assessment of Real-Business-Cycle Models', *Oxford Economic Papers*, 47,1, 24–44.

—— (2001). *The Methodology of Empirical Macroeconomics* (Cambridge: Cambridge University Press).

Hough, Dan (2013). *Corruption, Anti-Corruption and Governance* (Basingstoke, UK: Palgrave Macmillan).

Huberman, M., and C. Minns (2007). 'The Times They Are Not Changin': Days and Hours of Work in Old and New Worlds, 1870–2000', *Explorations in Economic History*, 44,4, 538–567.

Hugemark, Agneta (1994). *Den Fängslande Marknaden: Ekonomiska Experter om Välfärdsstaten*, Lund Studies in Social Welfare, 8 (Lund: Arkiv).

Hume, David (1987). *Essays Moral, Political, and Literary* (Indianapolis: Liberty Classics).

Humphrey, Thomas M. (1996). 'The Early History of the Box Diagram', *Federal Reserve Bank of Richmond Economic Quarterly*, 82,1, 37–75.

Hutchison, T. W. (2000). 'From the *Wealth of Nations* to Modern General Equilibrium "Theory": Methodological Comparisons and Contrasts', *On the Methodology of Economics and the Formalist Revolution*, ed. T. W. Hutchison (Cheltenham, UK: Elgar), ch. 10, 313–354.

Hutchison, T. W., ed. (2000). *On the Methodology of Economics and the Formalist Revolution* (Cheltenham, UK: Edward Elgar).

ILO (2013). 'ILO Comparable Estimates—Adjusted Annual Average Employment and Unemployment Estimates', http://laborsta.ilo.org/STP/guest.

—— (2014). 'G20 Labour Markets: Outlook, Key Challenges and Policy Responses', 10–11 September 2014 (Geneva: International Labour Organization).

IMF (1981). 'Supply-Oriented Adjustment Policies', SM/81/78, Ref. no. 178109, 3 April 1981 (Washington, DC: Executive Board Documents\Staff Memoranda\1981—Staff Memoranda International Monetary Fund, Research Department), http://archivescatalog.IMF.org/detail.aspx?parentpriref=125004358.

Ingrao, Bruna, and Giorgio Israel (1990). *The Invisible Hand: Economic Equilibrium in the History of Science* (Cambridge, MA: MIT Press).

Ioannidis, J.P.A. (2005). 'Why Most Published Research Findings Are False', *PLOS Medicine*, 2,8, 696–701.

Ivry, Sara (2006). 'Did an Exposé Help Sink Harvard's President?', *New York Times*, 27 February 2006.

Jackson, Tim, and Nic Marks (1994). *Measuring Sustainable Economic Welfare: A Pilot Index, 1950–1990* (Stockholm: Stockholm Environment Institute).

Jackson, Walter A. (1990). *Gunnar Myrdal and America's Conscience: Social Engineering and Racial Liberalism, 1938–1987* (Chapel Hill: University of North Carolina Press).

Jacobsson, E. E. (1979). *A Life for Sound Money: Per Jacobsson: His Biography* (Oxford: Clarendon Press).

Jael, Paul (2015). 'Socialist Calculation and Market Socialism', MPRA Paper 64255, 10 May 2015 (Munich: Munich Personal RePEc Archive) http://mpra.ub.uni-muenchen.de/64255/.

Janssen, Maarten C. W. (1993). *Microfoundations: A Critical Inquiry* (London: Routledge).

Jensen, Michael C., and William H. Meckling (1976). 'Theory of the Firm: Managerial Behavior, Agency Costs and Ownership Structure', *Journal of Financial Economics*, 3,4, 305–360.

Jensen, Michael C., and Kevin J. Murphy (1990). 'CEO Incentives—It's Not How Much You Pay, but How', *Harvard Business Review*, 68,3, 138–149.

Jones, Owen (2014). *The Establishment* (London: Allen Lane).

Jonung, Lars (1979). 'Knut Wicksell's Norm of Price Stabilization and Swedish Monetary Policy in the 1930's', *Journal of Monetary Economics*, 5,4, 459–496.

——— (1993). 'Riksbankens Politik 1945–1990', *Från Räntereglering till Inflationsnorm: Det Finansiella Systemet och Riksbankens Politik 1945–1990*, ed. Peter Englund and Lars Werin (Stockholm: SNS), 287–419.

——— (1993). 'The Rise and Fall of Credit Controls: The Case of Sweden 1939–89', *Monetary Regimes in Transition*, eds. Michael Bordo and Forrest Capie (Cambridge: Cambridge University Press), 346–370.

Jonung, Lars, ed. (1991). *The Stockholm School of Economics Revisited* (Cambridge: Cambridge University Press).

Jonung, Lars, and Elving Gunnarsson (1992). 'Economics the Swedish Way 1889–1989', *Economics in Sweden: An Evaluation of Swedish Research in Economics*, ed. Lars Engwall (London: Routledge), 19–48.

Jonung, Lars, Jaakko Kiander and Pentti Vartia, eds. (2009). *The Great Financial Crisis in Finland and Sweden: The Nordic Experience of Financial Liberalization* (Cheltenham, UK: Edward Elgar).

JSTOR (2012). 'Data for Research', http://dfr.JSTOR.org/.

Kanbur, Ravi (1990). 'Projects versus Policy Reform', *Proceedings of the World Bank Annual Conference on Development Economics* (Washington, DC: World Bank), 397–413.

Kapeller, J. (2010). 'Some Critical Notes on Citation Metrics and Heterodox Economics', *Review of Radical Political Economics*, 42,3, 330–337.

Karacuka, Mehmet, and Asad Zaman (2012). 'The Empirical Evidence against Neoclassical Utility Theory: A Review of the Literature', *International Journal of Pluralism and Economics Education*, 3,4, 366–414.

Karier, Thomas Mark (2010). *Intellectual Capital: Forty Years of the Nobel Prize in Economics* (New York: Cambridge University Press).

Kaufmann, D., and P. C. Vicente (2011). 'Legal Corruption', *Economics & Politics*, 23,2, 195–219.

Kay, John (2011). 'The Random Shock That Clinched a Brave Nobel Prize', *Financial Times*, 18 October 2011.

Kearl, J. R., Clayne L. Pope, Gordon C. Whiting and Larry T. Wimmer (1979). 'A Confusion of Economists?' *American Economic Review*, 69,2, 28–37.

Kendrick, J. W. (1970). 'Historical Development of National-Income Accounts', *History of Political Economy*, 2,2, 284–315.

Kincaid, Harold (1997). *Individualism and the Unity of Science: Essays on Reduction, Explanation, and the Special Sciences* (Lanham, MD: Rowman & Littlefield).

Kincaid, Harold, and Don Ross, eds. (2009). *The Oxford Handbook of Philosophy of Economics* (Oxford: Oxford University Press).

King, J. E. (2012). *The Microfoundations Delusion: Metaphor and Dogma in the History of Macroeconomics* (Cheltenham, UK: Edward Elgar).

Kirman, Alan P. (1992). 'Whom or What Does the Representative Individual Represent?' *Journal of Economic Perspectives*, 6,2, 117–136.

Klamer, Arjo (1984). *The New Classical Macroeconomics: Conversations with the New Classical Economists and Their Opponents* (Brighton, UK: Wheatsheaf).

Klein, Daniel B. (2013). 'The Ideological Migration of the Economics Laureates: Introduction and Overview', *Econ Journal Watch*, 10,3, 218–239.

—— (2013). 'James A. Mirrlees', *Econ Journal Watch*, 10,3, 466–472.

—— (2013). 'Thomas C. Schelling', *Econ Journal Watch*, 10,3, 576–590.

Klein, Daniel B. and Ryan Daza (2013). 'Franco Modigliani', *Econ Journal Watch*, 10,3, 472–493.

—— (2013). 'John R. Hicks', *Econ Journal Watch*, 10,3, 366–377.

—— (2013). 'Robert W. Fogel', *Econ Journal Watch*, 10,3, 316–325.

Klein, Daniel B., and Charlotta Stern (2007). 'Is There a Free-Market Economist in the House? The Policy Views of American Economic Association Members', *American Journal of Economics and Sociology*, 66,2, 309–334.

Klein, Daniel B., et al. (2013). 'Ideological Profiles of the Nobel Laureates', *Econ Journal Watch*, 10,3, 255–682.

Klein, Naomi (2007). *The Shock Doctrine: The Rise of Disaster Capitalism* (London: Allen Lane).

Ko, K., and C. F. Weng (2012). 'Structural Changes in Chinese Corruption', *China Quarterly*, 211, 718–740.

Kohn, M. (2004). 'Value and Exchange', *Cato Journal*, 24,3, 303–340.

Koopmans, Tjalling C. (1947). 'Measurement without Theory', *Review of Economics and Statistics*, 29,3, 161–172.

Korpi, Walter (1978). *The Working Class in Welfare Capitalism: Work, Unions, and Politics in Sweden* (London: Routledge & Kegan Paul).

—— (1996). 'Eurosclerosis and the Sclerosis of Objectivity: On the Role of Values among Economic Policy Experts', *Statsvetenskaplig Tidskrift*, 99,4, 369–389.

Korpi, Walter, and J. Palme (1988). 'The Paradox of Redistribution and Strategies of Equality: Welfare State Institutions, Inequality, and Poverty in the Western Countries', *American Sociological Review*, 63, 5, 661–687.

Korpi, Walter, and Carl Bildt (1992). *Halkar Sverige Efter?: Sveriges Ekonomiska Tillväxt 1820–1990 i Jämförande Belysning* (Stockholm: Carlsson).

Kregel, Jan (2006). 'Negative Net Resource Transfers as a Minskiyan Hedge Profile and the Stability of the International Financial System', *Money, Financial Instability and Stabilization Policy*, eds. L. Randall Wray and Mathew Forstater (Cheltenham, UK: Edward Elgar), 1–21.

Kreps, David M. (1990). *Game Theory and Economic Modelling* (Oxford: Oxford University Press).

Krueger, Ann O. (1974). 'Political Economy of Rent-Seeking Society', *American Economic Review*, 64,3, 291–303.

—— (2004), 'Meant Well, Tried Little, Failed Much: Policy Reforms in Emerging Market Economies', 23 March 2004, https://www.IMF.org/external/np/speeches/2004/032304a.htm.

Krugman, Paul (2009). 'How Did Economists Get It So Wrong', *New York Times*, 6 September 2009.

—— (2011). 'Irregular Economics', *New York Times*, 25 August 2011.

—— (2013). 'What They Say Versus What They Mean', *New York Times*, 2 October 2013.

Krussell, Per (2013). 'Naiv Kritik av Ekonomipris Missgynnar Saklig Debatt', http://www.dn.se/debatt/naiv-kritik-av-ekonomipris-missgynnar-saklig-debatt/.

Kunstler, Howard (2015). 'The Clash of Civilizations', http://kunstler.com/clusterfuck-nation/the-clash-of-civilizations/.

Lal, Deepak (2002). *The Poverty of 'Development Economics'*, 3rd ed. (London: Institute of Economic Affairs).

Landgren, Karl-Gustav (1960). *Den 'Nya Ekonomien' i Sverige: J. M. Keynes, E. Wigforss, B. Ohlin och Utvecklingen 1927–39*, Ekonomiska Studier, 3 (Stockholm: Almqvist & Wiksell).

Landsorganisationen (1946). *The Postwar Programme of Swedish Labour: A Summary in 27 Points and Comments* (Stockholm: Landsorganisationen).

Lane, Melissa (2013). 'The Genesis and Reception of *The Road to Serfdom*', *Hayek: A Collaborative Biography, Part 1: Influences, from Mises to Bartley*, ed. Robert Leeson (Basingstoke, UK: Palgrave Macmillan), 43–60.

La Porta, R., F. Lopez-De-Silanes, A. Shleifer and R. Vishny (1999). 'The Quality of Government', *Journal of Law Economics & Organization*, 15,1, 222–279.

Lavoie, Don (1985). *Rivalry and Central Planning: The Socialist Calculation Debate Reconsidered* (Cambridge: Cambridge University Press).

Lawson, Tony (1997). *Economics and Reality* (London: Routledge).

Leamer, Edward E. (1983). 'Let's Take the Con Out of Econometrics', *American Economic Review*, 73,1, 31–43.

——— (2010). 'Tantalus on the Road to Asymptopia', *Journal of Economic Perspectives*, 24,2, 31.

——— (2010). 'What Have Changes to the Global Markets for Goods and Services Done to the Viability of the Swedish Welfare State?' *Reforming the Welfare State: Recovery and Beyond in Sweden*, eds. Richard B. Freeman, Birgitta Swedenborg and Robert Topel (Chicago: Chicago University Press), 285–325.

LeBor, Adam (2013). *Tower of Basel: The Shadowy History of the Secret Bank That Runs the World* (New York: Public Affairs).

Leeson, Robert (2013). 'Introduction', *Hayek: A Collaborative Biography, Part I: Influences, from Mises to Bartley*, ed. Robert Leeson (New York: Palgrave Macmillan), 1–42.

Leigh, David, James Ball, Juliette Garside and David Pegg (2015). 'HSBC Files: Swiss Bank Aggressively Pushed Way for Clients to Avoid New Tax', *Guardian*, 10 February 2015.

Leijonhufvud, Axel (1973). 'Life among the Econ', *Western Economic Journal*, 11,3, 327–323.

Lenin, Vladimir Ilich (1904/1947). *One Step Forward, Two Steps Back: The Crisis in Our Party* (Moscow: Progress Publishers).

Leontief, Wassily (1937). 'Implicit Theorizing: A Methodological Criticism of the Neo-Cambridge School', *Quarterly Journal of Economics*, 51,2, 337–351.

——— (1971). 'Theoretical Assumptions and Nonobserved Facts', *American Economic Review*, 61,1, 1–7.

Lerner, Melvin J. (1980). *The Belief in a Just World: A Fundamental Delusion* (New York: Plenum Press).

Leslie, Christopher R. (2012). 'Revisiting the Revisionist History of *Standard Oil*', *Southern California Law Review*, 85,3, 573–604.

Levine, Yasha, and Mark Ames (2011). 'Charles Koch to Friedrich Hayek: Use Social Security!' *Nation*, 27 September 2011.

Levy, David M., and Sandra J. Peart (2008/2015). 'Socialist Calculation Debate', *The New Palgrave Dictionary of Economics*, 2nd ed., eds. Steven N. Durlauf and Lawrence E. Blume (London: Palgrave Macmillan). *The New Palgrave Dictionary of Economics Online*, Palgrave Macmillan, http://www.dictionaryofeconomics.com/article?id=pde2008_S000535> doi:10.1057/9780230226203.1570.

Lewin, Leif (1967). *Planhushållningsdebatten* (Stockholm: Almqvist & Wiksell).

Lewis, P., and H. Stein (1997). 'Shifting Fortunes: The Political Economy of Financial Liberalization in Nigeria', *World Development*, 25,1, 5–22.

Lewis, W. A. (1954). 'Economic Development with Unlimited Supplies of Labour', *Manchester School*, 22,May, 139–191.

Leys, Colin, and Stewart Player (2011). *The Plot against the NHS* (Pontypool, UK: Merlin Press).

Lilien, Gary L., and Arvind Rangaswamy (1997). *Marketing Engineering: Computer-Assisted Marketing Analysis and Planning* (Reading, MA/Harlow, UK: Addison-Wesley).

Lin, Justin Yifu (2011). *Demystifying the Chinese Economy* (Cambridge: Cambridge University Press).

Lindahl, Erik (1929). *Penningpolitikens Mål* (Malmö: Fahlbeckska Stiftelsen).

——— (1930). *Penningpolitikens Medel* (Malmö: Fahlbeckska Stiftelsen).

——— (1957). 'Riksbankens Avpolitisering', *Stockholmstidningen*, 17 May 1957.

——— (1957). 'Riksbanken och Regeringen', *Stockholmstidningen*, 13 May 1957.

——— (1958). 'Bankoutskottets Dom', *Stockholmstidningen*, 16 March 1958.

Lindbeck, A. (1959). 'Att Förutse Utvecklingen', *Inför 60-Talet: Debattbok Om Socialismens Framtid*, ed. Roland Pålsson (Malmö: Rabén & Sjögren), 65–83.

——— (1971). 'The Efficiency of Competition and Planning', *Planning and Market Relations*, eds. M. Kaser and R. Portes (London: Macmillan), 83–107.

————— (1971/1977). *The Political Economy of the New Left: An Outsider's View*, 2nd ed. (New York: Harper & Row).

————— (1978). 'Förvanskningar om Ekonomerna och Arbetarrörelsen', *Ekonomisk Debatt*, 6,1, 34–39.

————— A. (1981). 'Problem i Industriländernas Strukturanpassning', *Ekonomisk Debatt*, 9,2, 83–90.

————— (1981/1993). 'Disincentive Problems in Developing Countries', *The Welfare State: The Selected Essays of Assar Lindbeck*, ed. Assar Lindbeck (Cheltenham, UK: Edward Elgar), 2, 77–95.

————— (1982). 'Emerging Arteriosclerosis of the Western Economies—Consequences for the Less Developed Countries', *India International Centre Quarterly*, 1, 37–52.

————— (1983). 'Interpreting Income Distributions in a Welfare State: The Case of Sweden', *European Economic Review*, 22,2, 227–256.

————— (1983). 'Mekanismer för en Bättre Samhällsekonomi', *Ekonomisk Debatt*, 11, 3, 149–160.

————— (1985). 'The Prize in Economic Science in Memory of Alfred Nobel', *Journal of Economic Literature*, 23,1, 37–56.

————— (1993). 'Overshooting, Reform and Retreat of the Welfare State', Seventh Tinbergen Lecture Delivered on 1 October 1993 at de Nederlandsche Bank, Amsterdam (Stockholm: Institute for International Economic Studies, Stockholm University).

————— (1994). *Turning Sweden Around* (Cambridge, MA: MIT Press).

————— (2009). 'Assar Minns: Mina Tre Perioder på IUI', *IFN/IUI 1939–2009: Sju Decennier av Forskning om Ett Näringsliv i Förändring*, ed. Magnus Henrekson (Stockholm: Ekerlids), 245–250.

————— (2012). *Ekonomi är att Välja: Memoarer* (Stockholm: Bonnier).

————— (2012). 'Reflektioner om Nationalekonomins Styrka och Begränsningar', *Ekonomisk Debatt*, 7, 17–25.

Lindbeck, A., S. Nyberg and J. W. Weibull (1999). 'Social Norms and Economic Incentives in the Welfare State', *Quarterly Journal of Economics*, 114,1, 1–36.

Lindbeck, A., and Dennis J. Snower (1988). *The Insider-Outsider Theory of Employment and Unemployment* (Cambridge, MA: MIT Press).

Linde, J. (2001). 'Testing for the Lucas Critique: A Quantitative Investigation', *American Economic Review*, 91, 4, 986–1005.

Lindert, Peter H. (2004). *Growing Public: Social Spending and Economic Growth since the Eighteenth Century*, 2 vols. (Cambridge: Cambridge University Press).

Lindström, Ulla (1969). *I Regeringen: Ur Min Politiska Dagbok 1954–1959* (Stockholm: Bonnier).

Lindvall, Johannes (2004). *The Politics of Purpose: Swedish Macroeconomic Policy after the Golden Age*, Göteborg Studies in Politics 84 (Göteborg: Göteborg University).

Lipsey, R. G. (2007). 'Reflections on the General Theory of Second Best at Its Golden Jubilee', *International Tax and Public Finance*, 14,4, 349–364.

Lipsey, R. G., and Kelvin Lancaster (1956). 'The General Theory of Second Best', *Review of Economic Studies*, 24, 11–32.

Little, I.M.D. (1950/1957). *A Critique of Welfare Economics*, 2nd ed. (Oxford: Clarendon Press).

Little, I.M.D., and James A. Mirrlees (1974). *Project Appraisal and Planning for Developing Countries*, paperback ed. (London: Heinemann Educational).

————— (1990). 'Project Appraisal and Planning Twenty Years On', *Proceedings of the World Bank Annual Conference on Development Economics* (Washington, DC: World Bank), 351–382.

Ljungqvist, Lars, and Thomas J. Sargent (2010). 'How Sweden's Unemployment Became More Like Europe's', *Reforming the Welfare State: Recovery and Beyond in Sweden*, eds. Richard B. Freeman, Birgitta Swedenborg and Robert Topel (Chicago: Chicago University Press), 189–223.

The Local: Sweden's News in English (2005). 'Nobel Descendant Slams Economics Prize', http://www.thelocal.se/20050928/2173.

Lönnroth, Johan (1993). *Schamanerna: Om Ekonomi som Förgylld Vardag* (Stockholm: Arena).

Lönnroth, Johan, Måns Lönnroth and Peter Jagers (2004). 'Ekonomipriset Förminskar Värdet på Alla Nobelpris', *Dagens Nyheter*, 10 December 2004.

Lovell, Michael C. (1986). 'Tests of the Rational Expectations Hypothesis', *American Economic Review*, 76, 110–124.

Lucas, Robert E., Jr. (1980). 'Methods and Problems in Business Cycle Theory', *Journal of Money, Credit, and Banking*, 12,4, 696–715.

—— (1981). *Studies in Business-Cycle Theory* (Oxford: Basil Blackwell).

—— (1987). *Models of Business Cycles* (Oxford: Basil Blackwell).

—— (1988). 'What Economists Do', http://home.uchicago.edu/~vlima/courses/econ203/fall01/Lucas_wedo.pdf.

—— (2002). *Lectures on Economic Growth* (Cambridge, MA/London: Harvard University Press).

—— (2003). 'Macroeconomic Priorities', *American Economic Review*, 93,1, 1–14.

—— (2004). 'The Industrial Revolution: Past and Future. 2003 Annual Report Essay', *Region*, May 2014, https://www.minneapolisfed.org/publications/the-region/the-industrial-revolution-past-and-future.

Lundberg, Erik (1953). *Konjunkturer och Ekonomisk Politik: Utveckling och Debatt i Sverige Sedan Första Världskriget* (Stockholm: Konjunkturinstitutet).

—— (1969), 'Award Ceremony Speech', http://www.nobelprize.org/nobel_prizes/economic-sciences/laureates/1969/press.html.

—— (1971). 'Simon Kuznets' Contribution to Economics', *Swedish Journal of Economics*, 73, 444–459.

—— (1977). 'Ekonomernas Debatt om Ekonomisk Politik. Strödda Synpunkter', *Ekonomisk Debatt och Ekonomisk Politik: Nationalekonomiska Föreningen 100 År*, eds. Jan Herin and Lars Werin (Stockholm: Norstedt), 159–181.

—— (1985). 'The Rise and Fall of the Swedish Model', *Journal of Economic Literature*, 23,1, 1–36.

Lundgren, Nils (2002). 'Tidsandan Framfödde *Ekonomisk Debatt*', *Ekonomisk Debatt*, 30,6, 505–510.

Macfarquar, Larissa (2010). 'The Deflationist: How Paul Krugman Found Politics', *New Yorker*, 1 March 2010, http://www.newyorker.com/magazine/2010/03/01/the-deflationist.

MacGilvray, Eric (2011). *The Invention of Market Freedom* (Cambridge: Cambridge University Press).

Macpherson, C. B. (1962). *The Political Theory of Possessive Individualism: Hobbes to Locke* (Oxford: Clarendon Press).

Magnusson, Lars (1993). 'The Economists as Popularizers', *Swedish Economic Thought: Explorations and Advances*, ed. Lars Jonung (London: Routledge).

—— (2000). *An Economic History of Sweden* (London: Routledge).

—— (2014). 'Globalisering och den Svenska Modellen—Tjugo År Senare', *Det Globaliserade Arbetslivet*, eds. Karin Becker, Marinette Fogde and Johanna Övling (Möklinta: Gidlund), 65–78.

Mäki, Uskali (2008). 'Realism', *The Philosophy of Economics: An Anthology*, ed. Daniel M. Hausman (Cambridge: Cambridge University Press).

—— (2009). *The Methodology of Positive Economics: Reflections on the Milton Friedman Legacy* (Cambridge: Cambridge University Press).

Mäki, Uskali, ed. (2012). *Philosophy of Economics*, Handbook of the Philosophy of Science, vol. 13 (Amsterdam: Elsevier North-Holland).

Mäler, Karl-Göran, ed. (1992). *Economic Sciences, 1981–1990: The Sveriges Riksbank (Bank of Sweden) Prize in Economic Sciences in Memory of Alfred Nobel*, vol. 2 (Singapore: World Scientific).

Mandeville, Bernard de (1714). *The Fable of the Bees: Or, Private Vices Public Benefits* (London: J. Roberts).

Mankiw, N. Gregory (1991). 'The Reincarnation of Keynesian Economics', Working Paper 3885, October 1991 (Cambridge, MA: National Bureau of Economic Research).
——— (2008). *Principles of Economics*, 5th ed. (Mason, OH: South-Western).
Mankiw, N. Gregory, Matthew Weinzierl and Danny Yagan (2009). 'Optimal Taxation in Theory and Practice', *Journal of Economic Perspectives*, 23,4, 147–174.
Manzetti, Luigi (1999). *Privatization South American Style* (Oxford: Oxford University Press).
Marchant, Josephine (2008). *Decoding the Heavens: Solving the Mystery of the World's First Computer* (London: William Heinemann).
Marchionatti, Roberto, and Lisa Sella (2015). 'Is Neo-Walrasian Macroeconomics a Dead End?', CESMEP Working Paper 21/15, May 2015 (Turin: Centro Di Studi Sulla Storia e i Metodi dell'Economia Politica 'Claudio Napoleoni').
Martimort, David, and Stephane Straub (2006). 'Privatisation and Changes in Corruption Patterns: The Roots of Public Discontent', Discussion Paper 147 (Edinburgh: Edinburgh School of Economics).
Martin, B. (2009). 'Resurrecting the U.K. Historic Sector National Accounts', *Review of Income and Wealth*, 55, 3, 737–751.
Mayer, Thomas (1990). 'The Twilight of the Monetarist Debate', *Monetarism and Macroeconomic Policy*, ed. Thomas Mayer (Aldershot: Edward Elgar), 61–90.
——— (1993). *Truth versus Precision in Economics* (Aldershot, UK: Elgar).
McCarty, Marilu Hurt (2001). *The Nobel Laureates: How the World's Greatest Economic Minds Shaped Modern Thought* (New York: McGraw-Hill).
McClintick, David (2006). 'How Harvard Lost Russia', http://www.institutionalinvestor.com/Article/1020662/How-Harvard-lost-Russia.html#.U_OBSMWSzh4.
McCloskey, D. N. (1985). *The Rhetoric of Economics* (Brighton, UK: Wheatsheaf).
——— (1991). 'Economic Science: A Search through the Hyperspace of Assumptions?' *Methodus*, 3,1, 6–16.
——— (1994). *Knowledge and Persuasion in Economics* (Cambridge: Cambridge University Press).
——— (2013). 'A Neo-Institutionalism of Measurement, without Measurement: A Comment on Douglas Allen's the Institutional Revolution', *Review of Austrian Economics*, 26,4, 363–373.
McEachern, William A. (2006). 'AEA Ideology: Campaign Contributions of American Economic Association Members, Committee Members, Officers, Referees, Authors, and Acknowledgees', *Econ Journal Watch*, 3,1, 148–179.
McLean, Iain (1987). *Public Choice: An Introduction* (Oxford: Basil Blackwell).
McLean, Iain, and Jo Poulton (1986). 'Good Blood, Bad Blood, and the Market: The Gift Relationship Revisited', *Journal of Public Policy*, 6,4, 431–445.
McLeay, Michael, Amar Radia and Ryland Thomas (2014). 'Money Creation in the Modern Economy', *Bank of England Quarterly Bulletin*, Q1, 1–14.
Medoff, Marshall H. (1989). 'The Ranking of Economists', *Journal of Economic Education*, 20,4, 405–415.
Meek, James (2014). *Private Island* (London: Verso).
Meidner, Rudolf. (1993). 'Why Did the Swedish Model Fail?' *Socialist Register*, 29, 211–228.
Meidner, Rudolf, Anna Hedborg and Gunnar Fond (1978). *Employee Investment Funds: An Approach to Collective Capital Formation* (London: Allen & Unwin).
Meller, Patricio (1990). 'Comment', *Latin American Adjustment: How Much Has Happened?*, ed. John E. Williamson (Washington, DC: Institute for International Economics), 32–35.
Mellstrom, C., and M. Johannesson (2008). 'Crowding Out in Blood Donation: Was Titmuss Right?', *Journal of the European Economic Association*, 6,4, 845–863.
Meyerson, Per-Martin, Kurt Wickman, and Ingemar Ståhl (1990). *Makten Över Bostaden* (Stockholm: SNS).
Milberg, William (1996). 'The Rhetoric of Policy Relevance in International Economics', *Journal of Economic Methodology*, 3,2, 237–259.

Millward, Robert (2000). 'The Political Economy of Urban Utilities in Britain 1840–1950', *Cambridge Urban History of Britain*, eds. P. Clark, M. J. Daunton and D. M. Palliser (Cambridge: Cambridge University Press), 3, 315–349.

Milner, Henry (1989). *Sweden: Social Democracy in Practice* (Oxford: Oxford University Press).

Mirowski, Philip (2002). *Machine Dreams: Economics Becomes a Cyborg Science* (Cambridge: Cambridge University Press).

——— (2004). *The Effortless Economy of Science?* (Durham, NC: Duke University Press).

——— (2009). 'Postface: Defining Neoliberalism', *The Road from Mont Pelerin: The Making of the Neoliberal Thought Collective*, eds. Philip Mirowski and Dieter Plehwe (Cambridge, MA: Harvard University Press), 417–455.

——— (2013). *Never Let a Serious Crisis Go to Waste: How Neoliberalism Survived the Financial Meltdown* (London: Verso).

Mirowski, Philip, and Dieter Plehwe, eds. (2009). *The Road from Mont Pelerin: The Making of the Neoliberal Thought Collective* (Cambridge, MA: Harvard University Press).

Mirrlees, James A., et al., eds. (2011). *Tax by Design: The Mirrlees Review* (Oxford: Oxford University Press).

Mises, Ludwig von (1920/1935). 'Economic Calculation in the Socialist Commonwealth', *Collectivist Economic Planning*, ed. F. A. Hayek (London: George Routledge & Sons), 87–130.

Mishel, Lawrence (2012). 'The Wedges between Productivity and Median Compensation Growth', *Issue Brief*, 330, 1–7.

Mishkin, Fred S. (1998). *The Economics of Money, Banking, and Financial Markets*, 5th ed. (Reading, MA: Addison-Wesley).

Mitchell, B. R. (2003). *International Historical Statistics: Europe, 1750–2000*, 5th ed. (Basingstoke, UK: Palgrave Macmillan).

Mlynar, Zdenek (1980). *Night Frost in Prague: The End of Humane Socialism* (London: C. Hurst).

Modigliani, Franco (1988/1997). 'The Monetarist Controversy Revisited', *A Macroeconomics Reader*, eds. Brian Snowdon and Howard Vane (London: Routledge), 247–261.

Modigliani, Franco, and Arun S. Muralidhar (2004). *Rethinking Pension Reform* (Cambridge: Cambridge University Press).

Monbiot, George (2000). *Captive State: The Corporate Takeover of Britain* (Basingstoke, UK: Macmillan).

Morgan, Mary S. (2012). *The World in the Model: How Economists Work and Think* (Cambridge: Cambridge University Press).

Mueller, Dennis C. (2003). *Public Choice III* (Cambridge: Cambridge University Press).

Myrdal, Alva (1941). *Nation and Family: The Swedish Experiment in Democratic Family and Population Policy* (New York: Harper & Brothers).

Myrdal, Alva, and Gunnar Myrdal (1934). *Kris i Befolkningsfrågan* (Stockholm: Bonnier).

Myrdal, Gunnar (1930/1990). *The Political Element in the Development of Economic Theory* (New Brunswick, NJ: Transaction Publishers).

——— (1968). 'Asian Drama', *Nationalekonomiska Föreningens Förhandlingar*, 29 April 1968, 41–72.

——— (1968). *Asian Drama: An Inquiry into the Poverty of Nations* (London: Allen Lane).

——— (1977). 'Ett Bra Land som Borde Kunnat Vara Mycket Bättre', *Nationalekonomiska Föreningen 100 År: Ekonomisk Debatt och Ekonomisk Politik*, eds. Jan Herin and Lars Werin (Stockholm: Norstedts Förlag), 235–248.

——— (1977). 'The Nobel Prize in Economic Science', *Challenge*, 20,1, 50–52.

——— (1978). 'Dags för ett Bättre Skattesystem!' *Ekonomisk Debatt*, 6,7, 493–506.

Nagel, Thomas (2014). 'Listening to Reason' [Review of T. M. Scanlon (2014), *Being Realistic about Reasons* (Oxford: Oxford University Press)], *New York Review of Books*, 9 October 2014.

Naím, Moisés (1993). 'Latin-America—Post-Adjustment Blues', *Foreign Policy*, 92, 133–150.

——— (1995). 'Corruption Eruption', http://carnegieendowment.org/1995/06/01/corruption-eruption/3248.

——— (2002). 'Washington Consensus: A Damaged Brand', *Financial Times*, 28 October 2002.

——— (2005). 'Missing Links: Bad Medicine', *Foreign Policy*, 147,March–April, 96–95.

Nasar, Sylvia (1998). *A Beautiful Mind* (London: Faber and Faber).

Neild, R. R. (2002). *Public Corruption: The Dark Side of Social Evolution* (London: Anthem).

Nellis, John (1994). 'Is Privatization Necessary?', *Public Policy for the Private Sector*, FPD Note 7 (Washington, DC: World Bank).

——— (2006). 'Privatization—A Summary Assessment', Working Paper Number 87, March 2006 (Washington, DC: Center for Global Development).

Nelson, Robert H. (1991). *Reaching for Heaven on Earth: The Theological Meaning of Economics* (Lanham, MD: Littlefield Adams).

——— (2001). *Economics as Religion: From Samuelson to Chicago and Beyond* (University Park: Pennsylvania State University Press).

Nisbett, Richard, and Lee Ross (1980). *Human Inference: Strategies and Shortcomings of Social Judgment* (Englewood Cliffs, NJ: Prentice-Hall).

Nobel, Peter (2001). 'Alfred Bernhard Nobel and the Peace Prize', *International Review—Red Cross*, 83, 842, 259–274.

——— (2011). 'Gökungen i Nobelprisens Bo', http://www.svt.se/opinion/gokungen-i-nobel prisens-bo.

Norrman, Erik, and Charles E. McLure Jr. (1997). 'Tax Policy in Sweden', *The Welfare State in Transition: Reforming the Swedish Model*, eds. Richard B. Freeman, Birgitta Swedenborg and Robert Topel (Chicago: University of Chicago Press), 109–153.

Nurkse, Ragnar (1945). 'Conditions of International Monetary Equilibrium', Essays in International Finance 4 (Princeton, NJ: Princeton University, Department of Economics).

Nurske, Ragnar, League of Nations, Economic, Financial and Transit Department, and United Nations (1944). *International Currency Experience: Lessons of the Inter-War Period* (Geneva: League of Nations).

Nycander, Svante (2005). 'A. Lindbecks Succé Skadar Nationalekonomin', *Dagens Nyheter*, 10 April 2005.

Oborne, Peter (2007). *The Triumph of the Political Class* (London: Simon & Schuster).

Obstfeld, Maurice, and Kenneth S. Rogoff (1996). *Foundations of International Macroeconomics* (Cambridge, MA: MIT Press).

OECD (2008). *Growing Unequal: Income Distribution and Poverty in OECD Countries* ([Paris]: Organisation for Economic Co-operation and Development).

OECD (2011). *Divided We Stand: Why Inequality Keeps Rising* (Paris: OECD Publishing).

——— (2012). 'Unit Labour Costs—Annual Indicators: Labour Income Share Ratios', http://stats.oecd.org/Index.aspx?queryname=345&querytype=view.

——— (2015). 'GDP per Capita, at Constant 2005 Prices and PPPs, US Dollars', *OECD.Stat*, National Accounts at a Glance, Pt. IX, Reference Series, http://stats.oecd.org/#.

——— (2015). 'General Government Spending by Destination (Indicator)', doi:10.1787/d853 db3b-en.

Offer, Avner (1989). *The First World War: An Agrarian Interpretation* (Oxford: Clarendon Press).

——— (1997). 'Between the Gift and the Market: The Economy of Regard', *Economic History Review*, 50,3, 450–476.

——— (2003). *Why Has the Public Sector Grown So Large in Market Societies?: The Political Economy of Prudence in the UK, c. 1870–2000* (Oxford: Oxford University Press).

——— (2006). *The Challenge of Affluence: Self-Control and Well-Being in the United States and Britain since 1950* (Oxford: Oxford University Press).

——— (2007). 'The Markup for Lemons: Quality and Uncertainty in American and British Used-Car Markets c. 1953–73', *Oxford Economic Papers: New Perspectives in Economic History*, 59,Supp. 1, i31–i48.

——— (2008). 'British Manual Workers: From Producers to Consumers, c. 1950–2000', *Contemporary British History*, 22,4, 537–571.

——— (2008). 'Charles Hilliard Feinstein', *Proceedings of the British Academy*, 153, 189–212.

——— (2012). 'The Economy of Obligation: Incomplete Contracts and the Cost of the Welfare State', Discussion Papers in Economic and Social History 103 (Oxford: University of Oxford), www.economics.ox.ac.uk/materials/papers/12255/offer103.pdf.

——— (2012). 'Self-Interest, Sympathy and the Invisible Hand: From Adam Smith to Market Liberalism', *Economic Thought*, 1,2, 1–14.

——— (2012). 'A Warrant for Pain: Caveat Emptor vs. the Duty of Care in American Medicine, c. 1970–2010', *Real-World Economics Review*, 61, 85–99.

——— (2014). 'Narrow Banking, Real Estate, and Financial Stability in the UK, c. 1870–2010', *British Financial Crises since 1825*, eds. Nicholas Dimsdale and Anthony Hotson (Oxford: Oxford University Press), 158–173.

Offer, Avner, R. Pechey and S. Ulijaszek (2010). 'Obesity under Affluence Varies by Welfare Regimes: The Effect of Fast Food, Insecurity, and Inequality', *Economics and Human Biology*, 8,3, 297–308.

'Ökad Frihet för Riksbanken Enigt Krav från Bankföreningen' (1957). *Dagens Nyheter*, 26 October 1957.

Okun, Arthur M. (1975). *Equality and Efficiency: The Big Tradeoff* (Washington, DC: Brookings Institution).

Olsen, Gregg M. (1992). *The Struggle for Economic Democracy in Sweden* (Aldershot, UK: Avebury).

Olson, Mancur (1965). *The Logic of Collective Action: Public Goods and the Theory of Groups* (Cambridge, MA: Harvard University Press).

Orszag, Peter R., and J. E. Stiglitz (2001). 'Rethinking Pension Reform: Ten Myths about Social Security Systems', *New Ideas about Old Age Security: Towards Sustainable Pension Systems in the 21st Century*, eds. Robert Holzmann, Joseph E. Stiglitz, M. Louise Fox, Estelle James and P. Orszag (Washington, DC: World Bank), 17–56.

Osberg, Lars (1995). 'The Equity/Efficiency Trade-Off in Retrospect' (Halifax, Nova Scotia: Dalhousie University), http://myweb.dal.ca/osberg/classification/articles/academic%20journals/EQUITYEFFICIENCY/EQUITY%20EFFICIENCY.pdf.

Östberg, Kjell (2010). *När Vinden Vände: Olof Palme 1969–1986* (Stockholm: Leopard).

——— (2010). *I Takt med Tiden: Olof Palme 1927–1969* (Stockholm: Leopard).

Ostry, Jonathan D., Andrew Berg and Charalambos G. Tsangrides (2014). 'Redistribution, Inequality, and Growth', SDN/14/02 (Washington, DC: International Monetary Fund Research Department).

Palley, Thomas K. (2013). 'Horizontalists, Verticalists, and Structuralists: The Theory of Endogenous Money Reassessed', Working Paper 121 (Düsseldorf: IMK [Institut für Makroökonomie und Konjunkturforschung]).

Patinkin, Don (1965). *Money, Interest, and Prices: An Integration of Monetary and Value Theory* (New York: Harper & Row).

Pastor, Manuel (1987). *The International Monetary Fund and Latin America: Economic Stabilization and Class Conflict*, Series in Political Economy and Economic Development in Latin America (Boulder, CO: Westview Press).

Peterman, William B. (2014). 'A Historical Welfare Analysis of Social Security: Who Did the Program Benefit?' (Washington, DC: Federal Reserve Board of Governors), http://william peterman.com/pdfs/Social_security_history.pdf.

Peterson, Peter G. (2009). *The Education of an American Dreamer: How a Son of Greek Immigrants Learned His Way from a Nebraska Diner to Washington, Wall Street, and Beyond* (New York: Twelve).

Philipsen, Dirk (2015). *The Little Big Number: How GDP Came to Rule the World and What to Do about It* (Princeton, NJ: Princeton University Press).

Pierce, James L. (1995). 'Monetarism: The Good, the Bad and the Ugly', *Monetarism and the Methodology of Economics: Essays in Honour of Thomas Mayer*, eds. Kevin D. Hoover and Steven M. Sheffrin (Aldershot, UK: Edward Elgar), 27–48.

Piketty, Thomas (2014). *Capital in the Twenty-First Century* (Cambridge, MA: Harvard University Press).

Piketty, Thomas, and Emmanuel Saez (2012). 'Optimal Labor Income Taxation', Working Paper 18521, November 2012 (Cambridge, MA: National Bureau of Economic Research).

Piketty, Thomas, Emmanuel Saez and Stefanie Stantcheva (2014). 'Optimal Taxation of Top Labor Incomes: A Tale of Three Elasticities', *American Economic Journal Economic Policy*, 6,1, 230–271.

Pinto, Manuela Fernandez (2015). 'Tensions in Agnotology: Normativity in the Studies of Commercially-Driven Ignorance', *Social Studies of Science*. 45,2, 294–315.

Polak, J. J. (1991). *The Changing Nature of IMF Conditionality*, Essays in International Finance no. 184 (Princeton, NJ: Princeton University, International Finance Section, Department of Economics).

Pollock, Allyson, and Colin Leys (2004). *NHS Plc: The Privatisation of Our Health Care* (London: Verso).

Pollock, R. L., and J. P. Suyderhoud (1992). 'An Empirical Window on Rational-Expectations Formation', *Review of Economics and Statistics*, 74,2, 320–324.

Popper, Karl R. (1945/1957). *The Open Society and Its Enemies*, 3rd ed., 2 vols. (London: Routledge & K. Paul).

Poterba, James M. (2007). 'An Interview with Martin Feldstein', *Inside the Economist's Mind: Conversations with Eminent Economists*, eds. P. A. Samuelson and William A. Barnett (Malden, MA: Blackwell), 192–208.

Pritchard, Colin, and Mark S. Wallace (2011). 'Comparing the USA, UK and 17 Western Countries' Efficiency and Effectiveness in Reducing Mortality', *Journal of the Royal Society of Medicine Short Reports*, 2,60, 1–10.

Proctor, Robert (1995). *Cancer Wars: How Politics Shapes What We Know and Don't Know about Cancer* (New York: BasicBooks).

Proctor, Robert, and Londa L. Schiebinger (2008). *Agnotology: The Making and Unmaking of Ignorance* (Stanford, CA: Stanford University Press).

Pronin, E., T. Gilovich and L. Ross (2004). 'Objectivity in the Eye of the Beholder: Divergent Perceptions of Bias in Self Versus Others', *Psychological Review*, 111, 781–799.

Qin, Duo (2013). *A History of Econometrics: The Reformation from the 1970s* (Oxford: Oxford University Press).

Queisser, Monika (1999). 'Pension Reform: Lessons from Latin America', Policy Brief no. 15 (Paris: OECD), http://www.oecd.org/pensions/2407991.pdf.

Quigley, Carroll (1966). *Tragedy and Hope: A History of the World in Our Time* (New York: Macmillan).

Ramsay, Robin (2002). *The Rise of New Labour* (Harpenden, UK: Pocket Essentials).

Rawls, John (1971). *A Theory of Justice* (Cambridge, MA: Belknap Press of Harvard University Press).

Reddaway, Peter, and Dmitri Glinski (2001). *The Tragedy of Russia's Reforms: Market Bolshevism against Democracy* (Washington, DC: United States Institute of Peace Press).

Reder, Melvin W. (1982). 'Chicago Economics: Permanence and Change', *Journal of Economic Literature*, 20,1, 1–38.

Reinert, Erik S., and Arno M. Daastel (2004). 'The Other Canon: The History of Renaissance Economics', *Globalization, Economic Development and Inequality: An Alternative Perspective*, ed. Erik S. Reinert (Cheltenham, UK: Edward Elgar), 21–70.

Ricketts, Martin J., and Edward Shoesmith (1990). *British Economic Opinion: A Survey of a Thousand Economists*, IEA Research Monographs 45 (London: Institute of Economic Affairs).

——— (1992). 'British Economic Opinion: Positive Science or Normative Judgment?', *American Economic Review*, 82,2, 210–215.

Riksbankens Jubileumsfond (2004). *Hinc Robur et Securitas: En Forskningsstiftelses Handel och Vandel: Stiftelsen Riksbankens Jubileumsfond 1989–2003* (Hedemora/Stockholm: Gidlund/Riksbankens Jubileumsfond).

Rizvi, S.A.T. (2006). 'The Sonnenschein-Mantel-Debreu Results after Thirty Years', *History of Political Economy: Agreement on Demand: Consumer Theory in the Twentieth Century*, 38, Supp., 228–245.

Roberts-Hughes, Rebecca (2011). 'The Case for Space: The Size of England's New Homes' (London: Royal Institute of British Architects).

Robinson, Joan (1962). *Economic Philosophy* (London: C. A. Watts).

Rodrik, Dani (2006). 'Goodbye Washington Consensus, Hello Washington Confusion? A Review of the World Bank's Economic Growth in the 1990s: Learning from a Decade of Reform', *Journal of Economic Literature*, 44,4, 973–987.

———— (2012). 'Why We Learn Nothing from Regressing Economic Growth on Policies', *Seoul Journal of Economics*, 25,2, 137–151.

Rohter, Larry (2006). 'Chile's Candidates Agree to Agree on Pension Woes', *New York Times*, 10 January 2006.

Roine, Jesper (2013), 'Varför Har Balansen Mellan Kapital och Löner Förändrats?', http://ekon omistas.se/2013/02/18/varfor-har-balansen-mellan-kapital-och-loner-forandrats/.

Rooth, Ivar, and Gösta Rooth (1988). *Ivar Rooth, Riksbankschef 1929–1948: En Autobiografi* (Uppsala: G. Rooth).

Rose-Ackerman, Susan (1978). *Corruption: A Study in Political Economy* (New York: Academic Press).

Rosenau, Pauline Vaillancourt (1992). *Post-Modernism and the Social Sciences: Insights, Inroads, and Intrusions* (Princeton, NJ: Princeton University Press).

Rosenberg, Alex (2009). 'If Economics Is a Science, What Kind of Science Is It?', *The Oxford Handbook of Philosophy of Economics*, eds. Harold Kincaid and Don Ross (Oxford: Oxford University Press), 55–67.

Rosenberg, Alexander (1992). *Economics: Mathematical Politics or Science of Diminishing Returns?* (Chicago: University of Chicago Press).

Ross, L., and A. Ward (1996). 'Naive Realism in Everyday Life: Implications for Social Conflict and Misunderstanding', *Values and Knowledge*, eds. T. Brown, E. S. Reed and E. Turiel (Hillsdale, NJ: Erlbaum), 103–135.

Rothbard, Murray N. (1960). 'The Politics of Political Economists: Comment', *Quarterly Journal of Economics*, 74,4, 659–665.

Rothstein, Bo (2011). *The Quality of Government: Corruption, Social Trust, and Inequality in International Perspective* (Chicago: University of Chicago Press).

———— (2015). 'Ekonomipriset i Strid med Andan i Nobels Testamente', *Dagens Nyheter*, 11 October 2015.

———— (2015). 'Proposal for an Investigation by the Royal Swedish Academy of Sciences of Its Continued Involvement in the Awarding of the Sveriges Riksbank's Prize in Economic Sciences in Memory of Alfred Nobel', 10 October 2015 (Gothenberg: University of Gothenberg).

Rothstein, Bo, and Sven Steinmo (2013). 'Social Democracy in Crisis? What Crisis?' *The Crisis of Social Democracy in Europe*, eds. Michael Keating and David McCrone (Edinburgh: Edinburgh University Press), 87–106.

Rubin, Zick, and Letitia Anne Peplau (1975). 'Who Believes in a Just World?' *Journal of Social Issues*, 31,3, 65–89.

Rubinstein, Ariel (2012). *Economic Fables* (Cambridge: Open Book Publishers).

Rubinstein, W. D. (1983). 'The End of "Old Corruption" in Britain 1780–1860', *Past & Present*, 101, 55–86.

Ruccio, David F., and Jack Amariglio (2003). *Postmodern Moments in Modern Economics* (Princeton, NJ/Oxford: Princeton University Press).

Ruggles, Nancy (1949–1950). 'Recent Developments in the Theory of Marginal Cost Pricing', *Review of Economic Studies*, 17,2, 107–126.

Ruske, R. (2015). 'Does Economics Make Politicians Corrupt? Empirical Evidence from the United States Congress', *Kyklos*, 68, 2, 240–254.

Rydenfelt, Sven (1980). 'The Limits of Taxation: Lessons from the Swedish Welfare State', Mont Pelerin Society Papers 24/1, Hoover Institution Archives.

——— (1985). 'Trade Unions and Socialist Governments in Sweden: A Study of a Corporate Society', Mont Pelerin Society Papers 26/5, Hoover Institution Archives.

Ryner, Magnus (2002). *Capitalist Restructuring, Globalisation, and the Third Way: Lessons from the Swedish Model* (London: Routledge).

Sabadish, Natalie, and Monique Morrisey (2013). 'Retirement Inequality Chartbook: How the 401(K) Revolution Created a Few Big Winners and Many Losers', 3 September 2013 (Washington, DC: Economic Policy Institute), http://www.epi.org/publication/retire-ment-inequality-chartbook/.

Sachs, Jeffrey (1986). 'Managing the LDC Debt Crisis', *Brookings Papers on Economic Activity*, 2, 397–440.

——— (1987). 'International Policy Coordination: The Case of the Developing Country Debt Crisis', NBER Working Paper 2287 (Cambridge, MA: National Bureau of Economic Research).

——— (1994). 'Life in the Economic Emergency Room', *The Political Economy of Policy Reform*, ed. John Williamson (Washington, DC: Institute for International Economics), 501–523.

Sachs, Jeffrey, and H. Huizinga (1987). 'U.S. Commercial Banks and the Developing-Country Debt Crisis', NBER Working Paper 2455 (Cambridge, MA: National Bureau of Economic Research).

Samuelson, Paul A. (1958). 'Aspects of Public-Expenditure Theories', *Review of Economics and Statistics*, 40,4, 332–338.

——— (1958). 'An Exact Consumption-Loan Model of Interest with or without the Social Contrivance of Money', *Journal of Political Economy*, 66,6, 467–482.

——— (1962). 'Economists and the History of Ideas', *American Economic Review*, 52,1, 1.

——— (1985). 'Succumbing to Keynesianism', *Challenge*, 27,6, 4–11.

Sandbrook, Richard (2007). *Social Democracy in the Global Periphery: Origins, Challenges, Prospects* (Cambridge: Cambridge University Press).

Sapienza, P., and L. Zingales (2013). 'Economic Experts versus Average Americans', *American Economic Review*, 103,3, 636–642.

Sargent, Thomas J., and François R. Velde (2002). *The Big Problem of Small Change* (Princeton, NJ: Princeton University Press).

Sayers, R. S. (1976). *The Bank of England, 1891–1944*, 3 vols. (Cambridge: Cambridge University Press).

Schmitt, John, and Alexandra Mitukiewicz (2012). 'Politics Matter: Changes in Unionisation Rates in Rich Countries, 1960–2010', *Industrial Relations Journal*, 43,3, 260–280.

Schonfeld, Roger C. (2003). *JSTOR: A History* (Princeton, NJ/Oxford: Princeton University Press).

Schorfheide, F. (2011). 'Estimation and Evaluation of DSGE Models: Progress and Challenges' NBER 16781, February 2011 (Cambridge, MA: NBER).

Schumpeter, Joseph A., and Elizabeth Boody Schumpeter (1954). *History of Economic Analysis* (London: Allen & Unwin).

Sejersted, Francis, Richard Daly and Madeleine B. Adams (2011). *The Age of Social Democracy: Norway and Sweden in the Twentieth Century* (Princeton, NJ: Princeton University Press).

Selman, Donna, and Paul Leighton (2010). *Punishment for Sale: Private Prisons, Big Business, and the Incarceration Binge* (Lanham, MD: Rowman & Littlefield).

Sent, Esther-Mirjam (1998). *The Evolving Rationality of Rational Expectations: An Assessment of Thomas Sargent's Achievements* (Cambridge: Cambridge University Press).

Shalev, Baruch Aba (2002). *100 Years of Nobel Prizes* (Los Angeles, CA: Americas Group).

Shaxson, Nicholas (2011). *Treasure Islands: Tax Havens and the Men Who Stole the World* (London: Bodley Head).

Shiller, Robert J. (2003). *The New Financial Order: Risk in the 21st Century* (Princeton, NJ: Princeton University Press).

Shirley, Mary M., and John R. Nellis (1991). *Public Enterprise Reform: The Lessons of Experience*, EDI Development Studies (Washington, DC: World Bank).

Shleifer, A., and R. W. Vishny (1993). 'Corruption', *Quarterly Journal of Economics*, 108,3, 599–617.

Sims, Christopher A. (1980). 'Macroeconomics and Reality', *Econometrica (Pre-1986)*, 48,1, 1–48.

——— (1996). 'Macroeconomics and Methodology', *Journal of Economic Perspectives*, 10, 1, 105–120.

——— (2006). 'Comment on Del Negro, Schorfheide, Smets and Wouters', Seattle, 4 December 2006, http://sims.princeton.edu/yftp/DSSW806/DSseattleComment.pdf.

Sjöberg, Thomas (1999). 'Playboyintervjun: Kjell-Olof Feldt', *Playboy Scandinavia*, 5, 37–44.

Smets, F., and R. Wouters (2003). 'An Estimated Dynamic Stochastic General Equilibrium Model of the Euro Area', *Journal of the European Economic Association*, 1,5, 1123–1175.

Smith, Adam (1759/1792/1976). *The Theory of Moral Sentiments*, Glasgow Edition of the Works and Correspondence of Adam Smith (Oxford: Clarendon Press).

Smith, Adam (1776/1976). *An Inquiry into the Nature and Causes of the Wealth of Nations*, Glasgow Edition of the Works and Correspondence of Adam Smith (Oxford: Clarendon Press).

Smith, Noah (2014). 'The Most Damning Critique of DSGE', 10 January 2014, http://noahpinionblog.blogspot.co.uk/2014/01/the-most-damning-critique-of-dsge.html.

Smith, W. R. (2002). 'Privatization in Latin America: How Did It Work and What Difference Did It Make?' *Latin American Politics and Society*, 44,4, 153–166.

Snowdon, Brian, and Howard R. Vane (1999). *Conversations with Leading Economists: Interpreting Modern Macroeconomics* (Cheltenham, UK: Edward Elgar).

Söderberg, Gabriel (2013). *Constructing Invisible Hands: Market Technocrats in Sweden 1880–2000* (Uppsala: Acta Universitatis Upsaliensis).

Söderberg, Gabriel, Avner Offer and Samuel Bjork (2013). 'Hayek in Citations and the Nobel Memorial Prize', *Hayek: A Collaborative Biography, Part 1: Influences from Mises to Bartley*, ed. Robert Leeson (Basingstoke, UK: Palgrave Macmillan), 61–70.

Solow, Robert M. (2003/2009). 'Solow: Dumb and Dumber in Macroeconomics', http://economistsview.typepad.com/economistsview/2009/08/solow-dumb-and-dumber-in-macroeconomics.html.

——— (2007). 'Chapter 12. Reflections on the Survey', *The Making of an Economist Redux*, ed. David Colander (Princeton, NJ: Princeton University Press), 234–238.

——— (2008). 'The State of Macroeconomics', *Journal of Economic Perspectives*, 22,2, 243–249.

——— (2010). 'Building a Science of Economics for the Real World', House of Representatives, Committee on Science and Technology, Subcommittee on Investigations and Oversight, Serial No. 111–106 (Washington, DC: US Government Printing Office).

Spanos, Aris (2006). 'Econometrics in Retrospect and Prospect', *Palgrave Handbook of Econometrics*, eds. Terence C. Mills and Kerry Patterson (Basingstoke, UK: Palgrave MacMillan), 1, 3–58.

——— (2012). 'Philosophy of Econometrics', *Philosophy of Economics*, ed. Uskali Mäki (Amsterdam: Elsevier North Holland), 329–393.

Sproul, Allan (1964). 'The "Accord"—A Landmark in the First Fifty Years of the Federal Reserve System', *Federal Reserve Bank of New York, Monthly Review*, 46,11, 227–236.

Ståhl, Ingemar (1990). 'The Prize in Economic Science and Maurice Allais', Paper Delivered at the Mont Pelerin Society Meeting, Munich; Hayek Papers, 28/3, Hoover Institution Archives.

Ståhl, Ingemar, Kurt Wickman and Claes Arvidsson (1993). *Suedosclerosis: Marknadsekonomisk Rapport* (Stockholm: Timbro).

Steinmo, Sven (2010). *The Evolution of Modern States: Sweden, Japan, and the United States* (Cambridge: Cambridge University Press).

Stenfors, Alexis (2014). 'The Swedish Financial System', Studies in Financial Systems 13 (Leeds, UK: FESSUD [Financialisation, Economy, Society and Sustainable Development]).

Stigler, George (1959). 'The Politics of Political Economists', *Quarterly Journal of Economics*, 73,4, 522–532.

Stigler, G. J. (1971). 'Theory of Economic Regulation', *Bell Journal of Economics and Management Science*, 2,1, 3–21.

Stiglitz, Joseph E. (1990). 'Roundtable Discussion', *Proceedings of the World Bank Annual Conference on Development Economics* (Washington, DC: World Bank), 430–433.

—— (1991). 'The Invisible Hand and Modern Welfare Economics', Working Paper 3641 (Cambridge, MA: NBER).

—— (1994). *Whither Socialism?* (Cambridge, MA: MIT Press).

—— (2002). *Globalization and Its Discontents* (London: Penguin).

—— (2002). 'Keynesian Economics and Critique of First Fundamental Theorem of Welfare Economics', *Market Failure or Success: The New Debate*, eds. Tyler Cowen and Eric Crampton (Cheltenham, UK: Edward Elgar), 41–65.

Stone, Richard, and Donald A. Rowe (1954). *The Measurement of Consumers' Expenditure and Behaviour in the United Kingdom 1920–1938* (Cambridge: Cambridge University Press).

Straub, Ludwig, and Ivan Werning (2014). 'Positive Long Run Capital Taxation: Chamley-Judd Revisited', Working Paper 20441 (Cambridge, MA: NBER).

Studenski, Paul (1967). *The Income of Nations: With Corrections* (New York: New York University Press).

Sugden, Robert (2009). 'Can Economics Be Founded on "Indisputable Facts of Experience"? Lionel Robbins and the Pioneers of Neoclassical Economics', *Economica*, 76,304, 857–872.

Suskind, Ron (2004). 'Faith, Certainty and the Presidency of George W. Bush', *New York Times Magazine*, 17 October 2004.

Svenska Bankföreningen (1957). 'Riksbankens Ställning och Uppgifter. Diskussion Vid 1957 Års Ordinarie Bankmöte Den 25 Oktober 1957', Skrifter utgivna av Svenska Bankföreningen (Stockholm: Svenska Bankföreningen).

Svensson, Torsten (1996). *Novemberrevolutionen: Om Rationalitet och Makt i Beslutet att Avreglera Kreditmarknaden 1985: Rapport till Expertgruppen för Studier i Offentlig Ekonomi* (Stockholm: Fritze).

Swedish Bureau of Statistics (2013). 'Utrikes Födda 2012. Fortsatt Ökning av Utrikes Födda i Sverige', http://www.scb.se/sv_/hitta-statistik/artiklar/fortsatt-okning-av-utrikes-fodda-i -sverige/.

Syll, Lars P. (2013). 'Self-Righteous Drivel from the Chairman of the Nobel Prize Committee', https://rwer.wordpress.com/2013/12/23/self-righteous-drivel-from-the-chairman-of-the -nobel-prize-committee/.

—— (2015). *On the Use and Misuse of Theories and Models in Mainstream Economics* (Bristol, UK: World Economics Association Books).

Taleb, Nassim Nicholas (2007). 'The Psuedo-Science Hurting Markets', *Financial Times*, 23 October 2007.

Tanzi, Vito (1987/1989). 'Fiscal Policy, Growth, and the Design of Stabilization Programs', *Fiscal Policy, Stabilization, and Growth in Developing Countries*, eds. Mario I. Bejer and Ke-young Chu (Washington, DC: International Monetary Fund), 13–32.

—— (2003). 'Corruption around the World: Causes, Consequences, Scope, and Cures', *Governance, Corruption & Economic Performance*, eds. George T. Abed and Sanjeev Gupta (Washington, DC: International Monetary Fund), 19–58.

Tanzi, Vito, and L. Schuknecht (1997). 'Reconsidering the Fiscal Role of Government: The International Perspective', *American Economic Review*, 87,2, 164–168.

Taylor, A.J.P. (1975). *English History, 1914–1945* (Harmondsworth, UK: Penguin Books).

Taylor-Gooby, Peter (2013). *The Double Crisis of the Welfare State and What We Can Do About It* (Houndsmill/Basingstoke, UK: Palgrave Macmillan).

Taylor-Gooby, Peter, and Rose Martin (2008). 'Trends in Sympathy for the Poor', *British Social Attitudes*, eds. Alison Park, John Curtice, Katarina Thomson, Miranda Phillips, Mark C. Johnson and Elizabeth Clery (Los Angeles: Sage Publications/National Centre for Social Research), 24, 229–258.

Thomas, Brinley (1936). *Monetary Policy and Crises: A Study of Swedish Experience* (London: G. Routledge and Sons Ltd.).

Toniolo, Gianni (2005). *Central Bank Cooperation at the Bank for International Settlements, 1930–1973* (Cambridge: Cambridge University Press).

Tovar, Camilo E. (2008). 'DSGE Models and Central Banks', BIS Working Papers 258, September 2008 (Basel: Bank of International Settlements).

Transparency International (2011). 'Cabs for Hire', http://www.transparency.org.uk/publica tions/cabs-for-hire-fixing-the-revolving-door-between-government-and-business-2/.

——— (2013). 'Corruption Perceptions Index', http://cpi.transparency.org/cpi2013/in_detail/ cpi2013_Databundle.zip.

Tullock, Gordon (1978). *Svenskarna och Deras Fonder: En Analys av SAP-LOs Förslag* (Stockholm: Timbro).

Turner, Adair (2015). *Between Debt and the Devil: Money, Credit, and Fixing Global Finance* (Princeton, NJ: Princeton University Press).

Urban, Scott Andrew (2012). 'Gold in the Interwar Monetary System: Evolution of the Gold-Standard Regime', D.Phil. dissertation (Oxford: University of Oxford).

Vane, Howard R., and Chris Mulhearn (2006). *The Nobel Memorial Laureates in Economics: An Introduction to Their Careers and Main Published Works* (Cheltenham, UK: Edward Elgar).

Vanoli, Andre (2005). *A History of National Accounting* (Washington, DC: IOS Press).

Varoufakis, Yanis (2002). 'Deconstructing Homo Economicus? Reflections on Postmodernity's Encounter with Neoclassical Economics', *Journal of Economic Methodology*, 9,3, 389–396.

Varoufakis, Yanis, Joseph Halevi and Nicholas Theocarakis (2011). *Modern Political Economics: Making Sense of the Post-2008 World* (New York: Routledge).

Velupillai, Kumaraswamy (2000). *Computable Economics: The Arne Ryde Memorial Lectures* (Oxford: Oxford University Press).

——— (2010). *Computable Foundations for Economics* (London: Routledge).

Vickers, John, and George K. Yarrow (1988). *Privatization: An Economic Analysis* (Cambridge, MA: MIT Press).

Viktorov, Ilja (2009). 'The Swedish Employers and the Wage-Earner Funds Debate during the Crisis of Fordism in the 1970s and 1980s', Conference Paper (Stockholm: Stockholm University, Department of Economic History), https://apebhconference.files.wordpress. com/2009/09/viktorov1.pdf.

Viner, Jacob (1937). *Studies in the Theory of International Trade* (New York: Harper & Brothers).

von Neumann, John (1955). 'Method in the Physical Sciences', *The Unity of Knowledge*, ed. Lewis Gaston Leary (Garden City, NY: Doubleday), 157–164; *Collected Works VI* (New York: Pergamon Press), 491–498.

Vreeland, James Raymond (2003). *The IMF and Economic Development* (Cambridge: Cambridge University Press).

Wade, Robert (1990). *Governing the Market: Economic Theory and the Role of Government in East Asian Industrialization* (Princeton, NJ: Princeton University Press).

Wadensjö, Eskil (1992). 'Appendix D. Doctoral Theses in Economics in Sweden 1895–1989', *Economics in Sweden: An Evaluation of Swedish Research in Economics*, ed. Lars Engwall (London: Routledge), 200–232.

——— (1992). 'Recruiting a New Generation', *Economics in Sweden: An Evaluation of Swedish Research in Economics*, ed. Lars Engwall (London: Routledge), 67–103.

Wallander, Jan (1982). 'En Effektivare Kreditpolitik', *Ekonomisk Debatt*, 10,8, 507–517.

Walpen, Bernhard (2004). *Die Offenen Feinde Und Ihre Gesellschaft: Eine Hegemonietheoretische Studie Zur Mont Pelerin Society* (Hamburg: VSA-Verlag).

Ward, Benjamin (1972). *What's Wrong with Economics?* (London: Macmillan).

Watson, Mark W. (1993). 'Measures of Fit for Calibrated Models', *Journal of Political Economy*, 101, 1011–1041.

Wedel, Janine R. (1998). *Collision and Collusion: The Strange Case of Western Aid to Eastern Europe, 1989–1998* (Basingstoke, UK: Macmillan).

Wedeman, Andrew Hall (2012). *Double Paradox: Rapid Growth and Rising Corruption in China* (Ithaca, NY: Cornell University Press).

Weyland, Kurt Gerhard, Raul L. Madrid and Wendy Hunter. (2010). *Leftist Governments in Latin America: Successes and Shortcomings* (Cambridge/New York: Cambridge University Press).

Whaples, Robert (2009). 'The Policy Views of American Economic Association Members: The Results of a New Survey', *Econ Journal Watch*, 6,3, 337–348.

Whyman, Philip (2003). *Sweden and the 'Third Way': A Macroeconomic Evaluation* (Aldershot, UK: Ashgate).

Whyte, David (2015). *How Corrupt Is Britain?* (London: Pluto Press).

Wigforss, Ernst (1960). 'Den Nya Ekonomiska Politiken', *Ekonomisk Tidskrift*, 62,3, 185–194.

Wikiquote (2015). 'Talk: John Von Neumann', http://en.wikiquote.org/wiki/Talk:John_von_ Neumann.

Williams, John (2014). 'John Williams' Shadow Government Statistics: Primers and Reports', http://www.shadowstats.com/primers-and-reports.

Williamson, John E. (1990). 'What Washington Means by Policy Reform', *Latin American Adjustment: How Much Has Happened?*, ed. John E. Williamson (Washington DC: Institute for International Economics), 5–20.

–––––– (2003). 'Our Agenda and the Washington Consensus', *After the Washington Consensus: Restarting Growth and Reform in Latin America*, eds. John Williamson and Pedro-Pablo Kuczynski Godard (Washington, DC: Institute for International Economics), 323–331.

–––––– (2008). 'A Short History of the Washington Consensus', *The Washington Consensus Reconsidered: Towards a New Global Governance*, eds. N. Serra and J. Stiglitz (Oxford: Oxford University Press), 14–30.

Williamson, O. E. (1979). 'Transaction-Cost Economics—Governance of Contractual Relations', *Journal of Law & Economics*, 22,2, 233–261.

Willsher, Kim (2012). 'Christine Lagarde, Scourge of Tax Evaders, Pays No Tax', *Guardian*, 29 May 2012.

Wittman, Donald A. (1995). *The Myth of Democratic Failure: Why Political Institutions Are Efficient* (Chicago: University of Chicago Press).

Wolf, Charles (1993). *Markets or Governments: Choosing between Imperfect Alternatives*, 2nd ed. (Cambridge, MA: MIT Press).

Woodford, Michael (2003). *Interest and Prices: Foundations of a Theory of Monetary Policy* (Princeton, NJ/Oxford: Princeton University Press).

Wooldridge, Adrian (2013). 'Special Report: The Nordic Countries: Northern Lights', *Economist*, 2 February 2013, 1–16.

World Bank (n.d.). 'Alden Winship ("Tom") Clausen', http://web.worldbank.org/WBSITE/EX TERNAL/EXTABOUTUS/EXTARCHIVES/0,,contentMDK:20487071~pagePK:36726 ~piPK:437378~theSitePK:29506,00.html.

–––––– (1993). *The East Asian Miracle: Economic Growth and Public Policy* (New York: Oxford University Press for the World Bank).

–––––– (1994). *Averting the Old Age Crisis: Policies to Protect the Old and Promote Growth* (Oxford: Oxford University Press).

–––––– (1997). *World Development Report 1997: The State in a Changing World* (New York: Oxford University Press for the World Bank).

–––––– (2014). 'External Debt Stocks, Total (Dod, Current US$)', http://data.worldbank.org/ indicator/DT.DOD.DECT.CD.

Wray, L. Randall (2012). *Modern Money Theory: A Primer on Macroeconomics for Sovereign Monetary Systems* (Basingstoke, UK: Palgrave Macmillan).

Zagha, Roberto, Gobind T. Nankani and World Bank (2005). *Economic Growth in the 1990s: Learning from a Decade of Reform* (Washington, DC: World Bank).

Zingales, Luigi (2012). *A Capitalism for the People: Recapturing the Lost Genius of American Prosperity* (New York: Basic Books).

INDEX